D1233451

THE YALE-HOOVER SERIES ON AUTHORITARIAN REGIMES

# CATHOLICS ON THE BARRICADES

POLAND, FRANCE, AND "REVOLUTION,"

1891–1956

PIOTR H. KOSICKI

*Hoover Institution*
*Stanford University*
*Stanford, California*

Yale UNIVERSITY PRESS
New Haven and London

Yale University Press books may be purchased in quantity for educational, business, or promotional use. For information, please e-mail sales.press@yale.edu (U.S. office) or sales@yaleup.co.uk (U.K. office).

Set in Sabon type by Integrated Publishing Solutions, Grand Rapids, Michigan.
Printed in the United States of America.

Library of Congress Control Number: 2017939048

ISBN 978-0-300-22551-8 (hardcover : alk. paper)

A catalogue record for this book is available from the British Library.

This paper meets the requirements of ANSI/NISO Z39.48-1992 (Permanence of Paper).

10 9 8 7 6 5 4 3 2 1

*to Lidia and Henryk Kosk—*
*the grandparents who taught me*
*to ask questions*

# Contents

# Acknowledgments

*Pensiamo in secoli*—so repeat the cardinals who walk the halls of the Vatican, brushing aside the fact that a given matter has not yet been resolved: "We think in centuries."

This book has been a long time in the making, and it has often felt like *secoli*. I did my first research on the Catholic Church in the summer of 2002, in Italy and Poland, following my freshman year at Stanford. I lucked into a small papal audience at Castelgandolfo with John Paul II—visibly suffering from Parkinson's—and was caught up in the electric atmosphere: scores of twenty-to-thirty-year-olds chanting, call and response, first in Italian, then in Spanish. "GIOVANNI PAOLO!" "JUAN PABLO SEGUNDO!" I wanted to understand the ardor of those around me—why that pontiff commanded such devotion. I traveled on to Poland, where I read archival documents and interviewed bishops, philosophers, and statesmen, beginning to investigate how Poland has shaped the global Catholic Church.

Over the next fourteen years, many wonderful people and generous institutions made possible my journey from that papal audience to the completion of this book. It is deeply gratifying that the man who supervised that first project, Stanford history professor Norman Naimark, later solicited this book for the Yale-Hoover Series on Authoritarian Regimes. When I was an undergraduate, Norman nurtured my interest in the historical profession, and he helped me find my voice as a writer. Ever since, Norman has been there as a source of counsel and friendship, in times good and bad.

I count my blessings that I completed my PhD at Princeton in a department rich in brilliant mentors who taught me how to practice the craft of history. Jan Gross's generosity as an advisor and fearlessness as a scholar have inspired me; I learned from him that a historian should write in as many languages and for as many audiences as he can, challenging taboos and prejudices that erect artificial barriers to the pursuit of knowledge. Anson Rabinbach and Philip Nord have been great friends, extraordinary advisors, and challenging critics. Stephen Kotkin has offered important and earnest counsel over the years. While at Princeton, I also benefited from the tutelage and generosity of, among others, Peter Brown, Michael Gordin, Anthony Grafton, Irena Grudzińska-Gross, Harold and Marzenna James, Kim Lane Scheppele, the late Paul Sigmund, Jeffrey Stout, Maurizio Viroli, and the late C. K. Williams. Timothy Snyder joined my PhD committee from Yale and offered indispensable advice.

After finishing the PhD, I taught briefly at American University and then the University of Virginia. At American, I am grateful to Lisa Leff, Eric Lohr, and Pamela Nadell. At Virginia, Jeffrey Rossman made available funding—originally endowed by Blanka Rosenstiel—and encouraged me to organize conferences that brought fresh perspective to my own research. I am deeply grateful to him and to other colleagues who helped me feel welcome there: Edith Clowes, Gabriel Finder, Gerald Fogarty SJ, Paul Halliday, David Herman, Krishan Kumar, Erin Lambert, Melvyn Leffler, James Loeffler, Ekaterina Makarova, Allan Megill, Jonah Schulhofer-Wohl, Dariusz Tołczyk, and Joshua White.

Since I joined its faculty in 2013, the University of Maryland has been my haven. Outside my department, Vladimir Tismaneanu and Karol Sołtan have been generous interlocutors. In my home Department of History, every colleague deserves my thanks for fostering a wonderful intellectual community that welcomed me from day one. Philip Soergel has been a generous and supportive chair, and Antoine Borrut, Holly Brewer, Sarah Cameron, Mikhail Dolbilov, Arthur Eckstein, Kenneth Holum, John Lampe, Sonya Michel, David Sartorius, Donald Sutherland, Stefano Villani, Peter Wien, and Colleen Woods have been great sources of counsel. I thank especially Jeffrey Herf and Marsha Rozenblit, whose mentorship has been invaluable and whose friendship has meant a great deal to me.

This book would not have been possible without input from col-

leagues and confidants the world over. Jean-Dominique Durand and Andrzej Friszke have long been my mentors "in the field," so to speak. Zbigniew Nosowski has for years been a generous source of insight and advice on the Polish Catholic intellectual world. I owe a great debt to the late René Girard and to Martha Girard, whose friendship, counsel, and concern for the future of the Catholic Church convinced me to persist in my choice of research subject. The book has bene-fited, moreover, from exchanges with Nicolas Bauquet, Annette Becker, Masha Belenky, Agnieszka Bielak, James Bjork, Jens Boysen, Joseph Bradley, Robert Brier, Jennifer Burns, Mark Carlson, Holly Case, Giuli-ana Chamedes, James Chappel, Philippe Chenaux, Winson Chu, Kath-ryn Ciancia, Emily-Jane Cohen, Sarah Cramsey, Jane Curry, Norman Davies, Gregory Domber, Martin Dornbach, Ofer Dynes, Jerzy Eisler, James Ramon Felak, Małgorzata Fidelis, Mirosław Filipowicz, Étienne Fouilloux, Mayhill C. Fowler, Alice Freifeld, Łukasz Gałecki, Timothy Garton Ash, Michael Gehler, Stefanos Geroulanos, Jerzy Giebułtowski, Idesbald Goddeeris, Emily Greble, Udi Greenberg, Brad Gregory, Jan Grootaers, Michael Gubser, Malachi Hacohen, Paul Hanebrink, Jeffrey Hardy, Daniel Heller, Ellen Hinsey, Gershon Hundert, Wanda Jarząbek, A. Ross Johnson, Katherine Jolluck, Ari Joskowicz, the late Tony Judt, Tom Junes, Wolfram Kaiser, Artemy Kalinovsky, Brendan Karch, Dun-can Kelly, Padraic Kenney, Kathryn Kleppinger, Arpad Klimo, James Krapfl, Kyrill Kunakhovich, Mikołaj Kunicki, Jessie Labov, Marc Lazar, Nicholas Levy, Jan Lityński, Józef Lorski, Lorenz Lüthi, Kamila Łepkowska, Helena Łuczywo, Sławomir Łukasiewicz, Michael and Petra McGillen, Anna and Paweł Machcewicz, Ioana Manolache, Ag-nieszka Marczyk, Małgorzata Mazurek, Elidor Mëhilli, Maribel Morey, Anna Müller, Jan-Werner Müller, David Ost, Andrzej Paczkowski, Ag-nieszka Pasieka, Susan Pearce, Marcin Pera, Krzysztof Pomian, Marian Pospieszalski, Molly Pucci, Camille Robcis, Rachel Rothstein, Izabella Sariusz-Skąpska, Katrin Schultheiss, Anatol Shmelev, Sarah Shortall, Maciej Siekierski, Sara Silverstein, Victoria Smolkin, Daniel Steinmetz Jenkins, Chelsea Stieber, Dariusz Stola, Noah Strote, Krzysztof Śliwiński, Paul Thibaud, Misza Tomaszewski, Joanna Urbanek, Ian Ward, Jean-Philippe Warren, Amir Weiner, Odd Arne Westad, Lora Wildenthal, Larry Wolff, Zofia Wóycicka, Julia Young, Tara Zahra, and Paweł Ziętara.
The greatest intellectual influence on this book comes from the leg-endary Polish dissident and public intellectual Adam Michnik, with

whom I had the privilege of spending three months as a "sidekick" during his first visiting appointment at Princeton in 2007. Adam has opened to me an intellectual world at once Polish and transnational, which I would have been hard-pressed to discover any other way; he has been a generous advisor, critic, and friend.

Several scholars in the field have gone out of their way again and again to offer their friendship, to provide feedback on drafts of my work, and to launch my career. I am immensely grateful to John Connelly, Atina Grossmann, Samuel Moyn, Brian Porter-Szűcs, Marci Shore, and Timothy Snyder for their steadfast support over the years.

I have been very fortunate to have the opportunity to present portions of this work at various conferences and workshops and to receive extensive feedback in those venues. For their invitations, I thank the American Institute of Polish Culture; the Catholic University of Leuven's KADOC Center; the German Historical Institute in Warsaw; Harvard University's Center for European Studies; the Hoover Institution; the John Paul II Catholic University of Lublin; the Konrad Adenauer Foundation; the London School of Economics IDEAS Center; the Luigi Sturzo Institute; the Notre Dame Institute for Advanced Study; NYU's Kandersteg Seminar; NYU's Remarque Institute; the Program on Modern Poland at Oxford's St. Antony's College; Princeton University's Center for Human Values; Stanford University's Kruzhok; the *Tygodnik Powszechny* Club in Poznań; the University of California, Berkeley's Krouzek; the University of Virginia's Center for Russian, East European, and Eurasian Studies; and the joint Woodrow Wilson International Center for Scholars/National Council for Eurasian and East European Research Junior Scholars' Training Seminar.

Several fellowships and institutions have supported the research and writing of this book. The Department of History at the University of Maryland has been generous with research funding, as was the Graduate School at Princeton University. I also thank the Institute for International Education for a Fulbright Fellowship, hosted by Jan Malicki and Leszek Zasztowt of Warsaw University's Center for East European Studies; the Republic of France for a Chateaubriand Fellowship, hosted by Sciences Po; John Lampe, Christian Ostermann, and Kristina Terzieva of the Woodrow Wilson International Center for Scholars, for multiple East European Studies Title VIII scholarships; the American Council of Learned Societies and the Andrew W. Mellon Foundation, for the New Faculty Fellowship that funded my year at the University of Virginia; Robert Brier, Ruth Leiserowitz, and Miloš Řezník of the German Historical Institute in Warsaw for a research fellowship; and Stephen Langlois and Eric Wakin of the Hoover Institution—for a W. Glenn Campbell and Rita Ricardo-Campbell National Fellowship, as well as several follow-up grants. I finished revising the book as a guest of McGill University's Department of History and Classical Studies, for which I thank its chair David Wright.

At Yale University Press, I thank Jaya Aninda Chatterjee, who welcomed and championed my work; Margaret Otzel, who patiently guided me through production; and Beverly Michaels, whose copy-editing has made this a better book. For their rapid and methodical reading of the proofs, I thank Guy Aldridge, Danuta E. Kosk-Kosicka, Jordan Luber, Samuel Miner, Joshua White, and Miłosz Wiatrowski. For having read and offered extensive feedback on the entire book while it was still in manuscript, my deepest thanks go to James Chappel, Jeffrey Herf, Norman Naimark, Brian Porter-Szűcs, Molly Pucci, Marsha Rozenblit, Marci Shore, and a third reader for Yale. The Hoover Institution has generously subsidized the publication of this book, and for that I thank Eric Wakin, as well as the Yale-Hoover series' co-editors—Paul Gregory and Norman Naimark.

This book is based on a wide range of sources, encompassing published materials, interviews, and archival documents gathered in three different countries. I am deeply indebted to the staffs of the following archives for their assistance: in France—Archives de l'Institut Mémoires de l'Édition Contemporaine (St-Germain-la-Blanche-Herbe), Archives Jacques et Raïssa Maritain (Kolbsheim), Archives de la Province Dominicaine de France (Paris), and Archives de la Province Jésuite de France (Vanves); in Poland—Archiwum Akt Nowych (Warsaw), Archiwum Instytutu Pamięci Narodowej (Warsaw), Archiwum Katolickiego Stowarzyszenia *Civitas Christiana* (Warsaw), and the manuscript collections of the Biblioteka Narodowa (Warsaw) and the Biblioteka Uniwersytecka Katolickiego Uniwersytetu Lubelskiego Jana Pawła II (Lublin); and in the US—the Hoover Institution Archives (Stanford), the Archives of the Polish Institute of Arts and Sciences of America (New York), and the Jacques Maritain Center at the University of Notre Dame. Thanks to the generosity of Wojciech Mazowiecki, I was also granted privileged access to hundreds of documents from among the private papers of the late Tadeusz Mazowiecki. The Mazowiecki family has indicated that it will ultimately make these papers available for consultation at the Archiwum Akt Nowych, but in this work they appear as the Tadeusz Mazowiecki Private Papers.

This book derives from the PhD thesis that I prepared at Princeton University. Parts of the dissertation, revised and updated, have also appeared in Polish as *Personalizm po polsku: Francuskie korzenie polskiej inteligencji katolickiej* (Warsaw: IPN-KŚZpNP, 2016), translated by Jerzy Giebułtowski. While in the beginning my goal was to create a single, comprehensive work, two distinct works have grown out of the same dissertation, each written from a different perspective. While they overlap in content, each presents a unique view, making its own arguments tailored to different audiences. I thank Cambridge University Press for allowing me to use in chapter 7 of this book material from "The Soviet Bloc's Answer to European Integration: Catholic Anti-Germanism and the Polish Project of a 'Catholic-Socialist' International," *Contemporary European History* 24, no. 1 (2015). I am also grateful to Patrycja Bloch, Anne-Lorraine Bujon, Jean-Luc Domenach, Hélène Favard, Jerzy Illg, Elżbieta Jogałła, Katarzyna Kętrzyńska, Dominika Kozłowska, Tomasz Łubieński, Jacek Łukasiewicz, Wojciech Mazowiecki, Radosława Podgórska FSK, Michał Rosenberg, Jan Skórzyński, Zygmunt Skórzyński, Michał Smoczyński, Wanda Widmańska, Leszek Widmański, Rut Wosiek FSK, Marta Wójcik, Barbara Zezula, and Martins Zvaners for their assistance with permissions. My thanks also go to Lisa Klein of the University of Maryland's History Department for her advice and help with the logistics.

This book is a labor of love, but such labors come at a cost. Family and friends understand the cost only too well, and I remain eternally grateful to them for their indulgence and support. Jason Berto, Julia Alves, Roberto Madrid, and Twingo Wahba looked after me for weeks at a time in Washington, DC when I was lost in the most intense writing of the book. Anne-Marie Marrache and Daphnée and Johanna Azoulay have cheered me on unfailingly in my final year of work. Jim Bishop and Lexi White, Marikka De Tristan, Will Hudson, Kyrill Kunakhovich, Nicolas Patin, Phoebe Prioleau, Gary Raichart, Dorothy and George Strohecker, Mateusz Syczewski, Heidi and Michael Tworek, Joshua White, and Miłosz Wiatrowski—thank you for seeing me through difficult times. Since childhood, I have been privileged to enjoy the support and encouragement of Teresa and Beata Czajkowska and Stanisław Śliwiński; of Ayse, Mustafa, and Mehmet Dosemeci; of Grażyna Kosk-Wiśniewska and Jan and Wojciech Wiśniewski; and of Grażyna and Bogusław Sikora. I am grateful to Jeļena Šamoņina for her years of loyal and passionate support.

My closest family deserve the credit for fostering the intellectual and creative energy that have made me a better historian. My maternal grandparents, Lidia Kosk and the late Henryk Kosk, taught me as a child to love history, and they encouraged me to practice the craft as an adult; it is to them that I dedicate this book. The late Helen and James Timmers showed me the joy of story-telling. My parents, Danuta E. Kosk-Kosicka and Andrzej J. Kosicki, have advised me every step of the way with honesty and love, reading more than they probably ever could have conceived about the Catholic Church. Finally, I draw strength from the courage, patience, and wisdom of my wife, Melissa Azoulay.

# Abbreviations

| | |
|---|---|
| AAN | Archive of Modern Records (*Archiwum Akt Nowych*) |
| AIPN | Archive of the Institute of National Remembrance (*Archiwum Instytutu Pamięci Narodowej*) |
| AAJT | Anna and Jerzy Turowicz Archive (*Archiwum Anny i Jerzego Turowicza*) |
| AJRM | Jacques and Raïssa Maritain Archive (*Archives Jacques et Raïssa Maritain*) |
| AKSCC | Archive of the *Civitas Christiana* Catholic Association (*Archiwum Katolickiego Stowarzyszenia "Civitas Christiana"*) |
| APIASA | Archives of the Polish Institute of Arts and Sciences of America |
| APJF | Archives of the Jesuit Province of France (*Archives de la Province Jésuite de France*) |
| BN | National Library of Poland (*Biblioteka Narodowa*) |
| BUKUL | University Library of the John Paul II Catholic University of Lublin (*Biblioteka Uniwersytecka Katolickiego Uniwersytetu Lubelskiego im. Jana Pawła II*) |
| CPSU | Communist Party of the Soviet Union |
| FSK | Franciscan Sisters Servants of the Cross (*Siostry Franciszkanki Służebnice Krzyża*) |
| HIA | Hoover Institution Archives |

| | |
|---|---|
| ILCIP | International Liaison Committee of Intellectuals for Peace |
| IMEC | Institute for the Documentation of Contemporary Publishing (*Institut Mémoires de l'Édition Contemporaine*) |
| JOC | Young Christian Workers (*Jeunesse Ouvrière Chrétienne*) |
| KIK | Catholic Intelligentsia Clubs (*Kluby Inteligencji Katolickiej*) |
| KN | Confederation of the Nation (*Konfederacja Narodu*) |
| KUL | Catholic University of Lublin (*Katolicki Uniwersytet Lubelski*) |
| MBP | Ministry of Public Safety (*Ministerstwo Bezpieczeństwa Publicznego*) |
| MP | Member of Parliament |
| MRP | Popular Republican Movement (*Mouvement Républicain Populaire*) |
| NATO | North Atlantic Treaty Organization |
| NEI | New International Teams (*Nouvelles Équipes Internationales*) |
| NKVD | People's Commissariat for Internal Affairs (*Narodnii Komissariat Vnutrennikh Del*) |
| ONR | National-Radical Camp (*Obóz Narodowo-Radykalny*) |
| OP | Order of Preachers (The Dominican Order) |
| PCF | French Communist Party (*Parti Communiste Français*) |
| PDP | Popular Democratic Party (*Parti Démocrate Populaire*) |
| PKOP | Polish Committee of Defenders of Peace (*Polski Komitet Obrońców Pokoju*) |
| PKWN | Polish Committee of National Liberation (*Polski Komitet Wyzwolenia Narodowego*) |
| PPR | Polish Workers' Party (*Polska Partia Robotnicza*) |
| PSL | Polish Peasants' Party (*Polskie Stronnictwo Ludowe*) |
| PZPR | Polish United Workers' Party (*Polska Zjednoczona Partia Robotnicza*) |
| SJ | Society of Jesus |
| SP | Christian Labor Party (*Stronnictwo Pracy*) |
| STO | Compulsory Labor Service (*Service du Travail Obligatoire*) |
| TC | Christian Witness (*Témoignage Chrétien*) |
| TMPP | Tadeusz Mazowiecki Private Papers (by permission of the Mazowiecki family) |
| UCP | Union of Progressive Christians (*Union des Chrétiens Progressistes*) |

| | |
|---|---|
| UK | United Kingdom |
| UN | United Nations |
| US | United States |
| USSR | Union of Soviet Socialist Republics |
| WTK | *Wrocław Catholic Weekly* (*Wrocławski Tygodnik Katolicki*) |

# Cast of Characters

THOMAS AQUINAS OP (1225–1274)—Dominican monk, theologian, Doctor of the Catholic Church, and author of dozens of texts in philosophy and theology. His two major works—*Summa Theologiae* and *Summa contra Gentiles*—have been foundational to all subsequent doctrine of the Catholic Church. Called the "Angelic Doctor," he has inspired centuries' worth of disciples who call themselves "Thomists." Twentieth-century French and Polish thinkers saw his writings as the key to Roman Catholicism's renewal and reform.

JEAN BOULIER (1894–1980)—French Catholic priest and law professor, known after World War II as the "Red Priest" for his tireless advocacy of Communist political causes. A cofounder of the Young Christian Workers (JOC), he became a "worker-priest" in the 1940s. An active member of the Communist-inspired movement for world peace, he visited Poland regularly beginning in 1946. Defrocked in 1953 for his political activities, he returned to the priesthood a decade later as an advocate of social justice for the Global South.

MARIE-DOMINIQUE CHENU OP (1895–1990)—one of the authoritative Thomist theologians of the twentieth century and a principal theorist of *ressourcement*. Chenu was professor and rector of the Dominican seminary called Le Saulchoir, which he moved from Belgium to Paris in 1937. The banning of his guide to Saulchoir's methodology in 1942 marked the beginning of the Vatican's turn against "new theology." Although supported by French primate Emmanuel Suhard, Chenu was stripped of his rectorship and ultimately banned from teaching and publishing. These bans were reversed in the 1960s, when he became a prominent invited expert at Vatican II.

YVES CONGAR OP (1904–1995)—like his Dominican brother Marie-Dominique Chenu, one of the twentieth century's leading Catholic theologians and Thomist reformers. As professor at Le Saulchoir seminary during Marie-Dominique Chenu's rectorship, he elaborated theologies of labor and the laity. Silenced by Pope Pius XII's Holy See in the 1950s, he famously called it "a police regime of betrayal." His invitation to participate as an expert at Vatican II signaled a sea change in Church politics. In 1994, he was elevated to the rank of cardinal by John Paul II.

JEAN-MARIE DOMENACH (1922–1997)—one of the principal lay intellectuals of the Catholic vanguard. Born in Lyon, he studied briefly at Vichy's Uriage academy before joining the Christian Witness resistance movement. A devotee of Emmanuel Mounier's personalism, he joined the staff of *Esprit* in 1946. As editorial assistant, then managing editor, then executive editor of *Esprit*, he maintained a deep interest in Poland. His partnership with *Dziś i Jutro* was one of the cornerstones of the short-lived Catholic-socialist international. In 1954 he received PAX's Pietrzak Prize for his campaign against German rearmament. When his Catholic-socialist friends left PAX, he shifted his support to the new Catholic Intelligentsia Clubs. He was an *Esprit* editor until 1976, then an editor of the Seuil publishing house and a professor at France's *École Polytechnique*. In the 1980s, he promoted Poland's Solidarity movement and the cause of anti-Communist dissidents.

WOJCIECH KĘTRZYŃSKI (1918–1983)—philosopher, historian, diplomat. After completing part of high school in Belgium, he fought in the Polish army in 1939 against the invading Germans, then joined Bolesław Piasecki's underground Confederation of the Nation. After the war, he helped to define the *Dziś i Jutro* movement as the architect of its foreign policy, launching, for example, the Catholic-socialist international. In the Stalinist years, he was one of Poland's most promising and erudite young Catholic thinkers, a tireless advocate of personalism. He left PAX in 1956, but instead of joining the Catholic Intelligentsia Clubs, he cofounded the Christian Social Association. He wrote little after 1956, working as a diplomat in Montreal and in Paris. In the final years of his life, he served as an MP in the Polish parliament.

WŁADYSŁAW KORNIŁOWICZ (1884–1946)—pastor, theologian, and

Thomist. Born in Russian Poland, he studied theology at Fribourg. Ordained in 1912, he served as a chaplain during World War I and the Polish-Bolshevik War. In 1917 he founded a Thomist seminar that ran for almost three decades. Between the wars, he was a professor of liturgical theology at the Catholic University of Lublin and advisor to the Renaissance movement. From 1930, he served as pastor of the Laski community, where he pioneered a new method of catechism based on face-to-face dialogue with non-believers. He was responsible for propagating Jacques Maritain's work in Poland and for hosting the French Thomist in 1934.

André Mandouze (1916–2006)—a key lay activist of the French vanguard. He completed his PhD before the war, specializing in the thought of Augustine of Hippo. In 1937, he became an editor of the short-lived journal *Sept*. During the war, he co-organized the Christian Witness resistance movement. A theorist of "progressive" Christianity, he was a founding member of the Union of Progressive Christians and a key anti-colonial voice in the world peace movement. In 1946, he moved to Algeria, where he agitated for independence and became involved with the National Liberation Front. In 1965, he returned to Paris to teach at the Sorbonne.

Jacques Maritain (1882–1973)—one of the great Catholic thinkers of the modern era. Together with his wife Raïssa, he was baptized as a Catholic in 1905. He moved through several distinct phases as a philosopher and public figure—Bergsonianism, integralism, humanism. A devoted Thomist, Maritain was one of the founders of modern Catholic personalism. He was well-regarded in the Vatican until he protested the bombing of Guernica during the Spanish Civil War. He served as an important early mentor to Emmanuel Mounier. Maritain was in North America when Germany invaded France, and he spent the war teaching and writing in exile. His books were airdropped into France and circulated among anti-Nazi resistance fighters—both in France and in Poland. A long-time critic of liberalism and republicanism, he turned toward democracy and against anti-Semitism as a result of the war. He served as French ambassador to the Vatican from 1945 to 1948 before assuming a professorship at Princeton. After his retirement, Maritain returned to France, served as a prominent expert at Vatican II, and—at the end of his life—took monastic vows.

Tadeusz Mazowiecki (1927–2013)—one of the defining figures of twentieth-century Poland. He was the son of a 1930s Catholic Action activist. After World War II he briefly joined a Christian Democratic party, but having witnessed its co-optation he turned instead to *Dziś i Jutro* (later renamed PAX). Mazowiecki rose quickly through the movement's ranks, developing an expertise in personalism. By 1952, together with his friend Janusz Zabłocki, Mazowiecki had become a leading young radical. As editor of *WTK* in 1953–54, he prominently condemned Kielce bishop Czesław Kaczmarek, who had recently been convicted in a show trial following a harrowing two years of interrogation and torture. One year later, Mazowiecki led the young radicals' effort to de-Stalinize PAX, for which he was ejected from the movement. He cofounded the Catholic Intelligentsia Clubs in 1956 and the *Więź* monthly in 1958. From 1961 to 1972, he served as an MP. He became a dissident in the 1970s, advising hunger strikers and writing for *Esprit* about Communist Poland's infringement on human rights. A top advisor to Solidarity, he was interned following its suppression. In spring 1989 he played a leading role at Poland's Round Table negotiations, and in August of that year he became the Soviet Bloc's first non-Communist prime minister. He resolved the disputed Polish-German border, liberalized the Polish economy, and set Poland on a track to NATO and EU membership. He stepped down after losing the presidential elections of 1990 but remained active in public life until his death. In 1995, Mazowiecki resigned his UN commission as special rapporteur for Yugoslavia after the UN failed to prevent the Srebrenica Genocide.

EMMANUEL MOUNIER (1905–1950)—prominent philosopher, public intellectual, and founder of the journal *Esprit*. Mounier was the icon of the mid-century vanguard. After abandoning his studies to support his family and devote himself to writing, he became the architect of "personalist revolution." In the 1930s, he opposed fascism and Stalinism alike, but was consistently "totalistic" in his personalism, railing against liberalism, capitalism, and individualism. Under Vichy, he taught at Uriage until the regime turned on him. Thereafter, he served as a mentor to the Christian Witness underground. After World War II, he became a leading advocate of Catholic support for Communist regimes in the Soviet Bloc—especially in Poland (which he visited in 1946)—and argued for a joint Catholic-Marxist "revolution" on behalf of the "human person." He succumbed to a heart attack at the age of forty-five.

BOLESŁAW PIASECKI (1915–1979)—*éminence grise* of twentieth-century Polish politics. A National Democrat in his youth, he was radicalized into a fascist in the mid-1930s. One of the founders of the National-Radical Camp and leader of its Phalange faction, he was a leading anti-Semitic author and organizer of paramilitary violence. During World War II, he founded and led the Confederation of the Nation. He was arrested by the NKVD in 1944, but was released in 1945 under murky circumstances after presenting Poland's new Communist regime with blueprints for a pro-Marxist Catholic movement. He created and led *Dziś i Jutro*, later renamed PAX, until his death three decades later. Charismatic, megalomaniacal, and a prolific writer, Piasecki believed that he understood Catholic theology better than anyone. His 1954 *Essential Questions* landed on the Vatican Index, together with the *Dziś i Jutro* journal. In the 1960s, Piasecki returned to open anti-Semitism, making PAX co-responsible for the Communists' persecution of Polish Jews in 1968.

KAROL POPIEL (1887–1977)—leader of Poland's Christian Democratic movement. An elected official throughout the interwar years, he was briefly imprisoned by Piłsudski's regime in 1930. Cofounder of the Christian Labor Party in 1937, he became its leader in 1939. A member of the wartime government-in-exile, Popiel returned to Poland in 1945, hoping to compete electorally with the Communists. Unable to stop the co-optation of his party, he left Poland in time to avoid the arrests and show trials that swept up other Christian Democrats. For the next three decades, he led a small group of die-hard Polish Christian Democratic exiles funded by the American Free Europe Committee, who traveled the world waging "political warfare." In the wake of de-Stalinization, Popiel tested the waters for a return to Poland. When this proved infeasible, his Christian Democrats instead organized cross-Iron Curtain travel for hundreds of Polish Catholic intellectuals, assuring regular communication between Catholic activists in Poland and Western Europe. Cut off from American funding in the early 1970s, Popiel died in Rome, on the verge of penury.

STANISŁAW STOMMA (1908–2005)—publisher, legal scholar, co-creator of the journal *Znak*. Born in present-day Lithuania, Stomma studied law in Wilno. A long-time Renaissance activist, he was recruited by Jerzy Turowicz after the war to write for *Tygodnik Powszechny*. His 1946 essay on "minimalism" positioned the Kraków intellectuals of

*Tygodnik Powszechny* and *Znak* against Catholic socialism. In 1956, he cofounded the Catholic Intelligentsia Clubs and was later elected to represent that movement in parliament, which he did continuously for two decades. Stomma resigned in 1976 in protest against pro-Soviet constitutional reforms. He became an advisor to the Solidarity movement, and after 1989 served as a senator.

ANTONI SZYMAŃSKI (1881–1942)—one of the creators of social Catholicism in Poland, a prolific writer, and one of Poland's first personalists. Born in German Poland, he was sent to Louvain by his seminary professor Idzi Radziszewski to complete a doctorate. He returned to partitioned Poland an expert on the French Christian Democrats of the 1890s. In 1918, he cofounded the Catholic University of Lublin. He was a co-organizer of Poland's Renaissance and Catholic Action movements. In 1933, he became rector of the Catholic University. Following the German invasion of Poland in 1939, occupying forces—which had shuttered the university—kept Szymański under house arrest until just before his death.

JERZY TUROWICZ (1912–1999)—one of the great Catholic publishers of twentieth-century Europe. He studied engineering in the 1920s and 1930s before turning to Catholic philosophy as a student activist in Renaissance. Beginning in the 1930s, he was an ardent exponent of Maritain's and Mounier's personalist philosophies. He joined the Christian Democratic resistance during World War II, and made his home a refuge for clandestine activists. He served as editor of various Catholic publications from 1939 until his death sixty years later. He cofounded *Tygodnik Powszechny* with Jan Piwowarczyk in 1945, and edited it for the next fifty-four years. He was an ardent advocate of ecumenism and Catholic-Jewish dialogue. Together with Stanisław Stomma, he created Stalinist Poland's Catholic intellectual alternative to *Dziś i Jutro*. The future Pope John Paul II, Karol Wojtyła, was his staff writer from 1948 until receiving a bishop's miter in 1958. Turowicz cofounded the Catholic Intelligentsia Clubs in 1956, traveled internationally on the movement's behalf, and advised Solidarity in the 1980s.

KAROL WOJTYŁA, JOHN PAUL II (1920–2005)—Roman Catholic pontiff and saint, one of the defining global figures of the twentieth century. Left with no immediate family after his father's death in 1941, he survived by laboring in a limestone quarry and a chemical factory. He became active in the Christian Democratic resistance and was a member of an underground theater troupe. Wojtyła found spiritual guidance in a reading group run by the tailor Jan Tyranowski, who inspired the future pope to seek the priesthood. His wartime seminary mentor, Kraków archbishop Sapieha, sent him to Rome in 1946 to study at the Collegium Angelicum. Well-versed in Thomism, inspired by France, Wojtyła became a personalist and a pastoral radical. He returned to Poland and launched parallel careers as pastor and philosophy professor. Appointed auxiliary bishop of Kraków in 1958, he became protector to the Catholic Intelligentsia Clubs. Appointed archbishop in 1964 and cardinal in 1967, Wojtyła made a name for himself in the global Church at Vatican II, helping to draft *Gaudium et Spes*. He was an advocate of pastoral reform and lay activism in the Church, and was close to Pope Paul VI. In 1978, after the thirty-three-day pontificate of John Paul I, Wojtyła was elected Roman pontiff. Famous for his anti-Communism, his suppression of liberation theology, and his teachings on human life, John Paul II was a global advocate for Solidarity, which he considered a winning strategy for combating Communism and liberalism alike.

STEFAN WYSZYŃSKI (1901–1981)—pastor, professor, and leader of the Church in Poland from 1948 to 1981. He graduated from the Catholic University of Lublin, then studied in France and Italy. A disciple of Antoni Szymański, he became one of the defining figures of the Renaissance movement. He spent World War II running clandestine seminars and prayer groups, including gatherings at Laski. In 1946, he was appointed bishop of Lublin, and in 1948 he succeeded August Hlond as Primate of Poland. Initially he tried to reach a modus vivendi with the Communist regime, but in 1953 he protested the regime's overreach and the conviction of Bishop Kaczmarek. He was kept under house arrest for three years and was prevented from exercising his duties. Released in 1956 by Władysław Gomułka, he dedicated Poland to the Virgin Mary in celebration of 1000 years of Polish Christendom (1966). His turn to popular devotion made for uneasy coexistence with the lay intellectuals of the Catholic Intelligentsia Clubs. He lived to see his Kraków colleague Karol Wojtyła become pope.

JANUSZ ZABŁOCKI (1926–2014)—leading Catholic intellectual and politician of Communist Poland. Active as a Scout, he joined the Gray Ranks anti-Nazi resistance, and in 1943, at the age of seventeen, became a platoon leader. While in the resistance, he discovered Jacques Maritain's personalism. After World War II, he studied law in Kraków under an assumed name until he was amnestied in 1947. Initially suspicious of *Dziś i Jutro* founder Piasecki's fascist background, he ultimately joined the movement in 1949–50, embracing its Catholic socialism and rapidly establishing himself as one of its young radicals. He and Tadeusz Mazowiecki attracted a host of other young Catholic socialists who initially defended Stalinism, only to turn against it in 1955. Zabłocki was a cofounder of the Catholic Intelligentsia Clubs and later *Więź*, but in the mid-1960s he and Mazowiecki fell into conflict, fracturing both the movement and the journal. An expert on personalism and Catholic social thought, Zabłocki edited successive Catholic journals from the 1950s through the 1980s. He was an MP from 1965 to 1985. In 1967, he created a center for the study of social Catholicism. Zabłocki attempted to create a concessioned Christian Democratic opposition to the Communists, but in the mid-1980s, he was pushed out of politics by the secret police. In 1988, he briefly reactivated the Christian Labor Party, only to find himself on the outside once Solidarity took power.

JERZY ZAWIEYSKI (1902–1969)—playwright, statesman, catechumen. Zawieyski was gay, and his birth father was Jewish. Raised Catholic, he resented the Church's opposition to these core parts of his being. He was an active socialist throughout the interwar and spent three years in Paris, where he got to know Mounier and other Catholic nonconformists. During World War II, Zawieyski dialogued intensively with the priests Władysław Korniłowicz and Jan Zieja, and he returned to the Catholic faith. After the war he advocated for Catholic-Marxist coexistence. Rejecting Stalinism, he withdrew from public life in 1948, returning in 1956 to co-found the Catholic Intelligentsia Clubs. From 1957 to 1969, he served as an MP and a member of the powerful Council of State. Zawieyski tried, and failed, to normalize the Church's place in Communist Poland. In 1968, after "civic militia" beat student protesters, he delivered a speech of protest from the parliamentary rostrum. Harangued, denounced, and stripped of his public functions, he suffered a stroke and landed in a convalescent home, where—under suspicious circumstances—he fell to his death from an open window.

# Introduction

*To defend oneself from totalitarianism, one does not have to return to individualism.*

—*Tadeusz Mazowiecki*[1]

IN 1944, the Red Army was advancing westward across Eastern Europe, chasing the retreating forces of Nazi Germany. By the fall, Soviet authorities had a secure hold over much of the territory of prewar Poland. Having announced the formation of a Soviet-backed Polish Communist government in July, the Red Army waited out the Warsaw Uprising on the eastern banks of the Vistula, until Germans had crushed the resistance and set the Polish capital ablaze.[2]

In mid-October, a week after the Uprising's collapse, British prime minister Winston Churchill was in Moscow, meeting Joseph Stalin at the Kremlin. Churchill advised the Soviet dictator that he should take care not to mistreat the Catholic Church in Poland, in order to avoid angering the pope. Stalin retorted, "And how many divisions does the pope have?"[3] This was, of course, a rhetorical question: in Stalin's eyes, since the Vatican had no military might to back its international agenda, it did not count.

Fourteen years later, Pius XII (1939–58)—the pope whom Stalin had mocked—succumbed to heart failure. On hearing of the pontiff's passing, Jean-Marie Domenach, the Catholic editor of the respected French journal *Esprit* (*The Spirit*), made a note in his diary: "The Stalin of the Church is dead. It is a joy."[4]

Oddly enough, Stalin the atheist autocrat and Domenach the Catholic editor agreed on two crucial points: that social justice was the goal of political action, and that the Vatican was actually harming the cause of a just society. Stalin believed that the world should look to him for the answer, as the latter-day personification of Hegel's and Marx's march of History. Meanwhile, thirty-six-year-old Domenach thought that Pius XII shared Stalin's worst qualities: persecuting dissenters and pursuing absolute power in world affairs under the pretext of helping the poor and downtrodden—all while casting aside the ideals of the faith. Instead, Domenach saw the only chance for a just society in what he called the "Catholic *avant-garde*"—younger generations of Catholic activists, born in the 1910s and 1920s, inspired by their shared experience resisting fascism to work together with Marxists toward a better future.[5]

It was one and the same country that helped to convince Domenach and Stalin to write off the Vatican: Poland. The French editor and the Soviet dictator alike respected the singular clout of Polish Catholics. And yet, the way in which Polish intellectuals encountered the Catholic Church in the first half of the twentieth century was a function of what they had learned from generations of French Catholics like Domenach—and what they had taught the French in return. This book reconstructs these spaces of overlap and encounter between Poland, France, and the Catholic Church.

*Catholics on the Barricades* is a work of twentieth-century European history. It begins with the collapse of dynastic empires and the rising tides of nationalism and socialism in the *fin-de-siècle*, followed by Europe's failed experiment with liberal democracy after 1918 and the chaos and genocide of World War II. Then comes the core of the book: the establishment of Communist regimes in postwar Central and Eastern Europe, the rise and fall of Stalinism in the Soviet Bloc, and finally de-Stalinization.

This European master narrative frames the book's central story. Its subjects are several generations of Catholics from France and Poland who believed that they had found the key to building a just society. They pioneered a new kind of Catholicism that took Marxism seriously, and they intended to remake European social and political life in their own image. Their proposed method was revolution—not with guns, but with pens and typewriters. Seeing themselves as the bringers of "total" revolution—encompassing religion, politics, and society—they ended up serving twin evils: first exclusionary (or integral) nationalism, and then Stalinism as well.

This is a book about ideas, politics, faith, and the way in which all three shaped the everyday lives of intellectuals in impossible situations —whether setting deadly traps for German patrols in 1943, struggling to survive secret police beatings in 1949 without denouncing their friends, or justifying the arrests of bishops in 1953 on the misguided assumption that they were helping the Church in the long run.[6] Yet this is a story of life, not death, and of the creative ways in which several generations of Catholic activists refused to let themselves be trapped—whether by a partitioning imperial power, the decline of a republic, conquest by a fascist government, or the foreign imposition of a Communist autocracy. In response, they turned to utopian projects of social and political transformation. Seeking to use Roman Catholicism as their starting point for building a more just human civilization, they styled themselves "revolutionaries." Though most ultimately abandoned their utopian experiments, these Catholic intellectuals remained—to borrow from Padraic Kenney—"resourceful shapers of their own destiny."[7]

This book is a conceptual history of "revolution." It tells the story of the "political radicalization and deradicalization" of European intellectuals whose *fin-de-siècle* and interwar educations took on new meaning in the resistance to Nazism. For all, wartime anti-fascism led to, at a minimum, giving the benefit of the doubt to postwar Communist regimes—if not active involvement in their construction. In the end, all of these intellectuals were disappointed.[8] On the other hand, the book is their collective intellectual biography: a profile of generations of deeply religious people whose faith drove them into politics—and into friendship and intellectual partnership with one another.[9]

The main characters in this story include some of the most vivid and notable personalities of twentieth-century Europe—as well as near-forgotten figures who have not gotten the attention that they deserve. They include, from France, Jacques Maritain, arguably the twentieth century's most influential Catholic philosopher; and his one-time disciple Emmanuel Mounier, founder of one of Europe's most important opinion-making journals, *Esprit*.[10] The most accomplished Poles, mean-

while, were Jerzy Turowicz, who edited the only independent periodical to survive over forty years behind the Iron Curtain; Tadeusz
Mazowiecki, who went from being a Stalinist in his twenties to governing Poland in his sixties as the prime minister who ended Communism;
and one of the twentieth century's global household names—the future
Pope John Paul II, Karol Wojtyła.[11] But equally important to the story
are Wojciech Kętrzyński, a gifted Catholic philosopher whose career
effectively ended with the onset of de-Stalinization; and Antoni Szymański, who introduced turn-of-the-century Poland to France's first
experiments with Catholic "revolution." To help the reader keep track
of the book's most important protagonists, a series of brief biographi-
cal sketches precedes this introduction.

In 1891, a Roman pontiff admitted for the first time that the Industrial Revolution had thrown Europe's social and political order into
chaos. Over the next four decades, French Catholics responding to his
call exported new ideas to Poland. Those ideas, in turn, germinated on
Polish soil throughout World War II.[12] After the war, with Red Army
boots on the ground across Central and Eastern Europe, a few hundred
Catholics on both sides of the emerging Iron Curtain decided that, instead of resisting the new atheist, Marxist revolution, they would try to
work with it—perhaps even infiltrate it, like a Catholic "Trojan horse."
In Emmanuel Mounier's words, they devoted themselves to "making
the revolutionaries spiritual."[13]

In addition to their declared goals of social justice and peace, the
French and Polish Catholics were united by a shared fear of a resur-
gent Germany. For both nationalities, anti-Germanism built on, and
preserved, long-standing anti-Semitism. Their "revolution," then, was
poisoned from the outset. Seeking to create a model for export to all of
humanity, the transnational Catholic vanguard ended up reproducing
ethnonational hatreds.[14]

## TRANSNATIONAL POLAND

Too often, modern Poland has been studied in isolation, as an ir-
reducible *sui generis*. Following Brian Porter-Szűcs, I insist here that
Polish history can only be understood in virtue of its place in the wider
world.[15] That is why this book looks at Poland through a transnational
lens. Definitions of "transnationalism" abound, but in *Catholics on*

*the Barricades*, the word represents not a fully formed worldview, but rather a conceptual mold to be filled by empirical research spanning multiple nation-states.[16]

The twentieth century was devastating for Poland. Having been stateless for 123 years—partitioned by Austrians, Prussians, and Russians in the final decades of the eighteenth century—Poland regained sovereignty in 1918, only to lose it once again in 1939 to Nazis and Soviets working together to erase Poland from the map of Europe.[17] The Second Polish Republic, like much of interwar Central and Eastern Europe, featured a weak democratic culture marked by assassinations, coups, and paramilitary street fighting—all involving forces professing their dedication to defending Polish sovereignty from the nascent Soviet Union.[18] The multinational, multilingual, multiconfessional interwar republic saw a surge in ethnonational violence targeting especially Jews, but also Ukrainians and Germans. By the end of the 1930s, the vast majority of Polish political forces—strongly supported by their Catholic hierarchy—openly advocated the physical removal of Jews from Poland, in the interest of assuring that Poles would be "masters in their own home."[19]

Then came the Second World War. Within a month of signing the Molotov-Ribbentrop Pact of August 1939, Nazi Germany and the Soviet Union had invaded Poland from both sides, partitioning the country. The historic lands of the former Polish-Lithuanian Commonwealth became a site of deportations, ghettos, concentration camps, and the extermination of European Jewry. At the same time, six years of occupation brought a series of campaigns intended to wipe away Polish nationhood.[20]

The chaos of war bred social revolution.[21] As the Germans retreated in 1944–45, the Soviets stepped in to mold that revolution in their own image. At the Yalta Conference of 1945, Stalin promised "free and fair" elections for Poland.[22] Over the next three years, however, the fig leaf fell away, and Poland became part of the Stalinist system.[23] For the next decade, Polish Communists, closely monitored by Moscow, governed through a mix of terror and repression. Polish Stalinism outlasted even Stalin's death in 1953, finally relaxing only in response to the USSR's own de-Stalinization in 1955–56.[24]

Such has long been the conventional wisdom about twentieth-century Poland. It is accurate, but it is also incomplete—as a growing body of recent scholarship has shown by bringing gender history, labor history, cultural history, the history of emotions, and urban history into the historiographical mix.[25] Katherine Lebow is right to insist "that even coercion had its limits as an effective strategy of social control; that societies were never passive, even at the height of state repression and violence; that power structures comprised groups and individuals with competing agendas; and that [C]ommunist leaders, in order to achieve their goals, often sought popular participation and acquiescence, accommodating, in turn, to a variety of pressures from below."[26] One of the principal sources of pressure on the autocratic regimes governing modern Poland was Roman Catholicism.

Certain stories cut across national borders; these cannot be contained within the history of a single nation or nation-state. One of the most self-evidently transnational forces in world history is religion.[27] In Polish history, the Catholic Church has rightly been accorded pride of place in shaping the nation's trajectory. But its story goes beyond how Catholics living on Polish territory behaved, or how Rome and Warsaw interacted.[28] In the 1050 years since Christianity's introduction onto Polish soil in 966, Polish Catholics have traveled far and wide, encountering beliefs, ideas, and faith-practices that were often as little Roman as they were Polish. Likewise, Poles welcomed Catholic visitors from elsewhere, and these visits—and the ideas and memories they left behind—shaped the lives of Catholics in modern Poland.

Traditionally, Catholicism in Poland has been understood through the lens of the hyphenated identity of the "Catholic Pole" (*Polak-katolik*). The place of nationalism within Polish Catholic identity remains controversial. On the one hand, leading recent scholarship has decentered nationalism by examining Catholics' "national indifference" in the Polish borderlands.[29] On the other, nationalism remains central to scholars' explanations of how Polish Catholics positioned themselves in the wider world. In his path-breaking research, Brian Porter-Szűcs has shown how the "Catholic Pole" concept was manufactured between the world wars by a political movement known as National Democracy (*Narodowa Demokracja*, or *endecja*), which deployed a mixture of racial and religious criteria to define Polish nationhood.[30]

Theirs was an integral nationalism. Its exponents openly exploited religion in the service of politics, positing nationhood as an organic unity to be defended against external enemies. The pioneer of integral nationalism was a late-nineteenth-century French political movement called French Action (*Action Française*).[31] Its Polish admirer, *endecja* leader Roman Dmowski, proved an apt pupil, refashioning what in France had been a mass movement of monarchist anti-liberals into an anti-imperial vision that was at once pseudoscientific—Dmowski was a trained biologist—and spiritual. Dmowski grafted his integral nationalism onto a rich nineteenth-century tradition of national struggle, political messianism, and popular anti-Semitism. In fact, anti-Semitism was a central feature of both the French and the Polish movements.[32] Roman Catholicism reinforced those convictions: the Church had long held that Jews were collectively to blame for Jesus' death, and that Jews must convert in order to bring about the Second Coming. It was the contest between Dmowski's exclusionary, anti-Semitic vision and Józef Piłsudski's anti-Bolshevik, multicultural nationalism that defined Poland between the world wars.[33]

In retrospect, it seems that Dmowski was the victor. During World War II and in its aftermath, the drive for ethnonational purity remained central to the self-understanding of Catholics on Polish soil. Even in a post-Holocaust world, where most Polish Jews had been murdered, Polish Germans and Ukrainians expelled by postwar border shifts, and the apparatus of power seized by Communists, the idea of the "Catholic Poles" remained a staple of political mobilization. An ethnonational vision of Polish sovereignty united Catholics and Communists, ironically, just as it had the Catholic hierarchy and National Democrats before 1939. Michael Fleming rightly notes that "through the drive to national homogeneity, and nationality policy more generally, the [C]ommunists were able to secure sufficient acquiescence from Polish society to enable them to move forward with their social, political, and economic programs."[34]

One social class beat the ideological odds, re-establishing itself as a power-broker under the Communist regime. This was the gentry, defined by their "power to define patriotism and to authorize their own version of history."[35] After World War II, formerly landed classes worked with the new Communist regime to reinvent a social stratum that, since the mid-nineteenth century, had considered itself the vanguard of the Polish nation: the intellectuals.[36] In the nineteenth century, Polish intellectuals had followed their Enlightenment forerunners in looking to revolutionary France for the secret to a successful, "modern" future.[37] One hundred years later, reeling from war and imperial partition, the intellectuals of Communist Poland looked to the same source, considering themselves "closer to Paris than to Moscow, in spite of everything."[38]

## FRANCE, POLAND, AND THE CATHOLIC CHURCH

As with Poland, historians have recently begun to "transnationalize" France, looking beyond the borders of that nation-state to paint a fuller picture of France's role in world history. This narrative arc stretches from the French and Haitian Revolutions, through the Dreyfus Affair, to de-colonization, European integration, and beyond.[39] Catholicism and Poland together form an important—but as yet unexamined—strand of France's transnational story. By the mid-twentieth century, for many Polish Catholics, the immediate point of reference and inspiration in the Catholic world was not, in fact, Rome. Rather, Paris was where the action was. *Catholics on the Barricades* explains why.

France occupies a singular place in the history of Roman Catholicism. Ever since the French king Philip the Fair stood up to Pope Boniface VIII in the late thirteenth century, France has prided itself on an autonomous, "Gallican" tradition within the Catholic Church.[40] In the eighteenth century, this tradition helped to position the French "Old Regime" against the Jesuit order; in the nineteenth, it divided French Catholicism between "ultramontanes," who declared unquestioning loyalty to Rome, and "Gallicans," who believed that the Holy See's preferences ranked a distant second behind the needs of Catholics living on French soil.[41]

By the *fin-de-siècle*—defined roughly by the first four decades of the French Third Republic, from 1870 to the outbreak of World War I in 1914[42]—French activists saw themselves as a natural-born Catholic vanguard, unfettered by the Holy See's chain of command and the discipline that it imposed on the rest of the Catholic world. In the closing decades of the nineteenth century, French Catholics helped to develop democratic republicanism, the modern welfare state, and overseas empire.[43] By the start of the First World War, France stood in the vanguard of European Catholic social, political, and intellectual activism. It was also France that—in the course of the Dreyfus Affair—provoked a split that touched not only its own Catholic population, but the entire Roman Catholic world. As Émile Poulat argues, three distinct strains emerged: the integral nationalists (abbreviated "integralists"), the "modernists," and the "intransigentists."[44] Integralists, we have already encountered. "Modernists," meanwhile, believed that Catholics needed to recognize that the Reformation, the Scientific Revolution, and the Enlightenment had come to stay. The Catholic Church, therefore, needed to accommodate the "modern world"—not just its technologies, but also secularism, modern philosophy, and even new ways of interpreting the Bible.[45] To "intransigentists," modernists posed the gravest danger of all, far worse than the integralists. It was two separate intransigentist popes—Pius X in 1907 and Pius XII in 1950—who brought the heavy hammer of anathema down in full force against the diverse array of Catholics they painted with the "modernist" brush.[46]

For centuries, France has arguably been the single strongest adhesive binding Poland to the wider European cultural imaginary. Out of the Polish gentry's long-standing attachment to French language and culture came genuine intellectual friendships in the era of the partitions, as France welcomed exiled Polish artists and writers such as the national bard, Adam Mickiewicz.[47] In the process, French attitudes toward Poland evolved profoundly. In the eighteenth century, the French had Orientalized the Poles; in the twentieth century, however, French and Polish Catholics worked together to forge a new, "revolutionary" worldview.[48]

## THE "HUMAN PERSON"

The "person," one of the founding categories of European legal and political thought, migrated from ancient Greco-Roman law into Christian theology courtesy of its greatest medieval master, Thomas Aquinas.[49] Leading Jesuit theologians of the Catholic Reformation drew heavily on Aquinas in their quest to renew Catholic theology after the devastation wrought by Martin Luther and Jean Calvin. By the mid-nineteenth century, the "person" had become an organizing concept of political sovereignty in German-speaking Europe.[50] In the early twentieth century, however, French Catholic thinkers reclaimed the idea, calling for a literal "reinvention of the Renaissance."[51] Their goal was to reclaim humanism for God, replacing the secular, anthropocentric legacy of the Renaissance with what Jacques Maritain called "theocentric humanism": "at once ancient and new, respectful of the success of science but also capable of tempering its radicalism and fundamentally supportive of human spirit and dignity."[52] For the Catholic personalists of interwar France, the stakes were a matter of life and death: to alleviate suffering and to restore meaning to human existence, the "person" needed to be reinstated to its rightful place at the center of statecraft, culture, and humanist thought—replacing the secular "individual."

The "human person"—Aquinas's term—though not exclusively or originally French, became one of France's most significant twentieth-century exports. Calling a human being a "person" meant emphasizing her or his transcendent value—the fact that God created every "person" in His image. No longer simple atoms of humanity, "persons" both demanded and secured their own dignity, as well as the dignity of their fellow persons. Use of the word "person" implied a commitment to social renewal, to the pursuit of a just society, undergirded by faith in Roman Catholicism.

In France and Poland alike, "personalisms" became the basis for a range of different intellectual enterprises, both Catholic and secular: a revival of the study of the sources of Christian thought, from the Bible, to Augustine of Hippo, to Aquinas; a turn to humanism; and a theory of revolution. Any "personalism" is a "philosophy of reconstruction," of renewal, of transformation.[53] In the modern philosophical tradition, however, personhood remains grounded in G. W. F. Hegel's idea of *Sittlichkeit*, or the "ethical life."[54] The "person" serves as the ontological link between any one individual and all of humanity, between the secular and the divine—literally, unifying and transcending a fragmented world, as God Himself does.[55]

The idea of the "human person" is one of the keys to this book. One of the challenges in historicizing this concept lies in the plurality of its usages—and their frequent incommensurability. Jacques Maritain rightly complained in 1947, "There are at least a dozen personalist doctrines, which at times have nothing more in common than the term 'person.'"[56] The plurality of self-described personalisms should not, however, obscure the fact that modern personalism's roots lie in the very same mid-nineteenth-century debates that gave rise to Marxism.

For mid-nineteenth-century German Protestants, Warren Breckman observes, personhood was "the most important point of intersection for the discussion of theological, social, and political issues."[57] One hundred years later, the same became true of Catholics in France and Poland. In a century defined by the "total"—total war, total mobilization, the total state—it is unsurprising that the prescribed cure shared the language of the symptoms.[58] As Jerry Muller reminds us, "The critique that European intellectuals voiced in the interwar decades of the twentieth century was more comprehensive and more shrill than that of their nineteenth-century predecessors."[59] Amidst the economic depression and rampant violence of the 1930s, a French Catholic philosopher named Emmanuel Mounier—author of the call to "reinvent the Renaissance"—diagnosed individualism, liberalism, and capitalism as conjoined evils responsible for humanity's alienation from itself. Mounier called these evils the "established disorder" (*le désordre établi*). In its stead, he prescribed a "total" reordering of politics, society, and economics, to be achieved through "personalist and communitarian revolution."[60]

Like his one-time mentor Maritain, Mounier believed that faith should trump sovereignty and that the "spiritual" held primacy over the "political."[61] Yet his hope for remaking the world according to his personalism repeatedly ran aground on practical questions of politics. Having condemned fascism in the 1930s, he then collaborated with Vichy. Having condemned Communism in the 1930s, he insisted ten years later that Catholics living behind the emerging Iron Curtain had an obligation to play a role in Marxist revolution. This is why Zeev Sternhell described Mounier as a classic example of "neither Right, nor Left" politics—in other words, a man so idealistic in his belief in a "third way" that he collaborated again and again with the extremes. Personalism, in other words, seemed to carry its own "total" aspirations.[62]

## PERSONALIST AND TOTALITARIAN?

In the 1930s, Mounier criticized the Nazi movement as "totalitarian," yet he himself followed in the footsteps of Weimar archconservative Carl Schmitt—author of the idea of the "total state"—in peppering his philosophy with the adjective "total." His revolution was to be "total," each human being's sense of his own personhood—"total" as well.[63] Was Mounier's personalism itself totalistic, if not indeed—"totalitarian"?

As a work of intellectual history, *Catholics on the Barricades* holds fast to the principle of immanent critique. In other words, I take the characters in my story seriously on their own terms, using their language, before analyzing the assumptions and the consequences of that vocabulary.[64] This book therefore concerns itself with "the attraction of intellectuals to movements *promising* total integration through political power."[65]

At first blush, "totalitarianism" and "personalism" make for strange bedfellows. "Totalitarianism," one might object, is an artifact of Cold War social science, while "personalism" derives from theology. Although "totalitarianism" as a heuristic framework has fallen out of favor among historians since the collapse of Communist regimes in Central and Eastern Europe, it still rings ominous, laden with a heavy charge of moral transgression, if not outright "evil." Many scholars have become allergic to the term. Slavoj Žižek has famously charged its exponents with semantic bankruptcy: "the notion of 'totalitarianism,' far from being an effective theoretical concept, is a kind of *stopgap*: instead of enabling us to think, forcing us to acquire a new insight into the historical reality it describes, it relieves us of the duty to think, or even actively *prevents* us from thinking."[66]

Žižek, however, has missed a crucial segment of the "totalitarian" genealogy: the Catholic Church. It is in the semantic space of the sacred that "totalitarianism" and "personalism" share certain roots. One early exponent of "totalitarianism," the Fascist ideologue Giovanni Gentile, described the Catholic Church as a "totalitarian state."[67] One of the cornerstones of the historical study of "totalitarianism" has been the assumption that it was a kind of secular religion. Meanwhile, social scientists have for decades used the term "personalist" to describe dictatorships predicated on ritual devotion to a state's leader—a constitutive element of most historical definitions of "totalitarianism" as well.[68] In other words, as "personalism" has been secularized by scholars at the end of the twentieth century, so "totalitarianism" has been sacralized.[69]

Well before journalist Giovanni Amendola coined the term *totalitarismo* to indict Mussolini's Fascism, European thinkers wrote about the "person" in terms of its "absolute" or "total" status.[70] They were intervening in debates about power and sovereignty provoked by the rise of liberalism and socialism in the wake of Europe's Industrial Revolution. Warren Breckman has shown that nineteenth-century German monarchists constructed a theology of the "person" focused first and fore-most on the political. Anticipating the writings of Carl Schmitt in the 1920s, they argued that only an autocrat exercising total sovereignty—like God Himself—could protect personhood. Meanwhile, their opponents from among the young disciples of G. W. F. Hegel—including Karl Marx—secularized the idea of the "person," dethroning God in favor of "radical collectivization."[71] Marx understood humanity as a species-wide secular community of "persons." Neither side in this nineteenth-century debate used the term "totalitarianism," but both anticipated it in their insistence that total control over sovereignty was a prerequisite to reshaping a given society—whether the desired goal was material or spiritual renewal, or both.

A century later, Catholic personalists from across French- and German-speaking Europe developed their own theory of "totalitarian-ism." James Chappel has shown that three mid-century personalists —Dietrich von Hildebrand, Waldemar Gurian, and Jacques Maritain —embedded a personalist anti-totalitarianism within the American so-cial-scientific community just as World War II was ending and the Cold War beginning. Driven by fear of growing Soviet power, their accom-plishment, as Chappel observes, was "to take the theory [of totalitari-anism] from a local description of Italy to a more general theory of the modern state and its pathologies."[72] In other words, "personalism" not only shares intellectual roots with "totalitarianism": the former is, in fact, partly responsible for the latter.

My goal is neither to rehabilitate "totalitarianism" from its detractors nor to indict "personalism." These words held contextual meaning for the men and women who used them, and those meanings evolved ac-cording to contingent circumstances. As Jerry Muller writes, "before it became a historical reality, totalitarianism existed as an idea and ideal, spawned by men who defined and prided themselves on their mastery of ideas and commitment to ideals."[73] In this book, both terms func-tion as a conceptual terrain on which historical actors at odds on other issues—such as their relationship to the emerging Communist estab-lishment—found common ground. When prominent Polish intellectual Adam Michnik used the term "totalitarianism" to describe the com-mitments of personalists in the 1950s, his point was not that they had built some "totalitarian" ideal-type, but rather that their drive for intel-lectual consistency blinded them to the political consequences of their ideals.[74] To speak the word "totalitarianism" about twentieth-century personalists, then, is to frame an all-too-human story of intellectuals' radicalization and deradicalization—and of "revolution" betrayed.

## CATHOLICS AGAINST CAPITALISM

Catholic personalists were consistent in their rejection of capitalism, but what they actually proposed in its stead varied tremendously. While the personalist theorists of "totalitarianism" often found themselves allied with economic liberalism out of fear of the Soviet Union—a marriage of necessity with the lesser of two evils, as they saw it—Emmanuel Mounier proceeded from the reverse assumption. In his mind, the Bolsheviks' success proved that it was possible for revolutionaries to succeed in capitalism's overthrow. In other words, Mounier's endorsement of the "total" resulted from his admiration for the very political forces that had so terrified his personalist elders. He passed this anti-fascist, philo-Soviet understanding of "totalitarianism" along to his acolytes in France and Poland alike. Mounier's personalist project, vague though it was, inspired several generations of Catholics to follow in his footsteps.

These Catholics—from France, from Poland, and elsewhere—saw themselves not only as revolutionaries, but in fact as Catholicism's answer to the Marxist-Leninist "vanguard." Like Marx, they sought liberation through praxis from the radical alienation that they experienced.[75] Unlike Marx, however, they felt this way because they had just witnessed—and survived—total war and genocide. Mounier's disciples of the 1940s considered themselves to be "model Christians and prophets," leading the charge to rehabilitate modernism and to force the Catholic Church to accept the consequences of a "modern world."[76]

The Catholic vanguard of twentieth-century Europe embraced neither Stalin nor Pius XII, whom they saw as cut from the same cloth. Jean-Marie Domenach called Pius XII "the Stalin of the Church" not out of spite, but out of anguish that, instead of welcoming and evangelizing to the forces of revolution around the world, the pope was "carrying on a rear-guard battle" against them.[77] Meanwhile, the vanguard believed that Catholics and Marxists could march forward, arm in arm, in the revolutionary effort to build a just social order on earth, without waiting to die and go to Heaven. At the heart of this new order, they saw the sacrosanct figure of the "human person." In effect, the Catholic vanguard sought to work with Marxists in order to stand Marx on his head, restoring the sacrality of the "person" that Marx himself had dethroned a century earlier.

Like Marx, these Catholics were critics of capitalism. But the same was true of the two popes who, in the late nineteenth and early twentieth centuries, developed a "social doctrine" for the Catholic Church: Leo XIII (1878–1903) and Pius XI (1922–39).[78] Like those pontiffs, the twentieth-century vanguard worried about Europe's poor and destitute. Arguably, however, the stakes were more personal for the vanguard, which had witnessed first-hand the chaos of republican collapse and the devastation of war and genocide on a continent already scarred by industrialization.

Where the vanguard differed dramatically from the popes who handed down the encyclicals *Of New Things* (*Rerum Novarum*, 1891) and *The Fortieth Year* (*Quadragesimo Anno*, 1931) was in rejecting private property as the basis for modern political economy. France's and Poland's self-styled Catholic revolutionaries—in the 1910s, as in the 1950s—believed that property condemned capitalism "to ignore the person and to organize itself for a single quantitative and impersonal goal, profit."[79]

For generations come of age in interwar and wartime Europe, social Catholicism—the late-nineteenth-century Church's corporatist answer to the excesses of industrial capitalism—would never suffice to establish a just society.[80] To the extent that social Catholicism had pushed for state intervention on behalf of popular welfare, it had done so by working with republicans; this, too, was unacceptable to Emmanuel Mounier and his disciples because it made Catholics complicit in the rigged, "established disorder."[81] The Catholic vanguard also rejected Christian Democracy, a transnational movement of Catholic politicians pioneered under Leo XIII, because those politicians were willing to collaborate with liberal democracy, while failing to embrace modernity— two profound errors in one.[82]

As of the start of the Second World War, neither social Catholicism nor Christian Democracy had truly made peace with the modern world—despite their spokesmen's willingness to speak out decisively against Communism.[83] Theirs were merely attempts at damage control, at stemming the attrition of Catholics who did not want to wait for Heaven to address their needs. Seeing the limitations of these options,

Mounier's leading Polish acolyte Wojciech Kętrzyński wrote in 1948, "Catholicism to this very day lacks any feasible means of making good on its social doctrine, nor does it possess the material or political power equal to the task of leading that fight."[84]

This was the point of Jean-Marie Domenach's condemnation of Pius XII: that, instead of encouraging its revolutionary vanguard, the Catholic hierarchy sought to enforce orthodoxy at the expense of a just society. To Domenach, this was a betrayal of the men and women lost in war and revolution, of the creative ethos of intellectual and political ferment that survived World War II. Once the pontiff began condemning one vanguard group after another in the early 1950s, the Poles understood exactly how Domenach felt. If we consider that many French and Polish Catholic revolutionaries alike already saw the pope as a German sympathizer—for his wartime refusal to condemn the Nazis, then his postwar refusal to recognize the cession of German territory to Poland—it becomes clear why they looked to each other, and not to the Vatican, to build a better future.

In Poland, following the end of the Second World War and the coming of Moscow-backed Marxist revolution, Catholic "revolutionaries" reversed the grammar of their Church's social-Catholic ideology. Theirs became a project of "Catholic socialism," and it was under these auspices that Polish activists reached out again to the French intellectuals who had inspired them. This transnational vanguard wanted to enact "revolution" in the here and now, on earth, without waiting for the Last Judgment. They failed.

ORGANIZATION OF THE BOOK

*Catholics on the Barricades* proceeds chronologically, albeit with occasional overlap between chapters when the action played out simultaneously in different settings. The book traces a single narrative arc from the 1890s through the 1950s.

In at least one sense, 1945 was a *Stunde null,* or "zero hour." The most devastating war in human history had just ended, and life had to begin again. And yet the first half of the twentieth century was not forgotten by Europeans after 1945.[85] This is why it is crucial to take what Philip Nord has described as a "transwar" perspective on twentieth-century European history—and, likewise, following Jan T.

Gross—to reconstruct the continuum of violent social and political revolution begun, but not ended, by World War II.[86] This mid-century "continuum of mobilization and violence" bred a collective state of mind that, following scholarship on the French Revolution, Marcin Zaremba has called the "Great Fear."[87] Collective trauma conditioned the lives of Central and Eastern Europeans as their societies transitioned from postwar revolution and civil war into the Stalinist period: 1948–56.

This book makes four principal arguments:

1) that, beginning in the 1890s, Roman Catholics responded to the ascendancy of nationalism and Marxism by developing and pursuing distinctive, Catholic projects of "revolution";
2) that the Catholic Church was to be both agent and object of "revolution"—a tension that doomed the project to preserve Catholicism's integralist and "totalitarian" content, anti-Semitism included;
3) that the establishment of the Iron Curtain and of Communist regimes in postwar Central and Eastern Europe not only did not inhibit, but in fact encouraged collaboration between Catholics across the Iron Curtain looking to carve out a theologically grounded space for Catholicism in the Communist world; and
4) that those Catholics appropriated and gave new power to the idea of the "human person," which, though it failed to save Catholic "revolution" from itself, succeeded in inspiring a turn to dialogue, solidarity, and a new vision of "ethical life" in the final stages of the Cold War.[88]

This is a story of Catholics seeking "revolution," but it begins with Thomas Aquinas. Leo XIII, the pope who announced *Rerum Novarum*, launched his papacy with a promise of "Thomist renewal." In response, a generation of Catholic students from across the continent developed their own visions of a just society rooted in their study of Aquinas. Chapter 1 looks to this generation, exploring both the French and the Polish Catholic turns to "revolution," first in the *fin-de-siècle* and again after World War I. French Catholic philosopher Jacques Maritain and his Polish counterparts, the priests Antoni Szymański and Władysław Korniłowicz, made a passionate case for the "human person," rooted in close readings and discussions of the *Summa Theologiae*. Their generation wrestled with powerful currents of integral nationalism, which—especially in Poland—inhibited most Catholics from joining the ranks of the Thomists. Their teaching laid foundations in France and Poland alike for the "revolutionary" pursuit of social justice. In the 1930s, as republics collapsed across Europe and fascist and Soviet power grew, the generation of laymen who had studied under Maritain, Szymański, and Korniłowicz began looking for more radical solutions. First and foremost among these budding revolutionaries was Emmanuel Mounier, and it was principally to him that subsequent generations turned.

During World War II, Mounier's writings inspired Catholic activists born in the 1910s and 1920s as they suffered the trials of occupation, armed resistance, and clandestine existence. Chapter 2 tells this story, showing how Maritain's absence from the European continent elevated his erstwhile disciple. In France, Mounier initially supported the Vichy regime, only to fall into disfavor and, by the end of the war, earn the reputation of a successful dissident. Some 1300 kilometers away, hundreds of young Polish Catholics who had taken up arms against the German occupants risked their lives each night reading Mounier by candlelight. At the same time, young Catholics still had an alternative to Mounier: Christian Democracy.

The course of the Second World War cast their choices into stark relief, as chapter 3 demonstrates. When the war ended with the Red Army encamped on Polish soil, Mounier remained a source of hope for many. Of course, contingent circumstance did its part. At the war's conclusion, Bolesław Piasecki, an avowed fascist before the war, left an NKVD prison having promised to create a movement of pro-Marxist Catholics.[89] Mounier's writings played a major role in guiding the ex-fascist's recruits. Many had looked initially to Christian Democracy, only to see it implode under Communist pressure. In the end, Piasecki's movement—built around the journal *Dziś i Jutro* (*Today and Tomorrow*)—took over the intellectual and political space of Christian Democracy.

After the war's end, we move from the reception of French thought in Poland to a story of vibrant transnational exchange. Chapter 4 explores Mounier's interest in and hopes for a postwar Poland run by Soviet-backed Communists. In his eyes, Poland—the most Catholic country in Europe following the Holocaust and the postwar border shifts—had the opportunity to bring Catholics and Marxists together to craft a master script of "revolution." On the heels of a 1946 visit to Poland, the French personalist declared it a laboratory for social revolution—and exhorted Catholics to sign up. Polish debates over how to respond filled the pages of three new Catholic journals—*Dziś i Jutro*, *Tygodnik Powszechny* (*Universal Weekly*), and *Tygodnik Warszawski* (*Warsaw Weekly*)—as Catholic intellectuals wrestled with how much of a role they were willing to play in the Communist ascendancy. Incredibly, the violence of the transition from World War II to Soviet-style Communism did not hamper the Poles' intellectual dynamism. Behind the nascent Iron Curtain, men and women got on with their lives, asserted their agency in shaping the postwar reconstruction of their respective countries, and attempted to build a new world out of the rubble.

The first major test of "revolution" in the postwar world was the cause of world peace. This is the focus of the book's fifth chapter. Though answering to Moscow, the group that became the Partisans of Peace held their first meeting in Poland, in the fall of 1948, at a congress that the French and the Poles organized together. For four days, Poland welcomed a cast of global cultural and intellectual icons, from Cubist painter Pablo Picasso to *négritude* poet Aimé Césaire.

The cause of peace created a political space for Catholic-Marxist collaboration in Poland, marking the first milestone of personalist "revolution." After all, there could be no protection of any "human person" if the world's population perished in nuclear holocaust. This peace activism was, however, not only anti-nuclear: it was also anti-colonial, anti-American, and anti-German. This last element proved particularly crucial to cementing Franco-Polish cooperation across the Iron Curtain, rooted in the two nations' shared fear of a revanchist Germany. Ethnonational hatred was the common denominator for every player in this story: French or Polish, Marxist or intransigentist, pro- or anti-Communist. That baseline brought together a coalition of intellectuals who guaranteed integralism a postwar career, all while providing political cover for the Soviet Bloc's transition to Stalinism.

Chapter 6 looks at intellectuals who, by 1948, had chosen a different path. The journal *Tygodnik Powszechny* shared its French counterparts' commitments to personhood, peace, social justice—even anti-German ethnonationalism. But its writers refused to proceed in lockstep with every whim of the Communist regime. As a result, they looked past Mounier, formulating their own visions of Catholic revolution. In Mounier's stead, they looked to both interwar Polish Thomists and postwar French pastoral reformers—especially the Dominican "new theologians" and the worker-priest movement. This chapter focuses on one priest and one layman, both of whom found an alternative to Stalinism in *Tygodnik Powszechny*: a Catholic playwright named Jerzy Zawieyski; and the young Rev. Karol Wojtyła—the future Pope John Paul II.

Chapter 7 returns to *Dziś i Jutro*, exploring the movement's attempt —successful, for a time—to build a transnational, cross-Iron Curtain network of pro-Marxist Catholics. After 1948, the ideology that the movement's members had been formulating since the war finally crystallized as "Catholic socialism." Inspired by both Mounier and the Cominform, devoted to both the "human person" and "revolution," *Dziś i Jutro* ideologue Wojciech Kętrzyński launched a project that he called the "Catholic-socialist international."

That there should have been such dynamic partnerships emerging across the rapidly forming Iron Curtain is astonishing. Perversely, however, Catholic socialists' greatest successes at transnational cooperation came in the darkest years of Stalinist repression. For Poland's Catholic socialists, this was a moment of unparalleled possibility. While tens of thousands of their countrymen languished in prisons or hid in forests, Catholic socialists had the opportunity to propose new avenues for engagement in public life: theirs was a real contest of ideas with the Marxist establishment. Chapter 8 tells their story.

In the end, it was the agency of the Polish Catholic vanguard that defined the terms of its ultimate withdrawal from Stalinism. In particular, following the onset of de-Stalinization in 1956, former young radicals—most notably, Tadeusz Mazowiecki—found ready partners in the writers who, refusing to follow the Stalinist path, had congregated around *Tygodnik Powszechny*. PAX's Stalinist turn laid bare the integralist core of "revolution," forcing Catholic intellectuals who remained active on a European (or global) scale beyond de-Stalinization to start anew—with a focus on dialogue, ecumenism, and solidarity.

# 1 The Roots of Catholic "Revolution"

## Thomism, the "Human Person," and Emmanuel Mounier

*The French version of Catholic culture not only cannot be dangerous for Poland, but, quite the opposite, familiarity with it can have only positive consequences for Polish Catholics, as French Catholicism is one of the most valuable. [. . .] [W]e must accomplish this naturally, not by merely following in France's footsteps, but rather by creating our own Catholic culture that corresponds to our national psyche and our cultural typology, keeping in mind, however, the great truth bequeathed to us by French Catholicism: that Catholic culture cannot be made, that it must develop on its own as a full, self-sufficient, and necessary expression of the Catholic human person.*

—*Jerzy Turowicz*[1]

THE YEAR WAS 1932. The setting was a small cottage in the southwestern suburbs of Paris. A twenty-seven-year-old Sorbonne dropout was trying to sell a dozen or so of France's most eminent Catholic thinkers on the idea behind the new monthly journal he was about to launch. This young thinker would transform the intellectual life of the Catholic Church in Europe. His name was Emmanuel Mounier.

In the course of a life cut short—Mounier would die of a heart attack in 1950, at the age of forty-five—the French philosopher argued consistently for a "personalist and communitarian revolution." His goal was to take Catholics out of the "ghetto" of their own making that had separated them from the rest of Europe's population for the lion's share of the modern era.[2] They had their own schools and their own trade unions, their own literature and their own youth leagues. With the Church's qualified acceptance of the democratic political process beginning in the 1890s, Catholics even created their own separate, confessional political parties.[3] And yet, even though Pope Leo XIII had announced in *Rerum Novarum* that Catholics should strive for "that justice which is called *distributive*—toward each and every class alike,"[4] there existed no protocol for Catholics to reach across the aisle to Protestants and atheists, Jews and Orthodox, republicans and Communists.

Four decades after *Rerum Novarum*, Mounier offered a solution to this problem. The young Frenchman was not the first Catholic thinker to do so, nor was he even the best-known of his time. In Germany, the phenomenologists Max Scheler and Dietrich von Hildebrand had reinscribed dialogue with non-Catholic philosophy into modern Catholic thought.[5] Meanwhile, Mounier's one-time mentor Jacques Maritain —perhaps the twentieth century's greatest authority on the writings of Thomas Aquinas—achieved much greater renown over the course of six decades of academic and intellectual labor. The house in which Mounier lobbied his elder colleagues in 1932 to support and write for his new journal *Esprit* in fact belonged to Jacques and Raïssa Maritain.

But unlike the Thomist Maritain, Mounier wrote with the express intent of reaching the widest possible audience: he actively sought to inspire activism. More than any Catholic philosopher before him, Mounier prioritized praxis over ideas—and even faith. These aspirations gained him an ardent transnational following across Europe—east and west— that a more traditional scholar like Jacques Maritain could never hope to match. Yet both men were at the center of a pivot to "revolution" in Catholic thought that was gradually making its way into Poland.

Poland, for its part, was no theological wasteland in the 1920s or 1930s. Thanks to a handful of pioneering priests who had left the turn-of-the-century partitions to study in Western Europe, the Polish state reconstituted in 1918 already had experts in Thomism and social Catholicism who, like Maritain, had trained in Francophone Europe's leading institutions of Catholic learning. The philosopher-priests Antoni Szymański and Władysław Korniłowicz educated generations of Poles in Thomism, directing the gaze of interwar Poland's Catholic youth toward French Catholicism.

What these French and Polish thinkers shared was a conviction that they needed to find a way to reinscribe the key Thomist concept of the "human person" into the heart of modern social and political thought. By the 1930s, Poland was witnessing the emergence of a homegrown turn to "revolution" among a select group of Catholic intellectuals. Those men and women, in dialogue with strong integralist traditions, created a fertile field for the reception of the personalisms that the Frenchmen Maritain and Mounier exported to Poland.

## THE BIRTH OF THOMISM

In the thirteenth century, a Dominican friar from the Italian peninsula revolutionized the intellectual pillars on which Christianity stood. Within fifty years of his death, he had been declared a saint, and the reflections on natural law, metaphysics, and ethics contained in his voluminous *Summa Theologiae* had become the reference point for Christian philosophy and theology. His name was Thomas Aquinas.

The "Angelic Doctor" assembled a compendium of knowledge, with his own reflections interspersed throughout, about God and His relationship to humanity. This was a work of both philosophy and theology: a "series of reflections based in revealed truth on the role of reason in faith" and a "natural proof of God's existence."[6] Taken as a whole, the three-part document contains over one-and-a-half million words, its analysis spread over 500 topics and almost 2700 "articles." Bernard McGinn is right: "No survey of the *Summa* can pretend to convey the richness of Thomas's exposition and the wealth of distinctions, qualifications, insights, arguments, and conclusions he brings to the thousands of theological issues and problems he treats."[7]

And yet, the very breadth of the text makes clear that Aquinas intended it as a guide for faithful Christians seeking both reassurance of God's existence and advice on how best to reach Him. The three sections of the tome follow a logical progression: from a proof of God's existence, to an exploration of what it implied for humanity's ordering of its affairs, to a doctrine of salvation defining Jesus as the literal "way" of return to God. The *Summa Theologiae* is a book of sacred doctrine, but, just as importantly, it lays out a methodology for future Christian thinkers to use in reasoning through the problems of existence and action—both natural (of this world) and supernatural. Aquinas always ended by returning to the source: "For Thomas there is a cycle of wisdom, a circular process of emanation and return to God, following the order of the circular model of the creation and return of the universe."[8] Six centuries later, the Dominican's French Catholic disciples adopted this method as their own way of engaging the world, calling it *ressourcement* (literally—a return to the sources).

For three centuries after Aquinas's death, "Thomist" (the adjective form of his name) learning constituted the shared foundation of the educational curricula of medieval and early-modern Europe's greatest institutions of higher learning—Bologna, Oxford, Paris, Salamanca— inspiring also new universities, such as Louvain (1425).[9] The *Summa* also became the point of departure for the first generations of Jesuit thinkers following the order's founding in 1540—including the intellectual leaders of the Catholic Reformation, Roberto Bellarmine and Francisco Suárez.[10]

Thomism retained its central place in Catholic pedagogy until the French Revolution. In 1797, by decree of occupying French forces, the Dominican-dominated University of Louvain was closed, and so it remained until 1834. In the eighteenth and nineteenth centuries, Thomist rationalism lost its primacy in the universe of European higher education, replaced by its secular, Enlightenment-driven counterpart.[11] Among Catholic scholars, Aquinas's writings took a back seat to centuries' worth of commentaries *about* those writings.[12]

## LEO XIII AND *RERUM NOVARUM*

When Vincenzo Pecci assumed the papacy in 1878, taking the name Leo XIII, the first goal that he declared was to restore Thomism to its central place in Roman Catholicism. The universities were Leo XIII's principal object of concern. He created an "Aquinas college" in Rome (the Collegium Angelicum) and promulgated the August 1879 encyclical *Aeterni Patris* (subtitled "On the Restoration of Christian Philosophy").[13] In *Aeterni Patris*, he wrote, "Let carefully selected teachers endeavor to implant the doctrine of Thomas Aquinas in the minds of students, and set forth clearly his solidity and excellence over others." The "carefully selected teachers" who assumed newly minted chairs of Thomist philosophy at Louvain and Fribourg received the full doctrinal, financial, and institutional support of the Holy See.[14]

In 1891, Pope Leo XIII published the encyclical *Rerum Novarum*.

This was the papacy sounding trumpets to Catholics worldwide to re-order their societies according to the teachings of Thomas Aquinas. The encyclical broke new ground by encouraging Catholics to engage with the world around them. With no precedents among papal and curial writings, the pope cited from the Bible and the *Summa*. Particularly telling was Leo XIII's interchangeable usage of "natural justice" and "social justice": his loyalties to Thomas Aquinas translated into a belief that all that is just must follow from and accord with natural law, as captured by Thomism.

The pontiff opened the 1891 text by defining the tasks facing the Catholic Church in light of the "conflict now raging"—the Industrial Revolution. As he put it, "At the time being, the condition of the working classes is the pressing question of the hour, and nothing can be of higher interest to all classes of the State than that it should be rightly and reasonably settled." This required a definition of "the relative rights and mutual duties of the rich and of the poor, of capital and of labor."[15]

The promise of a Catholic program of social justice did not presume total equality among men. Quite the opposite, the pontiff wrote, "unequal fortune is a necessary result of unequal condition." All human beings were made in God's image, but no two human beings reflected that image in exactly the same way. Justifying material and economic disparity in this way, *Rerum Novarum* insisted that Catholics respect work and property alike. Property, however, was not an end in itself, but a means of honoring God. Property, *Rerum Novarum* argued, provides security to the family unit, allowing for cross-generational transmission of the fruits of earlier generations' labor "in stable and permanent possession."

This was a gambit to take the wind out of Marxism's sails. Catholic thinkers had written before about the growing specter of revolutionary socialism across the European continent, but no pope had ever dignified Marxist arguments with a response. By 1891, however, the Second International was building a network of political cells across the continent, and the Holy See was genuinely worried. Leo XIII believed that it was high time to explain to Catholics that Marxists were "working on the poor man's envy of the rich" and elevating labor at the expense of property. Perversely, then, revolutionary socialism threatened the proletarian's ability to elevate himself from poverty through the accumulation of capital, "striking at the interests of every wage-earner, since they would deprive him of the liberty of disposing of his wages, and thereby of all hope and possibility of increasing his resources and of bettering his condition in life." To Leo XIII, all collectivism, all calls for a revolt against private property, sowed the seeds of the proletariat's own destruction by pulling workers away from God. By arguing that only Catholicism held the secret to ending the alienation of the working man, the turn-of-the-century pope was trying to stand Marx on his head.

Issued in Rome, papal encyclicals had a much easier time reaching the Western European faithful than the imperial-subject minorities of the Austro-Hungarian, German, and Russian Empires. The Thomist renewal and the Catholic call to address the social question reached Poland, but with a delay. It took the work of several generations of intermediaries, studying and writing in the French language, to disseminate the message of "renewal" across Central and Eastern Europe. In the meantime, Catholics seeking to effect real change in partitioned Poland looked overwhelmingly to one ideology: integral nationalism.

## ROMAN DMOWSKI AND CHARLES MAURRAS

Turn-of-the-century Roman Catholicism was rife with divisions and internal contradictions. Modernism, intransigentism, and integralism were all affected by Leo XIII's announcement of a Catholic "social teaching"—albeit in conflicting and complex ways that varied from country to country. Brian Porter-Szűcs is therefore right that "The importance of *Rerum Novarum* and the movement it spawned should be neither overstated nor understated."[16] Interwoven with the story of the Catholic answer to Leo XIII's call was the fate of nations in an imperial Europe destabilized by social transformation. The "national question," too, had its putatively Catholic answers in the form of integral nationalism, positing an essential intertwining of religious faith with exclusionary nationalism. Like the Thomist renewal, the rise of integral nationalism in early twentieth-century Europe was a story of cooperation, exchange, and mutual emulation by French and Polish Catholic intellectuals.

Instead of seeing their compatriots as lost sheep in need of a reminder of Catholicism's core tenets, integralists categorized entire populations in black-and-white terms: either inside or outside their nation. This brand of exclusionary pigeon-holing went hand in hand with public demonstrations of devotion to a "national faith." This was turn-of-the-century mass politics, and it often went hand in hand with street violence waged under the banner of Jesus Christ.

Like social Catholicism, integral nationalism aspired to help the Church shape public life. In fact, integralists pursued this role more aggressively and more directly than social Catholics. Instead of worrying about justice and equality, their principal concern was for defining and enforcing exclusionary boundaries around the national community. Poland's principal theorist of integralism, Roman Dmowski, wrote in 1905, "Only a strong national organization, based on a deep respect for tradition, is capable of guaranteeing human society's moral health over the centuries." Maintaining the health of the nation took precedence even over commands of the Gospels, for "national ethics is the foundation of interpersonal ethics."[17]

In the *fin-de-siècle*, parallel integralist movements emerged in France and in partitioned Poland. Both promoted organic, "blood and soil" ethnonationalism. Both publicized their ideology through manifestos, journals, and extraparliamentary leagues, and presented themselves as movements of choice for pious Catholics who belonged to their respective nations. Created in 1887, the Polish movement National Democracy came first. Its counterpart French Action (*Action Française*) followed in 1898. The chief ideologues of the two movements—respectively, Roman Dmowski and Charles Maurras—had not founded them. Yet the intensity and radicalism of these men's activism rapidly elevated them to positions of unmatched authority. Remarkably, despite the reliance of both movements on Roman Catholics, Maurras and Dmowski themselves remained avowed agnostics until they found faith on their respective deathbeds.

The *Action Française* movement developed out of the Dreyfus Affair as a nationalist, monarchist movement. From 1908 onward, the movement centered around a daily paper of the same name. The watchword of its principal ideologue Charles Maurras was "politics first" (*politique, d'abord*), though Maurras rejected all established political parties and indeed, the parliamentary system itself. The League of French Action that he founded in 1905 was designed not for parliamentary agitation, but for opinion-making and street protest; as such, it brought to life Maurras's vision of the essential form of legitimate political action.[18]

Since 1893, the young political agitator Roman Dmowski—only twenty-nine years old at the time—had argued that Poland must be consolidated through a "national faith." With Zygmunt Balicki, he created one political group after another, transforming the paramilitary National League into a cross-partition front of political parties loosely associated under the heading of National Democracy.[19] To avoid arrest, Dmowski moved frequently back and forth between the Austrian and Russian partitions in the first decade of his activism, until the Revolution of 1905 resulted in the relaxation of Russian laws on associations.[20]

Dmowski and Maurras followed parallel trajectories. In the final decade of the nineteenth century, both launched paramilitary leagues. In the first decade of the twentieth, both authored major political manifestos: Maurras, in 1900—*An Inquiry into Monarchy* (*Enquête sur la Monarchie*); and Dmowski, in 1903—*Thoughts of a Modern Pole* (*Myśli Nowoczesnego Polaka*). Both edited periodicals that became the nerve centers of their respective movements: Maurras's eponymous daily *Action Française* and Dmowski's *Przegląd Wszechpolski* (*Review of All Poles*). Both were virulent anti-Semites who blamed Jews indiscriminately for all of the ills experienced by their respective nations. Dmowski, for example, wrote in 1903, "It is Jews whose enormous presence in Poland creates its most serious problem."[21] The one major difference between the men lay in their desired form of government: unlike Maurras, Dmowski was no monarchist, and he did not oppose a parliamentary system; in fact, he even served as a deputy in the Russian imperial Duma.

Having spent 1891–92 studying in Paris, Dmowski closely followed the day-to-day affairs of the Third Republic. He saw a kindred spirit in Maurras, whose program he later described as the "quintessence of what a French movement should be."[22] Dmowski's advantage over Maurras was that, unlike the French monarchist, he did not openly advertise that he cared more about politics than about faith. Meanwhile, Maurras's 1914 *French Action and the Catholic Religion* did not mince words: whereas "traditional Frenchmen, separated politically from the Church, could not even understand their own thinking," French Action's relationship to the Catholic Church was one of "strategic alliance for the nation" rather than service in Christ.[23] Dmowski at least paid lip service to "Christian ethics" in *Thoughts of a Modern Pole*, though not for another two decades did he attempt to define the proper place of the Catholic Church in national life.[24] He would do so only after seeing Rome condemn his friends from French Action.

## THE POLITICS OF A POLAND REBORN

By the time Poland reappeared on the map of Europe in the closing days of the First World War, Catholics already had over a decade of experience wrestling with how to implement Catholic social teaching on Polish soil.[25] Tomasz Sikorski and Marcin Kulesza underscore that "Attempts to 'square' the popular nineteenth-century teachings of Karl Marx with the lessons of St. Thomas Aquinas were hardly rare—especially since, on Polish soil, socialism was treated as a step on the Christian path to the liberation of man and the construction of a just Divine order on earth."[26]

Just as Karl Marx secularized personhood in the mid-nineteenth century, so he "nationalized" class conflict in the lands of partitioned Poland. Marx and Engels alike wrote passionately in defense of the restoration of a sovereign Poland.[27] With even Marxists splitting over whether to prioritize nationalism or internationalism, it is clear that turn-of-the-century partitioned Poland's politics were remarkably complex. Many of Poland's revolutionary socialists were, in fact, committed nationalists: men like Kazimierz Kelles-Krauz and Józef Piłsudski believed that Polish national freedom had to precede the end of class conflict. Roman Dmowski's National Democrats, too, wedded the cause of justice to a program of national freedom. In Dmowski's mind, however, only "biological" Poles deserved justice; Jews, Germans, and others deserved exile.[28] Polish workers figured importantly into Dmowski's program of strengthening the nation. Norman Naimark's pithy assessment of the Russian partition therefore applies to all of partitioned Poland: "the Polish industrial revolution [ . . . ] recast the social and economic life of the Congress Kingdom to the point where the working class would stand at the center of any subsequent internal solutions to the 'Polish question.'"[29]

The coming of the Russian Revolutions of 1917 and the ultimate emergence of the Soviet Union positioned Poland in the front line of Catholic Europe's confrontation with Marxism. The interwar republic formalized by the Treaty of Versailles had a great admirer in the first papal *nuncio* to Poland, Achille Ratti, who following his return to Rome was elected Pope Pius XI. He later wrote, "I learned patience in Poland . . . I love Poland, as always."[30] The interwar pontiff's personal acquaintance with the key players of the Polish political elite—especially Józef Piłsudski—convinced him that the marshal's questionable piety and fraught relations with Poland's bishops were a small price to pay so long as Poland, the geopolitical gateway to Europe, remained a bulwark against Bolshevism.

Pius XI supported Piłsudski even after the marshal carried out a *coup d'état* against Poland's parliament and president on May 14, 1926, with close to 400 killed in an armed firefight.[31] Six months later, Piłsudski assumed the post of prime minister; over the next nine years, he moved in and out of government, a puppeteer pulling the strings of successive political and military leaders who had sworn loyalty to him. The quasi-authoritarian rule of Piłsudski's *sanacja* ("healing") camp provoked strong opposition across the political spectrum, but the National Democrats were the best organized of the opponents. Returning to its roots in paramilitary street violence, the *endecja* regularly clashed with government supporters. Violence between representatives of the different camps continued on and off until the outbreak of the Second World War.

Seven months after Piłsudski's coup, Pius XI condemned French Action in a widely publicized letter.[32] Though the two events might seem unconnected, in fact they conspired to cement integral nationalism's legitimacy in the eyes of the Polish hierarchy. Unlike their Roman pontiff, the vast majority of interwar Polish bishops detested Piłsudski, and National Democracy proved a ready alternative. Seeing the French Action movement that he had admired and emulated for decades condemned at the end of 1926, Dmowski hastened to distance himself from it.[33] Publicly disavowing Charles Maurras's dictum of "politics first," Dmowski penned a treatise asserting the primacy of the Catholic Church in Polish national life. In so doing, he marched National Democracy right into the waiting embrace of Poland's ecclesiastical hierarchy.

Of utmost significance in Dmowski's 1927 *Church, Nation, State* (*Kościół, Naród, Państwo*) is the sequence of the nouns in the title. Despite the cloud hanging over the *endecja* following Maurras's condemnation, Dmowski adopted a celebratory, rather than defensive tone: "It must be noted that the latest phenomenon in Catholic countries, beginning with France and ending with Poland, is the turn toward religion—heralding the dawn of a new era in European history."[34]

As for French Action, Dmowski confronted its blighted status head-on. While conceding that France and Poland had witnessed the rise of integral nationalism "simultaneously," he underscored that "in each of these countries this movement is born of its own accord, independently of external influences." In other words, although Dmowski's student years in Paris had inspired his reliance on extraparliamentary leagues, integralism crystallized in the National Democratic movement out of a homegrown, "organic need," not some coordinated international effort. By extension, then, National Democracy bore no responsibility either for Maurras's ideas or their implementation in French Action.

Drawing a contrast with the tactical view of religion that Maurras had articulated on the eve of the Great War, Dmowski credited the Catholic Church with Poland's very existence. He wrote, "Catholicism is not a supplement to Polishness, a decoration, but rather it is bound to the essence of Polishness; to a large extent, it constitutes that essence. To attempt to divide our Catholicism from Polishness, to tear the nation away from religion and from the Church, is to destroy the very essence of the nation."

In this text, we find the origins of the essentialist myth of the "Catholic Pole" (*Polak-katolik*). National Democracy propagated the notion that the "true" Pole had always been a Catholic Pole.[35] In his earlier writings, Dmowski had only alluded to the Church's role in Polishness; the "Catholic" identity had always been ambiguously spiritual, rather than pegged to the Roman institution. By 1927, however, Dmowski no longer treated "Catholicism" as an abstraction: it became a *sine qua non* of the Polish nation. *Church, Nation, State* closed with Dmowski's definitive disavowal of Maurras: "Politics is an earthly matter, and the political point of view is earthly, temporal. But even from this standpoint, religion in the life of nations is the highest good, which cannot be sacrificed in the pursuit of any goal."[36]

Dmowski's ideological pivot paid off. While Maurras's supporters reeled, National Democrats in the 1930s refashioned themselves into quintessential defenders of Catholicism in Poland. National Democracy never lost its standing as the principal opposition front against Piłsudski's motley crew of anti-Bolshevik socialists and military men.

In the wake of Dmowski's rapprochement with the Church, however, more and more fissures appeared within Poland's integralist camp. The most devastating act of heterodoxy came when a group of National Democratic agitators in their early twenties split off from Dmowski's movement, creating the National-Radical Camp (*Obóz Narodowo-Radykalny*, ONR). The premise of ONR was that Dmowski had failed to assimilate the lessons of major international developments in the 1920s and 1930s: to these young men, Benito Mussolini, not Roman Dmowski, held the keys to integralism's future.[37] Organized into violent street gangs, the ONR beat Jews, protested liberalism, and openly advocated the kind of marriage between Catholicism and fascism that Engelbert Dollfuss had briefly achieved in Austria.[38] At the extreme end of this radical movement was a small group that took the name Phalanx (*Falanga*), from the fascist *Falange* party created in 1933 to oppose the Spanish Republic. The leader of these young Catholic fascists was named Bolesław Piasecki.

## A NEW POLISH "RENAISSANCE"

Even as integral nationalism became stronger and more radical from the 1890s through the 1930s, a serious alternative emerged, propelled by thinkers who took Leo XIII's encyclicals as a clarion call. This alternative was social Catholicism. In the first decade of the twentieth century, dozens of Polish seminarians left the partitions separately to take part in the international Thomist revival. These philosopher-priests studied in Belgium, France, or Switzerland before returning to Polish lands on the eve of World War I. Their goal was to create a homegrown elite of Catholic intellectuals equipped to intervene in the debates gripping the wider Catholic world.

Born in the 1880s, these men were products of Europe's *fin-de-siècle*, bringing a Western European education and an agenda of renewal back to a partitioned homeland long defined by resistance to three occupying empires. After World War I, they became the priestly intellectual elite of a reborn Polish state. All understood their scholarly vocation as a quest for a socially just Catholic political economy. These Polish philosopher-priests insisted that Catholics had an edge over the growing wellspring of Marxist thinkers who promised justice through violent revolution. For Catholics, they claimed, belief in God was only the beginning: Catholics needed to take responsibility for the world around them. This meant that each Catholic needed to arrive personally at a principled vision of how to live an ethical life in keeping with the Gospels. Only then might Catholics be in a position to redress the rampant starvation and social anomie defining their industrialized world.

In 1910, one of this chapter's Polish heroes, Antoni Szymański, defined "social Catholicism" for Poles in eminently practical terms: as "the totality of [social] reforms to be carried out" by Catholics.[39] Szymański came from a respected small-town family in the German partition of Poland. In 1904 the young priest's mentor at the Włocławek seminary, Idzi Radziszewski, arranged for Szymański to attend his own *alma mater*, Belgium's Catholic University of Louvain.[40] Like his Polish mentor, Szymański studied under the great Thomist scholar and future cardinal Désiré-Joseph Mercier. The priest defended his dissertation in 1908 with highest honors, publishing it in Polish two years later. Its title was *The Ideas of Christian Democracy in France, 1892–1907.*[41]

The young Szymański was fascinated by the first French "Christian Democrats": priest-politicians of the 1890s who attempted to bring Thomism alive through politics. In his eyes, their entrance into public life was a logical consequence of *Rerum Novarum*. Social renewal meant more than charity; it meant organized action. Szymański defined Christian Democracy simply: "That, which it has studied and deemed positive, it wants to turn into reality; it wants to participate in the creation of a Christian social organization."[42]

With his writings on France, Antoni Szymański became one of the first Polish-language authors to sketch both the theory and practice of a Catholic political economy.[43] In 1910, he contended, "Christianity is not only a religion of the individual, it denotes not only the individual relationship of the human soul to God, but moreover relationships between people, as well as their social relationships with God (theories of labor, property, etc.). There thus exists a Christian economics." Thomas Aquinas might well have used these very words, if he had suddenly found himself in twentieth-century Poland.

The most important tool for building a Catholic political economy was the "human person"—a Thomist concept that Szymański had brought back with him from his studies in Belgium. Szymański's personalism was predicated on the argument that Catholicism should define human social relations because, thanks to Aquinas, it could offer the most complete picture of what binds human beings to God: person-hood. In the Polish priest's rendering, a "person" was a transcendent essence linked at once to God and man—precisely as Jesus had been, as Son of God and Son of Man. This is why Szymański believed that "Catholicism is the most perfect imaginable amplification of the human person, whom it affords the possibility of participation in the life of God through the Holy Sacrament." Economic liberalism had allegedly missed this essential feature of human relations, instead "[s]eparating work from the human person and considering it to be an independent entity." [44]

In 1918, Antoni Szymański became one of the founding faculty members of the Catholic University of Lublin (*Katolicki Uniwersytet Lubelski*, KUL)—alongside his mentor from seminary, Idzi Radziszewski, who designed the new university's curriculum. [45] In its first decade, KUL attracted the greatest Polish-language talent in Catholic education—professors who had trained all over Europe—who took on the task of training a new Catholic intellectual elite for the reborn Polish state. Between 1918 and 1939, the institution produced approximately 30,000 graduates. [46] The university's first graduating classes included many defining figures of the Church in twentieth-century Poland, for example future Łódź bishop Michał Klepacz (Class of 1922) and future Primate Stefan Wyszyński (Class of 1929).

The new university's faculty created the "Lublin School" of Catholic political economy, which became renowned throughout Europe. As its leader, Szymański became one of the principal brokers of Catholic life in interwar Poland. In 1930, eight years after Pope Pius XI announced an initiative called Catholic Action, Szymański helped to register the movement in Poland. Intended to involve laity the world over in the life of the Church, by 1939 Catholic Action succeeded in involving Poles as well: 750,000 had joined. [47]

As one of the few professors to teach at KUL continuously from 1918 until its shuttering by German troops in 1939, Szymański inculcated several generations of Lublin students with his blueprint for Catholic renewal. He recognized that a fledgling social Catholicism required committed educators to train future generations of social Catholics, in order to give the new approach to social justice a real chance of taking hold.

Antoni Szymański was not alone in articulating a Thomist, yet distinctively Polish, social Catholicism. His fellow Lublin School professors played a key role, as did a host of self-styled "Christian economists," including Leopold Caro, a convert from Judaism. Caro advocated for "solidarism," inspired partly by the French doctrine of the same name announced thirty years earlier by the republican welfare-state pioneer Léon Bourgeois.[48] To Caro, solidarism meant "cooperation not competition." This was an anti-capitalist as well as anti-Marxist ideology, directed against all exploitation, whether by "wealthier individuals (as liberalism practices without scruples) or for the benefit of the whole (as extreme socialism advocates)."[49] Influential as Caro was in Poland's Catholic Action movement, his reach outside Poland was non-existent. Yet his ideological leap to solidarism—inspired by French thought, like many interwar Polish Catholic initiatives—anticipated the "revolutionary" quest for a Catholic third way by Jacques Maritain, Emmanuel Mounier, and their acolytes.

Under Szymański's patronage, students from Lublin in 1919 launched a nationwide network of Catholic university students, faculty, and alumni. Christened "Renaissance" (*Odrodzenie*), this movement became the umbrella for a half-dozen Catholic journals of public opinion, discussion clubs, and an annual retreat known as the Social Weeks (*Tygodnie Społeczne*). All of these elements had French progenitors: the retreat, for example, copied the French *Semaines Sociales* that had been meeting in Lyon since 1904.[50] To the goal of designing a just society, the Renaissance activists added other normative questions: what content to incorporate into Catholic education, what ideals to define for the Polish family, and how to mobilize youth for collective action.[51]

To be clear, most Catholic university students in interwar Poland sympathized with the *endecja*. For those seeking an alternative to integral nationalism, however, Renaissance offered a viable path.[52] The movement never reached a mass scale—at its height in 1934, it had just under a thousand active student members—but it had wide geographical coverage, with sections for students and alumni at universities in Kraków, Lublin, Lwów, Warsaw, and Wilno.[53]

Generations of Polish youth coming of age after 1918 benefited both intellectually and politically from figures like Szymański and Caro, who were a world apart from National Democracy. And yet, saying no to integral nationalism did not translate into an embrace of ecumenism, liberalism, or pluralism. Neither the Lublin School nor Renaissance renounced traditional Catholic prejudices against Jews. In fact, when universities introduced restrictions on Jewish student enrollment—the so-called *numerus clausus*—many of Szymański's disciples applauded the move, seeing it as a gain for Catholics in a contest between the forces of right and the forces of error.[54] Theirs was a Catholic anti-Semitism, predicated on the unquestioned assumption that not every human being was a "human person." Rather, personhood was contingent on conversion and active participation in the faith. Persons, then, were justified in discriminating against non-persons.[55] And so, even those who sought an alternative to integralism remained under its influence.

## DIALOGUE AS REVOLUTION

One philosopher-priest from Szymański's generation saw things differently. His name was Władysław Korniłowicz, and he pioneered an approach to personhood that outlasted the interwar Polish republic, anticipating in many respects the Second Vatican Council of the 1960s.[56] On the one hand, like Szymański, he believed that personhood was contingent. On the other, Korniłowicz believed that the fact of that contingency meant that Catholics had a moral imperative to help all non-persons find their way to personhood. This was not some latter-day reversion to the Inquisition: instead, it meant dialogue, acknowledging non-Catholics as thinking subjects with their own life experiences, and meeting them halfway. The goal was still conversion, but on a basis of dignity, not violence.

Korniłowicz was a one-man network of dialogue. Spurred to action by the defeat of the Revolution of 1905, Korniłowicz developed a new model of ministry predicated on dialogues between Catholics and non-believers—Jews, atheists, agnostics.[57] The first men and women he sought to reach were Poland's aspiring Marxist revolutionaries. This was Korniłowicz's praxis: a retooling of the Catechism of the Catholic Church from a written document to a live, face-to-face dialogue between two "persons" recognizing each other's inherent dignity and transcendent value in the image of God.

Coined during the Council of Trent (1545–1563) that spearheaded the Catholic Counter-Reformation, the word "catechism" traditionally refers to a document designed to "faithfully and systematically present the teaching of Sacred Scripture, the living Tradition in the Church and the authentic Magisterium, as well as the spiritual heritage of the Fathers, Doctors, and saints of the Church, to allow for a better knowledge of the Christian mystery and for enlivening the faith of the People of God."[58] In other words, the catechism was a reference guide for catechetical instructors shepherding their catechumens—tutees in the study of the faith—through the process of catechesis.

The key to understanding Korniłowicz's role in our story is to acknowledge that a new Catholic political economy would be worthless if it could not be transmitted to others—across generations, across political divides, even across creeds. This process of transmission would be built upon personal dialogues intended to reinforce the Catholic mission of preaching the Word of God in an effort to save as many souls as possible. The founding goal of Christianity, after all, had always been conversion in the service of salvation, and Korniłowicz's method represented a new take on this oldest of precepts.[59]

He had made the choice to minister to individuals, not masses, all while relying solely on face-to-face dialogue. An elitist Korniłowicz was not, but he was a pragmatist: he recognized the improbability that one man alone could succeed in converting large masses. Asked once why he spent more time with intellectuals than with "simple folk," Korniłowicz replied, "My child, I would love to take them all into my care and to dialogue with them, but I do not know how."[60]

From 1922 onward, Korniłowicz taught regular seminars on the Catholic liturgy at KUL, a post to which he was recommended by none other than Cardinal Achille Ratti, soon to become Pope Pius XI.[61] Yet his real base as an educator was in the forests just north of Warsaw, at a center for the blind run by Franciscan nuns. At Laski, Korniłowicz joined forces—first as a regular volunteer, then from 1930 onward as pastor and full-time resident—with the center's remarkable founder, the aristocrat Róża Czacka, herself blind. Inspired by French Catholic writings on service to the poor, Czacka used her family money as start-up capital for both the center for the blind and a new cloistered order of nuns, the Franciscan Sisters Servants of the Cross.[62] As Czacka wrote in 1927, "In this day and age, much is made of social work and charitable organizations, and yet people are finding it harder and harder to live in the world, and they are worse and worse off. Harder and harder, worse and worse off, because people do not know the Lord Jesus and His teachings through the Church; people are rejecting the only thing that can teach them to live, the only thing that can bring them happiness. The idea behind our Work is to bring to life the King-dom of Christ on this earth."[63]

Young Catholic intellectuals found among the pines, birch trees, and sands of Laski a place of spiritual solace to which they happily re-treated from emotionally draining daily life in the city. Armed with books brought back from his studies in Fribourg, Korniłowicz led a cross-generational Thomist seminar, including professors as well as stu-dents, who came not only from nearby Warsaw, but also from Lublin and Kraków. This was Korniłowicz's Little Circle (*Kółko*): it had first met in 1917, but it was not until Korniłowicz took up full-time resi-dence at Laski in 1930 as its pastor that he restructured the seminar as a formal course of readings, paired with a lengthy syllabus. Beyond its evangelical aspirations, the seminar also addressed "gaps and de-formations in Polish religious education, above all the education of the intelligentsia, on the one hand still under the influence of anti-rationalist schools, and on the other steeped in the living traditions of Warsaw pos-itivism."[64] At Laski, Korniłowicz's reading group went back to the orig-inal source texts, poring—for example—over complete editions of the *Summa Theologiae*. In its methodology of *ressourcement*, then, Korniło-wicz's Thomist seminar followed the example of Aquinas's *Summa* itself.

Under the philosopher-priest's tutelage, nuns from Laski became accomplished philosophers and writers. Korniłowicz himself lectured widely on the theology of the liturgy, insisting on reforms that would make it easier for Catholics attending mass to feel like active members of the Church. Beginning in 1934, Laski produced a philosophical jour-nal named *Verbum* (*The Word*), featuring contributions not only from Poles, but from across Europe. Its authors included some of the leading lights of interwar French Catholicism: François Mauriac, Nikolai Ber-diaev, and Jacques Maritain—Korniłowicz's personal hero and friend.[65] Thomist scholars from around the world—including Maritain—came to the center throughout the 1930s as invited guests of Korniłowicz's seminar, sitting amidst the Franciscan nuns and lay acolytes from all over Poland.[66] This was an elite group, and it included some of the most recognizable names in the history of twentieth-century Poland, among them—future primate Stefan Wyszyński, future Nobel Laureate Czesław Miłosz, and future Catholic statesman Jerzy Zawieyski.

This was a living, breathing personalism. Władysław Korniłowicz repeated often that his mission in life was to bring the "personal experience of faith" to catechumens inside and outside the Church. The Polish pastor was evangelizing to one person at a time—Catholics, but also Jews, Protestants, and Communists—arguing that only self-aware persons could be saved. The priest repeated often, "Obedience must be conscious; one must obey not like a mechanical wheel, but like a human being."[67]

## JACQUES MARITAIN, THOMIST

The *fin-de-siècle* had been an era of experimentation and conversion across Europe. Converts and catechumens crossed national, social, confessional, and political boundaries in pursuit of truth and dialogue.[68] And so it came to pass that the Protestant-born French philosopher Jacques Maritain converted to Catholicism in 1905 together with his Jewish-born wife Raïssa Oumançoff, having benefited from the spiritual tutelage of two prominent Catholic writers: Léon Bloy and Charles Péguy—themselves converts. Across Europe, other prominent non-Catholics or agnostics were joining the ranks of the practicing faithful in the final years of the *fin-de-siècle*, including English novelist G. K. Chesterton and German philosopher Dietrich von Hildebrand.

It was in this context that Jacques Maritain's journey as a self-described Catholic philosopher began. In the fifty-seven years between his conversion and his death, Maritain revolutionized Catholic philosophy. Within a decade after having received his professorship at Paris's Catholic Institute in 1914, he had become an example for lay philosophers to emulate, not only in France, but on a continental scale.

Maritain's ideological trajectory was not linear, but led him over the course of his long life through intransigentism, integralism, and anti-republicanism, to a reluctant ultimate embrace of liberal democracy. From the moment of his conversion, the one intellectual constant in his life was Thomas Aquinas. For this reason, when an unexpected inheritance gave him the financial freedom in 1918 to found his own center of learning, unbeholden to any one educational institution, he launched a Thomist seminar for all of France. Like Władysław Korniłowicz, Maritain aimed to make this a nationwide seminar, serving the twin causes of evangelizing the faith and of deepening humanity's understanding of the *Summa Theologiae*. In fact, Korniłowicz and Maritain knew of each other's seminars, and they traded ideas in written correspondence about how to facilitate critical, thoughtful reading of Thomas Aquinas. Korniłowicz came to Maritain's seminar as a guest in 1921, and Maritain visited the Laski seminar in 1934. In the meantime, Maritain moved the seminar in 1923 to his home in the Paris suburb of Meudon, which for the last seventeen years of the Third Republic "became the center of the Thomist revival and welcomed a stream of philosophers, scientists, physicians, writers, poets, musicians—Catholics for the most part but also Orthodox, Jews, and Protestants, a veritable Who's Who of French Letters."[69]

Even as he wrote profusely and ran his weekly seminar, Jacques Maritain went through a serious integralist phase, spending the first half of the 1920s as a friend and confidant to Charles Maurras. Maritain was neither a nationalist nor a monarchist, yet he shared with Maurras a deep distrust of republicanism. Their political partnership shaped a whole generation of French Catholic intellectuals who completed their studies in the 1920s.[70] Anti-republican, anti-liberal politics drew this generation to French Action in the decade following the catastrophic population and material losses of World War I.

Maritain's first systematic presentation of his thoughts on contemporary republican culture was his 1925 work *Three Reformers* (*Trois Réformateurs*). According to Maritain, the ills of the modern world followed from Martin Luther's individualism, René Descartes's skepticism, and Jean-Jacques Rousseau's ignorant manipulation of the rationalism inherited from the scholastics. The greatest of these sins was individualism: "Look with what bombastic piety the modern world has announced the sacred rights of the individual and what price it has paid."[71] Yet, despite its pride of place, "never had the individual been more at the mercy of the nameless powers of the State, Money, and Opinion" than in Maritain's own time. The young Thomist's diagnosis became the linchpin of modern Catholic personalism: "The modern world has simply confused two notions that ancient wisdom held as distinct: it mixes *individuality* and *personality*." Indeed, "the modern order sacrifices the person on the altar of the individual."[72]

*Three Reformers* represented both the zenith of Maritain's spite for modernity and republicanism and the first stepping stone on his path to ultimate reconciliation with both. Maritain's first papal supporter, Pius X, had died in 1914, his successor Benedict XV in 1922; the mid-1920s were the era of Pius XI, of Catholic Action, of engagement with the world by a growing lay apostolate. Pius XI was no lover of modernity, but, rather than fight it tooth and nail, he sought to use Catholic Action to re-evangelize the modern world, to win it back over to Catholic truth.

When Pius XI condemned French Action in December 1926, Maritain immediately broke with Charles Maurras. He then set out to reflect on the significance of this development for his own understanding of the relationship between faith and politics. The outcome was his great 1927 opus *Primacy of the Spiritual* (*Primauté du Spirituel*).[73] This work deconstructed the logic of Maurras's motto *politique, d'abord*, insisting instead on the "primacy of the spiritual" as a guiding force in all action. Cardinal Pietro Gasparri, Pius XI's Secretary of State, wrote personally to Maritain to thank him on the pontiff's behalf: "His Holiness thanks you from the bottom of his heart and can only congratulate you on the passion with which you have countered the factual and other errors and demonstrated the incompetence of the *Action Française* writers."[74] In just a few years, Maritain went from being one of the primary spokesmen for French Action to its most outspoken Catholic critic. *Primacy of the Spiritual* also helped Maritain to find his voice as a political philosopher.

At the turn of the 1920s and 1930s, Maritain began writing shorter essays for French journals of public opinion like *La Vie Intellectuelle* (*Intellectual Life*). These writings migrated across Europe, serialized, to Poland. Beginning in 1929, Maritain's essays appeared regularly in Polish translation in the Renaissance movement's flagship journal, *Prąd* (*The Current*). In these years, the Renaissance movement held a virtual monopoly on Polish-language distribution of the French Thomist's publications.

These essays introduced to Polish Catholic intellectuals the need to seek "revolutionary," yet distinctively Catholic, solutions to the pressing problems of the world. Of particular concern to Maritain was the rise of Bolshevism, which reflected a deeper ill of the modern world: a materialist compulsion brought on by secularization. To his mind, the root of all evil in the modern world was the dethroning of God within humanist thought. In 1929, he insisted that humanity "was beginning to feel more fragmented than ever before, at odds with others and with itself, for the material world, being a source of division, can produce only fragmentation. Nations against nations, classes against classes, passions against passions, until finally the human personality is torn apart."[75]

Maritain saw only one viable solution: that intellectuals must lead Catholics back to God by showing, through their own example, that Thomism could satisfy the faithful in their lives on earth. Thomism now promised not only spiritual renewal, but also social and political "revolution."[76]

## PIUS XI AND *QUADRAGESIMO ANNO*

The Thomist "revolution" that Maritain proposed was to be the work of every person, rather than a top-down executive order from the Holy See. And yet the interwar papacy also responded to Maritain's calls. Pius XI held the French Thomist in high regard, and the personalist vocabulary that Maritain helped to reintroduce into mid-century Catholic intellectual life appeared in all of Pius XI's most important encyclicals of the 1930s.

Although Pius XI issued qualified reprimands to Fascist Italy in 1931 and the Third Reich in 1937, the principal target of his political ire was the Soviet Union.[77] The Church's campaign against Europe's political Left had begun already during the mid-nineteenth-century pontificate of Pius IX, but the rise of the Soviet Union in the 1920s had made Marxism an imminent existential threat. As *nuncio* to Poland, the future Pope Pius XI had seen firsthand the Polish-Bolshevik battle for Warsaw in August 1920. The violence and the fear that he had witnessed colored his entire pontificate, inclining him to work with anyone willing to tolerate the Catholic Church and to denounce the USSR—Mussolini and Hitler included.[78]

In 1931, for the fortieth anniversary of *Rerum Novarum*, Pius XI offered his own anti-socialist encyclical, *Quadragesimo Anno*. In it, Pius intended not only to provide the definitive Catholic settlement of the social question, but also to expose the spiritual dangers that socialism—whether utopian, parliamentary, or revolutionary—posed to the world's working classes. Workers could count only on "the Christian reform of morals" to improve their living and working conditions.[79]

Despite his blanket indictment of all socialists, Pius XI explicitly recognized the difference between Marxists and other socialists. The former, in the pontiff's eyes, had already "laid waste vast regions of eastern Europe and Asia." For this reason, Pius deemed it "superfluous to warn upright and faithful children of the Church regarding the impious and iniquitous character of Communism." To those Catholics who believed in the possibility of meeting socialist revolution halfway, Pius XI replied in no uncertain terms, "Whether considered as a doctrine, or an historical fact, or a movement, Socialism, if it remains truly Socialism, even after it has yielded to truth and justice on the points which we have mentioned, cannot be reconciled with the teachings of the Catholic Church because its concept of society itself is utterly foreign to Christian truth. [ . . . ] Religious socialism, Christian socialism, are contradictory terms; no one can be at the same time a good Catholic and a true socialist."[80]

At the time of *Quadragesimo Anno*'s promulgation, few Catholics openly dissented from the Vatican's position. By the end of the 1930s, however, an increasing number of Catholic intellectuals seeking an alternative to capitalism, liberalism, and republicanism began to grow exasperated with the pope's choice to prioritize anti-socialism at all costs. In the face of an intransigent Holy See, a self-styled Catholic vanguard began to form that, while strongly disapproving of Marxism, nonetheless felt that Catholics needed to do more than simply denounce socialists of all stripes. Instead of anathema, the dissenters wanted reform and serious dialogue—with social democrats, with Marxists, with all people of good will. In the course of the 1930s, with Fascist Italy and Nazi Germany growing in power on the international stage, and with the Spanish Civil War breaking out in 1936, Poland seemed more and more important as a potential site of dialogue at the margins of European Catholicism. After all, interwar Poland straddled the boundary between Catholic Europe and the territory already lost to Marxism.

## MARITAIN IN POLAND

In January 1921, a thirty-seven-year-old priest from Warsaw knocked on Jacques Maritain's door. The two men had never met, but the legendary philosopher welcomed the Pole into his home, inviting him to join a gathering of philosophers that was about to begin inside the house. The topic of discussion—as always, in the Maritain household—was the *Summa Theologiae* of Thomas Aquinas.[81]

The priest was Władysław Korniłowicz, and through him that evening had tangible consequences for Catholic intellectual life in interwar Poland. Korniłowicz's seminar back in Poland benefited tremendously from the priest's newfound friendship with France's leading Thomist philosopher. The two men did not correspond frequently—Maritain actually responded more quickly than Korniłowicz—yet the French Thomist mailed his new friend one book after another for the Polish seminar's library. Thanking Maritain for a signed edition of the philosopher's tract *Antimodern (Antimoderne)*, the Polish philosopher-priest confessed that, "for me, memory of you will forever remain a great source of encouragement in this work."[82] Those present at Korniłowicz's seminars heard about Maritain almost weekly. One of the seminar's participants later recalled the philosopher-priest describing his French hero's path: "from an atheist and a rebellious partisan of official Sorbonne philosophy, he made himself into a Catholic and a wonderful force behind the renewal of Thomist philosophy."[83]

In the end, Władysław Korniłowicz was only one of Maritain's Polish apostles. The partitions may have been a thing of the past, but interwar Poles still lived in a geopolitical vise. Theirs was a world defined by Bolshevism to the east and, after 1933, National Socialism to the west. Their own political system was in chaos throughout the two decades of the interwar Second Republic, torn between Piłsudski's authoritarian social democracy and Dmowski's xenophobic integralism, which continually scarred the landscape of Poland's cities with pitched street violence.[84] For young, bookish Catholic activists in the 1930s, there was a great temptation to lose oneself in dreams of a (Catholic) just society in order to escape the secular cacophony and chaos of the immediate environment. French philosophy thus became a sort of intellectual comfort food for young Polish thinkers of the time.

Stefan Swieżawski, born in 1907, was the first layman in the Renaissance movement to complete a PhD in Christian philosophy, with a specialty in Thomism. From the moment he entered Jan Kazimierz University in Lwów, he avidly followed Maritain's intellectual output. Between 1925 and 1932, as he prepared first his master's thesis and then his PhD, he traveled regularly between Poland and France. In 1929–30, he spent an entire year living with his mother in Paris, where he took courses with Maritain's colleague, medievalist Étienne Gilson. Thanks to a warm introduction from Korniłowicz, whom Swieżawski had met at one of Renaissance's annual retreats, the young Pole joined the fabled Thomist seminar of Meudon. Jacques and Raïssa Maritain took to him instantly, and he became a regular guest at their home. In fact, this was the beginning of a lifelong friendship, culminating three decades later when Maritain and Swieżawski worked side by side as experts at the Second Vatican Council.[85]

Active in the Renaissance movement from his first day at university, Stefan Swieżawski served as its nationwide student president in the 1927–28 academic year. The following year, he led the first seminar on Thomism at Lwów, which was reprised in the 1932–33 academic year, after his return from Paris.[86] This seminar ultimately produced a "Thomist platform" for the entire movement.[87]

Swieżawski was an academic humanist *par excellence*, the first internationally renowned Polish Thomist who came from the laity, rather than the clergy. Given this background, he made for a particularly striking illustration of the fact that the Renaissance activists remained trapped within a contingent, exclusionary understanding of the "human person." In a February 1930 essay for the movement's *Prąd* journal, the twenty-three-year-old wrote, "We do not agitate against Jews for racial or religious reasons, but we must defend ourselves from the materialism of their culture and the anti-Polish bent of their international interests." He continued, "we must defend our special Polish culture from a deluge by the bankrupt Jewish culture, particularly in education, art, and social mores, and at the same time strengthen and expand our economic wealth as energetically as possible."[88] As an organization, Renaissance supported the *numerus clausus*, grafting the justification for that exclusionary policy into a larger claim in its statute about the need to reject "materialism"—read: "Jewish materialism"—and consolidate Polish national culture. Swieżawski's diatribe against a "bankrupt Jewish culture" makes clear that, between the world wars, learned Thomism was compatible with the denial of personhood to Jews.

Eleven months after Swieżawski defended the *numerus clausus*, his friend and fellow Thomist, the nun Teresa Landy, published a lengthy analysis of Thomism in the same journal. A Jewish convert to Catholicism, Landy had apparently "earned" her personhood in the eyes of her Renaissance colleagues, and she herself subsequently preached Korniłowicz's Thomist catechism as a leading member of his seminar. The future Franciscan sister had met Jacques and Raïssa Maritain in 1917, as an undergraduate studying at the Sorbonne. The two women—both Jewish converts, both Thomists, both Francophones from Slavic countries—developed a deep bond of friendship.[89] Thirteen years later,

Landy penned an essay arguing that Thomism held unique power and promise for Poland's spiritual salvation. Aquinas could, for example, disabuse Poles of their preference for secular ideology over what they considered to be a mass of medieval "ignorance."[90] Drawing on Maritain's 1925 *Three Reformers*, Landy explained that the Thomist renewal was already succeeding worldwide at reversing the secularization that had followed the Reformation and the Enlightenment. Like Maritain and Korniłowicz, Landy wanted to see God restored to Poles' understanding of personhood.

Neither Maritain nor the Poles of the Renaissance movement were liberals. Swieżawski's case casts into stark relief the fact that—even for Jewish converts like Landy—Thomist commitments implied neither ecumenism, pluralism, nor even religious toleration. To militate on behalf of human dignity was not to abandon conservatism or nationalism. Maritain and his Polish disciples sought to strike a balance between rationalism and faith. And yet, Polish Catholic ideas of personhood and social justice remained mired in ethnonationalism. Even Maritain himself did not denounce anti-Semitism until 1937, in the face of deepening Nazi persecution of Germany's Jewish population.[91]

The 1930s were nonetheless a decade of great success for Maritain in Poland. Between 1929 and 1939, nineteen of his shorter texts were published in Poland, as were complete Polish-language translations of five books (*Three Reformers, Science and Wisdom, Art and Scholasticism, Religion and Culture,* and the lecture that he delivered at Laski in 1934).[92] Maritain's intellectual influence on Poland over the course of the 1930s—in tandem with a range of homegrown Polish personalisms—defined a new vocabulary of Catholic engagement with the modern world.

In late August and early September 1934, Jacques Maritain spent two weeks in Poland. He came at the invitation of Polish primate August Hlond to speak before the International Thomist Congress, hosted by the western Polish city of Poznań between August 28 and 30, 1934. Besides attending the congress, the French philosopher traveled to Częstochowa, to pray before the sacred icon of the Black Madonna; to Wilno, to see the Marian icon at the Gate of the Heavenly Dawn (*Ostra Brama*); and to Warsaw, to relax for a few days and take in a seminar at Laski led by his friends Korniłowicz and Landy.[93]

When Maritain arrived, Poland was eight years into the quasi-

Fig. 1: Rev. Władysław Korniłowicz (third from left) and Jacques Maritain (third from right) in Warsaw in September 1934, surrounded by participants of Laski's Thomism seminar. Photograph held in the Rev. Władysław Korniłowicz Archive. Reproduced by permission of the Congregation of Franciscan Sisters Servants of the Cross (Warsaw, Poland).

authoritarian rule that followed the May 1926 *coup d'état*. The country had witnessed *endecja* and *sanacja* paramilitary groups in the streets, the conclusion of a non-aggression pact with Nazi Germany, and the imprisonment of Poland's Christian Democratic and Peasant party leaders (among many others).[94]

Not only Poland, however, but indeed all of Europe seemed to be ablaze in 1934. On February 6, violent paramilitary demonstrations in Paris nearly brought down the Third Republic.[95] On June 30, Adolf Hitler consolidated power by eliminating the leaders of Ernst Röhm's *Sturmabteilung* (better known as the SA) in the "Night of the Long Knives."[96] On July 25, just one month before Maritain's journey to Poland, Austria's Catholic fascist leader Engelbert Dollfuss was assassinated by Nazis.[97] Finally, the Spanish Republic—where Maritain had lectured in Santander just before traveling to Poznań—was on the verge of collapse.[98]

Maritain had not originally planned to make any political statements in Poland. He came to Poznań having prepared a lecture on intuition in the philosophy of his erstwhile mentor Henri Bergson. Under the weight of the year's events, however, he changed his mind.[99] Before attending the congress's opening session, the Thomist wandered the streets of Poznań, reflecting on the seeming inevitability of French, Spanish, and Polish republican collapse. His young friend Stefan Swieżawski spotted him from afar, but instead of calling to Maritain, he watched "the philosopher's shadow moving through the streets of Poznań, lost in a profound, melancholic meditation. I cannot forget the pained look on his face, his ardent prayer, his eyes raised to the sky in a church where he believed himself to be alone, as I, unseen, recorded in my memory this image of my hero, my friend."[100]

In the end, Maritain made it to the congress hall.[101] So many people came to hear him that the organizers needed to change the lecture's location three times in order to accommodate what proved to be an audience of 900. In a session chaired personally by the Primate of Poland, the French philosopher challenged his listeners to absorb a radical message. His intellectual biographer Michel Fourcade has eloquently recreated the scene:

> Pronounced in front of the Catholic intellectual elite of the entire country, in a session chaired by Primate Hlond, in the presence of Czech,

Slovak, and Croat Thomists as well as representatives of the Collegium Angelicum (notably, Father Garrigou-Lagrange) and the Pontifical Gregorian University, of the Catholic institutes of higher learning of Milan, Louvain, and Fribourg, and before two monastic Masters-General, the Dominicans' Martin Gillet and the Jesuits' Włodzimierz Ledóchowski, as well as numerous theologians of both orders, this decision was of course not without its risks, constituting indeed a sort of test run: to what extent, in effect, would this *new historical ideal* be compatible with the "corporatist Christian state" to be found here and there, derived from encyclicals? Six months after the suppression of riots in Vienna, only a month after the assassination of Chancellor Dollfuss by the Nazis (July 25, 1934), the question had a particular resonance, especially in Poland, where the corporatist project had mobilized significant forces.[102]

Maritain gave this lecture almost off the cuff, but it proved to be one of the most important that he had ever given. Revising and expanding on his talks from Santander, Maritain delivered in Poznań the text of what later became chapters 4 and 5 of one of his defining works as a political philosopher: the 1936 tract *Integral Humanism* (*Humanisme Intégral*).[103] Philippe Chenaux calls this the "veritable 'little red book' of an entire generation of Catholics."[104] It was Maritain's most comprehensive statement on the proper nature of the Catholic's engagement with the modern world, and in it he defined the mission of the era's Catholic intellectuals: reclaiming humanism from a bankrupt "anthropocentric" tradition by restoring Roman Catholicism's God to humanism's core.[105]

The very notion of "dignity" was losing its meaning. Materialism was behind the ascendancy of a secular humanism that destroyed the essence of what it meant to be human. *Integral Humanism* was to be the answer to these dilemmas—the definitive Thomist vision for Catholics looking to save humanity from its own folly, to reorder the political and to build a just society without waiting for the Last Judgment. What made Maritain's humanism "integral," or complete, was its aspiration to be *total*: to "meet the whole range of human needs—physical, emotional, mental, and spiritual."[106] To become "theocentric" humanists, Catholics needed to remember that they were made in the image of God as "human persons." After all—Maritain reasoned—it was only the "person," rather than the individual or the collective, that could avert the impending social and political catastrophes facing the modern world.

Renaissance was responsible for publicizing Maritain's work in Poland and for organizing his Polish sojourn. The students and graduates of Renaissance flocked to Poznań to hear him in 1934, and they not only absorbed the lessons of his treatises and lectures, but indeed produced their own critiques, adaptations, and responses. Renaissance's flagship journal *Prąd* therefore had the privilege of debuting in print texts that later went into Maritain's 1936 tract. In "The Historical Ideal of a New Christendom," he set about to debunk the myth that medieval Christendom had sufficed to safeguard personhood.[107] Instead, Maritain demanded a new, modern ideal for Catholics. Embracing modernity whole-heartedly, he declared, "nothing seems more dangerous to me than an unequivocal conception of the Christian temporal order that would bind this order to dead forms from the past."[108]

The arrival of *Integral Humanism* in bookstores in 1936 coincided with one of the defining events of interwar European history: the outbreak of the Spanish Civil War. The death toll—which included thousands of massacred priests and nuns—confirmed the Vatican's fears of the anti-religious "barbarism" of socialists and Communists.[109] Many French Catholic intellectuals—most notably, the poet Paul Claudel—argued that Catholics had a moral obligation to support the insurgent Franco regime. Maritain, though well-known as an anti-Communist, responded in 1937 that Church teaching was very clear on the definition of a "just war," and the Spanish Civil War did not meet this standard. As a result, Catholics were obliged to stay neutral, rather than side with any one belligerent.[110] Letters piled up, some attacking, some supporting Maritain; his detractors nicknamed him the "Red Christian" for his refusal to denounce the Spanish Republic.[111] Famed Catholic novelist François Mauriac came to Maritain's defense, as did the entire intellectual circle of *Esprit*.[112] Following the bombing of Guernica, Maritain shared the outrage of fellow travelers like Pablo Picasso, and Maritain drew up a manifesto of protest entitled *For the Basque People*, circulating it for signatures among his friends.[113] Under pressure from world events, the Catholic intellectual world had fractured.

## BETWEEN JESUS AND THE FRENCH COMMUNIST PARTY

When he published *Quadragesimo Anno* in 1931, Pius XI believed that the "evil" of Soviet Communism was an established fact among

Catholics. Six years later, however, the pontiff issued a new encyclical denouncing said "evil" as a "satanic scourge."[114] The pontiff was, of course, reacting to the Spanish Civil War and to the divisions it had created among Catholics. But there was a deeper question at stake: whether or not any Communist project could ever be "good," perhaps even deserving of Catholic support when it had the potential to improve or save lives. Pius XI answered this question loud and clear: no.

*Divini Redemptoris* was published in March 1937. Pius XI laced the encyclical with Maritain's language of Thomist personalism, arguing that Communism "robs human personality of all its dignity" and "denies the rights, dignity, and liberty of human personality." Finally, the pontiff denounced the collective basis of society in Communism, countering, "Only man, the human person, and not society in any form is endowed with reason and a morally free will." A collectivist social program could only do harm, for "each individual man in the dignity of his human personality is supplied with all that is necessary for the exercise of his social functions."[115]

At this point, the Great Terror and its attendant show trials were in progress in the Soviet Union, yet they played only a small role in the Vatican decision to hand down *Divini Redemptoris*. Pius XI was thinking of Spain, but he also looked to France. He saw France's first socialist prime minister, Léon Blum, assembling a "popular front" coalition with the support of the French Communist Party. Even more distressingly, he saw those very same French Communists reaching out across the aisle to Catholic workers, insisting that Catholics and Communists had every reason to work together toward a just society.[116]

On April 17, 1936, France's leading Communist, Maurice Thorez, declared over the airwaves of Radio Paris, "We reach out to you [*Nous te tendrons la main*], Catholic, worker, employee, artisan, peasant; we, who are outside the faith, because you are our brother, and you are, like us, plagued by the same concerns."[117] It is unclear whether or not Thorez actually hoped to welcome thousands of Catholic workers into his party's disciplined ranks. Nonetheless, the prospect of those workers' attrition from the Church gave the Holy See such a fright that—even faced with militaristic expansionism by both Fascist Italy and Nazi Germany—it focused above all on stepping up its campaign against Communism.

On the eve of the Second World War, the specter of potential Trojan horses haunted the Catholic Church. All the while, subversive as its intentions likely were, the French Communist *main tendue* helped to shift the boundaries of Catholic orthodoxy at mid-century. A year after his radio address, Thorez elaborated the principles behind the "outstretched hand" in a Communist Party pamphlet. Calling his April 1936 speech a "Profession of Materialist Faith," Thorez reaffirmed the Communist creed of rationalist, materialist atheism. At the same time, he offered a litany of citations from Marx, Engels, and Lenin to the effect that Communists must respect the religious beliefs of individual members of the working class. Thorez reminded Party members that Lenin had considered priests as well as workers to be welcome in workers' parties, so long as "the priest comes to us to deliver himself into shared political work" and "he consciously accepts his task, without placing himself above the program of the Party."[118]

Thorez then turned to Catholic sources, including *Rerum Novarum*, *Quadragesimo Anno*, and Paul's epistles, using a litany of quotations to emphasize the shared anti-capitalism of Catholics and Communists. He asserted that "class warfare was not proclaimed by some ill-willed Communists"—after all, even the Catholic Church had recognized it since *Rerum Novarum*—but only Communism could, by "liberating man from economic and political servitude [ . . . ] permit him to taste of the bread of the Spirit."[119]

Thorez's point was to encourage Communists assembled in France's biggest trade union—the General Confederation of Labor (*Confédération Générale du Travail*)—to seek cooperation with Christian workers associated with the French Confederation of Christian Workers (*Confédération Française des Travailleurs Chrétiens*). The only class that Thorez's radio address had mentioned was the proletariat, so Catholics outside the working classes were arguably of no interest to the PCF. Yet it was precisely the Communists' targeting of workers that led the Vatican to take the speech so seriously. When the Dominican journal *Sept* (*Seven*) published an exclusive interview with Prime Minister Léon Blum, on February 19, 1937, the Vatican instructed the Master-General of the Dominican order to shut the journal down immediately, without warning. As Oscar Arnal has underscored, the Spanish Civil War made Pius XI deeply sensitive to Catholicism's Left flank.[120] He was not willing to countenance what he saw as a new method of subverting the Catholic Church from within: openness to dialogue with the Left.

Whatever the pope's fears, there were no masses of Catholic workers flocking to the French Communist Party. Quite the opposite—respected Catholic voices like the Jesuit philosopher Gaston Fessard stepped in to offer damning critiques of the "outstretched hand." Turning Hegel and Marx against the French Communist, Fessard insisted that Thorez could not possibly be serious, given the PCF's long record of doctrinaire atheism. Fessard's *Outstretched Hand? Is a Catholic-Communist Dialogue Possible?* ultimately enjoyed a wider readership than Thorez's own writings on the matter.[121]

Yet the PCF stepped up its press campaign in 1937, attempting to discredit individual French bishops and prominent lay leaders. The PCF newspaper *L'Humanité* (*Humanity*) printed a series of commentaries reminding French Catholics that they enjoyed a long heritage of Gallican resistance to Rome. In other words, it was the historical prerogative of French Catholics to ignore the Holy See altogether.[122]

This was the immediate context for Pius XI's decision to publish *Divini Redemptoris*, which unequivocally condemned any Communist outreach to Catholics. Although the pope did not name Thorez or the PCF, he warned against Communists making a pretense of dialogue: "without receding an inch from their subversive principles, they invite Catholics to collaborate with them in the realm of so-called humanitarianism and charity; and at times even make proposals that are in perfect harmony with the Christian spirit and the doctrine of the Church." The lesson that Pius XI wanted the faithful to take away was that "Those who permit themselves to be deceived into lending their aid towards the triumph of Communism in their own country, will be the first to fall victims of their error."[123]

## THE FUTURE OF THE RENAISSANCE

Four months after Pius XI handed down *Divini Redemptoris*, a twenty-five-year-old Polish Catholic activist named Jerzy Turowicz strolled along the Seine. It was July 1937, and the young Pole had come to France to attend a congress of the international Catholic organization Pax Romana. He had two intellectual heroes, both French, both Catholic philosophers: Jacques Maritain and Emmanuel Mounier. Since he first encountered an issue of *Esprit* in 1933, Turowicz had been a devoted reader.[124] Not having had the opportunity to meet Maritain during the Thomist's 1934 visit to Poland, Turowicz decided to write to Mounier in advance of his trip to Paris. Remarkably, Mounier replied, and the two men met at *Esprit*'s annual summer retreat, held in the Paris suburb of Jouy-en-Josas.[125] It was a day that remained dear to Turowicz for the remaining six decades of his life.

Born in Kraków in 1912, Jerzy Turowicz studied first in Lwów, then returned home to continue his studies at Jagiellonian University. Although active in the Renaissance movement from the beginning of his studies, he did not publish in the movement's journals until asked in 1935 to join the staff of its newest, eponymous monthly. Turowicz cowrote this journal's mission statement, asserting the "enormous and largely unappreciated role of the Renaissance movement in the growth and deepening of the Catholicism of the younger generation."[126] The next year, he penned an article describing Maritain's thought as "the very best that Catholicism had to offer."[127] The essay appeared in the pages of the National Democratic journal *Prosto z Mostu* (*Straight from the Hip*), which had offered the young Renaissance activist a few columns to defend his hero. Two issues later, however, one of Poland's leading National Democrats pushed back against Turowicz, denouncing Maritain's thought as "decadent" and the philosopher himself as "a hack and a Jew."[128]

Despite his young age, then, Turowicz quickly made a name for himself within Polish Catholic intellectual circles of the late 1930s as an up-and-coming French-style personalist. And yet, as the decade drew to a close, Turowicz increasingly looked beyond Thomism, to a promise of Catholic "revolution" made by Maritain's erstwhile protégé, Emmanuel Mounier.[129]

## EMMANUEL MOUNIER'S "REVOLUTION"

Mounier's time in the sun came at a moment when European Catholic intellectual life was in disarray. Catholic thinkers broadly agreed that liberalism was doomed, but they disagreed on what should take its place. In France, the responses ranged from integral nationalism to cautious support for new, yet-to-be-defined democratic forms—as long as those recognized the primacy of the Catholic Church.[130] Corporatism was the order of the day, and its fixation on the "health" of the body politic lent itself to fascist tendencies. Christian Democratic political parties were weak.[131] Clergy and laity alike, then, had to choose their affiliations based largely on contingent factors like world events.

In this time of division and perceived decline, the younger of Turowicz's two personalist heroes established himself as a maverick voice of "revolution." When he co-founded the journal *Esprit* in 1932, the twenty-seven-year-old became a serious broker of French public opinion. Mounier thought of himself as both a Catholic philosopher and a "non-conformist"—ecumenical, antinomian, critical of a decaying bourgeois civilization, and seeking to fashion a "New Man."[132] Over the course of the 1930s, Mounier's avowed non-conformism gave him a unique platform from which to launch a social and political philosophy centered on the "human person." His personalism went beyond Thomism, to collectivism.

In the 1930s, Emmanuel Mounier, though critical of *Divini Redemptoris*, was no friend to Marxists. At the same time, he proudly lauded Maritain in the pages of *Esprit* when Maritain protested the bombing of Guernica. In fact—unlike his old mentor—Mounier wore proudly the epithet of "Red Christian." The philosopher drew a clear distinction between the Left—which Catholics should welcome—and Marxism, which Catholics should oppose. He became known for fiery rhetoric that gained him a growing international following, especially among the younger generations. By 1939, the Spanish Civil War had helped to establish Mounier as the clarion Catholic voice of a new approach to ordering human society.

Born in Grenoble in 1905, the son of a pharmacist, Mounier began studying philosophy at the Sorbonne in 1927, but financial constraints and his devotion to his writing led him to quit his studies. And yet, within five years, he had joined the Catholic intellectual elite of Paris, earning a place alongside Maritain, existentialist philosopher Gabriel Marcel, and the future Jesuit priest and cardinal Jean Daniélou.

Mounier created *Esprit* in 1932 with the help of a diverse crew of writers of different denominations and political persuasions. He and Maritain grew apart as *Esprit* became an overnight sensation. The journal was Catholic without being exclusively so, personalist without being Thomist, and "progressive" without being socialist. Though Mounier's intellectual peers were university-educated elites, he and his family lived in near-poverty, in a working class-dominated suburb of Paris. He commuted for years between the French capital and a high-school teaching job in Brussels, as running *Esprit* became for him an unpaid second full-time job—a labor of love. He thus understood the dilemmas of the working poor from personal experience.

Though Mounier had promised in 1932 that *Esprit* would belong to "neither the right, nor the left," but instead restrict its work to spiritual life, that vow faded into oblivion over the course of the 1930s.[133] Thomas Bokenkotter is right that Mounier's personalism was "a grab-bag of ideas drawn from many sources."[134] His passion for the working poor was visible already in his early writings, which contain no small amount of affection for the political Left. In his 1935 *Personalist and Communitarian Revolution* (*Révolution personnaliste et communautaire*), Mounier wrote, "On the Left [ . . . ] have appeared the majority of new forces, every example of social progress, almost all of the multitude of new things in art and in literature, and what is more than all of that, the immense influx of desire for justice maintained without compromise, even without eloquence, at the heart of the working masses."[135]

In his 1936 *Manifesto in the Service of Personalism* (*Manifeste au service du personnalisme*), Mounier insisted, "Personalism is the only terrain on which an honest, effective struggle can be launched against Marxism."[136] Two years later, frightened by the ease with which France and Britain simply surrendered the Sudetenland to the Third Reich, Mounier turned against fascism, too, drafting a "Statute of the Human Person" that he envisioned as the basis for all future democracy—to be neither liberal, nor Marxist, but ecumenical, humanist, and pluralist. This is what he meant by "personalist democracy."[137]

Whatever Mounier promised about making *Esprit* "neither right nor left," Lucien Pélissier rightly identifies him as a man of the Left—and, above all, an anti-capitalist.[138] In 1930s France, what that meant was that his journal refrained from any hint of support for a particular political party. The French republic was falling apart, and Mounier wanted no part of what he saw as a corrupt, co-opted system on the verge of collapse. For Mounier, the downward spiral of French republicanism between 1870 and 1940 showed that Marx, unfortunately, had a point. This is why Mounier came to believe unequivocally in a commonality of Catholic and socialist interests—where socialism meant neither the Soviet, nor the mainstream republican version. In 1934, he explained that *Esprit* would "never be for money because the world of money cannot cease to be evil."[139]

However we choose to label Mounier, it is clear that he was very different from Maritain.[140] Mounier was not a politician, but he believed in action, engagement, and service, three words repeatedly regularly throughout his writing. The underlying message was the same in 1935's *Personalist and Communitarian Revolution*, 1936's *Manifesto in the Service of Personalism*, 1946's *What is Personalism? (Qu'est-ce que le personnalisme?)*, and 1950's *Personalism (Le personnalisme)*: fight capitalism's "established disorder" through "affirmation of the primacy of the human person over material necessities and the collective apparatus that sustains its development."[141]

Interwar France had a Christian Democratic party: the Popular Democratic Party (PDP, *Parti Démocrate Populaire*).[142] It was marginal to mainstream politics, never topping 4 percent of the vote in elections to the interwar French National Assembly, yet it represented a Catholic effort to work within the political system of the Third Republic. Frightened by the emergence of Fascist Italy, the Christian Democrats followed Jacques Maritain's turn away from French Action toward personalism, which became a core element of their ideology—even though Maritain himself made it clear that he did not consider himself to be a "Christian Democrat."[143] The PDP's fundamental goal was to assure the protection of personhood in a democratic political system.

According to Emmanuel Mounier, this was ridiculous. Although there was some personnel overlap between *Esprit* and Christian Democracy before, during, and after World War II, Mounier himself would have none of it. His whole philosophy of the "established disorder" prevented him from even countenancing the possibility that human dignity could be squared with liberal democracy. In this respect, Mounier's Catholicism was quite traditional. In his mind, "Republican political culture became a kind of secular religion," and it could not co-exist with Catholicism in the long term.[144] It was Mounier's anti-republicanism that led him after 1939 to flirt with the Vichy regime, then later with Communism.

In place of Christian Democracy, Mounier's thought provided grounds for the emergence of a new personalist approach to Catholic politics, which came to be called "Catholic socialism." That said, Mounier was not the first French Catholic intellectual whose anti-capitalism brought him closer to Marxism. From 1935 to 1939, a handful of Catholics and Protestants published a journal called *Terre Nouvelle*

(*New Land*), which dismissed everyone outside the ranks of the proletariat as either "bourgeois and capitalist oligarchy" or "its mercenaries and dupes."[145] Simply put, *Terre Nouvelle* wanted France to become Communist, but with an allowance for religious faith. Not coincidentally, this was also Maurice Thorez's position. Meanwhile, Mounier situated himself and his journal *Esprit* neatly "between Thorez and Jesus Christ."[146]

Mounier envisioned a personalist communitarianism that could rise above existing political and ideological divisions. Communists could join, too, but on *personalist*, rather than Marxist terms. Like Maritain, Mounier put theocentric humanism front and center in his envisioned reordering of politics and society. However, the younger personalist considered "revolution" to be almost on par ontologically with personhood. This was a dangerous conclusion for a Catholic to reach. The erstwhile disciple departed from Maritain's "new Christendom" by casting aside the need for a Christian vision of history: what mattered most was the moment at hand.[147]

His sense of an *Augenblick*—of an existentially decisive moment—led Mounier to shift his politics dramatically after World War II.[148] The violence and suffering of war brought his communitarianism more in line with collectivism, his personalism more in line with Marxism. Mounier himself wrote in 1948, "Personalism, in fact, believes that capitalist structures today are an impediment to the movement towards the liberation of man, and they must be abolished and replaced by a socialist organization of production and consumption. It is not we who have invented socialism. It was born of man's suffering and his reflections on the disorders that oppressed him."[149]

What Mounier loved in Marxism was its promise of revolution. By the end of the Second World War, seeing in the Soviet Union the only viable alternative to capitalism and fascism, he would go so far as to claim that the best in Marxism was actually personalist: "The Marxist critique of the alienation and life of the workers' movement is pregnant with personalism."

To be clear, Mounier was not rereading Marx through the lens of mid-nineteenth-century German debates on personhood. He did not understand that Marx had consciously secularized the "person" and dethroned religion in response to G.W.F. Hegel.[150] Mounier, rather, was making a far weaker claim: that Marx's writings on the suffering of the proletariat simply anticipated his own Catholic personalism. In one of his final texts—published posthumously in 1950—Mounier proclaimed, "Communism and Christianity reinforce each other like Jacob and the angel, with a rigor and brotherhood-in-arms that infinitely surpass the struggle for power."[151]

In the final years of his life, Jacques Maritain looked back on the 1930s, and he faulted himself for not seeing the seeds of the Marxist turn in the young Mounier. While Mounier had been right to agitate for a "personalist and communitarian revolution [ . . . ] when I see the way that it is used now, I am not very proud of it. For after lip-service is paid to 'personalist,'" it is clear that what is really cherished is 'communitarian.'"[152]

Mounier escaped criticism on the part of the Holy See in his lifetime, in large part because *Esprit* did not request the Church's imprimatur. According to one of Mounier's successors at the helm of *Esprit*, Jean-Marie Domenach, by the time that Pope Pius XII died in October 1958, the Holy Office had already drafted an official condemnation of *Esprit*.[153] Until the Vatican opens its archives for the pontificate of Pius XII, we cannot know for sure.

## CONCLUSIONS

On the eve of the Second World War, France and Poland both had well-established Catholic intellectual communities with strong ties to one another. Since the late 1890s, select groups of Polish priests had trained in French-speaking Western Europe, returning to Poland deeply committed to Thomist renewal. Reverend professors like Antoni Szymański and Władysław Korniłowicz educated the reborn Polish state's first generations of Catholic intellectuals. Whatever their course of study, Jerzy Turowicz and his fellow men and women of Renaissance left university armed with a deep appreciation for Thomas Aquinas. For these interwar Polish Catholic intellectuals, Thomism was no mere hobby: it was a path to God, and it also held the key to a just society.

The experience of being a catechumen—of appreciating the return to the faith by lapsed believers, the conversion impulse of non-believers, and, most importantly, the willingness of believers to dialogue with non-believers—was central to the inception of Thomist personalism. The great Thomist Jacques Maritain was himself a convert from Protestantism, and his wife Raïssa Oumançoff entered the Catholic faith as a converted Jew. The idea of "catechesis" guided gifted educators like Korniłowicz and Maritain from the *fin-de-siècle* through the 1930s as they ran Thomist seminars that assembled the best and brightest of their respective countries.

Even before Maritain first set foot on Polish soil in August 1934, a plurality of affinities bound him to the country: Korniłowicz's seminar, Swieżawski's research, the parallels between French Action and National Democracy. Polish intellectuals' understanding of Maritain's intellectual and spiritual journey ensured him a warm reception. In turn, his Thomist personalism provided Polish Catholic activists with the foundation for elaborating their own homegrown philosophies of the "human person."

John Hellman is correct that "Polish personalism was not merely derivative."[154] Interwar Polish personalisms constituted a mixed bag of nationalism, Thomism, and exhortations for spiritual renewal. Catholic education, the life of the family, and the dignity of the "human person"—all central tenets of Catholic Action, all elaborated and transformed by Maritain into a promise of engagement with the modern world—marked an attempted escape from integral nationalism. And yet, anti-Semitism remained a central part of Polish Catholics' exclusionary politics, reinforced by the Church's long-standing anti-Judaism. Even the educated Catholics of Renaissance consistently linked the imagined community of "Jews" with the worst of the world's ills—capitalism, Communism, and the dethroning of Catholicism's God by modernity.

And so, despite the strength of homegrown Polish personalisms, as well as the enthusiasm for Jacques Maritain's writings in interwar Poland, integral nationalism threatened to derail the new ethics of the "human person" from its very inception. On the one hand, Catholic Poles began in the interwar years to contribute substantively to a burgeoning transnational discourse on the "human person" and to pursue new forms of catechism and liturgy that crossed confessional boundaries, reconceptualizing faith as a personal encounter. On the other, they could only imagine a just world of "human persons" from which non-persons—meaning non-Catholics, and especially Jews—were excluded.[155]

The nascent Catholic vanguard of the early twentieth century remained wedded to an exclusionary definition of the "human person." On the eve of the Second World War, then, personhood remained contingent on active membership in the world community of Catholics. Prevailing norms disqualified from personhood anyone who was not a baptized Catholic participating in the life of the Church. This is why Korniło-wicz's personalism was predicated on his desire to multiply the population of the world's "persons" by converting more souls to Catholicism. This is also why Maritain and Mounier alike insisted on reestablishing the "person" as the ontological core of humanism in European intellectual life. To them, personhood was the key both to a better life on earth and to salvation in Heaven.

# 2 Personalism at War

## Clandestine Intellectual Life and Anti-Nazi Resistance in World War II

*France is the nerve center of the conscience of Europe [ . . . ]. Its historical mission and its strength in the period after the war will be to determine and to stabilize the destiny of Europe.*

—*Jacques Maritain*[1]

IN THE FALL OF 1942, a twenty-year-old near-sighted bookworm dashed down an alley in occupied Warsaw to avoid German patrols. Only a year earlier, he had been released from the concentration camps at Auschwitz, where he had landed after getting caught in a random round-up in the Warsaw neighborhood of Żoliborz. Immediately enrolling in underground university courses, he came into contact with Catholic youth activists who were recruiting for a new underground campaign called *Żegota* (the Council to Aid Jews), which would work for three years smuggling Jewish children out of the General Government.[2] He later recalled that, when misidentified as a Jew during the 1940 round-up, he did not protest, because "Anti-Semitism and philo-Semitism made no sense to me at the time, just that these were two extreme versions of the same nonsense. For me, it was obvious that people cannot be reduced to their background—whether nationality, class, or creed."[3]

In 1965, Yad Vashem would honor Władysław Bartoszewski as "Righteous Among the Nations," a rescuer of Jews from the Holocaust. Exactly three decades later, following the fall of the Iron Curtain, he would become Poland's foreign minister, and he would serve in successive government posts until his death in 2015 at the age of 93.

Bartoszewski ran down that alley in November 1942 not simply because he was afraid, but to protect what he was carrying: the first issue
of *Prawda Młodych* (*The Truth of the Young*), an underground journal that he produced almost single-handedly for the next two years.
He succeeded in soliciting articles from resistance figures as diverse as
Żegota founder Zofia Kossak-Szczucka and underground sociologist
Maria Ossowska. Bartoszewski became—despite his young age—a distinctive, recognizable Catholic voice in the wartime world of Warsaw
underground publishing.[4] As fate would have it, the figure who made
this success possible was none other than Emmanuel Mounier.

In school, Bartoszewski had studied German, not French, but
Mounier's writings circulated to such an extent among occupied Warsaw's underground youth that personalism became a defining feature
of their thinking. Bartoszewski, too, became a personalist. According
to his own later testimony, personalism inspired him to become a Holocaust rescuer, to work after the war in Catholic publishing, and to
become a tireless advocate of Catholic-Jewish dialogue. In an era when
age-old anti-Semitic prejudice led many Catholics to blackmail and pogroms, Bartoszewski's case can hardly be construed as representative
of Polish Catholicism on the whole—or even of Catholic personalism.[5]
In fact, the chapter that follows says little about the Holocaust, largely
because—Żegota aside—most Catholic intellectuals in wartime Poland
consciously lived a life apart from the Jewish neighbors who had been
marked for death. As of the war's outbreak, Catholic personhood was
reserved for the baptized—with some Catholics even questioning the
personhood of converts.[6] The French personalist Jacques Maritain
began during the war to shift his views slowly toward a more inclusive,
ecumenical personalism that *might* include the Jews.[7] In neither the
French nor the Polish Catholic resistance, however, did reflections on
the Jewish question play any substantial role.

And yet, marginal as Żegota is to our story, Bartoszewski represented
a living link between French and Polish Catholic intellectual worlds
at war with Nazism. Like thousands his age in France and Poland,
Władysław Bartoszewski read Maritain and Mounier while at war, and
what he read inspired him to take action. In an era when Europe seemed
to have fallen apart, Mounier's interwar theory of revolutionary, communitarian personalism took on new meaning, as Catholics assembled

communities of resistance to German occupation out of localized, clan-destine social networks. Those who survived the war would continue to pursue the dream of "revolutionary" transformation, believing that it was their mission to create a civic order wildly different from that which had buckled so easily under pressure from Nazi Germany. This chapter tells the story of France's influence on the Polish underground.

## PIUS XII AND THE WAR

Prior to his elevation to the papacy, Cardinal Eugenio Pacelli had served as Vatican Secretary of State to Pius XI. It was in this capacity that he negotiated a concordat with Nazi Germany.[8] Pius XII came to the papacy as intent as his predecessor had been on fighting Commu-nism. World War II, however, took Catholicism's fate out of the pa-pacy's hands. Less "Hitler's pope" or "deputy" than bystander, Pius XII mostly kept the Holy See on the sidelines throughout the war. He failed to condemn the Holocaust, and he also opted for a hands-off approach to the Nazi puppet state of Slovakia, run by a Catholic priest, Jozef Tiso.[9] As Polish primate Hlond wrote in an August 2, 1941 letter to Pius XII, "the Poles are complaining that the pope does not pro-test against crimes when the Germans have 3,000 Polish priests killed in concentration camps, that he does not speak out in condemnation when hundreds of priests and members of Catholic Action, including papal chamberlains, are shot to death, all exterminated without the slightest offense on their part."[10] There was no response from Pius XII.

As the war unfolded, fundamental decisions about the life of the Church were made increasingly "in the field," rather than at the top of the ecclesiastical hierarchy. *Divini Redemptoris* was forgotten, and Catholics resisting German occupying forces and puppet states worked with anyone willing to lend a hand—including the Left. Oscar Cole-Arnal may have gone too far in concluding that "the Vatican welcomed the Cold War as one means of liberating Pius XII from the stain of collaboration with the Nazis and Italian fascists."[11] But there is no doubt that the hierarchy's wartime inaction in the face of brutalization and genocide on an unprecedented scale came at a tangible cost to its postwar legitimacy. This opened the door to more systematic long-term cooperation between Catholics and socialists across the European continent.

## FRENCH AND POLISH CATHOLICS AT WAR

The Catholic episcopates of Europe were thus left by and large to fend for themselves in the face of very different approaches adopted by occupying German forces, ranging from largely respectful co-existence (France) to harassment, persecution, and mass violence (Poland). Across Europe, men and women faced the choice between collaboration and resistance every day.[12] Horizontal networks of Catholic activism formed: almost all ultimately opted for resistance against German occupiers and their national proxies like Vichy.[13]

In Western Europe, Catholics and Communists worked together in the underground after 1941, when Hitler's invasion of the Soviet Union abrogated the Molotov-Ribbentrop Pact. Europe's Communist parties once again became anti-fascist, as they had been for the better part of the 1930s. In France, Communists and Socialists alike participated in the National Council of the Resistance (*Conseil National de la Résistance*) from the moment of its creation by Jean Moulin, and they were among the more accomplished of the guerrilla resistance fighters who comprised the French *maquis*.[14]

In underground Central and Eastern Europe, meanwhile, such cooperation was possible only in rare instances. In Poland, resistance to the Nazi occupation fractured along ideological lines, making cooperation between the Home Army (*Armia Krajowa*) and the Communist-led People's Army (*Armia Ludowa*) virtually impossible. Bands of guerrilla fighters proliferated on the margins of both movements, and the animus between them meant that the armies were as eager to fight each other as they were the Germans.[15]

France and Poland experienced World War II completely differently. France saw no Soviet occupation or Nazi death camps, no Warsaw Ghetto Uprising or Warsaw Uprising; its resistance fighters gained Anglo-American recognition even as Poland's Home Army lost that recognition.[16] It is therefore perhaps remarkable that, despite their divergent experiences of war and occupation, France and Poland both saw the emergence of a new model of Catholic resistance fighter: the guerrilla-*cum*-personalist.

Wartime activism in resistance networks often paired clandestine intellectual life with violent resistance in armed partisan units.[17] Living both theory and practice in their daily lives, Catholic activists experienced war and occupation as a call for the revolutionary transformation of the world that had allowed Nazism to come to power in the first place. Invariably, one of the political outcomes was a strong leftward turn. In France, the Lyonnais network of Christian Witness (*Témoignage Chrétien*) and, in Poland, a number of clandestine youth resistance groups became incubation sites for the vanguard of postwar Catholicism. In both cases, this vanguard was forged in the crucible of violent anti-German struggle.

## MARITAIN IN EXILE

One day in the fall of 1942, the sixty-year-old Jacques Maritain was en route from Columbia University to Princeton. He was guest lecturing at both schools as often as their faculties would permit, trying to piece together an income sufficient to support him and his wife Raïssa. They were now two years into the unplanned exile that France's "strange defeat" at German hands had forced upon them.[18] Lecturing in Toronto in advance of France's capitulation, the Maritains moved on to the United States thereafter, fated to wait out the remainder of the war in North America.

Jacques Maritain's wartime absence from French soil deprived the Resistance of a powerful intellectual leader. In the summer of 1940, the Thomist philosopher immediately set about forging ties with other exiled European intellectuals intent on supporting the anti-German war effort from abroad.[19] He co-founded the Free School for Advanced Studies (*École Libre des Hautes Études*) in New York as an academy-in-exile where he and other expatriate French scholars—including Claude Lévi-Strauss—met and gave regular public lectures.[20] He also became closely acquainted with exiled intellectual leaders from other occupied countries—including the great Polish historian Oskar Halecki.[21]

Despite a difficult material situation, Maritain wrote prolifically, publishing his work with the New York-based exile press *Éditions de la Maison Française.*[22] In 1941, he published *Through the Disaster* (*À travers le désastre*), a study of the reasons behind France's overnight collapse in 1940; in 1942, *The Rights of Man and Natural Law* (*Les Droits de l'homme et la Loi naturelle*); and in 1943, *Christianity and Democracy* (*Christianisme et démocratie*). Smuggled into France and reproduced on a large scale on clandestine printing presses, these volumes furnished a growing underground—reaching Catholics and non-Catholics alike—with propaganda material. Once France's Christian Democratic movement began to coalesce and build a field organization under the auspices of the wartime National Council of the Resistance, Maritain became required reading for its recruits.[23]

The circulation of Maritain's wartime writings also helped the Free French movement under Charles de Gaulle to mobilize Anglo-American support. The pride taken by Maritain in the ends served by his wartime writings is clear from his January 1942 letter to his friend, political philosopher Yves Simon: "my book is being printed clandestinely in France, the latest news received tells me, in 10,000 copies, which attests to a serious underground organization [ . . . ]. It is also necessary that a certain corpus of political and international doctrine be prepared here under conditions of freedom so that it may exert an influence on the French in London and on General de Gaulle himself, whom we must try to help."[24]

## VICHY COLLABORATION AND CHRISTIAN WITNESS

In Jacques Maritain's absence, the personalists who remained in France were hardly unambiguous in their opposition to Nazi Germany and its Vichy collaborators. In fact, some personalists—Emmanuel Mounier among them—immediately joined the ranks of those collaborators. In the summer of 1940, he and his *Esprit* colleague Jean Lacroix, a philosophy professor from Lyon, began teaching part-time at Vichy's Leadership School (*École des Cadres*) in the spa town of Uriage. Their students were groomed to be future leaders of Vichy France.[25] Mounier threw himself completely into work on behalf of Vichy's National Revolution, continuing to produce *Esprit* out of Uriage.[26]

According to Vichy's own Catholic luminary Henri Massis, however, it was precisely Mounier's prioritization of faith over the nation—what Maritain had called the "primacy of the spiritual"—that necessitated his dismissal from Uriage in April 1941. Overnight, *Esprit* ceased to appear.[27] Once out of the Vichy mainstream, Mounier quickly became a favorite punching bag of the Vichy authorities, who kept him either imprisoned or under house arrest for most of 1942 pending charges of involvement with the Resistance. Paradoxically, it was only when these charges were dropped—following a hunger strike by the besieged

Mounier—that the philosopher actually made contact with the under-ground.[28] Mounier thereby became one of many French Catholic intel-lectuals who, as the war advanced, turned from Vichy collaboration to resistance activities. These dramatic reversals meant that, by the time of Paris's liberation in August 1944, "the resistance served as an incubator of a new, transnational vision of France."[29]

Throughout the war years, the city of Lyon attracted significant num-bers of French thinkers of different political and religious backgrounds who looked to join the Resistance. Beginning in the fall of 1941, a small group of young Catholics supervised by two Jesuit priests, Gas-ton Fessard and Pierre Chaillet, published the bimonthly clandestine journal called *Cahiers du Témoignage Chrétien* (*Notebooks of Chris-tian Witness*). In parallel, the group produced also a more compact, mass-audience bulletin entitled *Courriers du Témoignage Chrétien* (*Letters of Christian Witness*), whose print run, at its height, reached 100,000 copies. Each issue consisted principally of a single extended essay meditating on contemporary events and their philosophical and spiritual implications.[30]

For its authors and editors, joining the Christian Witness (*Témoig-nage Chrétien*, TC) group was a way of taking a stand as Christians against the injustices of Nazi rule in occupied France. Following Mari-tain, TC drew a distinction between Christian confessionalism and Christian ethics. As their Thomist icon put it, this was the difference between wearing their Christianity on their sleeves (*en tant que chré-tien*), complete with discrimination against non-Christians, and simply trying to follow Christian ethics in their everyday choices (*en chrétien*). Like the exiled Maritain, they believed that actions, not labels, were a measure of authentically Christian behavior.

Simply put, TC sought to convince Christians that anti-totalitarian-ism and confessionalism should not go hand in hand: the point was to follow Christian ethics in opposing autocracy, not simply to evangelize on the Church's behalf. TC thereby took on the task of repairing the "spiritual" damage done to France by Vichy's collaboration with Nazi Germany. The subtitle of the first issue was *France, be on your guard against losing your soul* (*France, prends garde de perdre ton âme*), with Nazism and Vichy identified as the titular soul-snatching forces. Over the course of 1942, the young clandestine group attracted prominent Catholic contributors, including the publisher Stanislas Fumet and the novelist Georges Bernanos. For the January–February 1943 issue, the featured author was none other than Cardinal August Hlond, primate of Poland, who had escaped Poland in early 1940, arriving in France just in time to be taken into custody by the new German occupation authorities.[31]

Christian Witness openly promoted Catholic-Socialist-Communist cooperation in the Resistance. In 1944, the *Cahiers du Témoignage Chrétien* became a weekly journal, its name shortened to *Témoignage Chrétien*. More and more articles began to sound in tone and content like a Catholic answer to the "outstretched hand" that Maurice Thorez had offered almost a decade earlier. For example, the twenty-eight-year-old firebrand André Mandouze declared that anti-fascism had created a durable "spiritual front" that trumped confessional divisions—showing how much Catholics and Communists gained by working together.[32]

The great influx of vitality into the Lyon-based Catholic underground came with several of Mounier's and Lacroix's former students from Uriage. Most notable among these were Gilbert Dru and the Lyon native Jean-Marie Domenach.[33] Equally prominent was Mandouze, who in his Parisian graduate-school days had cut his teeth in Catholic publishing by joining the staff of the Dominican journal *Sept*, just before the Vatican ordered it shut down. A young historian of Augustine of Hippo, Mandouze was promoted in 1943 to deputy editor of the *Cahiers du Témoignage Chrétien*, yet he maintained a regular teaching load in the Humanities Department at the University of Lyon. Domenach wrote in admiration of Mandouze, "His elevated clandestine position in no way interrupted his official conduct."[34]

These young radicals were fiercely devoted to Emmanuel Mounier. After his hunger strike, Mounier spent the rest of the war years nursing his health and writing in the village of Dieulefit. That village became a mecca for the *Témoignage Chrétien* crew, who visited Mounier regularly, consulting him on their goals for TC and planning with him for the postwar reactivation of *Esprit*. In the end, Mounier's journal reappeared only following his return to Paris, at the city's liberation in the summer of 1944.

For Domenach and Mandouze, two future pioneers of Catholic socialism, clandestine publishing in wartime Lyon entailed not only active resistance, but also study and self-examination—a spiritual exercise in the sense intended by Ignatius Loyola.[35] Young activists got to know themselves, each other, and iconic elders like Mounier. Reflecting back on this period two decades later, Domenach captured its essence: "Many young Christians, obliged to rely on their consciences and sometimes even to challenge the directives of certain bishops, discovered the eternally new face of the Gospel teachings, and threw themselves whole-heartedly into the Liberation movement, which, after freeing their land and institutions, was also to be a liberation of souls."[36]

Lofty rhetoric aside, wartime personalism was deeply marked by the violence and tragedy of occupied Europe. Gilbert Dru, Domenach's best friend and a leading clandestine activist of the Young Christian Students (*Jeunesse Étudiante Chrétienne*), was identified and summarily executed in the *Place Bellecour* in late July 1944, only a month before Lyon's liberation. He was twenty-four years old. Domenach was so shaken by the circumstances of Dru's demise that he devoted an entire book to his friend, published in 1947. For Domenach, Dru's death was a wake-up call to become, in his words, "a partisan of peace."[37]

With Maritain in exile and Mounier caught between Vichy and physical exhaustion, the real center of gravity of the French Catholic intellectual resistance to German occupation was in Lyon. Mounier and Lacroix taught at Uriage, and Domenach and Dru studied there, but instead of becoming nationalists and fascists, they embraced humanism and personalist revolution. For them, as for many young writers belonging to Christian Witness, anti-fascist resistance was a first step toward Catholic socialism.

## FRANCE IN POLAND

The Polish story of Catholic resistance was more complex than the French story, but the example of France was absolutely critical to wartime Poland. By the time of the German invasion of Poland, Catholic intellectuals in Poland had been importing, teaching, and debating French innovations to Roman Catholicism for nearly twenty years. Warsaw's own wartime young radicals drew inspiration, like their counterparts in Lyon, from Mounier's personalist thought. It was during World War II that Catholic theories of "revolution" began to prove relevant to young activists' everyday lives.

At the start of the Second World War, few young Polish intellectuals had more experience with France than Czesław Miłosz. Though disaffected in his Catholicism, Miłosz had throughout the 1930s passed in and out of Władysław Korniłowicz's Thomist reading group at Laski. Guided by the Thomist priest, the young Miłosz developed a deep appreciation not just for Aquinas, but even more so for Jacques Maritain. After the German attack on Poland, Miłosz immediately became active in clandestine publishing, where he circulated his own poetry.[38] Far less known is Miłosz's major contribution to Polish Catholic intellectual life: a complete translation of Jacques Maritain's *Through the Disaster*, to which the future Nobel Laureate added his own preface.

The poet, in the words of his biographer Andrzej Franaszek, considered Maritain to be the "author who proved that it is possible to harmonize Catholicism with modernity and to liberate it from ties to nationalist ideology."[39] Though he had attended Korniłowicz's seminars, Miłosz had not proven a particularly devoted catechumen: together with the writer Jerzy Andrzejewski, with whom he frequented Korniłowicz's seminar, "we confessed to each other that the asceticism and the depth and nobility of spiritual self-reflection awakened only our appetites for vodka and juicy steaks."[40] Nonetheless, he retained close ties with Laski. This is how a copy of Maritain's *Through the Disaster* came into Miłosz's possession, having been printed in New York and smuggled into Poland in the fall of 1941 by a Dutch merchant.

When Miłosz heard that his friend Zenon Skierski was starting an underground press, he lobbied hard to make Maritain's book the press's first publication. In less than six months, he had translated the whole text from the French. As it turned out, Miłosz was faster than the French underground: his translation was in print well before *Through the Disaster* went into circulation in France.[41] Miłosz's translation appeared in 1640 copies; within six weeks, 1300 had been sold. His was a triumph of underground publishing, particularly given the logistical difficulties of procuring paper. Most clandestine printings had an average per-copy readership in the double digits, passed from hand to hand within organizations and among friends and family, so the actual wartime readership for Miłosz's translation was likely in the tens of thousands.

Writing his preface in January 1942, only a year after Maritain had finished writing the tract, Miłosz underscored how important it was that Poles continue to trust in France. Despite the country's ignominious defeat in battle in 1940, the strength of long-standing Franco-Polish cultural ties would play a great role in anti-German resistance. Miłosz presented Maritain's diagnosis of the French collapse as an antidote to any Polish temptation to turn away from France: "When as eminent a writer as Maritain takes the floor, we have the right to expect an explanation. And, for the most part, that is what we have received. [ . . . ] It is not true that the faults that resulted in the collapse of France are faults indelibly tied to democracy—this is the first certainty that Maritain explains."[42]

The trust that Miłosz recommended Poles place in Maritain followed from Maritain's status as "the leading representative of contemporary Catholic philosophy." The Thomist held a "place of honor" among thinkers seeking to make sense of "the wilderness of contradictory visions bogging down contemporary humanist thought."[43] Maritain's personalism would remain important after the war, too, as a bridge between different generations of activists and thinkers, especially between interwar leaders and novices who had been too young to play a serious role prior to 1939. Miłosz, though he had grown apart from the Catholicism of his childhood, single-handedly kept Maritain's thought alive in Poland during the war years.[44]

## CATHOLIC PHILOSOPHY AND VIOLENT RESISTANCE IN OCCUPIED POLAND

After first Nazi Germany and then the Soviet Union invaded Poland in September 1939, Polish sovereignty was gone within the month. For the generations of Poles who were raised and came of age in the interwar era, the only world they had ever known had come to an end. Like Stefan Zweig writing about World War I's erasure of the cosmopolitan life of *fin-de-siècle* Europe, so legendary Polish resistance courier Jan Karski recounted the illusions of interwar Poland's eternal grandeur dispelled by the Molotov-Ribbentrop Pact.[45] Of the night of his mobilization, one week before World War II began, Karski recalled, "We drank wine and danced interminably, mostly the airy, mobile European dances, first a waltz, then a tango, then a figured waltz. [ . . . ] I came home tired but so full of intoxicating plans that it was difficult to fall asleep. It seemed my eyes had hardly closed when there was a loud hammering at the front door. I dragged myself out of bed and began to walk down the steps, breaking into an angry run as the hammering

increased in volume. I yanked open the door. An impatient, surly po-
liceman standing on the steps handed me a slip of red paper, grunted
unintelligibly, and turned away. It was a secret mobilization order."[46]

The swift, comprehensive, and violent imposition of the occupying
General Government in central Poland—the western- and eastern-most
thirds of the country were subject to annexations—came as a shock to
the Polish citizenry. For the younger generations, however—particularly
Poles born between 1918 and 1924—war and occupation became the
centerpiece of everyday life. Paweł Rodak has called this the "wartime
generation": high-school students and recent graduates who, instead
of merely beginning their adult lives, assumed responsibility for their
country's very existence.[47] These were the Polish counterparts of Domenach and Mandouze, living the ignominious collapse of Poland's
Second Republic just as the young Frenchmen had France's Third.

This generation inherited a dual legacy of resistance from the recent
Polish past. On the one hand, the failure of the January Uprising of
1863–64 had cost the Russian partition of Poland an entire generation of aspiring young national leaders. In its wake, cultural authorities such as Maria Konopnicka and Henryk Sienkiewicz had insisted
on the priority of cultural and intellectual resistance through "organic
work," "positivism," and the preservation of a certain cultural canon of
Polish nationhood.[48] On the other hand, the successful anti-Bolshevik
campaign of 1920 had demonstrated that organized violent resistance
could work for Poland.[49]

Warsaw's capitulation left the wartime generation with a dual imperative: not merely to prepare clandestinely for armed combat, but
also to continue their education, in order to keep Poland alive as a
system of ideas and cultural practices.[50] Because the German *Blitzkrieg*
and the subsequent creation of the General Government led to a prohibition on all post-elementary instruction of Poles, it cut the wartime
generation off from access to formal education just at the time when
they were—depending on their age—preparing to finish high school,
to enter university, or to graduate with their master's degrees. Jadwiga
Biskupska observes that "Of all the many Polish responses to occupation, the underground university in Warsaw most directly took up the
challenge raised by Nazism's anti-intelligentsia policies in Poland, and
in doing so united much of the educated elite toward training a new
Polish-educated intelligentsia."[51]

In addition to following their partition-era forebears in "organic work" designed to preserve the continuity of Polish culture, these young Poles developed their own political projects. The collective assumption was that the war would end with Poland's successful reconstitution as a sovereign state, at which point they themselves would assume leadership positions in that state. The crucial task before them thus concerned not only their immediate fight, but also the long-term obligation to plan for a collective future in which they must avoid the mistakes that had left the Second Republic so vulnerable in the first place. As the anonymous young authors of the short-lived, but influential, clandestine wartime journal Dziś i Jutro declared in their 1941 mission statement: "We live amid chaos, faced with a new order that is still taking shape. We are on the brink. We are beginning to see many issues and concerns differently than they have ever been seen before. We also see points of commonality in places where others have so far seen only differences; contradictions, where harmony had supposedly reigned; we see new roads opening before us, where there supposedly had been nowhere to go. To understand the world of today—that is not simply to understand that it has grown out of yesterday's world, but also to anticipate the kind of tomorrow to which it aspires and to demand, for us and the world alike, a particular kind of tomorrow."[52]

Beyond long-term planning, education also served immediate needs. For teenagers and young adults expected to assume extraordinary responsibilities in society with their male elders in captivity, in exile, or in the forests, it was a matter of the utmost urgency to learn how to cope with the pervasive trauma and death that permeated everyday life: "education not only provided knowledge about the world, but in fact became a font of answers to the question of greatest urgency: how, in the face of humanity's total catastrophe, can the world continue to exist, and life go on within it?"[53] This was particularly true in Warsaw, which from the moment of its capitulation on September 28, 1939 through the end of the Warsaw Uprising of 1944 consistently suffered one of the most violent occupation regimes in the whole of the General Government. The trauma of capitulation loomed heavily in the background throughout these years.[54]

In practice, clandestine education (tajne komplety) could take many forms. Usually it involved secret coursework organized around lectures by renowned university professors who volunteered their time and risked their lives in the process. These academic authorities offered revised and condensed versions of their prewar courses, often tailoring lessons to the realities of war and occupation. Complementing these lectures were clandestine study groups, reading groups, and question-and-answer sessions with prominent literary figures like the poets Jarosław Iwaszkiewicz and Czesław Miłosz.[55] Finally, many students continued the discussions from their study groups in the pages of clandestine journals funded by the Polish underground and printed and distributed in secret. Some of these journals produced as many as several dozen issues over the course of two or three years, while others produced only a single issue.

Of course, not every Pole born into the wartime generation participated in clandestine activities. Likewise, not everyone who attended secret classes worked in clandestine publishing or belonged to guerrilla partisan units: unlike men, women were highly constrained in the paths of resistance they could pursue, making them a majority among underground students who succeeded in obtaining degrees.[56] Due to the nature of conspiratorial activity, students in the same classes were often entirely unaware of just how many of their classmates were active in the underground or its various affiliated armed resistance units. In Warsaw alone, there were almost a dozen major underground organizations focused on politics and culture, rather than guns and dynamite. These ranged from the ex-fascist-led Confederation of the Nation (KN, *Konfederacja Narodu*) to the Communists of the Polish Workers' Party (PPR, *Polska Partia Robotnicza*), as well as the Boy Scouts (*Związek Harcerstwa Polskiego*).[57] Meanwhile, the Home Army coordinated a wide range of armed organizations through its command structures, including battalions of former Scouts, as well as combat units attached to some of the political and cultural movements, including KN. Entirely separate was the Communist-inspired People's Guard (*Gwardia Ludowa*)—created in 1942, and from 1944 onward known as the People's Army.[58]

Warsaw's wartime generation thus lived and died within a complex latticework of conspiratorial activities—some violent, some nonviolent. The field of opportunities open to young Poles narrowed as the occupation continued, so the reconstruction of their story requires careful attention to periodization: 1941 was not 1939; 1943 was not 1941; and October 1944 was not January 1944. Speaking of turning points within the history of Warsaw's wartime generation, Paweł Rodak argues, "The stakes of their daily lives had become unprecedentedly high by the end of 1941, and this was also the time when the terror of the occupation began to intensify. From the fall of 1943 onward, one can no longer speak of it as ominous or troublesome; by then, it was cruel and inhuman. Round-ups and mass executions in the streets, whose victims were chosen entirely at random, became a daily sight. Whether a resident of the nation's capital lived or died increasingly became a matter of random chance."[59]

As the terror of life in occupied Warsaw increased, some of the wartime generation began to feel that they had less and less to lose in open combat. Yet, even then, the tasks of self-education and preparation for the future did not fall by the wayside. Only the outbreak of the Warsaw Uprising interrupted these tasks, channeling as it did all of Warsaw's resources into a single, concentrated resistance fight.

## EMMANUEL MOUNIER AND THE YOUNG POLISH RESISTANCE FIGHTERS

Despite his enthusiasm for Maritain, Czesław Miłosz had no patience for the Thomist's erstwhile disciple, Emmanuel Mounier, whom he considered derivative: neither a real philosopher like Maritain, nor a real activist. More than five decades after the war's end, Miłosz wrote, "Mounier was, in fact, known in Poland only second-hand, and his legend did not really correspond to reality."[60] This was, however, simply not the case. Already published in Poland before the war, Mounier in the course of the occupation became one of the most important Western European voices speaking to Poland's wartime generation.

The three resistance movements that engaged with Mounier's writings most directly and substantively were the Gray Ranks (*Szare Szeregi*), formed in late September 1939 by former Scouts[61]; the Flames (*Płomienie*), composed of non-Marxist socialists inspired by the writings of turn-of-the-century Polish philosopher Stanisław Brzozowski,[62] and the Confederation of the Nation. Founded after the fall of France in the spring of 1940, KN was a 10,000-strong Home Army-affiliated guerrilla organization.[63] The Confederation drew all of its leadership and much of its membership from the interwar ONR, particularly its league of young fascist militants, the Phalanx.[64] KN's leader Bolesław Piasecki had, before the war, been a rebellious disciple of Roman Dmowski.

During the war, he toned down his fascist, anti-Semitic rhetoric, putting patriotism and anti-Germanism front and center.[65] For him, the integralism of National Democracy was merely a starting point. As Mikołaj Kunicki demonstrates in his biography of Piasecki, the "chief" (*wódz*) consistently blazed his own path to power through bold, maverick moves.

The Confederation's declared wartime mission was to "stand on the ideological grounds of a strong, national, Christian, and just Poland, without serving any one political party or clique, but instead drawing on the strength of the whole Polish Nation."[66] KN members had, broadly speaking, two expectations for the future: first, victory against the occupier; second, an opportunity to sit in judgment over their compatriots. The goal was to weed out all unrighteous, to ensure the "purity" of postwar Poland by opposing "decisively all attempts at taking power by people who have shown themselves to be lacking in true love for the Fatherland, or good character, or have shown criminal negligence."[67] By "criminal negligence," the KN leaders meant all those aligned with the Piłsudskite *sanacja* camp, which had allegedly allowed the interwar Polish state to fall like a house of cards.

Even Piasecki's most ardent political opponents refer again and again to his personal magnetism. Numerous accounts describe his almost seductive power to draw recruits into his movement, winning their loyalty to himself personally, as well as to the organization.[68] Holdovers from the Phalanx of the 1930s welcomed into KN a new wave of non-fascists drawn to Piasecki's personality, his Catholicism, and his militant patriotism.

Piasecki kept a tight organizational leash on his disciples, but he also recognized and nurtured talent among them. He welcomed young recruits from the dispossessed Polish gentry, who proved apt pupils for integral nationalism. At the same time, the KN leader encouraged Wojciech Kętrzyński, Andrzej Krasiński, and other young KN members to join in the cultural and intellectual ferment of Warsaw's wartime generation. Evidence gathered by the postwar Polish state security apparatus in the early 1950s shows that extensive intellectual crossover and exchange played out among KN, Flames, and the Gray Ranks.[69]

How to explain the crossover between circles of such different ideological backgrounds—so different, indeed, that encounters between them prior to 1939 would likely have ended in violence?[70] As Wacław

Auleytner—member of the wartime generation, clandestine student, subsequent Warsaw Uprising fighter, and after 1956 a cofounder and leading member of Poland's Catholic Intelligentsia Club movement—wrote, "Circles of Catholic youth in Warsaw were governed by an unwritten rule that each of us could join a combat or political organization, but he did so at his own risk, without endangering the rest of his circle. The result was parallel participation in one ideological circle—for example, Catholic youth—and in another political organization."[71]

Underground units were mentored by some of Poland's most prominent humanist scholars. These professors delivered closed-access lectures and led seminars for their respective resistance groups, exerting a decisive influence on the young resisters they encountered. For example, Jan Strzelecki, the leader of Flames, invited Stanisław Ossowski, his mentor and an internationally renowned sociology professor at Warsaw University, to meet with and educate Flames.[72] Strzelecki and Ossowski shared an avid passion for the writings of Emmanuel Mounier.

Bogdan Suchodolski, eminent philosopher and—after the war's end—Łódź University rector, packed one Warsaw apartment after another with a loyal following of men and women in their teens and twenties attending his clandestine lectures. These "illegal" students somehow managed to shift back and forth from manual labor or guerrilla fighting by day to attentive note-taking and candlelight reading by night. Studying meant far more than idle curiosity or a desire to hide from the brutal reality of war and occupation. As one of Suchodolski's students later recalled, "our attitude toward education had undergone a radical transformation. [ . . . ] For we considered education as our civic duty, our fight for freedom."[73] Students read "by the light of candles and hissing acetylene lamps, at night, while also nervously listening for the lockstep march of German patrols or the roar of a car engine."

Among their assigned authors were the Polish socialist misfits Edward Abramowski and Stanisław Brzozowski, the Danish proto-existentialist Søren Kierkegaard, Karl Marx, and—Suchodolski's favorites—the German sociologist Karl Mannheim and the French personalist Emmanuel Mounier. Suchodolski himself later explained what it was that had drawn him to Mounier in the first place: "faith in the human being, respect for his personhood, the pursuit of equality, confidence in freedom and in creativity—these were the right values then, and they remain so today."[74]

Mounier cut more effectively across the old prewar political and ideological divisions than any Polish author could. Strzelecki, Suchodolski, and other future luminaries of Communist Poland found in Mounier an ethical guide to the new world ushered in by the events of 1939. Catholic and socialist resistance circles connected over Mounier. This unlikely confluence meant that Strzelecki's and Piasecki's respective followers were not only talking to each other, but in fact shaping each other's views on the fundamental questions of human dignity and social justice.

## FROM BRZOZOWSKI TO MOUNIER

In 1941, Strzelecki became the first Pole to undertake translation of Mounier's personalist magnum opus, the 1936 *Manifesto in the Service of Personalism*. Strzelecki only got halfway through the manifesto, but he then turned over to Suchodolski both his notes and the French original from which he had been working. The great professor, in turn, found someone to translate the whole book: a Warsaw-based advisor to the Scout-trained fighters of the Gray Ranks—a woman named Aniela Urbanowicz.

Years later, Strzelecki described in great detail why he took on the translation of Mounier's manifesto. For the thirty-four-year-old socialist, it was an act of solidarity with the spirit of ecumenism and non-conformism that *Esprit* had represented since 1932, over and against the intolerance and anti-Semitism of interwar Polish Catholicism. According to Strzelecki, "for us Leftist students sharing the bread of the *numerus clausus* with our Jewish friends, measuring with each passing day the rising tide of nihilist revolution, yet at the same time gladly making the sign of the cross, reading *Esprit* brought some promise of possible brotherhood with those in Poland who might perform a task similar to that which in France was being carried out by the group gathered around the figure of Mounier."[75]

Strzelecki's wartime Flames movement was a continuation of his prewar Independent Union of Socialist Youth (*Niezależny Związek Młodzieży Socjalistycznej*). Neither Marxist, republican, nor Piłsudskite, Strzelecki and his colleagues were at once humanists and non-conformists. Their hero was not Karl Marx, but instead the beleaguered *fin-de-siècle* Polish socialist Stanisław Brzozowski, who had bitterly contested Marx's materialist philosophy of history.[76]

Though baptized, Brzozowski was not a believer. Though he spent the final years of his brief life (1878–1911) insisting on the spiritual importance and historical role of the Church, he died fearing that he had not found faith, despite having taken Last Rites.[77] Like Władysław Korniłowicz, Maritain, and their fellow Thomists, the *fin-de-siècle* renegade socialist lived in an intellectual space that bridged the geopolitical chasm separating Poland from Western Europe. An instinctive anti-clericalist whose writings unabashedly mocked the Polish clergy as a privileged class with a vested interest in opposing Poland's national liberation—the Holy See's 1905 condemnation of Polish Catholics who joined the anti-tsarist revolution only confirmed his fears—Brzozowski found in the teachings of French Catholic reformers a more open, humanist spirituality.[78] Unlike what he called the "Jesuitism of the Church," the condemned French "modernists" of the early twentieth century drew him toward reconversion to the Catholic fold.

Brzozowski called on Catholics and socialists to work together toward Poland's "national strengthening": not to exclude a non-Polish "other," but instead to remind Poles of the universal dignity and ontological priority of human work.[79] Only by properly valuing work, he argued, could Poles achieve both interpersonal solidarity and salvation in God.[80] Leszek Kołakowski rightly contends that "the intellectual history of twentieth-century Poland cannot be understood without reference to the bizarre and disparate effects of his dynamic writings and personality."[81]

For the young wartime socialists of Flames, Emmanuel Mounier was a fitting successor to Stanisław Brzozowski. What so drew this movement to the French personalist was his writing, which Strzelecki described as "overflowing with beautiful passion in the struggle for the dignity and development of the human personality." These qualities fostered "respect and a sense of closeness" among personalism's adherents.[82]

The Flames group read, alongside Brzozowski and Mounier, Hendrik de Man, André Malraux, Georges Bernanos, Florian Znaniecki, Joseph Conrad, and Stefan Żeromski. It invited as speakers the leading young Polish poets of the day, including Jarosław Iwaszkiewicz, Czesław Miłosz, and Krzysztof Kamil Baczyński—soon to become a martyr of the Warsaw Uprising.[83] The group took a socialist stance against Marx by resurrecting turn-of-the-century Polish debates in which Brzozowski had squared off against not only Rosa Luxemburg, but also

Józef Piłsudski and his trusted colleague Kazimierz Kelles-Krauz.[84] Flames' approach to socialism demanded that human dignity go hand in hand with an *inclusive* nationalism: if oppressed nations could not be respected and protected, then oppressed classes did not stand a chance either. This stance made Strzelecki's take on Mounier an exact fit with the needs of occupied Poland, caught in the crosshairs of war and revolution.

In the minds of Strzelecki and his fellow Flames activists, a patriotic commitment to the nation corresponded to a universal commitment to humanity. The communitarian personalism of Emmanuel Mounier dovetailed with the group's view that, "incorporated into the field of essential humanistic values, nationality is understood in the same terms in which members of 'Flames' see the core of all values: their ability to form bonds of solidarity."[85] For Flames, "personalism was a defining issue, and Emmanuel Mounier's *Manifesto* was one of its principal points of reference. This is because persons form bonds with one another, and personalism brings them closer together."[86]

Examples of the humanist commitments of the Flames grace the pages of the group's eponymous clandestine journal (*Płomienie*), in which communities transcending the nation—"Europe," "humanity" —take center stage. This emphasis gave Flames the necessary tools to reflect meaningfully on Poland's place in the world. In 1942, Strzelecki drew an important distinction between the wartime generations of France and Poland: "We believe in Europe. This faith rests on a strong foundation—not a vision of the national character, but rather the strength of the idea of 'liberty, equality, and fraternity' [ . . . ] abandoned by the forces of reaction currently in power, by the return of the old regime to power in Vichy."[87] Wartime Poland did not have the baggage of a Vichy regime, and as such, Poland's youth had greater prospects for radical action—all while retaining the best of what the French had taught them.

Strzelecki was not a practicing Catholic. That said, he played a crucial role in shaping the wartime debates of Poland's young Catholic intellectuals. Suchodolski's student Wacław Auleytner recalls his clandestine studies as the time when he first met both Strzelecki and Szare Szeregi member Jan Józef Lipski, read his first copy of *Płomienie*, and understood the moral power of the encounter between Catholicism and socialism: "I think that this was the moment when Catholic youth began to develop their first inkling of what today we call openness. It was then that we encountered people who, like us, were young and engaged in both education and combat against the occupier, but predicated that engagement on an ideology different than our own."[88]

## MOUNIER AND THE WARSAW UPRISING

When in May 1941 Aniela Urbanowicz completed her translation of Mounier's *Manifesto in the Service of Personalism*, Suchodolski took the manuscript and immediately arranged for the mimeographing of 200 copies. These were distributed as widely as possible across underground resistance networks.[89] The Home Army soldier Wiesław Chrzanowski, though a devotee of Roman Dmowski, nonetheless became an enthusiastic participant in the discussion initiated by Strzelecki and Urbanowicz. When Chrzanowski looked back on those times six decades after the war's end, the "lively discussions surrounding the clandestine translations" still rang loudly in his ears.[90] Urbanowicz's translation had afforded him access to a foundational text from abroad, and Mounier's thought provided common ground for dialogue with a wide spectrum of his fellow resisters—believers and non-believers alike. These clandestine wartime discussions assured that, despite the violence to which Roman Dmowski and their other prewar elders had defaulted, those young National Democrats who remained in Poland after World War II were at least willing to countenance dialogue and cooperation with their ideological opponents.[91]

Suchodolski's plan was to arrange for a mass printing of Urbanowicz's translation, at least on the scale of Miłosz's translation of Maritain. Yet two separate misfortunes thwarted this goal. First, the text's mass reproduction was interrupted by the late 1942 arrest of its underground mimeographer, Konrad Zembrzuski of the Gray Ranks. Next, the clandestine publisher Crew (*Załoga*), which was to have released the *Manifesto*, shut down when the Warsaw Uprising began on August 1, 1944. Indeed, the original manuscript and the corrected proofs of Urbanowicz's translation were both lost in the chaos of the Uprising. Only two printed copies—uncorrected, with preface and introduction missing—survived the war to make their way back into Urbanowicz's possession.[92]

Nonetheless, in the years leading up to the Warsaw Uprising, Polish readership of Mounier was widespread. A growing network of acquaintances allowed Mounier's thought to flow unhindered between Flames and the Gray Ranks, turning revolutionary personalism into a basis for intellectual friendship.[93] According to literary critic Tadeusz Sołtan, "Mounier was welcomed as a virtual prophet of rebellion against the different forms of alienation wrought by the development of capitalism and bourgeois society."[94] Sołtan was a liaison of sorts between the different resistance groups. So was Władysław Bartoszewski, known to us from the opening of this chapter.

## "TODAY AND TOMORROW"

Having worked with Strzelecki to launch Flames, Sołtan moved on to found *Sztuka i Naród* (*Art and the Nation*), a journal supported by Bolesław Piasecki's Confederation of the Nation.[95] The premise of *Sztuka i Naród* was that, for "young people authentically engaged in matters of national culture and art, it was not enough—in the face of intensifying Hitlerite terror—to fight only with the pen, the written word, or the clandestine concert of Polish music. They would not be able to look at themselves in the mirror, if they could not join in combat with a weapon in hand."[96]

Given both Piasecki's prewar fascist politics and the Confederation's own wartime commitment to a program of radical violence, KN was a world apart from other Warsaw-based youth resistance movements. One of its battalion leaders has explained that the organization prioritized a "philosophy of combat": "The Confederation of the Nation was an organization encompassing a wide range of activities constituting key areas of the life of the Nation. It served above all in the day-to-day fight against the enemy—the most important task at hand—but it also adopted a realistic approach to planning the future shape of an independent Poland."[97]

And yet, despite the movement's singularities, the Confederation of the Nation, too, belonged to the intellectual ferment of wartime Warsaw, a world in which debates on personhood and social justice were consistently front and center. It was prepared to take advantage of all of occupied Poland's available cultural and intellectual resources to prepare its members for an active role in the postwar elite. Piasecki and his colleagues committed the Confederation to "behaving loyally and, whenever possible, working together" with other clandestine organizations.[98]

Extensive personal contact in clandestine study groups afforded many opportunities for the passing back and forth of the mimeographed copies of the *Manifesto in the Service of Personalism*. The intellectual crossing and re-crossing of paths of the three clandestine youth networks, particularly in the summer and fall of 1943, created the opportunity for them to work out their respective ideologies, planning for life after the war.

For members of Flames, Mounier was a gateway to a "more properly humanistic socialism, being a very clear form of secular personalism," while the KN fighters likewise became "very close to personalism, more in its Catholic version, but always personalism."[99] After the war, the Confederation's combat regulars, too, credited personalism with having guided them in their efforts to prevent the rise of a new "totalitarianism."[100] An attentive reading of KN's mission statement makes clear that Mounier achieved a significant influence within the movement well before the war ended. The movement remained nationalist, but it began also to incorporate references to a larger human community of "persons" transcending the nation. For example, the seventh point of KN's May 1944 *Programmatic Points of a New Poland* reads, "Personal human rights fall under the heading of human dignity, as does the right to creative labor. Human dignity entails freedom of spiritual development, in the sense that social community represents brotherhood with other persons, legal autonomy. Legal autonomy means that a human being cannot be a slave to other human beings, cannot be exploited by others. The sign of a human being's dignity is his development as a person, his readiness for service to the nation, for sacrifice."[101]

In this spirit of sacrifice, the Confederation of the Nation counted many martyrs in the course of the Second World War. The young writer Włodzimierz Pietrzak, who perished in the Warsaw Uprising on August 22, 1944, gained a reputation on par with Christian Witness's Gilbert Dru in France. Pietrzak became the namesake of a literary prize awarded annually by Piasecki's postwar *Dziś i Jutro* movement (later PAX) from 1948 until the end of the Communist period.[102]

As witness their choice of the phrase "today and tomorrow" for the name of their postwar successor organization, Piasecki's Confederation of the Nation was deeply embedded in wartime planning for the future. Talking about "today" and "tomorrow" was a popular shorthand among resistance fighters: "The agenda 'for today' was clear—this was struggle against the occupier. Yet after 'today' would come 'tomorrow.' And this 'tomorrow' had to be built according to new rules. The independent Poland that was to come into existence after the war's conclusion was to be different from what had come before the war."[103] It was the young Scouts and fighters of the Gray Ranks who systematized this impulse into a clandestine motto: "Today—tomorrow—the day after tomorrow" (*Dziś—jutro—pojutrze*). This motto encapsulated the young resisters' programmatic commitment to "education through struggle," by means of conspiracy and armed preparation (today) for an open uprising (tomorrow) in order to be able to work in a free Poland (the day after tomorrow). As Paweł Rodak has argued, "To pose this question about today and tomorrow was to take responsibility for them."[104]

In the meantime, however, these ideas shaped the self-understanding of an entire generation. Władysław Bartoszewski has become one of its most celebrated figures.[105] Beginning in 1942, he single-handedly ran the clandestine journal *Prawda Młodych*. By the spring of 1943, he was publishing 3000 copies of each issue.

Two years earlier, he had enrolled in a clandestine course in Polish studies led by the eminent sociologist Maria Ossowska. In her seminars, Bartoszewski met the leaders of Flames, entering into lively debate with them about personalism.[106] An article that he published in February 1943 captures the extent to which wartime dialogue had opened up a space for self-styled "revolution" in the fight against an evil occupier:

> Once upon a time, in the decades that came after Marx, in industrializing nations suffering from the worst that capitalism had to offer, one could speak a single word—"socialism"—to the educated, and everything would be clear. Here, over the course of a century of servitude, in our daily struggles against the entrenched invaders, one could feel what mattered—"independence, above all"—and that was clear, too. Even over the past two [interwar] decades, one could still draw a conclusion: "things are bad"—or (in another person's opinion) "things are good." In other words—the same pattern, a choice between two alternatives: either to keep or to change as radically as possible the existing state of

affairs. Yet the enthusiasm of reactionaries for that which was unjust revolutionized our thought into one steady stream, leading in one clear direction: to unsaddle the evil by building up the good.[107]

This was Emmanuel Mounier's lesson for occupied Poland: that protecting human dignity required a willingness to "build up the good" by forming partnerships across confessional and political divides. The wartime generation internalized this so well that certain Catholics in postwar Poland were even willing to take the new Moscow-backed Communist government seriously as a potential partner.

## THE RESISTANCE LEGACY OF CHRISTIAN DEMOCRACY

Before 1939, Poland, like most of interwar Europe, featured a self-styled Christian Democratic party. Poland's was called the Christian Labor Party (SP, *Stronnictwo Pracy*). Founded by Wojciech Korfanty and Karol Popiel in 1937, the party was, in fact, a coalition of different regional groupings from around interwar Poland that shared a Christian Democratic identity. Facing severe repression from Piłsudski's *sanacja* regime, interwar Polish Christian Democratic leaders spent years in prison or in exile.[108] By the time Germany invaded Poland, then, SP leaders could already draw on a substantial reservoir of experience with dissidence and exile as they prepared to resist, once again—both on Polish soil and abroad.[109] Unlike the leaders of France's prewar Popular Democratic Party, who remained on French soil throughout the war, SP's top leaders—its president Karol Popiel, chief party ideologue Zygmunt Kaczyński, and executive committee chair General Józef Haller[110]—left the continent following Poland's capitulation and joined the London-based Polish government-in-exile, in which all three served as ministers.[111]

When these leaders went into exile, they left behind an extensive network of disciplined party activists. This entire network had to go underground to avoid arrest, imprisonment, and execution at German hands.[112] Although several waves of arrests depleted the ranks of SP leaders who remained on Polish soil—mostly in the territory annexed to the German Reich, rather than under the General Government ruled by Hans Frank—politicking and in-fighting persisted among the surviving leadership. A pro-Soviet group under Zygmunt Felczak and Feliks Widy-Wirski gained ascendancy through SP's underground print media, particularly the journal *Zryw* (*Jolt*), which came to be identified with them.[113]

The historian Waldemar Bujak wrote in 1981 of the Jolt group: "there was not a trace of partisan blinders in the way that Z. Felczak and his colleagues looked at the world. Their honest analysis led them to conclude that the USSR would be the deciding player [at war's end], and they were ready to act accordingly."[114] If we strip away the Communist-era historian's own ideological blinders, we see the makings of a conflict that, once the dust settled over the Yalta Accords in Poland, would spell SP's doom. In the fall of 1942, however, SP's London leadership responded to Felczak's pro-Moscow stance by ordering his expulsion from the party. Felczak and Widy-Wirski formed their own splinter group, fragmenting the party's underground structures. At least for the time being, however, the conflict appeared to have been settled.

After the Polish army's surrender to Germany in the late fall of 1939, clandestine resistance organizations sprang up all over Poland, each consisting of two staple elements: an armed unit—incorporating trained Home Army regulars as well as untrained guerrilla fighters—and an intelligence unit.[115] Following the expulsion of the Jolt faction, SP needed to beef up its intelligence and ideological profile. The Christian Democratic leadership elected to join forces with another movement: the Union (*Unia*).[116] Its leaders were, for the most part, intellectuals over the age of forty who, like the young Warsaw resistance fighters, were working on an intellectual, cultural, and political program for the postwar.[117]

The ideology of interwar Polish Christian Democracy had been a blend of Catholic personalism and exclusionary nationalism. Its legendary leader was Wojciech Korfanty, a political revolutionary whose career began in the 1890s in the German Reichstag. In 1921, a German-Polish plebiscite mandated by the League of Nations rejected Polish claims to Upper Silesia; Korfanty did not like the result, so he led an armed uprising, which won more territory for Poland.[118] He had no problem spending money and fomenting violence in the service of his convictions. Hated by Józef Piłsudski, Korfanty spent much of the interwar era in court, in prison, or in exile. At the same time, he wrote prolifically and published his essays regularly in the Katowice-based journal

*Polonia.* These became the basic source texts of Polish Christian Democratic ideology. Deeply respectful of Thomism, Korfanty read Maritain and considered himself a personalist.

But, at the end of the day, integral nationalism trumped his personalism. Korfanty not only thought of Poland's non-Catholics as non-persons—this, after all, was the norm among prewar Catholics—but he in fact targeted them as alleged detractors to the Polish nation. Korfanty blamed Poland's Jewish population for everything he hated about Piłsudski's rule over Poland—to the point of calling for ethnic cleansing.[119] In its 1937 political program, Polish Christian Democracy proposed the Jews' deportation to Madagascar. According to Korfanty, Poles' top priority should be to establish themselves as unequivocal "masters in their own home." Even as he insisted that "respect for the dignity of human personhood" and "the inviolability of the natural rights of man" were "definitively Christian claims," Korfanty insisted that "Polish authorities and society must work together to execute the planned mass Jewish emigration."[120]

The onset of war pushed this agenda to the side. In the face of Nazi policy toward Jews—first ghettoization and exploitation, then extermination—Poland's Christian Democrats turned away from active anti-Semitic advocacy, and their personalist claims became more spiritually minded. The merger of the Christian Labor Party and the Union in the Polish underground elevated *Unia* leader Jerzy Braun, a poet and philosopher by training, to a leading role in Polish Christian Democracy. A long-time devotee of nineteenth-century Polish messianic thinker Józef Hoene-Wroński, Braun believed that liberalism ignored the organic unity of all existence. In this sense, his thought fit nicely with the Catholic Church's traditional corporatist political economy: "every whole is not merely a simple unit, but a complex system unto itself, and it consists of parts whose diversity and vivacity attest to the richness of forms of being of the larger organism."[121]

Some postwar Christian Democrats have argued that Jerzy Braun succeeded in adapting personalism to "Polish realities."[122] Given his obsession with metaphysics and messianism, however, this is a tough sell. Important as Braun may have been intellectually to the Christian Democratic elite, he fell far short of the kind of mass reception and ideological power that Korfanty had enjoyed prior to his death in 1939. Braun achieved a high-ranking position in the Polish underground—at the time of the 1945 armistice, he was the exile government's official delegate for all of occupied Poland. Yet Braun's penchant for the metaphysical inhibited the promotion of his program of "unionism." As a result, most Christian Democrats drifted ideologically between Korfanty's writings and a view of political economy inspired by other currents in the Polish underground.[123]

Like the French-inspired youth of Warsaw, the combined SP-Union movement insisted on planning for Poland's future in order to prevent the corruption, decadence, and incompetence responsible for the interwar republic's implosion. The postwar Catholic lay activist Krzysztof Kozłowski, whose family manor at Przybyszewice outside Kraków provided safe harbor for the Union's leaders, captured succinctly the movement's priorities for after the war: "I think it is in the nature of most clandestine projects that . . . Utopian dreams constitute their motive force, free us for a moment from the heavy weight of the everyday, allow us to persist with a sense of purpose . . . But in the Union's project we can see also a realistic assessment of the problems that the Second Polish Republic failed to handle. The reconstruction of the economic order, the universalization of property ownership and education, the strengthening of local self-government."[124]

The Union brought together multiple generations of Poland's cultural and intellectual luminaries under the wider umbrella of anti-German resistance. One of its most important voices in assuring the preservation of Polish culture was Jerzy Turowicz, the Renaissance activist who had met Mounier in Paris in 1937. At the time of SP's merger with the Union, Turowicz was barely thirty years old, an engineer by training whose student activism in Renaissance had redefined his career goals. After Turowicz moved back from Lwów to Kraków, he took a job in 1939 as deputy editor of the Christian Democratic paper *Głos Narodu* (*Voice of the Nation*), run by the priest Jan Piwowarczyk.[125] A mere six months later, Turowicz became editor-in-chief of the paper, which he soon had to shutter following the outbreak of war.[126] With his wife Anna, Turowicz—exempted for medical reasons from military service—withdrew to her family country house at Goszyce, twenty kilometers outside Kraków.

For the next five years, Goszyce served as a haven of cultural and intellectual life, especially for members of the Union underground. Though averse to the exclusionary nationalism of interwar Christian

Fig. 2: Jerzy Turowicz and his fiancée Anna Gąsiorowska, on the steps of her family home at Goszyce, outside Kraków, in 1937. Married in November 1938, they turned their new home into a haven of clandestine cultural activity during World War II, throughout the German occupation of Poland. Reproduced by permission of the Turowicz family.

Democracy, Turowicz joined the Union in 1940 and approved of its merger with SP two years later. From his base in Goszyce, Turowicz worked with Jerzy Braun to plan issues of the movement's clandestine journal *Kultura Jutra (The Culture of Tomorrow)*. The pages of that journal reflect both men's true passions: for Braun, metaphysics; for Turowicz, culture. In an unsigned essay from March 1943, Turowicz insisted that work for the nation's future must retain the creative spark of artistic and cultural inspiration. The young editor wrote, "Creativity is the greatest joy available to man on this earth, a true taste of Heaven to come. The entire economic and political organization of society makes sense only as a set of circumstances offering as many people as possible the power to participate in the beauty and moral dignity of creation."[127]

Turowicz's chief task within the Union was to draw up plans for a "Catholic social and cultural journal" to be launched with episcopal support immediately after the war's end. The creation of *Tygodnik Powszechny* (*Universal Weekly*) in 1945 would, in fact, follow these plans to the letter. Already two years earlier, in the pages of the Warsaw-based *Sztuka i Naród*, Turowicz had spelled out clearly the ideological foundations of that future project: "more important than resting on the laurels of our achievements thus far is to note the fact of the existence of an ever-greater longing for a 'third force.'"[128] For the thirty-one-year-old writing from Goszyce, this "third force" was Catholic personalism, defined by both Maritain and Mounier.

In the interim, the Turowicz family housed and fed fugitives from across occupied Poland, including many of the Union elite. One of Turowicz's visitors was the young Karol Wojtyła, not yet twenty-five years old, with seminary and priesthood still ahead of him. Wojtyła belonged to an underground theater troupe protected by the Union.[129] After the Warsaw Uprising ended in an almost-total razing of the city by the victorious German forces, the poet Czesław Miłosz, too, spent nearly a month at Goszyce along with his family.[130] All of these activists came and went from Goszyce while risking their lives in the course of their clandestine duties.

## CONCLUSIONS

In the fall of 1939, it would have been difficult to foresee the stature that Emmanuel Mounier—then thirty-four years old—would achieve in the Polish underground over the next six years. Tadeusz Sołtan called Mounier a "suprapolitical, suprapartisan patron of many reflections and actions directed toward the salvation of humanity in a time of disdain."[131] Maritain, Mounier, and a strong Christian Democratic resistance constituted three vectors of a transnational Catholic personalism that France and Poland came to share by 1945. Maritain lent Thomism's credibility to a humanist vision of anti-Nazi resistance—a product of the singular circumstances of World War II. Meanwhile, Mounier left a more permanent legacy: the sense that out of the ashes of war and occupation there could emerge a revolution in which Catholics and socialists could work together in solidarity.

The experience of wartime resistance in both France and Poland demonstrated the tremendous flux that characterized Catholic thought and activism during World War II. On the one hand, established figures —from Jacques Maritain to Karol Popiel—proved significant in their public contributions to the war efforts of their respective nations. On the other, the chaos of war allowed new organizations—Christian Witness, the Union, the Confederation of the Nation—to enter the field of play with contributions that would help to empower the Catholic vanguard in the immediate postwar period.

In both France and Poland, personalism at war was anti-German, and thereby anti-fascist. At the same time, Catholic youth became confessional and ideological "border-crossers" by virtue of their resistance activities.[132] Their underground encounters with personalism opened their horizons to the possibility of Catholic-socialist cooperation. Despite their confessional and political differences, the generation of 1914–24 ensured that wartime debates and lessons about human dignity were firmly implanted in the postwar intellectual, political, and social orders. As Wacław Auleytner has put it, "Among those who survived the Uprising there remained one common trait—and this is what helped us to get through life after the war—the inclination to understand and respect other views, and perhaps sometimes even to engage in dialogue with people of other convictions."[133]

# 3 Catholicism in a Newly Communist World

## Between Christian Democracy and Catholic Socialism

*Catholic Poland, the Polish Catholic nation, shies away from no sacrifice for the good of the Republic. [ ... ] We fear neither modernity nor social transformation, nor people's governments, so long as they continue to respect the unchanging principles of Christian morality. We want Poland to be the most progressive and the most cultured of countries, and we will do our part.*

—Cardinal August Hlond, Primate of Poland[1]

IN 1967, A VENERABLE eighty-year-old gentleman had the humiliating experience of writing to the United States Social Security Administration to protest the termination of a pension that had been promised to him for life.[2] Only briefly did this Polish émigré actually reside in the United States, yet he and his colleagues had played a serious role in the American Cold War effort. This was Karol Popiel, and his story casts into stark relief the choices faced by Poland's Catholic activists as World War II ended and the Cold War began.

1945 was not simply a "zero hour" in European history, but an unprecedented *Augenblick* of collective decision-making.[3] This defining moment was experienced differently across Europe, but a closer look reveals an underlying baseline. The Soviet Union—after 1941, the wartime ally of the United States and the UK—had spread its army across the eastern half of the continent, from Moscow to Berlin to Bucharest, as it did its part in "liberating" the continent from German occupation. At the February 1945 Yalta Conference, Joseph Stalin famously promised Winston Churchill and Franklin D. Roosevelt "free and fair" elections across territories occupied by the Red Army; this, however, was a promise that Stalin had no intention of keeping.[4] Elections were finally held after a few years, and their results falsified, with Soviet-backed Communist parties claiming a mandate to govern each country of the nascent Soviet Bloc.[5] In the meantime, men and women across Europe—those with and those without political power, those who had resisted and those who had collaborated, those who hid in the forests and those who helped to rebuild roads and factories—faced earth-shattering decisions, starting with whether or not to go home. They could choose to make peace with the new order of things, or count on—and count down to—the coming of a third world war.

In June 1945, Popiel was living in London, having spent the war there as a member of Poland's government-in-exile. He returned to Poland on the promise that the Communist-led transitional government would give his Christian Democratic party full access to the electoral process. Leaving the UK in June 1945, Popiel had to take a leap of faith that world powers would work together to make good on the promises of Yalta.

In the end, those promises proved empty. Popiel's party was broken apart from the inside by Communist infiltrators. In 1947, he left Polish soil for good, thereby avoiding torture, a show trial, and possibly death in prison. Going first to London to be with his ailing wife, he then passed briefly through New York and Paris en route to settling in Rome.

Cut off from the country whose Christian Democrats he had led since 1939, faced with leadership challenges from other political exiles within the same party, Popiel found solace in the Cold War embrace of the United States.[6] Securing a source of income for himself and a half-dozen loyal Polish operatives working for him in exile, this elderly Polish statesman presided over two decades' worth of vigorous campaigning to keep Central and Eastern Europe's exiled Christian Democratic parties relevant in a Cold War world. It was the US-based National Committee for a Free Europe (later renamed the Free Europe Committee) that bankrolled these activities, which ranged from speaking before the United Nations General Assembly to running clandestine workshops for aspiring anti-Communist statesmen from Latin America.[7]

Despite his movement's impressive list of accomplishments, by the mid-1960s the Americans were ready to cut this old-world gentleman off financially. Overnight, he was reduced from a world-class political operative to a senior citizen on the verge of penury. What explains this trajectory? Popiel's Christian Democrats had proven themselves adept operatives and loyal US allies throughout the 1950s and early 1960s, but by the time of the global turn to détente and human rights-talk in the late 1960s, their movement had outlived its Cold War usefulness. Nonetheless, SP remained active in exile until the collapse of the Soviet Bloc, serving as a reminder of the Allies' abandonment of Central and Eastern Europe in the wake of the Yalta Accords' catastrophic failure.

And yet, Christian Democracy's brief restitution on Polish soil in 1945 had opened the door for a new generation of Catholic political activists. These men and women of the wartime generation wanted to tap into the demographic strength of Roman Catholicism in postwar Poland, where Catholics represented over 90 percent of the population —a figure unprecedented in all of Polish history. This was the combined result of the Holocaust, the expulsion of Germans, and the loss of Ukrainians and Belorussians to the Soviet Union. After the Christian Democrats were permanently excluded from the postwar political arena, younger generations of aspiring Catholic activists turned to the only ideological alternative that they could find: Catholic socialism.

## AFTER YALTA

Poland was not the only Catholic country in postwar Central and Eastern Europe, but it did contain the largest and most active population of Catholic faithful. Among Czechs, Catholicism had been on the wane for centuries, while Catholic Slovakia suffered from its association with the wartime Nazi puppet government of the Catholic priest Jozef Tiso.[8] In ethnically and religiously divided Yugoslavia, the Catholicism of the Croats was easily marginalized.[9] Only Hungary rivaled Poland in the importance of Catholicism to its national and political culture. Its primate Cardinal József Mindszenty's conservative politics and close ties to the Holy See made the Hungarian Church a ready target for the emerging Communist establishment.[10]

In Poland, meanwhile, the war had transformed the ecclesiastical hierarchy's place in the social order. As Maryjane Osa puts it, out of a "feudal Church" was born an "activist Church."[11] At the war's onset, Primate August Hlond escaped into exile. Although another prelate—Adam Stefan Sapieha of Kraków—stepped into the spotlight to mediate between the Church and occupation authorities, Sapieha had no intention of supplanting the primate.[12]

In the absence of strong episcopal leadership, Catholic activists in wartime Poland relied on horizontal linkages that emerged in the wartime underground. By reading illegally printed copies of Maritain and Mounier, and by joining groups like the Union or the Confederation of the Nation, Catholics developed common cause in a high-stakes environment that made them mutually interdependent. The way they dealt with that interdependence often spelled the difference between living and dying; it also gave them the opportunity to reflect on the kind of country they wanted to see Poland become after the war.

The bonds among lay activists survived the war. Theirs was a different approach to Catholicism, averse to the strict, top-down control historically exercised by bishops and parish priests in these lands.[13] The Allies' conference at Potsdam in July–August 1945 shifted Poland's borders to the west, leading to a mass resettlement of Poles to formerly German lands. Misunderstandings between Polish Catholics and the Holy See multiplied as the Vatican refused to redraw diocesan lines. Poles settling the so-called "Recovered Territories" were, in the Vatican's eyes, under German jurisdiction. Even Poland's bishops—though loyal to the Holy See—found this situation intolerable. As Michael Fleming wryly observes, "The 'will of God' in this case was neatly aligned with Polish Church, state, and national interests but apparently had not been revealed to the Pope."[14] In the interim, the Polish episcopate developed a stopgap solution of appointing temporary Polish administrators. It was not until the 1970s that the Vatican would agree to recognize the postwar border shifts and formally transfer the affected territories from the charge of German bishops to Polish jurisdiction.[15]

For Catholics seeking a role in the public life of postwar Poland, wartime demographic and geopolitical shifts cut both ways. On the one hand, Polish Catholics alienated from their bishops were already one step closer to accepting the new Communist way of doing things. On the other, the lack of a strong ecclesiastical hierarchy meant that Communists had no simple path to co-opting the Church in a country now more than 90 percent Catholic. James Ramon Felak has noted that, among Slovaks in Czechoslovakia between 1945 and 1948, "The Communists, for instance, despite an atheistic outlook and a desire to cripple the influence of the churches, were not unequivocally hostile to Catholics in this period; rather, their attempts to weaken the Catholic Church ran simultaneously with efforts to build positive relations with Catholics and woo them into their camp."[16] If this was true in postwar Slovakia, it was all the more so in Poland.

On July 22, 1944, Moscow backed the creation of a Polish Committee of National Liberation (PKWN, *Polski Komitet Wyzwolenia Narodowego*) based in the eastern Polish city of Lublin. Four years later, many of that committee's successors fell from grace as postwar Poland's Communist-dominated government turned Stalinist, rooting out ostensible "enemies within." In the intervening years, Polish Communists installed by Moscow had spearheaded the country's reconstruction and transformation, couching both in the language of socialist revolution.

In 1945, their program involved no immediate leap to a dictatorship of the proletariat. Rather, it included tentative concessions for the creation of autonomous Catholic organizations, as well as invitations extended to two—as the PKWN termed them—"non-fascist" political parties that had survived the war in London as part of the government-in-exile: Stanisław Mikołajczyk's Polish Peasants' Party (PSL, *Polskie Stronnictwo Ludowe*) and Karol Popiel's Christian Democrats.[17] Initially, it seemed as though these two parties might serve as guarantors of Stalin's Yalta pledge to hold free elections. Within a matter of months, however, they had become little more than targets for the new order's security forces.

Even before Poland's postwar Communist government turned Stalinist in 1948, it already had teeth. Its major political party, the Polish Workers' Party, controlled access to all media and publicity in the country. This included a stranglehold over the new Ministry of Information and Propaganda, the Polish Press Agency (on which all other parties had to rely for news), radio broadcasting, the new "Reader" (*Czytelnik*) publishing house, and the army's propaganda division.[18]

Even more influential in daily life was the Ministry of Public Safety (MBP, *Ministerstwo Bezpieczeństwa Publicznego*), a name eerily reminiscent of Robespierre's Committee of Public Safety from the French Reign of Terror. The Soviet NKVD had remained active in the Polish countryside after the war, running a counterinsurgency campaign across Polish territory until August 1946. The MBP, created in January 1945, initially served as the NKVD's homegrown liaison and partner. In the fall of 1945, the MBP already had over 27,000 officers in its employ, with a rapidly growing network of agents and informants.[19] Even before the Soviet-backed postwar Communist party—the Polish Workers' Party (PPR)—went Stalinist, it could and did make systematic use of this ministry as a partisan police force against Catholics, as well as any other activists perceived to be endangering the new order.

The new government's growing propaganda arm marketed Communist authority to the Polish public as an ally intent on improving the proletarian lot. Before World War II, Dmowski's integral nationalists and Piłsudski's *sanacja* had regularly split the worker vote.[20] With both of those factions out of the picture after the war, social Catholicism suddenly held sway over the largest constituency that it had ever enjoyed in Poland. Rooted in papal encyclicals dating back to Leo XIII's 1891 *Rerum Novarum*, the ideology of social Catholicism—given its focus on social justice, elaborated over five decades—seemed to stand a chance of competing with Marxism for the hearts and minds of Polish workers.[21] As a result, the "social-Catholic" label became a sought-after prize for postwar Catholic activists, including both Christian Democrats and the self-styled Catholic socialists of the new *Dziś i Jutro* (*Today and Tomorrow*) movement.

These two groups proved unable to work together. In fact, Catholic socialists benefited directly in proportion to the establishment's quick and utter suppression of the Christian Democrats. Yet both groups ultimately developed extensive transnational networks of partners and acolytes. Their stories exemplify the political dilemmas of European Catholics at mid-century, navigating the treacherous straits between the promotion of social justice and the legitimation of Soviet-style autocracy.

## THE "GENTLE" REVOLUTION

After the war's end, the government installed in Poland by the USSR needed all the help it could get to consolidate power. In 1945, Polish Communists had no homegrown constituency: Stalin had sent most of the prewar Polish Communist Party membership to their deaths in the late 1930s.[22] The Soviet-backed postwar Communist party—the Polish

Workers' Party (PPR)—was a Frankenstein-like assemblage of different approaches and allegiances that took several years to find its footing. In its earliest postwar incarnation, however, the PPR leadership decided to offer its own version of Maurice Thorez's *main tendue* to Poland's Catholic activists.[23]

Reaching out to Catholics was the first step in a broader campaign by PPR "nationalists" like Władysław Gomułka, who wanted to make Communist Poland less dependent upon Moscow. General secretary of the PPR from 1943 to 1948, Gomułka also became deputy prime minister in postwar Poland's interim government. Initially, he pushed for a coalition government modeled on the prewar French Popular Front—with some ministerial posts, for example, even going to the PSL.[24]

Jerzy Borejsza, a French-educated one-time Zionist, was the man behind this approach. His wartime service in the Red Army and the Polish People's Army had earned him the rank of major. Loyal to Gomułka as well as the Communist cause, Borejsza would, until 1948, play the role of gatekeeper for postwar Poland's intellectual life. He single-handedly created the Communist establishment's flagship publishing house. Borejsza's voice could make or break not only careers, but lives: his support redeemed many a political prisoner from a path leading to torture and execution. One of his beneficiaries was the ex-fascist Bolesław Piasecki.[25]

In 1945, it was Borejsza who explained why the fledgling Communist establishment was seeking to partner up with "non-fascists." According to him, these partnerships reflected a shared interest in pursuing Poland's material reconstruction and political transformation, as well as a loftier goal: social justice, achieved through a classless society. Rather than follow the USSR's model of an immediate, violent leap to the dictatorship of the proletariat, Borejsza argued for a "gentle" revolution (*rewolucja łagodna*).[26] Three years later, when the PPR took a Stalinist turn against "right-wing nationalist deviations," Borejsza's long-standing program of gentle revolution would cost him his position in Polish public life.

To the extent that it really applied at all, the gentle revolution was a realistic option for only a select few in Polish society. As Marcin Zaremba has argued, for the overwhelming majority of Poles, the years 1944–47 were in fact a time of chaos, civil war, pogroms, and penury that he describes—on the example of the French Revolution—as the "Great Fear" (*Wielka Trwoga*).[27] In 1945, however, Borejsza's proposal to replace the revolutionary "guillotine" with some latitude for Poland's "progressive intelligentsia" allowed for at least a façade of cooperation with non-Marxists.[28]

This approach cracked the door open for Catholics looking to play a role in Polish public life. It was not clear, however, where the ecclesiastical hierarchy itself fit into the gentle revolution. Ambiguity turned to antagonism when, on September 12, 1945, Poland's Government of National Unity unilaterally abrogated the 1925 concordat with the Holy See. Suddenly, the Catholic Church became an extra-legal institution, with its diplomatic channels to the Holy See now seen by the new state as potentially subversive. The Church was poised to lose its legal privileges, tax-exempt status, ecclesiastical charities, and—of greatest concern to the Polish episcopate—the place of Catholic education in schools.[29] It did not help the Church's cause that the returning Primate Hlond was widely viewed by Communists as a wartime defector. Kraków's Archbishop Sapieha commanded the respect of establishment circles for his stalwart wartime opposition to the German occupation, but he was not the primate.

With the formation of new state structures after Poland's liberation by the Red Army, supervision of churches and religiously affiliated associations fell initially to the Ministry of Public Administration. Its first minister, Władysław Wolski, created a Department of Religious Affairs to handle day-to-day matters, while his office made political decisions in direct consultation with the Central Committee of the PPR and, later, its successor—the Polish United Workers' Party (PZPR, *Polska Zjednoczona Partia Robotnicza*).[30] In April 1950, the Polish parliament eliminated this ministry, turning the Department of Religious Affairs into an autonomous administrative unit answering directly to the prime minister.[31] From that point onward, the Polish secret police took over most of Wolski's portfolio.[32]

Already in 1945, then, the new Communist establishment had begun to replace the hierarchy's interwar privileges with an apparatus designed more to keep the Church in check than to work with it. It is therefore unsurprising that Hlond, Sapieha, and others looked to proven lay activists from the interwar and war years to represent the hierarchy's interests in public life. The regime and the hierarchy were both willing to accept the political parties invited back from wartime exile and clandestine life in the underground (in other words—the PSL and SP), as well as the new *Dziś i Jutro* movement spearheaded by Bolesław Piasecki.

## THE OPPOSITION

In June 1945, the PKWN invited back to Poland the two London-based political groups in the exile government that it classified as "non-fascist." One reason why Communists initially sought to attract the PSL and SP back to Poland was the influence that they might wield in persuading their former constituents that, rather than fight the Soviet-backed regime, they should lay down their arms and integrate into Communist Poland's civic life. The resulting political constellation had all of the trappings of a struggle for the soul of the nation. Despite good-faith pronouncements by leaders of both returning parties, Poland remained in a state of civil war through 1947, with NKVD and MBP officers working together to seek out and either arrest or execute partisans who remained in hiding throughout the countryside.[33]

The former prime minister of the London government-in-exile, Stanisław Mikołajczyk—leader of the PSL—had lent his full support to the Yalta Accords. Agreeing to reactivate the PSL on Polish soil, Mikołajczyk himself returned on June 27, 1945. Meanwhile, SP leaders disagreed over whether or not to return. The party's long-time president Karol Popiel prevailed, however, and he returned to Poland in July. Popiel described the decision tersely in his memoirs: "My country, via a telegram from the Executive Committee of SP, called me in 1945 to return home. I returned. We fought for a voice and for our active role in the life of the nation."[34] According to Popiel, it was in fact the priest Zygmunt Kaczyński—fated to die eight years later in a Stalinist prison—who had been the most dogged advocate of SP's legal reactivation in Poland. Their colleague Jerzy Braun later recalled that Kaczyński "returned from England to his homeland with boundless reserves of energy and faith in the possibility of participating in the new order, undergirded by the indefatigable, creative power of Polish Catholicism."[35]

Popiel's plan had been first to call a national party convention to obtain a vote of confidence for his leadership, then to prepare the party's field organization for a successful electoral campaign. All of this was predicated on the assumption that the postwar interim government actually intended to honor Stalin's Yalta promises. What Popiel wanted matched exactly the goals of Poland's Catholic bishops: to give "Catholic political representation" a real electoral chance against the Communists.[36]

When Popiel received his invitation to return home, he was fully aware of the show trial taking place in Moscow at that very moment (June 18–21, 1945). The accused were the "Sixteen," leaders of the Polish underground invited to Moscow for consultations, only to be arrested by the NKVD when they arrived—then tortured, sentenced in a show trial, and imprisoned. The most prominent among the Sixteen was Gen. Leopold Okulicki, last commander of the Polish underground's Home Army, who had made the decision to launch the Warsaw Uprising in August 1944. The general made a poignant speech at his show trial in defense of "soldiers of the Polish army who died at the hands of soldiers of the Red Army."[37] After his sentencing in June 1945, Okulicki disappeared from public view, his fate unknown to the wider world for over a decade. Only in 1956—in the midst of de-Stalinization—did Soviet authorities report that Okulicki had died on Christmas Eve 1946. The official version was that he died of a heart attack following a hunger strike, though Okulicki's fellow inmates variously claimed that he had either been executed or smothered in the dead of night.[38]

In the face of world governments' refusal to intervene on the Sixteen's behalf, Okulicki's disappearance from public view was an ominous portent to Polish leaders in Warsaw and London alike of what the future might hold for them. Karol Popiel, in particular, had a personal reason to feel traumatized by the Sixteen's persecution. Namely, one of his best friends, the Christian Democratic politician Józef Chaciński, was also among those arrested in Moscow. The prewar prime minister and wartime Auschwitz prisoner would be one of the few to survive his Moscow sentence and return to Poland, albeit in such ill health that he died soon thereafter.[39]

Show trials soon proved to be one of the most important weapons in the Communist arsenal—not only *against* particular individuals, but in the *service* of propaganda for the new regime. Whether we are looking at the Trial of the Sixteen in Moscow or the show trials of Polish clergy in the early 1950s, the goal was the same: "materializing an enemy."

Bishops and parish priests, farmers and statesmen—in their courtship of the postwar Polish nation, Communists could turn any of their fellow countrymen into "Gestapo collaborators, spies, and imperialist agents."[40]

While Popiel knew about the trial, his PSL counterpart Stanisław Mikołajczyk was actually in Moscow as it was taking place. His task there was to negotiate the PSL's exact share in Poland's new Government of National Unity, and he did not allow his colleagues' tragic fate to take his eyes off of that goal.[41] Unable to aid his condemned colleagues, Mikołajczyk in fact lent legitimacy to Poland's new Communist establishment. Over the next two years—until the day that, fearing for his life, he was smuggled out of Poland in the fall of 1947—he came to regret this decision. From 1945 to 1947 he presided over a party whose members faced mass arrests, kidnappings, and murder at the hands of the MBP.[42]

The fortunes of Popiel's party were less violent in the short run, though no more successful. Despite his deep disillusionment with Mikołajczyk's inability to aid the Sixteen, Popiel nonetheless went ahead with his planned repatriation. On July 15, 1945, he presided over a Christian Democratic national convention in Warsaw. The assembled party members confirmed Popiel's leadership, agreeing to hold further conventions to settle the details of the upcoming electoral campaign.

Not a single additional convention would come to pass, however. Polish prime minister Edward Osóbka-Morawski began pressuring Popiel—on Moscow's behalf—to merge SP with another political party close to the Communists: the Democratic Party (*Stronnictwo Demokratyczne*). Popiel refused, reiterating that his whole reason for returning to Poland had been to lead a confessional Christian party into parliamentary elections. For him, this precluded partnership with any party that did not base its program on social Catholicism.[43]

Just as the government was trying to force a merger on SP, Popiel confronted another challenge—this time, from within his own party. Jolt (*Zryw*), which had splintered off from the SP underground movement in 1943 under the leadership of Zygmunt Felczak and Feliks Widy-Wirski, demanded a power-sharing arrangement with Popiel within the party's executive committee. Unsurprisingly, the PPR was behind this challenge. The Christian Democrats' hands were tied, as Popiel locked in arduous, multi-month negotiations with Widy-Wirski.

Jolt demanded no less than 40 percent of the SP leadership, a figure at least double the faction's real numerical representation. In the end, Widy-Wirski withdrew entirely from negotiations on July 9, 1946. But instead of punishing him, the Polish government came after Popiel, withdrawing permission for a second SP convention and refusing to continue recognizing Popiel as the party's presiding officer.[44]

In the interim, the Jolt leaders consistently blocked Popiel's initiatives in postwar Poland's constituent assembly. Subsequently, they formed a new SP executive committee on their own, usurping the authority vested in Popiel's group by the first party convention. By the end of July 1946, Widy-Wirski had sent out dozens of letters informing SP's constituent assembly MPs that they had been stripped of their seats.[45] Under these circumstances, the party effectively descended into chaos. As a consequence, Popiel's executive committee passed a resolution to suspend the party *in toto* "until such time as the government changes its stance."[46] From this moment forward, SP participation in Polish politics was limited to the pro-Communist Jolt, which allowed itself to be absorbed into the Communist rank-and-file in 1950.

Widy-Wirski's SP made no attempt at "Catholic political representation." In December 1945, he published a book under the provocative title *Poland and the Revolution* (*Polska i Rewolucja*), dedicated to the "youth of Poland." Written by a self-described Christian politician from a Catholic political party, the book nonetheless made not a single mention of Jesus or the Bible. Instead, it was full of citations of Marx, Engels, and Lenin. It even referenced some of Lenin's philosophical *bêtes noires*, like Eduard Bernstein and Karl Kautsky. This was a Marxist tract that showed no interest whatsoever in Christianity.

The book began with the text of a speech given by Widy-Wirski in Warsaw for the twenty-eighth anniversary of the Bolshevik Revolution. In that speech, Widy-Wirski called upon Poles to take advantage of the "privilege" bestowed upon their nation by the liberating Red Army. In other words, he wanted to initiate a "Polish Revolution," imitating the Bolshevik example. Widy-Wirski thundered, "Tragic is the fate of those nations and individuals who are unable to fathom the great historical process unfolding before our eyes [ . . . ]. This is the problem of the Polish Revolution, which would conquer in one decisive leap our present backwardness." In the volume's conclusion, Widy-Wirski complained that Poles had great difficulty embracing "political realism."[47] His implication, of course, was that Jolt had no such trouble, and therefore deserved a role in leading the country.

To Popiel, *Poland and the Revolution* was anathema. The SP leader's commitment to Catholic confessionalism made him an easy target in postwar Poland, and it also made it more difficult for him to focus his energy on organization-building. Rather than forge relationships at home or network abroad, Popiel focused SP's resources on countering Jolt. In response, for example, to a spring 1946 memo from Felczak and Widy-Wirski demanding the removal of "religious education and the indissolubility of the family" from SP's draft party platform, Popiel vented his frustration on their disloyalty to key tenets of Catholic politics: "The deletion of these two principles from a draft of the party platform that had already been accepted by your representatives is an open declaration of war on these principles. Only a party founded on materialist ideology would dare to undertake this kind of war. It is, however, unacceptable within the parameters of a social-Catholic party. [ . . . ] In response to the proposals contained in your most recent correspondence—I can say only that I deeply regret that six weeks of exhaustive negotiations with you have borne no fruit in the pursuit of further democratization of Polish political life."[48]

Popiel's problems with Jolt illustrated a more general fact of Polish politics in the war's immediate aftermath. Less than a year after Borejsza's announcement of the gentle revolution, that revolution turned against the coalition partners who had been invited back to Poland. Throughout 1945 and 1946, the PPR aggressively pursued a monopoly on power—by means of the secret police, propaganda, and electoral fraud. In April 1946, Stanisław Mikołajczyk agreed to the PPR's proposal of a national referendum on three issues: the abolition of the Senate, support for land reform and nationalization, and recognition of Poland's new western borders. Despite questions framed to maximize the number of "Yes" votes cast, the PPR still had to falsify the results in order to claim an overwhelming victory in the so-called "three times 'Yes'" referendum.[49]

Five months after the referendum, at its September 9–10, 1946 plenary conference in Częstochowa, the Polish episcopate publicly protested the Jolt faction's usurpation of the SP name. The bishops demanded that the government permit the Catholic party to hold another national convention.[50] At this point, Bolesław Bierut—president of the constituent assembly and soon to become president of Poland—was still concerned enough about Catholic opinion to promise in an interview with the newspaper *Rzeczpospolita* (*The Republic*) that "Catholics possess and will continue to possess in Poland the same rights as other citizens. If they want, they can campaign to elect a separate Catholic bloc to the next parliament."[51]

Initially, it seemed that something might come of Bierut's declaration. Following its publication, Catholic activists representing very different agendas sat down at one table to negotiate the future of Catholic politics in Poland. In addition to Popiel's group, the participants included Bolesław Piasecki's new *Dziś i Jutro* group, as well as smaller delegations from other newly created Catholic journals.[52] Student activist Tadeusz Przeciszewski later recalled that Piasecki droned on incessantly about "the priority of our nation's existence and our obligations as Catholics to preserve that existence." Yet it was Piasecki who pulled the plug on the negotiations when SP and the other groups refused to concede to *Dziś i Jutro* a majority of the seats in the leadership of any new "Catholic" party.[53]

The failure of these negotiations dealt a deathblow to SP. In October 1947, Popiel went back into exile. While Popiel left Poland legally, Mikołajczyk, fearing prison or assassination, arranged to be smuggled out of the country one month later.[54] Violent recriminations against former SP activists did not begin until mid-1948. Meanwhile, first in London, then—successively—New York, Paris, and Rome, Popiel gathered around himself a small but devoted group of lieutenants who kept SP alive. SP's postwar life in exile existed not merely on paper, but as a set of transnational commitments to Christian Democracy worldwide and to the American side in the Cold War.

Led by Popiel and SP secretary-general Konrad Sieniewicz, who, like Mikołajczyk, had left Poland illegally, Popiel's team of exile operatives became a staple presence at international congresses of the "New International Teams" (*Nouvelles Équipes Internationales*, NEI), Western Europe's postwar Christian Democratic international.[55] Sieniewicz wrote in July 1948 to former Polish underground leader General Tadeusz Bór-Komorowski, requesting financial support for the SP exiles' project: "As the General undoubtedly knows, for some time now I have focused in my work—in keeping with instructions from my superiors, known personally to the General—on the international arena, above all in the *Nouvelles Équipes Internationales* [ . . . ]. I hereby permit myself to turn to the General with an ardent request for assistance in maintaining the international position of the social-Catholic option that I represent, which in my view is an important accomplishment for the entire camp of freedom."[56]

The following year, Popiel's group branched out across the Atlantic. The National Committee for a Free Europe, established in 1949 as a publicly supported private corporation, maintained an Exile Relations division, which recruited Popiel's team to wage "political warfare" against the Soviet Bloc.[57] Popiel, Sieniewicz, their disciples Stanisław Gebhardt and Janusz Śleszyński, and the rest of SP spent the next fifteen years in exile as a sort of Eastern European "A-team" on retainer for Free Europe. After 1956, they were even able to fund international travel for young Catholic intellectuals from Poland, who then returned to Warsaw and Kraków having seen the world and made long-term intellectual and political contacts.[58] The Christian Democrats' American handlers called these initiatives an example of successful "counter-penetration" of the Soviet Bloc.[59]

Before World War II, the "human person" had been an ideological anchor for Polish Christian Democracy, beginning with the writings of its founder Wojciech Korfanty. In the 1930s and early 1940s, Christian Democrats conceived of personhood as being at once contingent and ethnocentric: in other words, Catholic baptism and membership in the Polish ethnos were preconditions to personhood in Poland. As SP became less rooted in Poland and more focused on Cold War geopolitics, the "human person" disappeared from their writings and teachings, as did any reference to SP's origins in Catholic social thought.[60] Rather than a comprehensive philosophy of Catholic activism, what the Polish Christian Democrats had to offer at the end of the day was political acumen, American money, and the promise of access to global activist networks. They abandoned their own personalist tradition, but at the same time they helped to launch the careers of generations of personalists to come.

## INTEGRAL NATIONALISTS AS FELLOW TRAVELERS

It was a curious twist of fate that, among Catholic political movements in early Communist Poland, the one group to survive the implosion of the "gentle" revolution was also the one group that openly admitted its integralist roots. Arrested in 1944 as leader of the Confederation of the Nation, Bolesław Piasecki hatched a plan while under guard by the NKVD to re-enter Polish public life in the war's aftermath.

Contemporaries and scholars alike have loved to hate Piasecki. A fascist-turned-fellow traveler who simply walked out of NKVD custody? Of course he was a Soviet agent! Communist Poland's own high-level secret police defector Józef Światło was the first to broadcast this theory over the waves of Radio Free Europe, and it has held sway ever since.[61]

Mikołaj Kunicki's *Between the Brown and the Red* has capably defined the contours of Piasecki's character: an eternal integralist, a devout Catholic, and a megalomaniac with great charisma. But as important as the man himself was the world that he created in the first decade of Communist Poland's existence—beginning in 1945 with a weekly newspaper called *Dziś i Jutro* (*Today and Tomorrow*), which became the keystone of a financial and media empire that he built over the next decade.

It all began with an idea for a publication that would bring Catholics and Marxists together. *Dziś i Jutro* assembled a staff from among 1930s fascists, wartime guerrilla fighters, and nationalists of different ages and backgrounds—all looking for a political home in Communist Poland. *Dziś i Jutro* quickly spawned a movement of non-conformist misfits seeking to shape the "revolution" that their country was experiencing. In this respect, they were not unlike Mounier and his fellow founding editors at *Esprit*, with one significant difference: everything that happened at *Dziś i Jutro* happened with the full knowledge of, and in consultation with, representatives of the new Communist-dominated government.

Using Borejsza as an intermediary, Władysław Gomułka summoned Piasecki for a face-to-face meeting on July 4, 1945.[62] Although Piasecki made Gomułka uneasy, the PPR leader invited Piasecki back for a second meeting two weeks later, with instructions to draft a political program in the interim.[63] Following their second meeting, Gomułka approved Piasecki's project to start a Catholic lay association anchored in a journal. In subsequent consultations with Borejsza, Piasecki hammered out the details for his new weekly, launched on November 25.

To understand this journal, it is important to underline a few key phrases from the political program that Piasecki submitted to Gomułka. After committing to making Poland a "bridging, not a dividing, factor between the worlds of the East and the West" and to working on behalf of Polish-Soviet friendship, Piasecki concentrated on the area of greatest personal and institutional interest to him: Catholic-Marxist relations. Piasecki declared,

> Ideological elements of the governing camp harbor fears that allowing for the recognition of idealist circles and, ultimately, a movement, might end in the rebirth of reactionary elements on Polish soil. Christian idealist circles, on the other hand, lack faith in the good will of Marxist leaders, in their loyal commitment to involve them in shaping Polish life. We believe that this mutual lack of trust must be broken. We want to make this happen by a) sharing with Marxists in the crucial task of rebuilding and transforming the Polish state; and b) sharing with Marxists our ideologically pure and loyal struggle for the fullest development of the Polish idea in the service of humanity. Mutual relations between Marxists and idealists can only enrich both sides.[64]

Adopting Marxist terminology, Piasecki used the word "idealists" to refer to all religious people, a group in which he included himself. The operative terms in Piasecki's proposal were "sharing" and "mutual." His point was that, although Marxists controlled the "governing camp," Piasecki expected to build a partnership that would break down the wall between the two sides.

Though Primate Hlond was not entirely certain what to make of this motley crew of aristocrats and ex-fascists, he initially offered them his support, even contributing US$500 to help get their journal off the ground.[65] Borejsza, too, met regularly with Piasecki throughout the fall of 1945. The new movement subtitled its journal a "Catholic social weekly" (*katolicki tygodnik społeczny*). For *Dziś i Jutro*, combining the words "Catholic" and "social" signaled not an endorsement of nineteenth-century social Catholicism or corporatism, but instead a radically new fusion of Catholicism and the social. Thus was born Catholic socialism. Pius XI must have been spinning in his grave.

SP's co-optation inspired Piasecki to develop his own political designs. These included, among others, a place in parliamentary politics. After *Dziś i Jutro* walked out of the November 1946 meeting on creating a new Catholic party, Hlond cautiously supported Piasecki in his goal of putting up candidates for parliament. Alerted soon to the fact that this would likely hurt the PSL, however, the primate pulled his support.

Within a year *Dziś i Jutro* had made it clear that it was as interested in joining the new *nomenklatura* as in promoting Catholicism.[66] By mid-1946, the *Dziś i Jutro* staff had a government concession to run a private bus company serving the Warsaw area. Their commercial ventures soon multiplied, growing to encompass two trading companies, Inco and Veritas; a private high school; a daily newspaper; and the only publishing house in Poland with a concession to print the Bible in large quantities.[67] Already in its first year of existence, then, *Dziś i Jutro* seemed to be quickly drifting away from social Catholicism toward secular entrepreneurship.

At the same time, the external enemy by which the group defined its nationalism had also changed. In the course of the war, the anti-Semitism of the movement's old guard had been supplanted by fear and loathing of all things German. Anti-Semitism remained a feature of Piasecki's inner circle, but his new recruits trained their sights on a different target.[68] Germans were not only Nazis, according to this view, but also latent revanchists: after all, it was at Germany's expense that Poland had gained new western territories by Allied agreement at Potsdam. This created all sorts of complications for Polish Catholics moving to those territories, as the Holy See consistently sided with the German bishops who refused to relinquish their jurisdiction. In 1948, Pius XII addressed a long letter to the German bishops declaring full support for their claims under canon law.[69]

Anti-German sentiment formed a wellspring of inspiration for *Dziś i Jutro*, allowing Piasecki's old guard to direct their integralism against Poland's former occupiers. On this point, *Dziś i Jutro* in fact echoed a national consensus in postwar Poland: Communists and nationalists, bishops and laymen—all wanted to secure Polish sovereignty over the "Recovered Territories." Indeed, even the Polish episcopate refused to accept Pius XII's judgment with respect to Germany.[70] As Michael Fleming notes, "The practical basis of Church-state cooperation in the period leading up to 1947 was the shared objective of 'Polonizing' the 'Recovered Territories.'"[71] This remained the case even after the regime turned against the Church, accusing prominent ecclesiastical officials of having been German collaborators.

Historians have been quick to dismiss *Dziś i Jutro* as—at best—

hypocrites, at worst, Stalinist henchmen and traitors to Catholicism.[72] Yet leaving it at that ignores the fact that *Dziś i Jutro* is an integral part of any intellectual genealogy of Catholic activism on Polish territory in the twentieth century. Piasecki was no Maritain or Mounier, but many of the activists whom he gathered around him had a deep knowledge of the French Catholic vanguard. That knowledge, in turn, proved instrumental in shaping *Dziś i Jutro*'s own intellectual and political commitments—both nationally and transnationally.

The story of *Dziś i Jutro* also reveals that the fates of Christian Democracy and Catholic socialism were, in fact, intertwined. In France, the Catholic vanguard expanded in direct proportion to the fervor with which the country's postwar Christian Democratic "Popular Republican Movement" (*Mouvement Républicain Populaire*, MRP) pushed for Franco-German rapprochement and shifted away from its early designs to become a party of the working classes.[73] In France as in Poland, Christian Democracy and Catholic socialism both claimed to have led the Catholic wartime resistance. However, the Polish Catholic socialists —unlike the French—took parliamentary seats vacated by Christian Democrats who had been targeted for political repression.

Bolesław Piasecki's movement benefited directly from SP's muzzling and expulsion from Polish public life. True—his negotiations with Popiel and his fellow Catholic editors had failed to secure consensus for Piasecki to take a majority in the leadership of a new Catholic political party. Nevertheless, Piasecki leveraged these negotiations in his dealings with the PPR to obtain an allowance of three MPs for the *Dziś i Jutro* group in the 1947 Polish parliamentary elections: this, at a time when Catholic activists were either fleeing into exile or preparing themselves for prison sentences.[74]

The greatest gain made by *Dziś i Jutro* with the collapse of SP was the migration of a significant number of aspiring young Christian Democrats to *Dziś i Jutro*. Tadeusz Mazowiecki—at the time an ambitious nineteen-year-old Catholic activist, soon to become one of *Dziś i Jutro*'s most important voices, and, forty years hence, Poland's first non-Communist prime minister since the war—is one such example. The son of a doctor from Płock who had been active in Catholic Action in the 1930s, Mazowiecki in early July 1946 became head of the SP youth circle for his home region.[75] Over the next six weeks, however, he watched SP implode. To this recent high-school graduate, the long-standing dispute between Popiel and Widy-Wirski meant nothing. All that Mazowiecki wanted was to get involved in public life, to become part of a Catholic organization that would give him a chance to shape the world around him.[76]

When the SP door closed, Mazowiecki saw another one open in *Dziś i Jutro*.[77] At the time, Mazowiecki saw Piasecki's movement in the following terms:

> This was a thoughtfully crafted journal and a movement that proved really dynamic in reaching out to the younger generations, bringing them in. And this is how, in the course of my university studies, I found myself developing a fascination with this group—because *Tygodnik Powszechny* functioned on a celestial plane, never finding its way back down to earth, and on top of that was a fairly hermetic group. [ . . . ] But the *Dziś i Jutro* weekly actually reached out to the young, offering them a way of getting involved in the new reality—something that everyone was seeking because the division [between Communism and capitalism] seemed permanent. It seemed that Poland might be able to preserve a certain measure of distinctiveness, and so we should be searching for some kind of modus vivendi.[78]

By the time that *Dziś i Jutro* organized its first nationwide youth retreat—in August 1948, in rural northwestern Poland—Mazowiecki was already an integral part of Piasecki's staff. The young activist from Płock was certainly not alone in seeking a modus vivendi because the division of the world into two camps "seemed permanent." As Hanna Świda-Ziemba has written about Polish Stalinism, "The point was for society to feel that it had no choice—that things would stay this way, if not forever, then at least for the rest of the current generations' lives."[79]

The experience of Mazowiecki's friend, sociologist Zygmunt Skórzyński, is equally revealing. In 1946, Skórzyński was a twenty-three-year-old student in Kraków looking, like Mazowiecki, to become involved in public life without having to hide his Catholicism. Having just joined SP in the late spring of 1946, Skórzyński experienced a rude awakening when he saw the fallout from the bitter negotiations and disputes between Popiel's core group and the Jolt faction. To Skórzyński, Christian Democracy was one big disappointment. As he later explained, "since this party was supposed to bring Catholics together, I expected that it would be possible to combine in harmony a socially progressive, active stance with work for the intellectual advancement of young Catholics. I had no idea at the time about the political difficulties of that party and was shocked by the politicking that became the order of the day."[80] Many intellectuals in their twenties would feel the same way: a pox on both Popiel's group and Jolt. Why, then, not turn instead to *Dziś i Jutro*?

The cases of Mazowiecki and Skórzyński illustrate that, for many politically minded Catholics, *Dziś i Jutro* represented an organizational home where they could publicly express both their Catholicism and their desire to participate in the ongoing "Polish Revolution." Whatever Piasecki's personal magnetism—and, apparently, it was truly seductive—young postwar activists had little choice but to join Piasecki's enterprise if they wanted to stay active in public life as Catholics.

These were the ideal circumstances for recruitment to a fledgling Catholic socialism. For Poles looking to *Dziś i Jutro* in the late 1940s, Emmanuel Mounier's personalism would open a door to new ways of seeking social justice. In its openness toward a Communist establishment that offered the promise of active participation in the construction of a workers' state, *Dziś i Jutro* could seem like a promised land. Years passed before most of its recruits realized that this utopia was putting a good "Catholic" face on show trials and terror.

# 4 The Twilight of Social Catholicism?

## Emmanuel Mounier and Poland's Catholic Press, 1945–1948

*A great experiment is underway in Poland [ . . . ]. We would be remiss not to draw attention to the first steps of a Catholic vanguard whose mission will carry into the long term, for it must create an entire tradition that we in France already have behind us, along with its attendant trials and tribulations.*

—Emmanuel Mounier[1]

IN DECEMBER 1949, a thirty-six-year-old Catholic journalist sat down in his Kraków apartment to write a letter. Jerzy Turowicz was editor-in-chief of Poland's Catholic journal *Tygodnik Powszechny* (*Universal Weekly*). The letter that he began was one that he had thought about sending for almost four years, ever since its addressee—Emmanuel Mounier—had toured a Polish countryside still reeling from the devastation of war. Turowicz liked to say that he had two great heroes, both Frenchmen, both personalists: Jacques Maritain and Emmanuel Mounier. His devotion to Mounier began in 1933, when he encountered a copy of *Esprit* as a twenty-one-year-old engineering student in the Galician city of Lwów. Four years later, Turowicz traveled to France and met Mounier himself at a convention of *Esprit* acolytes.[2]

In May 1946, Turowicz was one of a handful of Catholic activists who welcomed Mounier to Kraków as the head of a delegation of French Catholic and Communist writers. The Polish editor personally showed his hero around the medieval capital's historic Wawel Castle. Together with four colleagues from *Tygodnik Powszechny*, Turowicz pitched to Mounier an idea for a Polish Catholic monthly modeled on *Esprit*. The French philosopher loved the idea, and he promised moral and logistical support.

Yet, in Turowicz's eyes, the events of the next three years made a liar of Mounier. In an article published on his return to France, Mounier named *Dziś i Jutro* as his favorite movement in Poland, while summarily dismissing the group managed by his Kraków host as an "aristocratic citadel."[3] As promised, Turowicz and company launched the journal *Znak* (*Sign*), and Mounier even delivered an article, but it was clear that his heart belonged instead to Poland's budding Catholic socialists. After two years, citing costs, his staff cut off a free subscription to *Esprit* that the staffs of *Tygodnik Powszechny* and *Znak*—which shared one set of offices—had been jointly promised.[4] Meanwhile, *Dziś i Jutro* would continue to receive free copies of the French monthly into the mid-1950s.

Not surprisingly, Turowicz was bitter that his icon had turned his back on the Kraków intellectuals. A decade after Mounier's visit to Poland, Turowicz remarked bitterly that the Frenchman "really had not seen very much from the Wawel."[5] Five months shy of the fourth anniversary of Mounier's trip to Poland, Turowicz finally mustered up the courage to confront Mounier with his disappointment. In painstakingly careful French, he expressed his hope that Mounier might give the Catholic activists of Kraków another chance to convince him of the genuine dilemmas facing Catholics in Communist Poland. Turowicz began with a statement of "regret that you could not extend your stay [in 1946], for there were still so many things for us to say to each other to be able to understand each other better, and I held out great hope for this understanding." Without mincing words, *Tygodnik Powszechny*'s editor went on to articulate the disappointment that had remained with him since Mounier's visit to Kraków: "Today, just as three years ago, it is impossible for me to share certain of your political opinions and positions, however well I might understand their origins; this is, undoubtedly, a consequence of our quite different experiences and situations." In the end, however, Turowicz explained that he continued to hold out hope that he and Mounier would "meet again someday, to talk more" about personalism, so that he might explain to Mounier the reality of the situation in Poland and in the Communist world more broadly.[6]

The tone of Turowicz's letter was emotional. The response that Mounier drafted one week later, however, was anything but. It was almost as though Mounier did not remember Turowicz, whom he asked to pass along the Frenchman's greetings to "anyone else I might have met" while in Poland. Since Mounier could not read *Tygodnik Powszechny* or *Znak*, he did not give them a second thought. Instead of sharing Turowicz's hope for another chance at a meeting of the minds, Mounier offered merely the generic wishes of a Catholic fellow traveler: "I hope very much that our work in our various countries on behalf of peace will allow us to maintain it, come what may."[7]

This was a blow for Turowicz, who wanted an actual dialogue, not an exchange of pleasantries. He resolved to try again after a respectful interval. Yet he would never get the chance. Within half a year, the legacy of Mounier's support for Catholic socialists in Poland—matched by lack of interest in all others—was set in stone. Mounier and Turowicz would never speak again, nor would they exchange any more letters. Less than three months after his curt dismissal of Turowicz's entreaties, Mounier was dead of a heart attack at the age of forty-five.

## THE CATHOLIC PRESS IN POSTWAR POLAND

Turowicz's abortive final exchange with Mounier shows that the postwar world of Polish Catholic publishing was bound up with French Catholicism. Misunderstandings abounded, yet French and Polish intellectuals built a vibrant network of bilateral exchange even as Communists consolidated a stranglehold on postwar Poland, while a divided Europe plunged into the Cold War.

Transnational contacts reshaped the face of Roman Catholicism at mid-century, as activists of Europe east and west put the "human person" and social justice front and center. This focus came not only from the postwar Catholic vanguard, but also from the old guard of Catholic politicians who now took the reins of Western European Christian Democracy. In a celebrated speech at the University of Cologne in March 1946, the German Christian Democratic Union's leader Konrad Adenauer declared, "The human person has a unique dignity, and the value of each individual is irreplaceable. This sentence gives rise to a concept of state, economy, and culture, which is new compared to one that has been usual in Germany for a long time."[8]

The key to tracing the postwar evolution of the "human person" in Poland lies in the journals established by Catholic intellectuals in the months following the German withdrawal. Their pages document clearly the eclipse of Christian Democracy and the rise of Catholic socialism. On both counts, Polish Catholic intellectuals were responding to tectonic shifts they observed among their French heroes and counterparts.

*Tygodnik Powszechny*—launched in March 1945—was only the first of three major lay Catholic weeklies to emerge on Polish soil in the year of the Second World War's conclusion.[9] Seven months later came *Tygodnik Warszawski* (*Warsaw Weekly*) and *Dziś i Jutro*. *Tygodnik Warszawski* began as a personal initiative of Poland's Primate Hlond. Throughout its three-year existence, it identified closely with Popiel's SP, continuing his Christian Democratic line even after the party's co-optation in 1946. Beginning already in 1945, Bolesław Piasecki, the man behind *Dziś i Jutro*, started building a "movement with no name" (*ruch nie nazwany*) around his journal. The movement would receive formal government recognition only in April 1952—taking the name "PAX"—but institutionally it had by far the most solid footing of any of the three journals.[10]

All three weeklies laid claim to the heritage of turn-of-the-century and interwar social Catholicism. All three were launched with mission statements promising to adapt the Catholic project of "revolution" to a postwar world. All three sought a mass readership, printing tens of thousands of copies of each issue. *Dziś i Jutro* had the lowest circulation, yet even it had an average print run of 10,000.

What followed was a contest to see who could most effectively sell social Catholicism as a viable approach in postwar Polish public life.[11] To that end, the editors and contributors to the three journals returned to French writings on the "human person," dusting off prewar and wartime translations of Maritain and Mounier and trying to turn those writings into a philosophy of action. The result of these efforts was the emergence of three dramatically different personalist programs for postwar Poland.

Communists controlled the transitional government that the Red Army had brought to Poland. Even so, in the wake of the Germans' departure, the vast majority of Catholic activists breathed a sigh of relief. In 1945, a window opened for debate among Catholics about what kind of a Poland they wanted. But Communist censors and secret police began to encroach on that freedom already within the year. *Tygodnik Warszawski* found itself a constant target of mainstream press attacks and police provocations, while *Tygodnik Powszechny* swore off politics, turning instead to literature, ecology, and hobbies. After 1948, only *Dziś i Jutro* could grow and flourish. In the meantime, however, the creative ferment of the three competing journals gave Polish writers the opportunity to lay out competing visions of "revolution" for the new era, not only for Poland, but for the Catholic Church and France as well.

The major figures behind these journals are already familiar to us from the wartime anti-German resistance—in particular, from the SP-Union underground and from Piasecki's Confederation of the Nation. Most of the postwar Catholic writers already knew each other: their paths had crossed and re-crossed throughout World War II. For much of the period 1945–48, they wrote simultaneously for multiple journals. Authors like the satirist Stefan Kisielewski, the historian Paweł Jasienica, and the literary theorist Stefania Skwarczyńska in effect took turns writing for *Dziś i Jutro*, *Tygodnik Powszechny*, and *Tygodnik Warszawski*. This was a world of peers, not competitors. To varying degrees, all three journals received financial support from the hierarchy, yet they were mostly the work of lay men and women. Editors and contributors did not feel beholden to their bishops, and even the most anti-Communist editors freely dissented from the episcopal line.

As they had since the *fin-de-siècle*, Poland's Catholic intellectuals looked to France as an example of both the best and the worst in Catholicism. Activists constituting a self-styled Catholic vanguard in both France and Poland entered into regular contact, visited each other, and shaped each other's approaches. The French inspired the Poles, who, in turn, attempted to draw both the French and other Western European groups into the "Polish Revolution," arguing for Marxist revolution on the one hand and Catholicism on the other.

Polish Catholic activists' path from Thomism to "revolution"—from Aquinas through Marx, from a simple message of charity to the dictatorship of the proletariat—began as the war was ending. Hand in hand with this revolutionary reframing of social Catholicism came a deep sociological shift within Catholic activism. Once the purview of priests, activism now became the dominion of the laity.[12]

Not everyone who began this journey went as far as *Dziś i Jutro*—in other words, all the way to Catholic socialism. And there were those who refused to take it altogether—in particular, National Democrats.[13] After World War II, Roman Dmowski's legacy bifurcated in the strangest of ways: while the most radical of the prewar National Democrats became ethnonationally driven Catholic socialists, the vast majority either took up arms against the new regime, or bided their time, convinced that a third world war was imminent.[14]

And so it was that by the late 1940s the lion's share of interwar Poland's integral nationalists had landed in exile, in prison, or in mass graves. Occasionally, *Dziś i Jutro* threw a lifeline to the more repentant among them.[15] On Polish soil, integral nationalism survived within Bolesław Piasecki's new movement—a fateful holdover that sowed the seeds of Catholic socialism's eventual undoing.

## KRAKÓW

*Tygodnik Powszechny* debuted over a month before Germany's capitulation to the Allies. This journal would average a remarkably high print run of 50,000—until its state seizure and transfer to Piasecki in 1953.[16] (The rightful editors were muzzled until the onset of de-Stalinization in October 1956.)[17] Although memory of the war's unprecedented violence and destruction weighed heavily on the journal's early issues, its articles from the outset sought to link Poland's spiritual and material reconstruction to a vibrant "social and cultural" program. In other words, its editors made the conscious choice not to dedicate the journal exclusively to social Catholicism or Catholic social teaching.[18] In so doing, *Tygodnik Powszechny* fulfilled the promise of a postwar cultural review that Turowicz had conceived at Goszyce back in 1943, at the behest of the Union's leadership. The new journal was at once humanist, personalist, and positivist, committed to exploring what it meant to be "Polish," to be "Catholic," and to be "human."[19]

Turowicz had maintained close ties throughout the war with his prewar employer, Jan Piwowarczyk, a priest and leading figure of SP in the 1930s. Rather than serve as an MP or minister, however, Piwowarczyk had taken upon himself the role of party ideologue. Having produced in the mid-1930s the authoritative Polish translations of *Rerum Novarum* and *Quadragesimo Anno*, he used his knowledge of Catholic social thought to write one social-Catholic manifesto after another for Poland's Christian Democrats.[20]

In January 1945, Kraków archbishop Adam Sapieha called Piwowarczyk and Turowicz to his office for a series of consultations. The archbishop wanted to create a new Catholic journal based on Turowicz's wartime design. Sapieha, who emerged from the war with a reputation of fierce antagonism toward the German occupiers, was in a position to provide political cover for the fledgling journal. Piwowarczyk and Turowicz, working in tandem to recruit a diverse staff, published the first issue immediately after Kraków's liberation.[21]

Most historical accounts of *Tygodnik Powszechny* neglect to mention that Sapieha asked Piwowarczyk to run the journal, though Jerzy Turowicz loyally repeated that the priest "was of course the No. 1 person in this enterprise."[22] Initially, the journal's masthead sported the phrase "Edited by the staff" (*Redaguje: Zespół*) instead of identifying Piwowarczyk by name. Seven months into *Tygodnik Powszechny*'s existence, however, government censors demanded a name for the journal's masthead. Turowicz asked Piwowarczyk to submit his, but the priest refused. He feared that, as a clergyman, he might mark *Tygodnik Powszechny* for attacks by the Communist press. By default, then, Turowicz's name went on the masthead. Despite the fact that the journal had come into being at the behest of an archbishop, its official face was that of a journal of the laity. Fact followed formality here: within a year, Piwowarczyk had been reduced to the role of token priest on a large, lay editorial staff.

Five decades later, when Pope John Paul II publicly commemorated the journal's fiftieth anniversary, he declared, "If I say that the initiative of creating *Tygodnik Powszechny* at a moment when the Second World War was still raging was a decision born of Divine Intervention, I mean also that it carried in itself a theology of the laity. A journal edited by laymen is one form of lay apostolate."[23] In the pope's mind, it was Turowicz and his fellow laity who had set the tone for Catholic publishing in postwar Poland.

The journal's first issue led with an essay by Piwowarczyk entitled "Toward a Catholic Poland" (*Ku katolickiej Polsce*). *Tygodnik Powszechny*'s mission statement combined Thomist personalism with a commitment to transforming Poland by revolutionary means. Piwowarczyk insisted that the Church needed to play a leading role in Poland's transformation, and that it was ready and willing to do so. He began, "Our entire attitude toward the events underway can be summed up in the following two truths: 1) The world, and Poland with it, must accept transformation as well as reconstruction; 2) The

Church has a particularly important role to play at this time. Thus far, we have divided history into three epochs: antique, medieval, and modern. Now it will be necessary to add a fourth: the one that we are currently entering."[24]

The priest went out of his way to persuade his readers that, not only was Catholicism compatible with democracy, but that in fact they were two sides of the same coin. For historical proof, Catholics needed look no further than the first Christian Democrats of the early 1890s, whom Pope Leo XIII encouraged to take an active role in the public life of Third Republic France in order to break the prevailing secularist monopoly. Those *fin-de-siècle* priests had also been heroes to the late Antoni Szymański, with whom Piwowarczyk worked closely in the 1930s.[25] Resurrecting an argument that his Belgian-trained old friend had made back in 1910, Piwowarczyk noted, "In a day when 'democracy' is synonymous with progress, let us recall that Leo XIII personally elevated and blessed at St. Peter's Basilica the banners of French democracy."

Piwowarczyk had felt at home in the prewar pontificate of Pius XI. At the same time, he followed Maritain in arguing for a more visible role for Thomist personalism in Catholic political philosophy. The Polish priest repeated the central tenets of two of the French Thomist's key treatises. In Piwowarczyk's eyes, Maritain's thought sufficed to justify—not just for Catholics, but for all citizens of a democracy—a principled rejection of "totalitarianism" in favor of its alternative: a personalism that would have the Church's blessing, yet aspire to being secular and pluralist. In other words, Piwowarczyk sought a form of personhood that would no longer be contingent on the promise of salvation through Catholic baptism. This was neither Marxism, nor an integralist fantasy of "revolution," but instead *actual* Catholic revolution. This option would lose out for another two decades, until Vatican II.

Acknowledging that Poland needed "a new type of culture into which we can fit Western values," Piwowarczyk evoked Maritain to define those values: "the primacy of the spirit over matter, the liberation of the human person from the tyranny of external conditions, the ethical meaning of life, etc." Piwowarczyk then continued by explaining the "rights and responsibilities" of citizens who were conscious of their status as "human persons." These derived from their civic bonds with each other, not from the state, which existed only to "offer security" to a "greater number of human persons having a purpose in themselves."

Piwowarczyk's political theory came straight out of natural law according to Thomas Aquinas: hence his preference for Jacques Maritain. Presenting Thomism as the answer to "totalitarianism," Piwowarczyk wrote, "In place of these [totalistic] addictions, the Church imprinted upon humanity Christian personalism, conscious of its responsibilities and rights, rendering unto Caesar that which is Caesar's, and unto God that which is God's." This passage paraphrased Maritain's *Primacy of the Spiritual*, whose English translation was in fact published under the title *The Things That Are Not Caesar's*.[26]

In his preface to a 1984 collection of Piwowarczyk's writings, Turowicz described *Tygodnik Powszechny* as the priest's proving ground for a "vision of personalist democracy based on the fulfillment of the principles of social justice."[27] This is exactly right: Piwowarczyk's exploration of the "rights and responsibilities" of the "human person" in a democracy could accommodate even the thought of Emmanuel Mounier, whose advocacies Piwowarczyk otherwise found indefensible in light of Church teachings.[28] In this instance, however, Piwowarczyk's argument unintentionally recalled Mounier's own 1938 Statute of the Human Person, in which the French philosopher called "for a coalition for a personalist democracy" to protect "THE PERSON" against all established interests.[29]

Piwowarczyk had been one of interwar Poland's experts on Thomist natural law. The Vatican had welcomed his 1933 Polish translations of *Rerum Novarum* and *Quadragesimo Anno*. His textbook *Catholic Social Ethics* (*Katolicka etyka społeczna*) went through four editions in the 1930s and 1940s. It is a curious twist of fate that made this priest, who personified interwar social Catholicism, the intellectual force behind Poland's first postwar Catholic "journal of the laity."

Piwowarczyk's lay colleagues shared his deep appreciation of Maritain, albeit to varying degrees. Between 1945 and 1948, Jerzy Turowicz put together a crack team of rising stars in the literary world of postwar Poland who left the theology and philosophy mostly to their elder colleague of the cloth. These lay writers included Antoni Gołubiew, Józefa Hennel, Paweł Jasienica, Stefan Kisielewski, Hanna Malewska, Zofia Starowieyska-Morstin, Stanisław Stomma, and Jacek Woźniakowski. This team of prose writers, poets, and journalists was assembled from among Kraków literary circles; Catholic University of Lublin alumni; Warsaw academics; and forcibly resettled figures from Wilno, interwar

Poland's cultural haven, who had made their way through the ruined countryside to Poland's medieval capital.[30] *Tygodnik Powszechny*'s eclectic staff wrote on a wide range of topics: from the historical roots of postwar Poland's new borders, to contemporary trends in poetry, religious iconography, and urban design. Neither Piwowarczyk nor Turowicz wanted to impose an ideological straitjacket on the staff. Some considered themselves social Catholics, others liberals, still others socialists. There were even writers who invoked turn-of-the-century French republican reformer and politician Léon Bourgeois's philosophy of "solidarism"—a pluralist adaptation of corporatism in which all citizens shared a "moral duty of solidarity," intended to transform the liberal republic into the "cooperative republic."[31]

The atmosphere in the *Tygodnik Powszechny* offices in the mid-to-late 1940s evokes a range of associations from different periods in twentieth-century Polish history. Most days, it recalled the smoky cafés of the interwar republic.[32] Yet a student of modern Poland might also be tempted to compare it with dissident student clubs and protests that came decades later—from the Warsaw "Commandos" like Adam Michnik who organized the great student protests of 1968, to Waldemar Fydrych and the other organizers of carnivalesque street protests in Wrocław in 1987 and 1988.[33]

The man who made this sort of diversity possible was Jerzy Turowicz. This legendary editor has been widely mischaracterized by scholars. Neither an "ideological indifferentist" nor a "political pragmatist," Turowicz sought simply to take full advantage of the public forum available to him and his staff for as long as possible.[34] This approach derived from the Union's wartime ethos of humanism, positivism, and personalism, which Turowicz consciously strove to preserve. The very fact that he had been part of the Union shows that he was not at all "indifferent" to ideology: when faced with the opportunity to oppose the Nazi occupation, he jumped at it. The collapse of the interwar republic had underlined for him—as for so many of his French counterparts in the same era—the bankruptcy of liberal democracy. This is why, without a hint of opportunism, Turowicz wrote already in the third issue of *Tygodnik Powszechny* that "it is necessary to replace the anarchy of liberal democracy with the order of a planned democracy."[35]

As Turowicz understood it, political opposition must focus first and foremost on support for Poland's continued cultural and intellectual development. This was the message of the texts that Turowicz had prepared together with Jerzy Braun during the war for the clandestine bulletin *Kultura Jutra*. And this is the path that Turowicz chose once again as *Tygodnik Powszechny* editor. In both cases, the model was the approach of "organic work" pioneered by late-nineteenth-century Polish intellectuals, who preferred to educate the young, rather than watch them die in failed uprisings against Russia.[36]

Piwowarczyk and Turowicz differed in approach, but together they established *Tygodnik Powszechny* as a pillar of intellectual life in Communist Poland. The philosopher-priest represented the rear guard of a social-Catholic school whose last hurrah in 1945–47 coincided with the acceptance by the bulk of his fellow Catholic intellectuals that the country had gone Communist. Yet Piwowarczyk, too, accepted this state of affairs, endorsing Poland's revolutionary transformation as a way of giving meaning to the sacrifice of the wartime "generation of heroes and martyrs who with unswerving manliness suffered for Faith and Nation."[37]

By 1948, *Tygodnik Powszechny* was the sole remaining outpost of Thomist thought in Poland outside the Catholic University of Lublin. The faculty there included both surviving interwar cadres and, starting in the 1950s, younger scholars like the future Pope John Paul II. Their elders had studied under interwar Thomists like Antoni Szymański and Władysław Korniłowicz. These were scholars deeply in conversation with French Thomist thought—Maritain, in particular—and they imparted the Thomist canon to their students, despite increasing ideological pressure and even physical intimidation from the Stalinist secret police.[38]

## THE TWILIGHT OF SOCIAL CATHOLICISM

In 1948, a middle-aged canon law professor named Stefan Wyszyński became Poland's head bishop, succeeding the recently deceased Cardinal August Hlond. He would prove to be one of twentieth-century Europe's most influential clerics, leading the Polish episcopate through almost the entire Communist period.[39] Known in Poland today as the "Primate of the Millennium" (*Prymas Tysiąclecia*), Wyszyński in the 1960s became the international face of the Catholic Church's resistance to Communist encroachment, representing Poland at Vatican II

Fig. 3: Archbishop Stefan Wyszyński, Primate of Poland, 1948. Reproduced by permission of the Primate Stefan Cardinal Wyszyński Institute (*Instytut Pryma-sowski Stefana Kardynała Wyszyńskiego*).

and organizing a nine-year jubilee leading up to the millennial anniversary of Polish Christendom in 1966. In the face of constant interference and provocation by the Communist party, the "Millennium" proved a testament to the strength of popular religious sentiment on a continent long confronted with the specter of secularization.[40]

In 1948, however, all of this was still far in the future. Wyszyński came to the post of primate with barely eighteen months of experience as a bishop. Before that, he had been a seminary professor and a Catholic youth organizer.[41] In the six months before he became bishop of Lublin, Wyszyński contributed regularly to the Warsaw-based *Tygodnik Warszawski*. The journal's editor-in-chief from 1945 until early 1947 was Rev. Zygmunt Kaczyński, but Wyszyński's writings proved equally important in defining the journal's relationship to social Catholicism. In early 1946, Wyszyński challenged Marxists with a Thomist reading of "social progress": "Social progress can be found in the evolution of forms of social coexistence in tandem with better adaptations of those forms to the needs of human personhood as it develops."[42] Wyszyński's Thomist personalism positioned *Tygodnik Warszawski* close to Piwowarczyk's *Tygodnik Powszechny*.[43] Their ideological affinity was, however, short-lived: unlike their Kraków colleagues, Kaczyński and *Tygodnik Warszawski* diverged sharply from the so-called "Polish Revolution."

In March 1946, Wyszyński published an essay in defense of Pope Pius XII, responding to months of denunciations of the pontiff by *Kuźnica* (*Ironworks*) and other Polish Communist journals. Wyszyński portrayed the beleaguered pope as a defender of the "rights of the human person" against "totalitarianism," rather than a puppet of American capitalists, as Marxists made him out to be: "The entire struggle of the Pope for the security of the personal rights of human beings, for a personalist social, political, and economic order, a struggle unappreciated by the person in whose defense it is waged, creates a certain chasm between the Holy See and the other side."[44]

The defense of Pius XII was not central to the ideology of *Tygodnik Warszawski*—too many Poles resented the pope's refusal to acknowledge Poland's new postwar borders—but personalism was. So were democracy and an embrace of Poland's revolutionary transformation —albeit on terms defined by social Catholicism, not Communism. In the lead article of the journal's first issue, Kaczyński had written, "if today democracy has become the new global motto, then cannot every Catholic subscribe to this motto, since in the very premise of Christianity there resides such a definitive idea of equality among people, identical rights for all who were previously deprived of them?" *Tygodnik Warszawski* impressed upon its readers that Catholics had a moral obligation to shape the "new world order," which, if "its structure is not to be one-sided, must be built with the hands of all people of good faith. No one is allowed today to stand passively off to the side, or to isolate himself in waiting."[45]

Just as *Tygodnik Powszechny* was funded by the Kraków archdiocese, *Tygodnik Warszawski* debuted as an arm of the Archdiocese of Warsaw. Three of the five principal founders of *Tygodnik Warszawski* were priests with a history of active political and social engagement.[46] The abundance of priests within *Tygodnik Warszawski* made it the first of the Catholic weeklies to arouse the Communist establishment's suspicions. Jan Piwowarczyk was the lone clergyman on the *Tygodnik Powszechny* staff, while *Tygodnik Warszawski* seemed to be awash with men of the cloth. Furthermore, its patron was Cardinal Hlond, who was a far less effective protector than Sapieha.[47] After all, the primate had fled to France in 1940 and spent the war in exile; the PPR had no respect for a man whom they saw as a wartime defector. The journal's editor-in-chief, Kaczyński, had also just returned from exile. Last but not least, pro-Vatican articles like Wyszyński's defense of Pius XII seemed designed to set the journal's readers at loggerheads with the new regime, given its antagonism toward the Holy See.

The laymen who did write for *Tygodnik Warszawski* were no friends of the PPR either. They included politicians who had returned from exile in London and SP leaders close to Popiel. On December 8, 1946, *Tygodnik Warszawski* began publishing a column written by pseudonymous contributors from among Poland's Catholic students.[48] The editors and authors of the *Youth Column* (*Kolumna Młodych*) came from either wartime clandestine organizations or the few surviving nodes of the prewar Catholic Action movement. Most had fought in the Warsaw Uprising in August and September 1944. A number had done time in Soviet labor camps in the Urals, arrested following the Red Army's liberation of Poland for involvement with the Home Army.[49] Although there was nothing illegal or even clandestine about the *Ty-*

*godnik Warszawski* enterprise, its authors' wartime experience and ties to SP and the Home Army destined the group for particularly harsh treatment at the hands of the authorities.

## THE POLITICS OF THE CATHOLIC PRESS

SP's short-lived return to Polish public life was central to the fates of the three postwar Catholic weeklies. Initially, both *Tygodnik Powszechny* and *Tygodnik Warszawski* were edited by prominent Christian Democrats. *Tygodnik Warszawski*'s editor Kaczyński had, in fact, served as SP's minister in the London government. Meanwhile, Piwowarczyk wrote part of the program approved at SP's July 15, 1945 national convention.[50] In early 1946, writing under the pen name Mikołaj Patkowski, the *Tygodnik Powszechny* editor published a lengthy pamphlet entitled *SP and Catholics* (*Stronnictwo Pracy a katolicy*). Its message was that SP—as the one official, legitimate party of Catholics in Poland—was best suited to lead country and Church alike through a time of revolutionary social and political transformation.[51] As Jan Piwowarczyk's case shows, Catholic publishing was bound up with Christian Democracy in the first postwar years.[52]

SP also had the episcopate's seal of approval as the "party of Polish Catholics." Both Cardinal Hlond and Archbishop Sapieha offered their personal support to Popiel and his colleagues. *Tygodnik Warszawski* published a series of brief notes advertising SP's platform, as well as a homily by Hlond calling on Poles to combine "Christian patriotism" with "the healthy revolutionary content of the times." The only political force in Poland in 1945 that claimed to do both was Christian Democracy.[53]

In fact, *Tygodnik Warszawski* went beyond stumping for SP, reflecting deeply on the ideology that had inspired the Christian Democrats' program: social Catholicism. Between its first issue on November 11, 1945 and its last on August 29, 1948, more than half of *Tygodnik Warszawski*'s content dealt with Catholic social teaching.[54] The authors of these texts were often former wartime Union leaders (such as Jerzy Braun), or Christian Democrats who had done hard time in German captivity (such as Konstanty Turowski). Some espoused a vanguard social Catholicism that did not differ much from Catholic socialism. Others, meanwhile, sounded like they were living in the 1890s rather than the 1940s, repeating again and again that Catholics needed to go back to *Rerum Novarum* and to charity—as though the Bolshevik Revolution had never happened.[55]

Landing somewhere in the middle, the former POW Konstanty Turowski took a more pragmatic approach, comparing Communist proposals with their corresponding social-Catholic alternatives. Drawing on the 1931 encyclical *Quadragesimo Anno*, the Christian Democrat attempted to prove that social Catholicism simply made more sense for Poland's peasants and farmers than did Communist proposals of collectivization.[56]

At the end of January 1947, Polish Communists held the parliamentary elections promised at Yalta, only then to turn around and falsify the results. With many of his colleagues facing arrest or exile, former Christian Democratic underground leader Jerzy Braun sat down with *Tygodnik Warszawski* editor-in-chief Kaczyński to figure out how to keep the journal alive. Together, the two men decided that the journal had a better chance of surviving with a layman in the charge. Thus Braun took the priest's place at the weekly's helm.

Although *Tygodnik Warszawski*'s ties to SP had politicized the weekly, the staff's politics also made it into a journal of the laity. With Popiel's disappearance from the public arena following SP's co-optation by Jolt, *Tygodnik Warszawski* became the last stand for Polish Christian Democrats using Catholic philosophy to debunk Communist promises of justice for the working classes.

Paradoxically, *Tygodnik Warszawski*'s turn toward the laity made it less personalist. The former SP politicians who took over the journal in 1947 were far less in touch with transnational Catholic thought than priests like Kaczyński, Piwowarczyk, or Wyszyński. SP's founder Wojciech Korfanty had shown in his writings a keen affinity for Jacques Maritain's Thomist personalism.[57] Yet the next generation of SP leaders, while sharing Korfanty's nationalism—even his anti-Semitism—lacked his facility with French Catholic philosophy. Not only did *Tygodnik Warszawski*'s deepening connection to SP politicize the weekly, but it also made the actual content of the journal read more like a party-political bulletin than a forum for high-brow cultural and intellectual debate.

*Tygodnik Powszechny* was entirely different. True—Piwowarczyk occasionally used the journal's pages to lend support to SP, as when he

backed the bishops' 1946 call for a confessional Catholic voice in parliamentary politics: "We know that there are also Catholics in other
parties. But we know, moreover, that, for the complete fulfillment of
a Catholic program, it is necessary to have a separate political camp.
For these reasons, we consider the only proper and purposeful course
of action to be recognition of the project of creating a separate political organization of Catholics."[58] Yet, just as he had used a pen name
when writing his pamphlet for SP, so Piwowarczyk preferred to keep
politics out of the pages of *Tygodnik Powszechny*. The priest showed
a remarkable talent for figuring out just how much the weekly's authors could say without incurring the wrath of Communist censors and
provocateurs.

In mid-1947, Piwowarczyk left the editorial staff of *Tygodnik
Powszechny*, staying on formally only as the journal's ecclesiastical advisor. He had received several visits at the journal's offices in early 1947
from Adam Doboszyński, an interwar National Democratic politician
who had returned from London illegally, evading border guards, in
hopes of launching a new integralist movement in postwar Poland.[59]
Though he had only met briefly with Doboszyński, Piwowarczyk was
caught in the crosshairs of the secret police team surveilling him. As a
result, he, too, came under investigation. On the advice of Archbishop
Sapieha, Piwowarczyk withdrew as editor and moved to the countryside. Although himself under constant scrutiny, he continued to write
prolifically and contribute regularly to *Tygodnik Powszechny* until its
forced shuttering in 1953.

What conclusions can we draw from the experiences of *Tygodnik
Powszechny* and *Tygodnik Warszawski*? Though both journals piv-
oted almost simultaneously toward lay control, these shifts played out
very differently. Piwowarczyk had argued in the pages of *Tygodnik
Powszechny* for an explicitly Catholic political party only when the
fate of such a party hung in the balance. Once it had become clear that
the party was doomed, Piwowarczyk ceased his political commentary.
Unlike the laymen who took over *Tygodnik Warszawski*, Piwowarczyk
wrote thoughtful and considered essays on Catholic social teaching before, during, and after the crisis of SP; his writings never smacked of
propaganda. Catholic social thought was his life's work. And, like the
lay authors of *Tygodnik Powszechny*, he wrote about what interested

him. Stanisław Stomma wrote about law, Antoni Gołubiew about literature, Zbigniew Herbert about poetry and aesthetics.

Meanwhile, the shift toward the laity in *Tygodnik Warszawski* politicized the journal. Its lay editors sought not to find a place in the new political order, but to indict the PPR. In its final years, *Tygodnik Warszawski* became, in effect, an ersatz press organ for the defunct SP. In contrast, *Tygodnik Powszechny*, for better or for worse, avoided the bloody arena of party politics, looking to continue bearing witness to Catholicism in the face of an increasingly authoritarian regime.

The fallout from the falsified parliamentary elections of January 1947 soon demonstrated just how dangerous that arena could be. *Tygodnik Powszechny* and its sister journal *Znak* suffered censorship, surveillance, and threats against the person of Rev. Piwowarczyk.[60] Meanwhile, *Tygodnik Warszawski* tested ever more aggressively the patience of the new Communist establishment's censors.[61] The Communists did not take this well.

The Communist response began with an *ad hominem* press campaign against Jerzy Braun, accusing the former underground leader of wartime collaboration with the Nazis. Within a few months, the campaign widened to take on the entire staff of what one Communist newspaper caustically dubbed "the *Wall Street Weekly*." According to an unsigned editorial in another Communist paper, everything in the pages of *Tygodnik Warszawski* reflected an "Anglo-Saxon orientation," bought and paid for by American "Judas's dollars." The editorial continued, "Longing for the Anglo-Saxon order—alongside spies, speculators, and tax criminals—are journalists and essayists philosophizing on behalf of foreign agents about personalism, the sovereign rights of the individual, the autonomy of the spirit."[62]

Seeing the writing on the wall, Braun and his fellow editors at *Tygodnik Warszawski* decided that the 100th issue of their journal, published on October 19, 1947, would pull no punches. Here they laid out all of what they considered to be the journal's contributions to postwar Poland. In contrast with *Tygodnik Powszechny*'s turn toward culture, *Tygodnik Warszawski* had "devoted a great deal of attention to Christian social, economic, moral, and political doctrine. Taking a stand on current problems and conflicts in public life, it was—of necessity—more 'maximalist' and therefore drew upon itself many insults and heavy thunder from one side or another." Taking exception to the accusation that they were serving a foreign power, the editors underscored, "Despite the stubborn libeling of us for some sort of 'Anglo-Saxon orientation,' we stand decisively on Polish ground, on a foundation of the eternal Christian tradition of our nation."[63]

The editorial reads today like the captain of a sinking ship trying to explain himself, while refusing to abandon his post. Written entirely in past tense, the essay makes clear that the *Tygodnik Warszawski* staff knew that their time was almost up. Eight months later, the PPR turned against its leader Władysław Gomułka and his fellow "right-wing nationalist deviationists" in the Party. The coming of Stalinism to Poland meant mass arrests, repression, and show trials. *Tygodnik Warszawski* was, in the words of its *Youth Column* editor Wiesław Chrzanowski, "locked up along with its staff."[64] Mass arrests touched both former SP activists and all of *Tygodnik Warszawski*.

One of the accusations lodged against the Warsaw journal was that it had "become home to an illegal group of enemies of the democratic order." As the accusation went, these were all puppets of Karol Popiel —even though he had been in exile for a year by the time of the journal's shuttering. News of the arrests reached the SP chairman in Paris, and he felt duty-bound to exonerate his friends and former colleagues. In September 1948, eleven months after leaving Poland behind for the final time, Popiel issued a two-page statement. Writing from France, Popiel explained that he had left Warsaw of his own volition. Only after seeing the political storm provoked by PSL leader Stanisław Mikołajczyk's illegal escape from Poland did Popiel conclude that, "very soon, well before the end of the present era, the Communist dictatorship will be a permanent feature of Polish life."[65]

As to his former colleagues, Popiel imagined that his "decision to stay in exile for a second time, taken while already abroad, had to have taken his old friends in Poland entirely by surprise, earning their disapproval." Dismissing the accusations against the *Tygodnik Warszawski* staff as "completely inexplicable," Popiel accurately diagnosed why authorities had closed the journal: "the security apparatus needs to be able—even if on entirely spurious terms—to lodge an accusation of alleged ties between Catholic media in Poland and my activities abroad, in order to provide a pretext for brutal repressions intended to destroy the last vestiges of Catholic publishing in Poland."[66]

Although *Youth Column* contributors like Wiesław Chrzanowski were treated less severely than *Tygodnik Warszawski*'s older leadership, all activists were subjected to multiple rounds of physically exacting interrogations. In the priest Zygmunt Kaczyński's case—and likely others, as well—this extended to systematic torture. In show trials held in January 1950, the *Youth Column* staff received from three to eight years' prison time on the paradoxical charge of "anti-state, anti-people, illegal activities conducted in a legal manner." In March and April 1951, the elder activists and editors of *Tygodnik Warszawski*—lumped together with the former SP leaders who, unlike Popiel, had remained on Polish soil—were given separate show trials. Their sentences ranged from fifteen years to life in prison, their punishment memorialized by the regime in a thick book entitled *Allies of the Gestapo* (*Sojusznicy Gestapo*).[67] Kaczyński, the wartime minister of the London exile government, died in prison under mysterious circumstances two years into his sentence.[68] The rest were amnestied in 1955–56 under the auspices of de-Stalinization, emaciated and often crippled.

## THE CATHOLIC-SOCIALIST ALTERNATIVE

Of the three postwar weeklies, *Dziś i Jutro* was the only one to take an overtly pro-Soviet line. At the same time, Piasecki and company professed a commitment to social Catholicism. The journal attempted to square the two by arguing that any commitment to social justice necessitated political realism. In the journal's first lead article, its founder asked his readers to look at the social responsibilities of postwar Polish Catholics through the lens of geopolitics. What he offered was a vision of how to position a newly Communist Poland vis-à-vis the USSR, the United States, France, and Germany. Piasecki reasoned, "If we predict an impending Anglo-Saxon–Soviet conflict and we believe that it will determine decisively and exclusively the subsequent course of Polish history, then the situation is not easy. [ . . . ] the expectation of an impending war has created a different situation: some Poles, though they live in Poland, find their hearts and minds already in the West, while others have long since emigrated psychologically to the East."[69]

Piasecki's message was that Poles, instead of worrying about whether or not the ongoing "Polish Revolution" was the work of Soviet agents, should focus on rebuilding their lives. Their obligation as both good

Poles and good Catholics was to live those lives committed to a program of "revolution." At the same time, Piasecki made a geopolitical argument, insisting that a Polish-Soviet alliance made sense for both countries. According to *Dziś i Jutro*'s founder, the USSR deserved credit for securing for Poland "the return of the western lands, the acceleration of social and economic transformation in the service of social radicalism, and a tradition of shared struggle against the Germans." In his reasoning, Piasecki showed a remarkable continuity with his interwar fascist writings, combining Catholic patriotism with the stance of a Russophile wrapping himself in the flag of Polish "*raison d'État.*"[70]

Mikołaj Kunicki is undoubtedly correct that *Dziś i Jutro*'s profession of social Catholicism reflected a certain recasting of its ex-fascist elders' integral nationalism. Yet this does not mean that the new journal's social Catholicism was a mere ideological head-fake. It was not Piasecki, but a younger generation of French-inspired activists who supplied the details of *Dziś i Jutro*'s ideology, filling in the gaps around Piasecki's broad strokes. Wojciech Kętrzyński and Andrzej Krasiński, the most prolific writers among Piasecki's wartime recruits, genuinely believed that the "Polish Revolution" was the fulfillment of Catholic social teaching.

What they brought to *Dziś i Jutro* was their aristocratic lineage and concomitant love of all things French. As Longina Jakubowska observes, "the gentry saw no contradiction between their cosmopolitan outlook and patriotism."[71] Translations of writings by Maritain, Mounier, theologians like Yves Congar, and novelists like Daniel-Rops and Georges Bernanos became common in the pages of Piasecki's journal. What this meant was that *Dziś i Jutro* editors kept up with cutting-edge trends in Western European Catholic life. En route to positing a heterodox Catholicism that met the needs of the Communist government, they sought to establish *bona fides* both in Polish nationalism and in European Catholic culture writ large.[72]

The legendary Communist poet Julian Tuwim penned many a couplet mocking Piasecki's megalomania and the convenient amnesia of his supporters: "Forgetting about their yesterday / With 'Today and Tomorrow' he flirts today."[73] Tuwim was hardly the only establishment luminary to see Piasecki this way. Even Władysław Gomułka expressed concern that Piasecki's fascist past was not past.[74]

It is perhaps too easy today to follow either Gomułka or Tuwim in their different rationales for seeing *Dziś i Jutro* as a group of power-hungry cynics. The fact of the matter, however, is that the journal's youngest contributors did serious philosophical writing, on par with their most renowned counterparts across Europe. They would become Poland's first Catholic socialists, putting the "human person" at the service of Marxist revolution for religious, as well as ethnonational, reasons.

At the beginning of May 1946, the young writers of the *Dziś i Jutro* movement received a pleasant surprise: Emmanuel Mounier, one of the cultural heroes of their KN guerrilla-fighting days, came to Poland and agreed to meet with them. Unlike Jerzy Turowicz, they had never before personally encountered Mounier or any of his *Esprit* colleagues. Now Piasecki's staff—Kętrzyński, Krasiński, and Konstanty Łubieński, as well as the leader himself—had the chance to learn face-to-face from the great Catholic theorist of "revolution."

## MOUNIER IN POLAND

It is easy to understand why Mounier was attractive to Polish Catholics who saw their faith as a reason to join the "Polish Revolution." Mounier believed that figuring out how to respond to Marxism required first-hand knowledge of how it was reshaping daily life. And so it was that Mounier ended up in Poland in 1946.

Goulven Boudic is right to describe postwar Poland as a "country of reference" for Mounier.[75] The French thinker felt so personally invested in the trip to Poland that, although he spoke no Polish, he became the delegation's leader.[76] At his side was the priest Alexandre Glasberg, a Ukrainian-born Jewish convert to Catholicism who spoke fluent Polish—as did the émigré sculptor Marek Szwarc and the historian Ambroise Jobert, who took turns translating for Mounier and the other travelers: priest and law professor Jean Boulier, Dominican editor Pierre Boisselot, *Humanité* editor Pierre Courtade, composer Elsa Barraine, journalist Gaston Fournier, the PCF's dedicated "Franco-Polish friendship" propagandist Maurice Thiédot, and Angèle Fumet—daughter of Catholic publisher Stanislas Fumet.[77] Emmanuel Mounier kept a day-by-day diary of the journey, which provides a detailed portrait of the delegation's travels, conversations, and conclusions.

Between May 6 and May 31, 1946, the delegation visited a handful of cities and several score towns and villages, making contact with statesmen, bishops (including Sapieha and Katowice bishop Stanisław Adamski), and factory managers.[78] The main event was a lecture delivered by Mounier in the Auditorium Maximum of Kraków's Jagiellonian University.[79]

On his return to France, Mounier devoted a long article in the June 1946 issue of *Esprit* to his travels around Poland. He expressed his sympathy for the wartime suffering of the Polish people, whose misery had been evident to the French delegation.[80] At the same time, however, Mounier and his French fellow travelers were by and large critical of the reticent, if not outright defensive, stance toward Marxism that they encountered among Poles. In Mounier's eyes, for example, "the overwhelming majority of the nation" was falling prey to an "obsession with Russia." Unfortunately—Mounier argued—this majority failed to understand Poland's unique "world-historical importance." Of all the nations of the world, the Poles alone had the power to "reconcile the Catholic Church and socialism."[81]

For Mounier, the historic opportunity afforded to Poland demanded certain compromises. Poles should insist neither on fidelity to the nation, nor on free and democratic elections in keeping with the letter of the Yalta agreement, for such elections "would be catastrophic if held today." According to the French philosopher, Poland was in no danger of becoming a "seventeenth Soviet republic." Poles, then, were supposed to let themselves be carried along by the current of history. The alternative meant denying so-called historical necessity.[82]

Seventy years on, Mounier's article is frustrating reading for anyone with even a basic knowledge of modern European history. In the two years following the French delegation's visit to Poland, Stalinism achieved a stranglehold over Poland, consolidating power on a wave of falsified elections and mass arrests. This was a decade of repressions, pogroms, and guerrilla fighting in Poland, what Jan T. Gross has called the "ghastly decade" (*upiorna dekada*—1939–48).[83] Mounier felt no qualms about pigeon-holing certain Catholics as "reactionary" during his visit. When they later found themselves in interrogation rooms or in prison, Mounier was long gone, and he paid their tragic fates no heed. The historian John Hellman's conclusion seems justified: "Mounier seemed rather short on memory and long on rationalization."[84] And yet, supporting a Marxist revolution in 1946 is not the same thing as apologizing for a Stalinism that had not yet begun in Poland.

Still, in his dealings with Poland, Mounier proved to be extremely naïve. He believed that the clergy, factory directors, and state functionaries whom he met were in a position to speak freely with him. Even some of Mounier's fellow delegation members criticized his gullibility. Particularly dangerous was his uncritical acceptance of his Polish guides' use of the word "reactionaries," a term that he then repeated in his writings to denote anyone opposed to the "Polish Revolution." Mounier thereby homogenized everyone who fell outside the boundaries of his emerging vision of Poland's Catholic-socialist future as a gray mass of political enemies. Politically, *Esprit* was right about many things in 1946, as it criticized France's Christian Democrats and other mainstream parties for supporting nuclear rearmament and for waging brutal colonial warfare in Indochina and North Africa.[85] On Poland, however, Mounier got it wrong.

## MOUNIER ON ANTI-SEMITISM

And yet, Mounier was spot-on in his diagnosis of a perverse consequence of the war's end in Poland: the revival of Catholic anti-Semitism. Mounier wrote in June 1946 of the German extermination of Poland's Jewish population:

> One might have believed that this hecatomb would have put an end to racial antagonism, all the more so since most Poles behaved admirably in their protection of the persecuted. However, we found in almost every circle, even Christian circles, indeed even among the most generous or the most highly placed among Catholics, an anti-Semitism as vigorous as if extermination had never been visited upon the nation of Israel. [ . . . ] But the hardened attitude adopted by all at the very moment this subject is broached, without anyone realizing that they are falling into the most common, worldwide patterns of anti-Semitism, contributes to a climate of contempt, distance, and diffuse hostility, in which acts of violence whose roots lie elsewhere encounter here, whatever anyone says, a sort of complicity.[86]

Mounier's diagnosis is remarkably accurate. Perhaps the explanation is his own experience watching friends, mentors, and disciples of his flirt with anti-Semitism: first in French Action; then in various "nonconformist" movements of the 1930s (especially the Young Right, or *Jeune Droite*); and, finally, in the Vichy regime.[87]

What is most striking, however, is that prewar anti-Semitism retained its currency in postwar Poland—even acquiring new power—after the Shoah. The scale of human trauma seemed to elude even Catholic activists who worked to divorce social Catholicism from the integral nationalism that had dominated Catholicism in prewar Poland. Postwar Poland's Catholic vanguard by and large rejected the pogroms that awaited scores of returning Holocaust survivors in 1945 and 1946. Nonetheless, they generally believed that prewar Poland had suffered from a "Jewish problem" and that the Holocaust had done much to resolve that problem.[88]

Paradoxically, these included even Catholics who had been actively involved in rescuing Jews from Nazi hands throughout the Second World War. The Catholic *Żegota* campaign to rescue Jewish children had been coordinated by members of Christian Democracy's "Union" movement. And yet it was none other than Union leader Jerzy Braun who, in July 1945, expressed relief that the war had "(finally!)" transformed Poland's social and demographic structures. By this he meant that economic power had passed from Poland's exterminated Jewish populations to Polish "peasant sons [ . . . ] to whom Jews could not even compare in terms of courage." Anticipating that his position might be described as anti-Semitic, Braun wrote, "Nonetheless, what some take to be anti-Semitism are 'simply economic laws of nature for which there is no alternative.'"[89]

Part of the explanation for Braun's perverse postwar stance lies in the anti-Semitism of SP founder Korfanty, whose writings formed the bread and butter of Polish Christian Democratic ideology. Braun's belief that "economic laws of nature" could explain the Jews' extermination shows that Korfanty's proposals for ethnic cleansing did not die with him nor with the end of the Second World War. Postwar anti-Semitism thus drew on both prewar ideology and the experience of war. Not all postwar Christian Democrats thought like Braun, but those who did believed that there was no contradiction between Korfanty's program and *Żegota*'s rescue campaign. It was both wrong to kill Jews and right to drive them out of Poland. This kind of thinking explained the widespread Catholic permissiveness toward, for example, the July 4, 1946 Kielce Pogrom, which resulted in the murder of approximately forty Polish Jews.[90]

Jan T. Gross is right to underscore that Catholic activists did not react uniformly to postwar pogroms. For example, the editors of *Tygodnik Powszechny* responded strongly to the Kielce killings: "As Catholic writers and journalists, we declare that no conditions can justify the trampling of divine law and the shaming of Poland's good name in the world."[91] Yet the Polish bishops virtually ignored the human tragedy and its underlying causes. Rather than condemn the pogrom as a gross violation of the Catholic social ethics that they were so ardently asserting in an era of Marxist revolution, almost all of the bishops treated it as a provocation: Communists taking "first shots against the Church in Poland" by impugning Poland's Catholic population. (Bishop Teodor Kubina of Częstochowa was the notable exception.[92]) Primate Hlond's statement was even more egregious than Braun's had been a year earlier: "I deeply desire that the Jewish problem of the postwar world shall at last find its proper solution."[93]

Aside from *Tygodnik Powszechny*, Poland's Catholic journals stayed silent on the Kielce Pogrom. Somehow no one thought to revisit what Mounier had written just a few weeks earlier. Although all of postwar Poland's Catholic writers participated in heated debates over the role that Mounier's philosophy should play in their country, not a single author returned to his diagnosis of Poland's persistent Catholic anti-Semitism. Mounier himself, in subsequent dealings with Polish Catholics over the next four years, seemed to have forgotten his own words. Catholic anti-Semitism evaporated from *Esprit*'s institutional memory.

Jacques Maritain, meanwhile, was appalled to hear of the Kielce Pogrom, and it prompted him to write to the Holy See's undersecretary of state Giovanni Battista Montini—the future Pope Paul VI—protesting Catholic complicity in the "unprecedented fury of humiliation and cruelty" visited upon Europe's Jews since 1939.[94] As French ambassador to the Vatican, the Thomist wanted to hear a clear denunciation from Pope Pius XII of the persistence of violent anti-Semitism in the aftermath of the Holocaust. No such statement was forthcoming, however, and Maritain's disgust played a role in his decision to resign his ambassadorship in 1948.

While Maritain's reaction to the Kielce Pogrom was one of principle, his "revolutionary" colleague seemed to prioritize tactical concerns. Mounier had made clear that, in Poland, he preferred *Dziś i Jutro*—with its anti-Semitic, ex-fascist leadership—over the less "hardy" writers of *Tygodnik Powszechny* and *Znak*.[95] Thus began a curious romance between the French progressives and the Polish ex-fascists. Piasecki's staff would, in fact, gain a reputation in Western Europe over the next decade as the most open-minded and tolerant among Polish Catholics. And yet it was not Piasecki's, but rather Turowicz's movement (which included the future John Paul II) that would play a role in the early 1960s in initiating Polish Catholic-Jewish dialogue.[96] Meanwhile, those who stayed with Piasecki beyond de-Stalinization would, in the late 1960s, join in an anti-Semitic campaign launched by the Communists themselves.[97] Mounier's accurate June 1946 diagnosis of anti-Semitism went nowhere, as *Esprit* lent its support to *Dziś i Jutro* and failed to follow up in the aftermath of the Kielce Pogrom.

## TAKING SIDES: "ARISTOCRATIC" KRAKÓW AND "HARDY" WARSAW

Why bother with Emmanuel Mounier? After all, he was a French public intellectual. His name was hardly on the tip of every Pole's tongue in 1946.

Yet it would be a mistake to underestimate Mounier's influence at this moment in Polish history. He was an authority, a French trailblazer of Catholic socialism. Polish intellectuals had a long-standing love affair with French intellectual life, and Mounier had made a small splash in the Polish literary press already in the 1930s. In 1934—two years before releasing his widely read *Manifesto in the Service of Personalism*—Mounier published an article in Poland's *Wiadomości Literackie* (*Literary News*). In that essay, he touted *Esprit* for "going beyond capitalism and Communism, but at the same time opposing Stalinism and fascist-inclined nationalism." His answer both to the "established order" of liberalism and to "totalitarianism" was the same: personalism.[98] Despite Mounier's declared opposition to Stalinism, the integral nationalists who dominated Poland's Catholic press in the 1930s derided him as a proponent of "Christian Communism."[99] After World War II, Mounier would prove them right.

But in 1934, for Jerzy Turowicz and his fellow young Polish Catholics who sought to reconcile Catholicism with the modern world, Mounier was a revelation. Their generation of Catholic activists was born between 1905 and 1915; they came of age between the two world wars. Throughout their high-school and university years, they had followed every new development in the philosophy of social Catholicism and in the Catholic Action movement. Yet the ascendancy of Emmanuel Mounier augured something entirely new.

Ten years later, Polish Catholic intellectuals were divided on Mounier once again. Some contributors to the three nascent postwar weeklies loved Mounier; others hated him. But all knew who he was and cared about what he had to say. As one-time Piasecki disciple Janusz Zabłocki later put it, "The influence of Mounier's stay in Poland cannot be measured only in terms of articles published or lectures given by him. His contact with representatives of Catholic circles—in their direct and open confrontation of traditional Polish Catholicism with the thought and attitudes of French Catholics—triggered a creative intellectual ferment that would continue to bear fruit long after his departure from Poland."[100]

In the end, Mounier was partially responsible for fissures within the Polish intellectual world. The activists of *Dziś i Jutro* would join forces with a Stalinist regime, while the writers of *Tygodnik Warszawski* went into Stalinist prisons. Meanwhile, *Tygodnik Powszechny* tried simply to keep its head above water, while staying true to its watchwords of dialogue and dignity.

In early 1946, the bulk of the Mounierian "true believers" in Poland had come from this last group. Jan Piwowarczyk, the clarion voice of interwar social Catholicism, disapproved of Mounier's revolutionary brand of personalism, but, within his journal, he was the exception. When Turowicz announced the group's intention to spin off a new Catholic monthly journal modeled on *Esprit*, Piwowarczyk took himself out of the equation.

Turowicz's point man for the new monthly *Znak* was the twenty-two-year-old philosophy student Jerzy Radkowski. Archbishop Sapieha took an interest in this young veteran of the underground, helping him to gain access to a range of French-language reading material. This included back issues of *Esprit*, which Radkowski devoured hungrily. When Mounier and his colleagues came to Kraków in May 1946, it was Radkowski who shuttled them around town. The young philosopher joined Turowicz in pitching the project for a Polish *Esprit* to Mounier, who reacted warmly, betraying no hint of the aloofness that he would later show.[101] This was the zenith of *Tygodnik Powszechny*'s fascination with Mounier. But all of this would change within a matter of weeks.

What soured Turowicz and his Kraków colleagues on Mounier and *Esprit* was the article that Mounier published on his return to Paris. On seeing their hero pronounce judgment on them in the pages of a journal that they had long idolized, the editors of *Tygodnik Powszechny* and the new *Znak* did not know what to do. The Mounier of 1946 was no longer the self-proclaimed anti-Stalinist of 1934. Instead, Mounier would defend Soviet policy in Central and Eastern Europe, entangle *Esprit* with Communism, and receive a warm invitation to join the PCF.[102]

Fascinated as they were with Mounier's promise of personalist "revolution," Turowicz and company were realists. Inspired by Mounier's energetic writing in their youth, they were nonetheless unprepared for his reckless endorsement of Soviet anti-capitalism after the war. They did not give up on French personalism, but neither did they agree to advocate on behalf of a Communist takeover.

*Dziś i Jutro*, on the other hand, did precisely this. However opportunistic their ex-fascist elders, the wartime and postwar generations were—by and large—men of principle. They had read Mounier for the first time either in Urbanowicz's underground wartime translation, or after the war had ended. For them, Mounier was more than a philosopher: he was a prophet of justice and dignity. The young Catholic "revolutionaries" who had come of age in the wartime Confederation of the Nation soon found the postwar Mounier compelling for the same reason that so troubled their Kraków elders like Turowicz. The problem was that Mounier's loyalty to "revolution" was so total that he ultimately proved willing to sacrifice the dignity of individual persons in the service of Soviet collectivism.

Mounier's travel diary from May 1946 shows just how differently he viewed *Dziś i Jutro* and *Tygodnik Powszechny*. According to Mounier, *Esprit* and *Dziś i Jutro* shared the same basic ethos. Both sought to fuse Catholicism with revolutionary socialism; both diverged from the teachings of the Church hierarchy. Meanwhile, Mounier described his admirers in Kraków as "encrusted in their ferocious patriotism and this same manner of being; despite their declared attitude of openness, [they are] in bitter opposition [to the regime], and this threatens to derail their project" (May 19). In contrast, the young activists of *Dziś i Jutro* "even seemed rather shy to us, these people reputed to have been 'paid off by the Marxists.'" They were, in any event, "the boldest young Catholic group" that Mounier had ever encountered. For this reason, "we promised each other that we would maintain very close ties" (May 29).[103] One month later, in the pages of *Esprit*, Mounier wrote, "Kraków, the aristocratic citadel of old Catholicism, is more timid than Warsaw."[104] By Kraków, he meant *Tygodnik Powszechny*; by Warsaw, Mounier meant the youth of *Dziś i Jutro*.

The difference in these two characterizations speaks for itself. Mounier was aware of Bolesław Piasecki's shady past—his bizarre conversion from fascism to philo-Communism and his reputation as a Soviet agent. In Mounier's eyes, this made the authentic revolutionary fervor of Piasecki's young followers all the more seductive. In fact, Mounier's own life experience inclined him to forgive Piasecki and the other *Dziś i Jutro* elders their dubious conversions to Catholic "revolution." His own wartime experience, after all, had its paradoxes: before he went on an anti-Vichy hunger strike, he spent a year teaching at Vichy's elite academy for future leaders. Mounier's interactions with Jerzy Turowicz's circle proved to be a mere courtesy, while the French thinker expected to exert a much greater influence on the youth of *Dziś i Jutro*. And he was right.

Meanwhile, disillusioned with Mounier and *Esprit*, the editors at *Tygodnik Powszechny* went out of their way to raise the Polish profile of Jacques Maritain, as well as other prominent French Catholic writers, including Daniel-Rops, Georges Bernanos, and François Mauriac.[105] Unlike Mounier, Maritain was no longer in fashion in postwar Poland. The personalist vocabulary that the Thomist had provided for Catholic social teaching sounded increasingly "reactionary" to the new Communist establishment. Promoting Maritain rather than Mounier between 1946 and 1948 was thus as much a political as a philosophical statement. It was *Tygodnik Powszechny*'s way of saying yes to personalism, but no to Catholic socialism.

The writers of *Tygodnik Powszechny* and *Znak* were not anti-Communist dissidents, but, in their eyes, Mounier had gone too far. Turowicz's wartime affiliation with the Union did not make him into a Christian Democrat, but it cemented his commitment to an older form of social Catholicism that he and his staff retained from Catholic activism in the interwar years.[106] The *Tygodnik Powszechny* staff set boundaries for themselves in their public activism, rejecting open political involvement in favor of what they considered to be Poland's "national interest."

## BETWEEN MINIMALISM AND MAXIMALISM

After the French delegation's departure, the newly constituted staff of *Znak* met to try to make sense of what had transpired during the visit. The contents were already set for the first two issues of the new monthly, but, when Mounier criticized the Kraków intellectuals in his June 1946 article, *Znak* had to respond. In their third issue, which appeared in mid-fall of 1946, the Poles published a lengthy essay by the new journal's co-editor, the law professor Stanisław Stomma. Adjacent to the essay was the transcript of a roundtable discussion featuring four of the new journal's contributors.[107] This was the last serious discussion that Mounier would receive for the next four years in either *Tygodnik Powszechny* or *Znak*, and it would define these journals' ideological profile for the next forty years. In their rejection of Mounier's total commitment to "revolution," the Catholic activists of Kraków drew a line in the sand. While colleagues elsewhere cast their lot either with ethnonational Catholic socialism or with anti-Communist dissidence, the men and women of *Tygodnik Powszechny* and *Znak* declared that, like Poland's late-nineteenth-century positivists, they would defend Poland's "national interest" by focusing on the preservation of Polish culture.

The title of Stomma's essay—"The Maximalist and Minimalist Social Tendencies of Catholics" (*Maksymalne i minimalne tendencje społeczne katolików*)—marshaled an ambiguous terminology that continues to confuse commentators to this day.[108] The scholarly consensus has been that the Catholic activists of Kraków unanimously embraced Stomma's essay as a mission statement. Their critics later accused them of having sold out—by becoming "minimalists."[109] Yet this careless parroting of Stomma's phrasing reflects a fundamental misunderstanding of what he was trying to do. His goal was to open a debate on whether or not Polish Catholics could and should continue to count on France—as Polish intellectuals had for centuries—to guide them in shaping the cultural, social, and political life of their country.

To be fair, Stomma did not make things easy for his readers. Rather than lead with his main argument, Stomma rambled for four pages about

STANISŁAW STOMMA: MAKSYMALNE I MINIMALNE
TENDENCJE SPOŁECZNE KATOLIKÓW — Z DYSKUSJI
REDAKCYJNEJ — DYSKUSJE MIĘDZY KATOLIKAMI
FRANCUSKIMI ● EMANUEL MOUNIER: PRZEKRÓJ IDE-
OWY FRANCJI ROKU 1946 — ODPOWIEDŹ NA ANKIE-
TĘ ● HANNA MALEWSKA: FARYZEIZM ● JERZY ZA-
WIEYSKI: MĄŻ DOSKONAŁY (c. d.)
ZDARZENIA — KSIĄŻKI — LUDZIE

KRAKÓW
ROK I. ● WRZESIEŃ - GRUDZIEŃ ● 1946

3

Fig. 4: Front cover of the
monthly journal *Znak* (*Sign*),
September-December 1946
issue. Stanisław Stomma's
programmatic article appeared
in this issue, as did an essay by
Emmanuel Mounier. Repro-
duced by permission of the
editors of *Znak*.

Oswald Spengler's *Decline of the West* (*Der Untergang das Abend-
landes*), considering it in reference to postwar Poland and France.
Stomma then referenced Maritain to show that Spengler had convinced
leading Catholic thinkers in Western Europe of the decline of occiden-
tal culture—of which Communism's spread, Stomma argued, was the
latest sign. Next came a fairly dense statement about the importance
of the debate that he was looking to start: "The recent visit of French
Catholic writers in Poland occasioned lively discussions in the Polish
press, and it should not be surprising that the Polish Left took advantage of the opportunity to renew its accusations against Polish Catholics, charging them with the mistakes of France's Catholic intellectual
elite, on which it pronounces summary judgment based on very limited
recent experience with one particular group of radicals."[110] Acknowledging that *Esprit* was, in fact, "radical," Stomma exhorted his readers to understand that one group alone cannot "constitute a basis for
drawing conclusions about the entirety of French Catholicism."[111]

What had radicalized *Esprit*, according to Stomma, was the question of how Catholics could best make their voices heard on social and political issues. Continuing the uncompromising anti-Communist line of Pope Pius XI seemed unrealistic in an era of Communist ascendancy over half of Europe.[112] But Stomma also blamed Mounier for undermining the traditional Catholic approach to social justice. This is what Stomma understood—and criticized—as the essential message of Mounier's May 1946 visit to Poland:

> Catholic social doctrine belongs to an old European civilization, while socialism must be acknowledged as the beginning and the basis of a new civilization. [ . . . ] Personal conversations with our French guests have confirmed the thesis that radical French groups live under the presumption of the inevitable victory of socialism, with all of its consequences. Anyone with a deeper familiarity with the attitude of the French masses knows how well this type of historiosophy corresponds to predominant French attitudes. The French proletariat, in large part self-consciously Communist, moves intentionally toward a great historical transformation, and lives according to its vision of the new socialist era.[113]

While the French proletariat was actively pushing for revolution, the French middle classes, according to Stomma, were inclined to "capitulate immediately" in favor of revolution's "inexorability." It was these French bourgeois whom Stomma described as "minimalist and pessimistic," particularly "compared with Polish Catholics."[114]

Meanwhile, the Poles, according to Stomma, suffered from a different flaw. This was "thoughtlessness," which Stomma described as "Poland's national trait."[115] Because Poles, as "maximalists," rejected any "Catholic ideology divorced from the living tissue of the national organism," with every new day they believed ever more inexorably in the coming of "a conflict in the immediate future."[116] This worried Stomma: "We do not know if, when, and how a conflict will play out in Poland between the Catholic camp and the camp of warring socialism."

It was here that *Znak*'s role became clear. The journal was to become a bulwark of "reservists" in the Catholic cause—a last outpost of social Catholicism.[117] As one of *Znak*'s leaders, however, Stomma believed in taking what was best in "the truly Catholic stance" of Maritain and Mounier. Whatever the flaws of their radicalism, French Catholics enjoyed a "greater civilizational maturity," which in turn made it easier for them to separate "social and political" from "religious and moral" issues.[118] Poles' failure to recognize this separation, meanwhile, resulted from their relative youth as a civilization compared to France.

Stomma's essay has been misread for decades—for example, as the carefully staged unveiling of a fully formed ideological alternative to social Catholicism. But this was no substitution of political realism for Catholic social teaching.[119] Stomma was deeply torn, and his argument in this seminal essay was neither linear nor fully articulated. Stomma's equivocation and ambivalence were clear, alternating as he did between genuflection and slaps across the face for both French and Polish Catholic thinkers and activists. His deterministic "civilizational" argument seemed to negate any possibility of a normative prescription for Polish Catholics. It is thus entirely unclear what the "reservists" of *Znak* would actually do if called upon to defend Catholicism in Poland.

What is clear is that Stomma wanted to help end the civil war in progress in Poland's forests, villages, and prisons. And yet, ironically, his article deepened, instead of healing, divisions within the very camp that he sought to consolidate: the Catholic activists. What Stomma rejected was any presumed Polish obligation to national tradition, arguing instead that the goals of personalism and social justice alone were enough to give meaning to Catholic activism. Stomma was trying to find a new basis for unity across confessional and ideological divides at the very moment when the drive to "revolution" was drawing new battle lines and reinforcing old ethnonational divides.

It is ironic that such an ambiguous exercise in circumlocution as Stomma's essay was received by Polish Catholic activists in 1946 as a declaration of war on social Catholicism.[120] In March 1947, Jerzy Braun, for example, chided Stomma for "overreaching indifferentism," a consequence—Braun surmised—of "how strong an influence Mounier's argumentation has had on Stomma's reasoning."[121] Braun argued that "social maximalism" must fight on, despite the French-inspired concerns of Stomma and his ilk. Braun's goal was for Polish lay activists to come to the opposite conclusions from Mounier, "with his thesis that the system can be Communist while the spirit will remain Catholic. This is a horrible misunderstanding that has led to the entire catastrophe of modern civilization."[122]

Unlike Stomma, Braun made a simple and straightforward argument. He also did an excellent job of poking holes in Stomma's exposition. Stomma had ignored Maritain and Mounier's distinction between "the individual" and "the person." Without this distinction, there could be no personalism.

Braun was not the only one to criticize Stomma in the pages of *Tygodnik Warszawski*. The young legal scholar Tadeusz Przeciszewski, too, criticized Stomma for not differentiating "between the Church and the social and political camp of the Catholic laity."[123] Even more than Braun, Przeciszewski manifested the moral indignation of a principled anti-Communist: "It is impermissible to conduct a discussion with Marxists on the question of whether the Church—as E. Mounier understands it in France—should swear off the attempt to fight for its own idea of the social order and capitulate to Marxism, retreating to the last line of defense—exclusively religious and moral values— or instead be tempted by its own program of social transformation and proceed to fight for that program over and against the Marxist alternative."

As political refugees from SP flooded the staff of *Tygodnik Warszawski* in 1946 and 1947, the journal took on an aggressively political tone. Indignant about the co-optation of their party, SP activists like Braun and Przeciszewski sought an opponent. This needed to be a fellow Catholic activist, someone whom they could attack without incurring the wrath of Communist press censors. In this respect, Stomma was an ideal scapegoat.

Several months had elapsed between the publication of the fateful issue of *Znak* in the fall of 1946 and *Tygodnik Warszawski*'s stinging rebuke in the spring of 1947. It is not the case that Braun read Stomma's essay and immediately responded to it. His attack on Stomma was less about Stomma himself, and more about the falsified elections of January 19, 1947, which revealed the bad faith underlying the Yalta Accords. When the Christian Democrats' hopes were crushed, they channeled their anger against Stomma. They knew that Stomma was no Communist, yet they saw in *Znak* a permissiveness, an unwillingness to fight, that they took as emblematic of their own exclusion from postwar Poland's revolutionary mainstream.

Despite a number of well-founded, biting criticisms of Stomma's thought, then, the passionate press debates surrounding his essay were not really about the essay itself. Jerzy Braun, for example, seemed unable to decide whether Stomma was actually a minimalist (like his presumed hero Mounier) or rather a "social indifferentist." The latter, according to Braun, implied belief that life on earth was relatively insignificant because true life would come only in union with God in the supernatural realm. Such metaphysical reflections, however, were a far cry from what Stomma had actually written. Stomma may have described Mounier's thought as "truly Catholic," but nowhere did he identify himself or *Znak* with Mounier, or for that matter, even speak approvingly of the French personalist.

Stomma became a *bête noire* of postwar Catholic debates, a scapegoat, after offering "ill-timed advice." Yet the passivity and the surrender to Communism by French lay Catholics were no reason for celebration, according to Stomma. Rather, it was only against the backdrop of looming civil war in Poland between the "Catholic camp" and "warring socialism" that France began to look good to Stomma. This was not pride in some new "minimalist" ideology, but instead an expression of regret that Catholic "revolution" had failed to eject integral nationalism.

## A BALANCING ACT

A decade later, writing under different political circumstances, Stomma would call himself a "neo-positivist."[124] What this implied was a principled commitment to an ethical life in the service of both the nation and humanity, without regard for ideology. Curiously, it was *Tygodnik Warszawski* that turned neo-positivism into a contentious issue in print polemics as early as 1947. To the Warsaw journal's *Youth Column* editor Wiesław Chrzanowski, neo-positivism, whatever its short-term strategic advantages, had one fatal flaw: it "blurred the lines between good and evil."[125]

What Stomma proposed for *Znak* was not for Catholics to run and hide from public debate, but rather to take on the greatest possible variety of issues without directly challenging either the bishops or the Communists. This was a delicate balancing act. Its intention was neither surrender nor mere survival, but rather a chance at shaping the country's future.

To what extent was this essay, and the debate that followed it, really about Mounier? Following a long tradition of Polish deference to

France, Jerzy Turowicz, Stanisław Stomma, and their colleagues had sought Mounier's guidance. When his attentions went elsewhere, they felt betrayed. Stomma's claim about France's "greater degree of civilization" was only partly ironic. His essay makes plain the dilemmas of having to choose between a suicidal Polish maximalism and a pessimistic French defeatism (with the fog of Vichy still hanging over Europe). The "maturity" that Stomma sought for Poland through his lugubrious, ironic borrowings from Oswald Spengler was one conditioned by national interest. He wanted Polish Catholics to see the difference between martyrology and national interest, so that they might choose the latter.

Even a brief glance at the transcription of an editorial roundtable that immediately followed Stomma's essay reveals the essential reason for Poland's fascination with the French. *Znak*'s editors wanted not to make Poland more like France, but instead to learn from France's historical experience dealing with the challenges of modernity. France, despite Stomma's indictment, still had a lot to offer in the way of reconciling "the Christian world" with "the modern world." As he planned the roundtable discussion, the philosophy student Jerzy Radkowski copied this theme from the August–September 1946 special issue of *Esprit*, using it as a springboard for discussion about the position that Poles should take.[126] In Radkowski's words, the Second World War had prevented Poland from overcoming its "civilizational backwardness" relative to, among others, France. Ironically, then, the war had placed several generations of unprepared Polish Catholics in the vanguard of a "revolution" that French Catholics had already been contemplating for decades.[127]

Poles were unprepared to deal seriously with this problem because— according to Radkowski—they felt like they had already suffered the worst that modernity could throw at them. Compared to more than a century of partitions and six years of brutal German occupation, "the modern crisis of values" did not seem especially frightening. Instead, Radkowski suggested, "The resolution of the conflict of 'Christian world' vs. 'modern world' lies in the Christianization of the modern world, not in passing it by and professing disinterest in it."[128] The young editor wanted Poles to continue learning from the French. The lesson in question, though, was how to juggle the eternal Catholic mission of saving souls with the everyday concerns of the modern world.

To resolve this quandary, *Tygodnik Powszechny* and *Znak* would have to wait two years for the return from Rome of a precocious student of philosophy: Karol Wojtyła, future pontiff.

The story of *Znak*'s debut is one of Emmanuel Mounier's broken promises. Turowicz, Stomma, and their colleagues felt that they were staying true to their principles, even as they fell out with *Esprit* over the question of what form the ongoing "Polish Revolution" should take. But an entire movement of Catholic intellectuals waited in Warsaw to shore up Mounier's "progressive" answer to this question. This is why our story now shifts to *Dziś i Jutro*.

# 5 World Peace on Nationalist Terms

## Progressive Catholicism and the Stalinist Turn of 1948

*In the present era, socialism is the most perfect material order. Catholicism is the only spiritual order. Just as there exists in worldly life a burning momentum carrying us toward socialism, so in the realm of spiritual life does Catholicism achieve impressive feats. Catholicism and the socialist movement are two forces, which, coordinated, will lead humanity to a great future and create a new "golden era," while—if turned against one another—will lead to a catastrophe such as history has not yet seen.*
—*Konstanty Łubieński*[1]

IN AUGUST 1948, legendary Spanish painter Pablo Picasso walked the halls of the Wawel Castle, studying the aging tapestries and portraiture. He was in Kraków, Poland's medieval capital. The Cubist even gave a spontaneous talk on the Wawel artwork's history to the half-dozen French intellectuals accompanying him. Together, they walked the very same halls explored two years earlier by Emmanuel Mounier, with *Tygodnik Powszechny*'s Jerzy Turowicz as his guide.

Picasso's cameo appearance in our story is no mere curiosity. The founder of Cubism was a prominent member of the French Communist Party. In 1948, he was decorated in Warsaw by Polish Communist president Bolesław Bierut; in 1950, he received the Stalin Peace Prize from the government of the USSR. He went to the Wawel in 1948 not as a tourist, but as part of a French delegation to the first-ever Communist-sponsored world peace congress. As he improvised a walking tour of the artistic creations of bygone times, Picasso was attended by a tight-knit group of Francophone luminaries: poet Aimé Césaire, philosopher Julien Benda, and Algerian independence advocate André Mandouze.

It is this last figure who brings us to the focus of this chapter. Mandouze was one of postwar France's leading theorists of Catholic socialism. A disciple of Emmanuel Mounier, Mandouze had spent the war's final years leading the underground Christian Witness enterprise. At France's liberation, he swore to make the twin causes of world peace and social justice his life's work. This is what brought him to Poland.

The Cold War had just begun. Funded and overseen by Moscow, the 1948 peace congress was nonetheless the work of French and Polish Communists. Although it was primarily by and for card-carrying Party members, the congress officially was open to all people of "good will" interested in advancing the cause of peace. Held in Wrocław, the largest city of the newly "recovered" territories of postwar Poland, it became one of the most important sources of ideological inspiration for transnational Catholic socialism.

The logic of Catholic socialism held that without peace, there could be no talk of the "human person." This was a minority position, but that minority filled a crucial void at the intersection of transnational Catholic activism and transnational Communism. Pablo Picasso did not believe in Catholic "revolution," but the international spotlight that he shone on Poland in August 1948 helped to make the Wrocław congress an effective launching point for active cooperation by Catholic socialists on both sides of the Iron Curtain. Starting in 1948, the French and Polish Catholic vanguards marched in lockstep with the Communist-inspired movement for world peace. That same year, the pursuit of peace became an essential part of the turn to Stalinism in the Soviet Bloc. In order to justify repressive policies in Central and Eastern Europe, activists cited American nuclear fear-mongering, age-old Western European overseas colonialism, and the alleged persistence of fascism in post-Nazi Germany. In the short term, the linchpin to preventing a third world war was not eliminating atomic power, but assuring that a defeated and divided Germany remained weak.

## COLD WAR EUROPE

Historians disagree exactly when the Cold War began, but already by 1947, foreign-policy experts in both the United States and the USSR saw the globe as having separated into two opposing camps. In June 1947, the United States offered Europe the Marshall Plan. The frontier between the American and Soviet camps materialized right down the middle of Europe, as every country playing host to Red Army troops— save for Germany, still divided into four occupation zones—turned down the American proposal.[2] Nine months later, conflict over the Allied governance of Berlin and of Germany led to the Berlin Blockade, which lasted for most of 1948 and half of 1949. In 1948 alone, the month of February had brought a Communist coup in Czechoslovakia, the month of April—a heated contest between Christian Democrats and Communists for control of the Italian Parliament, and the month of June—Stalin's decision to eject Yugoslavia from the Cominform for "nationalist deviation."

In July 1948, PPR general secretary Władysław Gomułka was accused of "right-wing nationalist deviation" and stripped of his duties. Four months later, Polish president Bolesław Bierut combined the PPR with what was left of the prewar Socialist Party (*Polska Partia Socjalistyczna*) into a new Polish United Workers' Party (PZPR, *Polska Zjednoczona Partia Robotnicza*). Communists thereby achieved one-party rule in Poland. Mass arrests and political murder were the order of the day.

The pre-Stalinist policy of allowing each country's Communist establishment the leeway to run its own revolution gave way to a tight leash held by Moscow. The coming of international Stalinism gave certain Central and Eastern European leaders a taste of their own medicine, as they themselves became prisoners and show-trial defendants. The Cominform, founded in 1947, proved its usefulness in 1948 as a weapon of discipline and exclusion.[3] The Cold War had begun, and internationalism within the constraints of a bipolar world was the new reality.

This was true on both sides of the emerging Iron Curtain. In Western Europe, Marshall Plan money jumpstarted European integration, including a provision for the plan's beneficiaries to create an Organization for European Economic Cooperation. At the same time, political parties began to seek transnational cooperation with their counterparts across Europe: Social Democrats built the Socialist International, and Christian Democrats built the vibrant *Nouvelles Équipes Internationales* (NEI).[4]

The quest for partners in other countries was a child of both economic promise and civilizational peril. Fear defined the geostrategic thinking of the early Cold War years.[5] Within just a few years, the world had witnessed mass genocide and atomic warfare, and no one wanted to repeat either. But the USSR did not yet have atomic weapons technology. Not only Soviet-backed regimes feared an American nuclear monopoly: when the new Cominform lent its support to an international peace movement, a global response ensued. At first, the movement met with substantial sympathy—extending well beyond the Communist fray. Then, in 1949, the Soviet Union got the bomb, and the movement lost all pretense of neutrality, remaining steadfastly anti-American while lauding the USSR.[6]

Among European Catholics, too, fear-mongering and hopes for peace drove social and political advocacy. Activists in their twenties and thirties—members of both the wartime and postwar generations—believed that recent history demanded a new approach. Unlike their celebrated elders Jacques Maritain, Waldemar Gurian, and Dietrich von Hildebrand—all of whom had spent World War II in exile in North America—these younger personalists believed that, in the face of a bipolar Cold War order, the prewar, anti-Bolshevik strategy of promoting the "human person" against "totalitarianism" was at odds with the goal of building a just society.[7] In the minds of the new self-styled Catholic vanguard, the sitting Roman pontiff, Pius XII, was also on the wrong side of history: rather than try to resolve the conflict through diplomacy, his instincts were to push the American camp to be even more aggressively anti-Communist.[8]

In a now-classic thesis, Stephen Kotkin has proposed that we should see the Soviet Union of the 1930s as a Stalinist civilization under construction. Neither a nebulous cloud of evil nor an abstract set of ideas, Stalinism in the Soviet Union brought a lived reality, oppressive and all-encompassing, yet also intimate and dynamic.[9] Kotkin's idea of Stalinist civilization is crucial to any serious history of the Communist world after 1948: the works of Padraic Kenney and Katherine Lebow have clearly established this for the "Polish Revolution" of the late 1940s. As Lebow writes, "within the constraints and unfreedoms of Stalinism, individuals creatively used the materials at hand to shape meaningful stories of their own experience."[10]

On the one hand, the Stalinist "civilizations" of the Soviet Bloc were but faint echoes of the Soviet Stalinism of the 1930s. On the other, as Czesław Miłosz documented in his 1953 masterpiece *The Captive Mind*, Stalinism forced Poles, Czechs, and Hungarians—among others —to wear a different face in their daily public lives than in the comfort of their own minds. Failure to do so could mean ostracism, prison, or death. People became actors in their everyday lives, and—for many— the pressure to be someone else began to erase their actual sense of self:

> It is hard to define the type of relationship that prevails between people in the East otherwise than as acting, with the exception that one does not perform on a theater stage but in the street, office, factory, meeting hall, or even the room one lives in. Such acting is a highly developed craft that places a premium upon mental alertness. Before it leaves the lips, every word must be evaluated as to its consequences. A smile that appears at the wrong moment, a glance that is not all it should be can occasion dangerous suspicions and accusations. Even one's gestures, tone of voice, or preference for certain kinds of neckties are interpreted as signs of one's political tendencies.[11]

Catholics, too, faced the choice of whether or not to become players in the Stalinist tragedy. The writers of *Dziś i Jutro* decided in the affirmative. In the process, Piasecki's movement was transformed from a motley crew of ex-fascists and aristocrats into a power-broker shuttling between the Stalinist establishment and the ecclesiastical hierarchy. Their trajectory evokes anthropologist Longina Jakubowska's observation that "the Polish gentry were quick to adapt to any new political order [ . . . ]. So although the regime forged the gentry as a punishable category, in practice it made use of them, employing their expertise and the prestige inherent in their historical capital to its own ends."[12]

After the Berlin Blockade began in 1948, a divided Germany became the focal point of Cold War hopes and fears, and *Dziś i Jutro* reiterated its staunch anti-German line. The blockade opened a door for Piasecki and company to capitalize on Polish fear of German revanchism, which was more or less universal among Polish Catholics. *Dziś i Jutro* spoke out at a time when the Polish bishops were scared to do the same, since the pope refused to recognize that the "Recovered Territories" of Silesia and Pomerania were now in Polish hands.

In 1948, *Dziś i Jutro* made its fateful leap from a prewar social Catholicism to an aggressive Catholic socialism. Like their French heroes at *Esprit*, they frequently described themselves as "progressive

Catholics." By "progressive," they meant pro-Communist and committed to the vision of a future just society. Any opponent was pilloried as a German collaborator. Since the new regime repeatedly stated that the unrepentant, American-sponsored Germans remained the greatest obstacle to world peace, anti-Germanism became one of the prerequisites for the pursuit of peace. Anti-Germanism was thus firmly established as a core tenet of the transnational Catholic-socialist enterprise. From the Polish perspective, in particular, "This rhetoric was extremely convincing when combined with the threat of the country being plunged into a third world war."[13]

Two intertwined stories played out. *Dziś i Jutro*—through the person of its leader Bolesław Piasecki—became a privileged power-broker in Stalinist Poland. Meanwhile, his recruits were developing a sophisticated ideology of Catholic socialism that found ardent fans on the other side of the Iron Curtain—most notably, in France. *Dziś i Jutro* forged a unique link between Western European personalists and the Soviet Bloc. Instead of breaking with the Church, the Poles styled themselves the ultimate pioneers of Catholic "revolution," which they redefined as the Christianization of Communism from within. Inspired by French Catholic philosophy and theology, the Poles argued that Poland's place as a Catholic country at the forefront of Marxist revolution made it the perfect laboratory for social justice. What brought *Dziś i Jutro* onto the international stage was the movement for world peace.[14]

## POLES AND GERMANS, CHURCH AND STATE

The relationship between Pius XII's Holy See and the postwar Polish episcopate was not a good one.[15] Pius XII knew Primate Hlond well from his own years as Vatican Secretary of State under Pius XI. The pontiff was angry at the cardinal for lending his support to the Polish claim to the Recovered Territories, yet he continued to respect the man as a Church elder. When Hlond died in October 1948, however, Pius XII pulled back from Poland, replacing the late primate with the episcopal novice Stefan Wyszyński.

In December 1948, Cardinal József Mindszenty, primate of Hungary, was arrested for the second time in under a year. Rather than simply threaten him, the Hungarian secret police imprisoned and tortured him, leading to a confession exploited at his February 1949 show trial. In June 1949, Archbishop Josef Beran of Prague met the same fate. Pius XII, who considered Mindszenty a friend, exploded with rage against the Communist governments of Central and Eastern Europe. On February 12, 1949, he excommunicated everyone involved in the Mindszenty affair.

The immediate result of Mindszenty's treatment was a new decree issued on July 1, 1949 by the Holy Office—the Vatican institution formerly known as the Inquisition. Vatican watchdogs threatened excommunication against any Catholics working together with Communists.[16] The decree, formulated as a series of four questions, culminated in the statement that "His Holiness Pius XII, pope by Divine Providence, in an ordinary audience accorded to the assessor of the Holy Office, approved the decision" that any Catholic "faithful professing materialist and anti-Christian doctrine as Communists and, above all, those who defend or propagate such doctrine incur, as apostates of the faith, the excommunication specially reserved to the Holy See."[17] The Vatican seemed to have shut the door not only on active Catholic-Marxist cooperation, but also on any Catholics seeking peaceful coexistence with Europe's new Communist regimes.

Stefan Wyszyński became primate only two months after Mindszenty's second arrest. Called to grow up fast as a Church elder, Wyszyński found himself going the opposite way from Pius XII in his first years as primate. At the very moment when the pontiff was recasting the Catholic hierarchy as a "resistance Church," Wyszyński was negotiating with Poland's Communist establishment.[18] The young bishop endorsed Communist claims to the Recovered Territories. In his quest to protect the Church in Stalinist Poland, the young primate used every willing intermediary—especially Bolesław Piasecki.[19] Seeking a modus vivendi, Wyszyński was himself arguably violating the spirit, if not the letter, of the July 1949 Holy Office decree.

In so doing, however, he was, in fact, faithfully representing the overwhelming majority of Poland's Catholics. All Poles could agree that the Polish claim to the so-called Recovered Territories was non-negotiable. All Catholic activists, regardless of their political or philosophical commitments, came out of the war with a firmly anti-German stance.[20] Even before the Cold War began in earnest, Poles genuinely feared that the international community would wrest these lands away from Poland.

Polish fear of German revanchism made the Soviet Union attractive as a guarantor of Poland's new western borders on the Oder and Neisse Rivers.[21] Following the division of Germany into two republics in 1949, Poland only became more dependent on the USSR to guarantee its borders with the "good" Germans of the German Democratic Republic.[22] The dispute over Poland's boundaries fueled a nationalist revival directed against Germans. This was the new face of integral nationalism.

Poland's postwar Catholic press had, from the start, been vocal in its support of the country's new borders. In the case of *Tygodnik Warszawski*, for example, anti-Germanism likely extended the journal's lifespan. The Christian Democrats made no secret of wanting to punish the German people for the Third Reich's wartime crimes against Poles. This reasoning echoed official Polish foreign policy. The journal's editor, Zygmunt Kaczyński, applauded both Poland's postwar borders and the state's campaign to expel by force the ethnic Germans living on those territories.

In the very first issue of *Tygodnik Warszawski*, Kaczyński wrote, "We must pay special attention to the problem of our lands on the Oder and Neisse, for without these lands we would become something like the Grand Duchy of Warsaw, a creature incapable of opposing the regenerated German hydra."[23] Kaczyński gestured toward Catholic ethics, noting, "I am not an advocate of revenge and 'eye for an eye' repayment by Germans." Yet, he declared, in the wake of their attempted "biological extermination of the Polish nation," the Germans simply could not be allowed to "live in one house with Poles."[24]

Arguably, when the first issues of *Tygodnik Warszawski*, *Tygodnik Powszechny*, and *Dziś i Jutro* called on Poles to invest their energy in "reconstruction" and "transformation," what they were really doing was encouraging Poles to establish their control over the Recovered Territories. The goal, then, was to present the formerly German lands as organically Polish.[25] Neither the start of the Cold War nor the Stalinization of Central and Eastern Europe tempered Polish Catholic thinking on the German question. In keeping with an emerging Stalinist consensus, Polish Catholics only became more dogged in their defense of the Potsdam settlement. *Tygodnik Powszechny* devoted a special issue to the German question on June 27, 1948, with a lead article by Piwowarczyk entitled "The Collective Responsibility of the German Nation." Drawing on the philosopher Karl Jaspers's writings about German guilt, Piwowarczyk explained, "there is no reasonable justification for releasing the majority of the German nation from all responsibility. Responsible are the German worker who produced weapons, who supplied the army with the aid of 'slaves' taken by force from neighboring nations; the trader, whose services enabled fighting Germans to arm themselves; the functionary, whose work enabled the entire criminal regime to run without the slightest hitch for so many years."[26]

Poland's postwar anti-German consensus resurrected certain prewar National Democratic ideas, substituting Germans for Jews as targets of Polish Catholic ire. In a country in which most of the Jewish population had just been either annihilated or driven into exile, anti-Germanism assumed the place that anti-Semitism had occupied before World War II. As Michael Fleming has argued, for the emerging postwar Communist establishment in Poland, "ethno-nationalism was also the only model available to restructure the social anger regime" to their own advantage.[27] The *Dziś i Jutro* movement readily followed their Communist patrons' lead. Ethno-nationalism became the linchpin of the Catholic socialists' global peace activism. In the end, this made the Poles even more attractive to a French Catholic vanguard indulging its own postwar anti-Germanism.

## BOLESŁAW PIASECKI, POLAND'S CATHOLIC DEALMAKER?

In September 1945, Poland's Provisional Government of National Unity unilaterally abrogated the country's twenty-year-old concordat with the Holy See. Formally speaking, the Catholic Church no longer had any legal standing on Polish soil. It was not until 1950 that Church and state reached an understanding as to how Catholicism would continue to function in a newly Communist Poland.[28] In the intervening five years, *Dziś i Jutro*'s leader Bolesław Piasecki positioned himself as a dealmaker who could help the two sides arrive at an agreement. Remarkably, he succeeded. The man who opened the door for Piasecki was Primate Stefan Wyszyński.

Piasecki and Wyszyński had met for the first time in February 1946, prior to the priest's installation as bishop of Lublin. Thereafter, Piasecki and Wyszyński met regularly until September 1953.[29] Piasecki could, in fact, do much that the primate could not. His word carried tremendous weight, for example, with Poland's Public Administration minister Władysław Wolski, as well as with legendary secret police mastermind Julia Brystygier.

Unsure of his footing and inexperienced in both episcopal and state politics, the new primate had a habit of sending mixed signals in his dealings with Catholics and Communists alike. He complained to the *Dziś i Jutro* editors in 1949 that they were acting like "social-Catholic schismatics," yet he continued to meet regularly with Piasecki and to act on the layman's advice.[30] In a sermon delivered on February 23, 1950, Wyszyński sent two completely contradictory messages to Piasecki's movement. First, he complained that a "certain faction of the press and the people concentrated around it, who call themselves 'progressive Catholics,' worry us by their lack of Catholic sensibilities and their ignorance of theology, and yet today they want to play the incomprehensible role of teacher and mentor to the bishops."[31] And yet, having just upbraided *Dziś i Jutro*, Wyszyński then turned around and made them a lucrative proposal: "We will gladly accept every offer of joint responsibility for the affairs of the Church, but our condition is that it be predicated on an understanding of Church teachings and an awareness of the order of things in the hierarchy."[32]

One reason for Wyszyński's ambivalence toward *Dziś i Jutro* was that its Catholic socialism bothered him less than its Communist-sponsored alternative: the Main Priests' Commission (*Główna Komisja Księży*). Organized in 1949, these were the so-called "patriot priests." Technically, they were an arm of a new nationwide World War II veterans' organization, the Union of Soldiers for Freedom and Democracy (*Związek Bojowników o Wolność i Demokrację*).[33] In practice, however, the patriot priests had a unique mission: to erode the bishops' authority among Polish clergy, supplanting it with blind loyalty to the Communist party-state. For all of his megalomania, Piasecki never intended to usurp the primate; meanwhile, the patriot priests, as a de facto arm of the Communist secret police, wished to do exactly this.

These were ordained priests, mostly former military chaplains. Many had been prisoners in German concentration camps. They openly denounced Pius XII's refusal to recognize Polish sovereignty over the Recovered Territories. To them, the Polish bishops, too, were complicit in German revanchism. Organized into regional units coordinated centrally out of Warsaw, the patriot priests created their own power structure parallel to the official Church hierarchy. Tending toward schism, the Main Priests' Commission grew in power until Piasecki stepped in to take them on. Piasecki wanted his own cadres of sympathetic clergy who would help him to market Catholic socialism to Church and state alike. He had no intention of seeing this plan derailed by competition.[34]

Having the patriot priests as a shared enemy helped to bind the episcopate and *Dziś i Jutro* together. This bond, however, was always tenuous. On the one hand, Piasecki became a behind-the-scenes architect of the accord ultimately signed between the episcopate and the Polish government on April 14, 1950. This agreement—of which the Vatican quietly, but firmly, disapproved—obliged the Polish bishops to rein in priests who supported any remaining anti-Communist guerrilla groups and to "oppose any activities antagonistic toward Poland."[35] These obligations, in turn, earned the Communists' de facto acceptance—in the absence of a formal concordat—of the pope as a legitimate authority to whom the episcopate had to answer. Of almost equal importance, from the episcopate's standpoint, was the government's pledge that public schools would continue to teach the Catholic catechism, with supervision by joint Church-state commissions.[36]

With this agreement in place, Piasecki continued to advise Wyszyński as the primate navigated the treacherous straits of Church-state cooperation in the early years of Communist Poland. In return, Wyszyński proved patient and accommodating of Piasecki's movement. For example, he overlooked the fact that, when the government seized the Catholic charity named Caritas, *Dziś i Jutro* directly benefited. In fact, the government simply replaced the bishops' appointees to Caritas with a combination of *Dziś i Jutro* editors hand-picked by Piasecki and so-called patriot priests. As a result, the one-time charity lined the pockets of both movements.[37]

Even as Piasecki conducted shuttle diplomacy between Wyszyński and the secret police, *Dziś i Jutro* was moving far afield of Catholic orthodoxy. By the summer of 1947, the Polish episcopate had excluded *Dziś i Jutro* from the official registry of the country's Catholic press.[38] Even though this step was tantamount to banning *Dziś i Jutro* from advertising itself as a "Catholic social weekly," the journal continued to carry this subtitle until its last issue, published in 1956. Yet, even faced with Piasecki's defiance, Wyszyński never imposed any sanctions. Clearly, heterodoxy was not a deal-breaker for the primate.

In effect, Catholic canon law gave the Catholic socialists of *Dziś i Jutro* a back door out of the Holy Office decree. In principle, that document threatened excommunication as punishment for any form of collaboration with Communism. Yet this threat could apply only to Catholics—in the Holy Office's words—"consciously and freely choosing such acts" of collaboration. Arguably, given the everyday reality of life under Stalinism, Catholics living in the Soviet Bloc could be construed as not being able to choose "freely" the nature and degree of their support for the new regimes. For the activists of *Dziś i Jutro*, the line between opportunism and the "acting" described in Miłosz's *Captive Mind* would remain fuzzy, at best.[39]

## CHRISTIANIZING THE REVOLUTION

When Emmanuel Mounier returned to France in 1946 after three weeks in Poland, he found himself at a crossroads in his journey as a Catholic. He wanted to follow the same path of Catholic socialism that he had just demanded of Polish Catholics in his June 1946 *Esprit* article. Yet, that same month, there appeared in print a book-length manifesto by the Jesuit priest Gaston Fessard, a wartime mentor of the Christian Witness underground. Fessard was the man behind the anti-Nazi, anti-Vichy call to arms that had launched the first issue of the *Cahiers du Témoignage Chrétien*: "France, be on your guard against losing your soul." Before the war, however, Fessard had been focused on anti-Communism: in a 1937 book-length tract, he had demolished the intellectual foundations of Maurice Thorez's *main tendue*, arguing that the essential atheism of the French Communist Party precluded any real partnership between Catholics and Communists.[40]

In the wartime Resistance, Fessard had accepted—conditionally—that Catholics, Socialists, and Communists must fight side by side against a common enemy.[41] Following the Liberation, however, elections to the postwar French constituent assembly had split three ways among the Christian Democrats, the Communists, and the Socialists, with the first two running neck and neck.[42] An attempt to create a unified "Third Force" (*Troisième Force*) government incorporating all three parties led to rancorous bickering, culminating in Charles de Gaulle's withdrawal from public life. This was the French political backdrop for Mounier's visit to Poland. As the PCF, with which Mounier sympathized, became increasingly radicalized, Gaston Fessard turned against the political Left altogether. In the end, he picked up his pen and declared war.

The form that declaration took was *France, be on your guard against losing your liberty*. Dedicating the book to the "memory of the executed and the deported dead in Germany" and "all of the activists of the clandestine teams of Christian Witness," Fessard tapped into the narrative of a Resistance nation: the founding mythology of France's Fourth Republic.[43] In the second paragraph of his preface, Fessard wrote, "Today, eighteen months after the Liberation, we must point out a new peril that, under the cover of the Resistance, threatens France: Communism."[44]

Each chapter of the book began by comparing the need for anti-Communist struggle with the all-too-recent fight against Nazi Germany. Fessard described the Communist as a "red Nazi." Anticipating that Communist critics might call him a fascist, the Jesuit declared, "Just as denouncing the hypocrisy of Nazism did not make us pro-Communist, we do not become pro-fascist by unmasking that of Communism."[45] The core message of Fessard's book, however, was that Marxism goes hand in hand with atheism. What Fessard sought was to redeem those Catholics who had strayed, the "Catholic fellow travelers and philo-Communist Christians," before it was too late.[46]

Fessard's manuscript was completed before Mounier had returned from Poland. Yet, given the article that Mounier published on his return, it is difficult to imagine a better example of the kind of Catholic Fessard wanted to redeem. Mounier and Fessard knew each other well. Mounier took the Jesuit's book very seriously, bringing out his own heavy artillery against the priest in a review essay published a few months later in *Esprit*. Mounier accused Fessard of trivializing "the real drama of those Christians who feel themselves torn between a total and lucid Christian fidelity and certain, no less constricting, historical or political considerations of the society in which they live."[47] Mounier had in mind the drama of those friends he had just made in Poland, such as the staff of *Dziś i Jutro*.

In this review essay, Mounier showed that he was no minimalist. Rather than put up his feet and let Communism take power on its own, the *Esprit* editor instead took a decisive step forward. His June 1946 reflections on the trip to Poland, his retort to Fessard, and his growing interest in socialist movements in France's colonies led him as close as he had ever been to joining a political party. Rather than sign up for the PCF, however, the personalist icon chose to advertise himself as a progressive Catholic.

After Mounier's May 1946 visit to Poland, *Esprit*'s editors showed considerably greater interest in Poland. For the first time ever, *Esprit* established a press exchange with Poland. *Tygodnik Warszawski*, however, held no interest for Mounier. None of its editors had paid him much heed until Stomma invoked him in the pages of *Znak* in 1946. For *Esprit*, then, there existed two centers of Catholic activism in postwar Poland: the "aristocratic citadel" of Kraków (*Tygodnik Powszechny* and *Znak*) and the "bold youthfulness" of Warsaw (*Dziś i Jutro*).

The *Dziś i Jutro* staff learned quickly how to play the game of international diplomacy. In the spring of 1947, Piasecki appointed one of his former KN lieutenants, Wojciech Kętrzyński, as director of foreign affairs for *Dziś i Jutro*.[48] Kętrzyński, a young man of aristocratic background with an excellent command of the French language, had already been tasked since Mounier's departure from Poland with keeping up the correspondence with *Esprit*. From 1947 onward, his responsibilities expanded significantly as *Dziś i Jutro* sent its first representative to the United States (Piasecki's sister-in-law, Janina Kolendo).[49]

What made *Dziś i Jutro* so attractive to *Esprit* was its placement at the crossroads of religion and politics, intellectual and political activism, Western Europe and the Soviet Bloc. Its international profile grew in 1947 because of unfavorable press in the British Catholic weekly the *Tablet*. Auberon Herbert, a wealthy British Catholic who adopted Poland as a sort of second homeland, served during World War II in a Polish uniform. Reputed to be related to Winston Churchill, Herbert made a huge splash in Warsaw when he briefly returned in February 1947.[50] As he was preparing an article for the *Tablet*, Herbert was approached by both Piasecki and Kętrzyński, who hoped that he would speak well of *Dziś i Jutro*.

Following the advice of his friend Karol Popiel, however, Herbert was deeply suspicious of the movement. Without attacking *Dziś i Jutro* by name, he dismissed Catholic socialism as a mirage. As Herbert saw it, a storm was brewing: "At this moment two systems profoundly opposed to one another, Christianity and Marxism, are existing side by side in Poland. It is difficult to see how such a situation can endure for any length of time. [ . . . ] Should a conflict arise, however, it is not with the Church alone that the Communists must reckon, but with the entire Polish nation."[51]

Over the next three months, the *Tablet* followed up on Herbert's articles with a series of direct attacks on Piasecki and *Dziś i Jutro*. For example, English-language readers learned here for the first time about Piasecki's shady past—specifically, that he "admitted in private conversation that he has been sentenced by a Soviet court and released on condition that he would co-operate with the Communists."[52] Word of the *Tablet*'s claims reached *Esprit*, and Mounier rejected them out of hand. If anything, the British journal's campaign against Catholic socialism only brought *Esprit* and *Dziś i Jutro* closer together.

While their "maximalist" colleagues from *Tygodnik Warszawski* were being rounded up in 1948, the staff of *Dziś i Jutro* made a political gambit to demonstrate that they were neither Christian Democrats nor acolytes of the old gentle revolution model of Communist rule. Remarkably, *Dziś i Jutro* succeeded in turning bad international press into a successful campaign to refashion itself. As much as political tactics on the part of the journal's staff, however, this gambit involved an actual embrace of the premise that Catholics should support Marxist revolution.

Wojciech Kętrzyński started the offensive in the summer of 1948 by posing a question: what should Catholics living through a Marxist revolution retain from the most important papal encyclicals of the modern era? Kętrzyński's response consisted of three basic claims. First, Catholicism could not be a "third force" alongside liberalism and Communism. Although it possessed an "unimpeachable moral and ideological position," it "lacks the resources to function on the world stage as a partner of equal stature." Second, Catholics seeking, as any good personalist should, to shape the world around them must "choose such methods of conduct as correspond to today's reality." Third and finally, Catholics had only one choice: the "Christianization of existing forces."[53]

The intent behind the article is clear: to affirm that the *Dziś i Jutro* movement had no desire to create a new Catholic party. SP and the Christian Democrats were the way of the past. To justify partnership with Communists, Kętrzyński invoked France's Gallican tradition. Since the Middle Ages, the French had retained for themselves a right

Fig. 5: Wojciech Kętrzyński,
late 1940s. Reproduced by
permission of Katarzyna
Kętrzyńska.

that no other Catholics had: to practice heterodoxy without courting
papal sanction.[54]

It was this type of compromise that was on the minds of the *Dziś i
Jutro* activists in 1948.[55] As a historical precedent for breaking with
Rome, but not the faith, Gallicanism allowed *Dziś i Jutro* authors to
think of themselves as loyal and faithful Catholics even as they embraced a Communist regime, in clear violation of the letter and spirit
of both *Quadragesimo Anno* and *Divini Redemptoris*. According to
Kętrzyński, Catholics were justified in embracing Communism because
it corresponded "to today's reality."

The phrase "Christianization of existing forces" was no empty slogan. Kętrzyński was trying to derive a generalizable Catholic philosophy from *Dziś i Jutro*'s political strategy. Like the editors of *Znak*,
Kętrzyński sought a blueprint for reconciling the modern world with
the Christian world. *Znak*'s approach had failed to make any head-
way, but Kętrzyński contended that a personalist mission to the Polish

proletariat held the key to unlocking the future of social justice world-wide. Without Catholicism's active involvement in Marxist revolution, however, this could never happen.

Kętrzyński argued that politics was the key in Poland. After all, the Communist claim to legitimacy was that, through the PZPR, the proletariat had taken the reins of power. Demonstrating *Dziś i Jutro*'s loyalty to the "Polish Revolution" was to give Catholics the opportunity to Christianize it, and thereby to fulfill several generations' dreams of Catholic "revolution."

But first, as *Dziś i Jutro* editor Konstanty Łubieński remarked a year later, it was "necessary to revise Catholic social and economic doctrine, which no longer had any grounding in prevailing social and economic conditions." Rather than stick to charity, corporatism, and other tenets of prewar social Catholicism, Łubieński lauded his circle for having "accepted the fundamental social and economic principles of the socialist order." Supposedly, *Dziś i Jutro* diverged from their Marxist patrons only on one point: the "categorical rejection" of materialism. What Łubieński was saying to his colleagues—in private, out of the reach of press censors—was that *Dziś i Jutro* had figured out how to "base the socialist social and economic order on the Catholic world-view."[56] Mounier himself could hardly have asked for more.

### PROGRESSIVE CATHOLICS UNITE!

*Dziś i Jutro* was not alone among European Catholics in defying the letter and spirit of key Vatican documents. Concerned as Mounier was by some of the events of 1948—the Prague coup, the falling-out between Stalin and Tito—*Esprit* toed the Party line, promoting Communists in France and people's democracies abroad.[57] Until 1948, however, the French and the Poles alike were missing a manifesto tailored to the circumstances of a divided Europe.

In the year that Stalinism came to the Bloc, thirty-two-year-old *Esprit* contributor André Mandouze published a "progressive" manifesto. During the war, Mandouze had been deputy editor for Christian Witness. In 1945, he joined the staff of a reactivated *Esprit*. In 1948, he became the canonical theorist of progressive Catholicism.

Mandouze's manifesto was a forty-one-page essay entitled "Take the outstretched hand" (*Prendre la main tendue*). From the outset, Mandouze made it clear that he intended not to create a new system of thought, but rather to assemble a compendium of reasons for Catholics to fight arm in arm with the political Left: "I have no intention of laying foundations for or justifying a Communist Christianity or a Christian Communism, but I collaborate closely with Communists in political combat: in other words, I am what it is known today as a progressive Christian."[58] Paraphrasing Maurice Thorez, Mandouze declared, "A hand has reached out to me, and I have taken hold of it."

Mandouze was clear that progressive Catholicism did not imply the loss of a distinctly Catholic identity: "We are marching hand in hand, but that means that there are two of us." For this reason, Mandouze resented certain Communists' tactics of praising Catholicism as a faith while heaping insults upon the Vatican. PCF luminary Roger Garaudy, for example, argued that Pius XII was a fascist who had turned Catholicism into a "religion of the dollar," allied the cross with the atomic bomb, and reduced the Vatican to little more than a "banking trust."[59] In reply, Mandouze confessed, "I will always resent those who pretend to be better Communists than Stalin or better Christians than Pius XII."[60]

And yet, Mandouze admitted, the Church hierarchy had "in fact accepted the good as well as the bad of the capitalist regime," thereby entering "dangerously into capitalist business."[61] To Mandouze, this was fundamentally antithetical to the pursuit of human dignity. He wanted to be a "Christian person," not a "Western pawn." In the realm of political economy, his statism and syndicalism did not distinguish him dramatically from the French Fourth Republic's political mainstream, Christian Democrats included—or even from Charles de Gaulle.[62] What made Mandouze different was the virulence of his call for anticapitalist revolution: that private property itself was to blame, and that the only way for Catholics to right their Church's wrongs was to enter into a committed partnership with Marxism.

Mandouze explained that Christians and Communists must remain true to themselves, while also taking one another seriously, on their own terms. To lend legitimacy to progressive Christianity, he drew, like Fessard, on the myth of the Resistance, calling it "the crucible in which all of these tendencies have taken form and the occasion of foundational encounters between Christians who previously had no idea about the political and Marxists who previously had no sense of the importance of the spiritual."[63]

Even more foundational to the progressive stance, however, was personalism, which Mandouze explicitly contrasted with anti-Communism. Mandouze declared, "Anti-Communism is a sort of attack on the human person that could qualify as political neo-Malthusianism. It renders infertile all that it touches, and the worst is that, most of the time, it works only thanks to unintentional complicities."[64] Without invoking the pope by name, Mandouze was blaming the Holy See for blocking Catholicism's modernization. His was a cry for the laity to step in and take charge.

Meanwhile, the politics of progressive Christianity spoke for themselves. Mandouze decried American foreign policy, following in Mounier's footsteps by calling for the peoples of the emerging Soviet Bloc to welcome Moscow with open arms. The essence of progressive Christianity, for Mandouze, lay in *recognition that no revolution is possible without the Communists but that the Communists cannot do it alone.*[65] Mandouze proposed "a policy of friendship with the USSR and of ferocious resistance against the ideological and military encroachments of the Marshall Plan."[66]

Although Mandouze had not yet personally been to the Soviet Bloc at this point, he insisted on the permeability of Churchill's "Iron Curtain." He lauded Western European travelers to the Communist countries, congratulating the "numerous Christians and even priests who can speak with familiarity of the religious situation in the people's democracies because they themselves have traversed the Iron Curtain without being able to say where it was, while others, for the needs of their own cause, imagine it to be impermeable."[67]

This was exactly the right approach at the right time for *Esprit*, and even more so for *Dziś i Jutro*. Mandouze himself was wary of the term "progressivism"—he insisted that "Christian" must be the noun, not the adjective—yet he succeeded in clearly delineating principled grounds for Catholic-Communist partnership. The term "progressive" was not new; a party of the same name had existed in the United States since before the First World War, and the term functioned also in the political discourse of France's Third Republic beginning with the Dreyfus Affair. Yet, in 1948, for the first time ever, to be "progressive" meant to be Catholic.

In December 1948, Konstanty Łubieński, inspired in large part by Mandouze's essay, published what was widely received as a programmatic declaration for *Dziś i Jutro*.[68] It came in the form of an open letter printed as a full-page response to the latest installment of bad press given Poland by the *Tablet*. Łubieński borrowed Mandouze's word "progressive" (*postępowy*) to describe the Catholic movement coalescing around *Dziś i Jutro*.

Chastising his colleagues at *Tygodnik Powszechny* and the now-defunct *Tygodnik Warszawski* for falling prey to "inferiority complexes," Łubieński proclaimed that Catholics lacked an "objective assessment of the Marxist camp's activities thus far." Marxists, too, needed to learn from Catholicism. Religion would be the "fundamental source of strength" for the project of "building a new order that would be based on justice and peace, in other words, on the same ideals for whose realization the Marxist camp has been fighting."

It is Łubieński who turned Mandouze's progressive Christianity into the political foundation of Catholic socialism. His goal was full-on evangelization under a Communist regime: Christ and Lenin as a match made in Heaven, so to speak. In Łubieński's view, "Catholicism and the socialist movement are two forces, which, coordinated, will lead humanity to a great future and create a new 'golden era,' while—if turned against one another—will lead to a catastrophe such as history has not yet seen."[69]

Celebrating the anniversary of *Dziś i Jutro* the following year, Łubieński made clear that Catholic socialism could not be an exclusively Polish enterprise. Without naming *Esprit*, Łubieński lauded "progressive movements in the capitalist camp" standing their ground against "governments that, in reality, smother social movements." He went on to promise *Dziś i Jutro*'s unwavering support for these movements.[70] *Esprit*, in Łubieński's eyes, was an ally not just for *Dziś i Jutro*, but for all of "People's" Poland.

Symbiotic as the relationship between *Esprit* and *Dziś i Jutro* had become by 1948, Mandouze, Łubieński, and their colleagues found the relationship threatened by clashes between the worlds of Catholic and Marxist orthodoxy. Mounier's public response to the July 1949 anti-Communist decree of the Holy Office was calm and equivocal. Yet his own personal commitment to the enterprise of Catholic socialism was firm: "socialism and the Church can cohabitate, each disposing of its own domain and, in their borderlands, work together toward the successful liberation of man."[71] These "borderlands" lay at the crossroads of personalism and "revolution," where both *Esprit* and *Dziś i Jutro* claimed to dwell.

Progressive Catholicism proved seminal to the projects of exchange and cooperation that French and Polish Catholic activists were just initiating across the emerging Iron Curtain. Rather than dampen this cooperation, the Holy Office decree seemed to accelerate it. Yet that decree haunted the entire Catholic-socialist enterprise. How could Catholic socialists call themselves "Catholic" while flouting the Vatican's Cold War policy? Mandouze had answered that every Catholic had the right to make up his own mind.

## CATHOLIC SOCIALISM AT WORK

The Catholic socialism of *Dziś i Jutro* was a unique blend of French vanguard thought and postwar Polish politics. When the year 1948 ended with a Stalinist PZPR governing Poland, *Dziś i Jutro* had to move beyond philosophy and geopolitical commentary to explain its role in the "revolution." Communists did not care about Catholics seeking to "Christianize" their revolution at some future date. They wanted to see a crypto-Catholic rationale for their own program. *Dziś i Jutro* did not disappoint them.

In the January 19, 1947 elections to the Polish parliament, *Dziś i Jutro* won three seats. In an assembly of over 400 MPs tightly controlled by the PPR (and, later, its successor, the PZPR), these MPs had no real chance of getting anything done. And yet, the mere fact that those three could wear their Catholicism out in the open—as elected officials, with state salaries and parliamentary immunity—gave their movement a certain cachet. This applied especially in *Dziś i Jutro*'s international dealings, where Kętrzyński, Łubieński, and others gave a convincing impression of being serious power-brokers in Polish public life.[72] For this reason, *Dziś i Jutro*'s leadership quickly reached the conclusion that it made tactical sense to incorporate both national and international concerns into their ideology. Catholic socialism was thus as much about national interest as about the future of humanity.

Even as the Communist establishment began aggressively intimidating the Polish Catholic press, the *Dziś i Jutro* movement took advantage of the situation to promote itself as postwar Poland's only "social-Catholic" option. They began using this adjective to describe everything connected to their group: journals, books, MPs.[73] The goal was to play both sides: to go all-in with the Communists, while making it seem that for social Catholics struggling to find their place in the "Polish Revolution" the only option was to move beyond the prewar Church's teachings, into Catholic socialism.

In so doing, the *Dziś i Jutro* activists were standing *Rerum Novarum* and *Quadragesimo Anno* on their heads. In 1891 and 1931, respectively, those encyclicals had been radically anti-capitalist in their own way, and the Polish Catholic socialists were happy to remind their readership of that fact. Yet the principal enemy of both popes was not capitalism, but socialism. Although Leo XIII and Pius XI legitimated the idea of limited state intervention in the social order, both popes used Thomas Aquinas to underscore that the Catholic Church believed in an ironclad natural right to private property. Leo XIII put it succinctly in 1891: "every man has by nature the right to possess property as his own."[74]

In the hands of Poland's Catholic socialists, "revolution" supplanted natural law, and Thomas Aquinas took a backseat to collectivism. More importantly, the Poles argued that this was what both Leo XIII and Pius XI had meant all along. Opportunistic as these claims sound, most *Dziś i Jutro* authors were earnest in their claims that only their movement understood the correct way to apply those encyclicals. After all, in the entire world, only their movement brought together Catholic intellectuals voluntarily seeking an active role in a predominantly Catholic country's Marxist revolution. In June 1948, Kętrzyński tried to turn this reasoning into an ideological trump card: "The encyclicals were written for Catholics living in liberal, capitalist orders, illuminating the correct path to reforming those orders, not falling into the opposite extreme."

Meanwhile, revolutionary socialism demanded a new interpretation of those encyclicals. Communists had made "objective" progress relative to the "liberal, capitalist" order, and serious Catholics could not ignore this. Therefore, Kętrzyński declared, "In our specific conditions, we demand that Catholics immediately undertake this work, taking as their point of departure the current social forms as they have emerged. For we see in them, aside from errors to be corrected, also values whose preservation is just as much the proper task of Catholics."[75] In claiming for itself the privilege of interpreting Catholic doctrine, *Dziś i Jutro* set itself on a collision course with Poland's bishops, to say nothing of the Vatican.

Every plank of the social and political platform advanced by *Dziś i Jutro* came packaged as a Catholic policy. Even before the shuttering of *Tygodnik Warszawski*, *Dziś i Jutro*'s Wojciech Kętrzyński was laying the foundations for his movement to lay claim to the title of Catholicism's guardian in Communist Poland. Kętrzyński complained, "The contemporary Catholic press in Poland is drowning in a flood of theoretical, abstract debates, erudite but entirely divorced from real life." Luckily for Polish Catholicism, the staff of *Dziś i Jutro*—"we, the young"—cared enough about the future "to undertake a methodical examination of the most burning issues framing the reality of the everyday life of Catholic society in Poland."[76] There was one overriding message for Catholic readers who were wondering how to react in the face of Stalinism: *Carpe diem*!

But *Dziś i Jutro* did more than just advertise itself as the Catholic political option in Communist Poland. The journal tackled specific questions of policy, claiming that its positions followed from a commitment to personalism and progressive Christianity. These declarations were no mere propaganda. They were clearly the product of methodical study and deep reflection on French and Polish personalisms of the interwar years. Their point of departure was to acknowledge work as the sole path to achieving universal respect for the dignity of the "human person."

At the end of 1948, with Gomułka deposed, the PZPR announced a six-year plan for the Polish economy. Following the Soviet model, collectivization of agriculture was to be one of the plan's cornerstones. Gomułka had opposed collectivization, arguing that Poland was historically different from the USSR, and so there was no need to replicate the Soviet trajectory. These objections, among others, landed him a one-way ticket out of the leadership and, three years later, into handcuffs. One of the PZPR's top propaganda priorities was to sell agricultural collectivization as the key to the next stage of the "Polish Revolution."[77]

The author chosen by Bolesław Piasecki to tackle this question in the pages of *Dziś i Jutro* was, curiously enough, Andrzej Krasiński. His surname was almost a household word in Poland: scion of an illustrious line of landed nobility, his ancestors had included the Romantic poet Zygmunt Krasiński. It was the Nazis, not the Soviets, who had destroyed Krasiński's family holdings. World War II turned the dispossessed young aristocrat into a committed disciple of both Bolesław Piasecki and Emmanuel Mounier. From 1948 onward, he served as a sort of deputy to Kętrzyński in matters of foreign policy.

Despite his aristocratic pedigree, Krasiński had nothing but praise for the PZPR program of collectivization. To sell it more effectively, he began his article by reframing the issue as one of the "cooperative organization of work." This creative turn of phrase drew on the long history of Polish socialism—especially the writings of early twentieth-century anarcho-syndicalist Edward Abramowski.[78] At the same time, Krasiński made an explicitly personalist argument, contrasting "cooperative" agricultural work with small farming—a supposedly capitalist, and therefore anti-personalist, way of doing things. Krasiński reasoned, "A fundamental assessment of the cooperative organization of work from the personalist standpoint demands its recognition as perhaps the highest form of action, in which the creative individual, in possession of his individual aspirations, voluntarily binds himself to the collective with the aim of multiplying his strength and achieving a better result for his actions." Taking a page from Mounier's *Personalist and Communitarian Revolution*, Krasiński insisted that Communist Poland had an ethical imperative to aggregate individual farmers into collectives.[79]

In the end, however, it was anti-Germanism that became the glue holding together *Dziś i Jutro*'s political program. Wojciech Kętrzyński, in particular, put the German question at the very top of his movement's agenda: "The defining task of our generation is the complete binding of the Recovered Territories to Poland, their assimilation into our economic, national, and political whole. And, what is most important and most difficult—convincing the entire world that these Territories need not and indeed must not be taken away from Poland."

This was not really about the Cold War or about Catholicism, but rather memory of World War II. And yet Catholic socialists made the German question the linchpin of their ideology. The implication was that social justice could never be achieved so long as the United States continued to protect a revanchist Germany. For it was the "fascist," western portion of German territory that had secured American protection: "Our task is to lead the *status quo* in western Poland through the years of uncertainty. This will be accomplished when Germany is finally vanquished and when the German question will no longer be a bone of contention between the two principal world powers: the USSR and the USA."[80]

Realistically, *Dziś i Jutro*'s ability to shape domestic policy was quite limited. In the international arena, however, the movement could make a name for itself that would then reflect well on Communist Poland. For Piasecki's movement, the best hope for the immediate future was to build international Catholic-socialist initiatives in partnership with Western Europe.

## THE DANGERS OF EUROPEAN INTEGRATION

In September 1947, top Soviet strategist Andrei Zhdanov announced that the world had split into two opposing camps.[81] By that time, however, *Dziś i Jutro* had already been arguing for over a year that only Communists could secure world peace. Its editors registered a simple appeal: "Poland needs peace. Peace among nations is necessary."[82]

Poland was to play a special role in assuring peace within Europe and the world. One of its first tasks was to help restore an exhausted and demoralized French nation. As one *Dziś i Jutro* author reported from Paris in late 1946, this would be no easy task: "Exhausted by fears, catastrophism, and nonsense, the Frenchman withdraws into the quiet of his own home."

This is where Poland came in. France supposedly had nowhere else to turn, reviling Russians and Americans, "whom they have come to know and consider barbaric. [ . . . ] They fear Germans, regarding whose fate they have almost as little to say as does Poland today." Because they shared a fear and loathing of Germany, France and Poland had good reason to form a bilateral partnership. Working in concert, Frenchmen and Poles would no longer have so "little to say" about Germany's fate, but would instead be in a position to shape postwar Europe, eliminating Germany's ability to do more damage.[83]

Events seemed to bear out these hopes. Even as the Iron Curtain became a geopolitical reality between 1946 and 1948, Western Europe played host to a series of initiatives aimed at developing a system of shared sovereignty on the continent. The potential pay-offs were clear: to increase European bargaining power with the looming giant of the

United States and to share resources across national borders, working from the assumption that everyone could help everyone else to rebuild. As a result, another war would be far less likely.

Western Europe's march toward integration had begun already in 1947, with the Marshall Plan. The idea of a united Europe had been floated for decades, but now mainstream political parties were getting involved from across the entire western half of the continent.[84] The question was how to treat Germany: as a partner, or as a threat. Christian Democracy went farthest in bringing the future political elite of West Germany into the process.

In 1948, the Christian Democratic NEI welcomed a German delegation headed personally by Konrad Adenauer, the esteemed, elderly Catholic leader of the nascent Christian Democratic Union (*Christlich Demokratische Union*). This center-right party had emerged in the war's aftermath as the only acceptable German alternative to the political Left, given that virtually the entire Right had been compromised by association with Hitler's regime.[85] That same year, the new European Movement lobby group, with assistance from the NEI and other transnational political movements, put on a major international "Congress of Europe" at The Hague. Winston Churchill gave the keynote address, and a host of European luminaries—from philosopher Bertrand Russell to medievalist Étienne Gilson—met and worked on a plan for uniting Europe.[86] Once again, Adenauer personally led the German delegation.

Meanwhile, on the eastern side of the Iron Curtain, European integration was seen from the start as a cause for concern. The big worry was that Germans would get free rein over the continent. On this point, *Dziś i Jutro* spoke for all Poles in 1948, denouncing Western European leaders for legitimating an unrepentant German nation. Adenauer, painted as a neo-fascist, became the symbol of German revanchism. For Poles, then, European integration threatened their country's new western border; the outcome that they feared was a new war over control of the Recovered Territories.[87]

Yet dissent against European integration did not come from the Soviet Bloc alone. Communists, Socialists, and many Catholics across Western Europe protested vehemently against what they saw as a voluntary surrender of sovereignty. The French opposed both (West) German power and a united Europe, which they felt would make the former irreversible. Fear of a rearmed and revanchist Germany bound these issues together. No French voice was more impassioned in its opposition to a united (Western) Europe than *Esprit*.[88] In a scathingly Euroskeptical article published in the November 1948 issue, Jean-Marie Domenach warned that rearmament would inexorably follow (West) Germany's strings-free entry into European political cooperation. West Germany did not have nuclear weapons, but the argument was that a rearmed Germany would start a third world war: any struggle that began as a continental conventional war would end in global nuclear winter.

Reading Domenach's article and various pieces that followed in its wake, Polish Catholic socialists came to believe in the real possibility of coordinated political action with their French heroes. The Poles only needed political cover to pursue this kind of a joint project. That cover came when Poles and Frenchmen began working together in the summer of 1948 to launch a global peace campaign.

### WHY PABLO PICASSO CAME TO POLAND

The campaign for peace began with Moscow, but it was Poland's Communists who actually launched it. None other than Jerzy Borejsza —father of the gentle revolution—planned the Congress of Intellectuals in Defense of Peace, held in Wrocław (formerly Breslau), the largest city of the Recovered Territories.[89] As it turned out, the congress would be Borejsza's last hurrah.[90]

With Communist establishments turning against "national deviation" after Tito's defection, Borejsza hoped to mount an event that would prove that he had made the leap into the "new, post-'gentle revolution' era" (read: Stalinism). In the end, however, he stayed true to himself, trying to be equally respectful of Soviet, French, and Polish cultures.[91] For Moscow, this was unacceptable. Taking place from August 25 to 28, 1948, the Wrocław congress not only heralded Borejsza's fall from grace, but in fact showed the world that Stalinism was on the rise, and that the global peace campaign would be one of its mainstays.

Borejsza worked tirelessly to prepare the congress. He offered the co-chairmanship of the upcoming event to Jarosław Iwaszkiewicz, one of Poland's leading poets and a long-time Marxist. In the postwar "Polish Revolution," he and his colleagues "now appeared as decidedly *engagé* poets on the correct side of the 'red barricade.'"[92] Together, Borejsza and Iwaszkiewicz planned an extensive international PR campaign to generate interest in the upcoming congress. It was Iwaszkiewicz who took the show on the road, and he proved to be an extremely effective promoter.

Iwaszkiewicz criss-crossed Europe several times over the course of 1948, exhorting the continent's cultural and intellectual elites to come to Wrocław in August. He was a natural. In May 1948, tears flowed in his Marseille audience as the poet described drawings made by Polish children—how the children, their psyches deformed by war, continually "return to the topic of Warsaw as a leveled city, giving a poignant, plastic form to the ruins."[93] A month later, in Rome, he passionately lauded the revolution's accomplishments in the fields of culture and education. The real point, however, was to scare his listeners into taking seriously the thought that it might all come crashing down any minute. Germans and Americans, after all, were preparing another war: "Books reach the peasant and the worker, the newspaper and the literary weekly have become his most basic need. [ . . . ] You can thus imagine how disturbing to such peaceful work are even the vaguest of whispers about a new war, how frightening are specific predictions and clear preparations for a new cataclysm, with what terror we follow the declarations of statesmen in the West who speak of a new war with no qualms."[94]

Borejsza made a decision early on to advertise the congress as a project of cooperation between Western Europe and the Soviet Bloc, rather than a Moscow-directed venture. In fact, official invitations to the congress were written on behalf of the "Franco-Polish Executive Committee," a roster of luminaries: the architect Le Corbusier; the artists Pablo Picasso and Ksawery Dunikowski; and a litany of writers, including Julien Benda and Vercors from France, and Maria Dąbrowska, Zofia Nałkowska, and Antoni Słonimski from Poland.[95]

Borejsza's principal French partner was Frédéric Joliot-Curie.[96] The French scientist's credentials were unmatched in Polish eyes: a Nobel Laureate in his own right, son-in-law of celebrated Franco-Polish Nobel Laureate Maria Skłodowska-Curie, and creator of France's postwar peaceful atomic energy industry, Joliot-Curie seemed to be the living embodiment of Franco-Polish cooperation in the pursuit of peace.[97] One year earlier, Joliot-Curie had been elected president of the Franco-Polish Friendship Association (*Association de l'Amitié Franco-Polonaise*). Under its auspices, he created a journal, *Peuples Amis* (*Friendly*

*Nations*), that became a propaganda machine for the global peace campaign, as well as a French-language promotional bulletin for Poland's Marxist revolution.[98]

Franco-Polish accents framed the Wrocław congress. Its official transcript was recorded in French. Iwaszkiewicz promised that pluralism and tolerance would be the watchwords of the congress, exhorting his Roman and Parisian audiences in June 1948 to "come join us in the greatest numbers possible, without prejudice toward political or religious convictions—keeping in sight only the matter most important to humanity at present: the matter of securing the peace." Official invitations called for "intellectuals of good will [ . . . ] to come in the spirit of mutual understanding." Pablo Picasso supplied artwork to grace the congress hall. After the congress, he drew the famous "dove of peace" that became the resultant peace movement's official logo.[99]

In the end, approximately 500 participants representing forty-six countries converged on Wrocław in August 1948. These included poets Aimé Césaire and Paul Éluard, biologist Julian Huxley, and philosopher György Lukács. Opening the assembly on August 25, Iwaszkiewicz appealed to the "spiritual" dimension of peace, recognizing that "many among you beginning these discussions will sigh, asking for the blessing of the 'God of Peace, who has led us through the valley of death.' And everyone without a shadow of a doubt will devote all of their strength and heart to triumphing over the curse of the modern Tower of Babel."[100]

However positive the impressions left by the poet's invocation, the mood soured dramatically when, three speeches later, Soviet author Alexander Fadeev launched into a vicious, crass attack on anyone who might dare to speak out against actions taken by the USSR. Polish novelist Maria Dąbrowska—a prewar Socialist who had refused to join the postwar Communist party—was in the audience for Fadeev's speech. That evening, she noted in her diary that he "spoke for an hour-and-a-half like a traveling salesman hawking his wares and heaping insults upon the competition. The content was nothing more than the highfalutin slogans of any establishment newspaper, while the tone and delivery were below the level not only of an intellectual, but of any normal human being."[101]

Fadeev's worst crime in the eyes of Western European participants had been to insult Jean-Paul Sartre, who was like a god to many of

Fig. 6: Pablo Picasso, in session at the Congress of Intellectuals in Defense of Peace, Wrocław, Poland, August 25, 1948. Reproduced by permission of the Polish Press Agency (PAP).

them. Fadeev lumped Sartre in with "literary agents of imperialist reaction" and blamed him personally for the "spiritual depravity" of the
West. The Soviet writer railed against existentialism, which he belittled
as seeking "to reduce man to an animal crouching on all fours."[102] At
this point, the congress witnessed Pablo Picasso "tearing off his head-
phones [ . . . ] Éluard takes his off slowly and starts to note something.
Vercors and Léger remain motionless." And in the background was
poor Borejsza, his hopes of redemption dashed, telling French journalist Dominique Desanti, "This is it, they've smashed my congress to
pieces."[103]

In point of fact, the congress did not fall apart. PPR luminary Jakub
Berman put in a call to Soviet foreign minister Vyacheslav Molotov,
and together the two did some serious damage control on Borejsza's
behalf. Luck also played its part: the man behind Fadeev's tirade—top
Stalin advisor Andrei Zhdanov—died in Moscow while the congress
was in session. In the end, Borejsza convinced almost everyone to remain at the conference. Ilya Ehrenburg then gave a conciliatory speech
on behalf of the Soviet delegation.[104]

Yet Fadeev's speech did not uniformly disgust or dishearten. The
existentialist legend Jean-Paul Sartre vigorously defended the Soviet
Union even in the worst years of Stalinism, and yet Communists criticized him as an exemplar of "bourgeois" decadence. In fact, criticism
of Sartre helped on various occasions in the postwar decade to create
a Catholic-Communist consensus in European intellectual life. In October 1945, both Catholic and Communist thinkers in France attacked
Sartre's widely publicized lecture "Existentialism is a Humanism." As
Edward Baring observes, "The Christians decried a humanism turned
atheistic in Sartre's work; the Communists, a humanism of the bourgeois. [ . . . ] In both cases it was a testing ground for a larger debate
being played out at the political level, a debate the result of which
would have profound consequences for the causes they held closest."[105] In August 1948, too, criticism of Sartre made common cause
for Catholic and Communist delegates. Though Éluard, Vercors, and
other French delegates objected to Fadeev's crass, propagandistic way
of denouncing a French literary icon, other delegates—non-believers
and believers alike—nodded their heads in agreement.

Even those who took exception to Fadeev left Poland feeling like
they had done something important to advance the cause of world

peace. Catholic activists in attendance were particularly pleased. The most prominent arrivals from abroad were André Mandouze—fresh off the publication of his treatise on progressive Christianity—and Jean Boulier, a pro-Communist clergyman who called himself "the Red Priest."[106]

Almost a year before rolling out his theory of progressive Christianity, Mandouze had taken the French intellectual world by storm with a scathing critique of French policy toward Algeria.[107] Overnight, Mandouze was offered and accepted the position of leader of the Action Committee of Algerian Intellectuals for Freedom and Democracy (*Comité d'Action des Intellectuels Algériens pour la Liberté et la Démocratie*). He also accepted a university position in Algiers, to which he relocated to campaign on behalf of Algerian independence.[108] Mandouze was thus wearing two hats at once in Wrocław, for "my Algerian struggle combined on the one hand with my progressive convictions, acquired and confirmed earlier in France, but drawing strength on the other hand from my independent participation in the international struggle waged for peace."

But Poland was more than a site of political agitation for Mandouze: he had the opportunity to see and thoroughly enjoy a country that had previously seemed exotic and foreign. With a group of Francophone colleagues, he took a road trip to Kraków and its surrounding area, enjoying the company of a "constellation of French intellectuals, writers, and artists whom I would otherwise have never dreamed of being able to approach."[109] One of them was Pablo Picasso, who gave them an unforgettable tour of artwork in the Wawel Castle. Meanwhile, Mandouze's roommate for the duration of the trip was Aimé Césaire, a legend of Francophone literature. Mandouze was pleasantly surprised to find Catholicism alive and well everywhere he looked: sacral artwork in Kraków, masses for schoolboys in Wrocław, chapels and statues of saints made of salt in the mines at Wieliczka. He and the rest of the French delegation requested that their Polish guides take them to Auschwitz, and it was his conversations there with Aimé Césaire that inspired the substance of his speech at the peace congress.

The poet from Martinique drew Mandouze's attention to the fact that their invitations to the congress had made no mention of "colonialism as a cause of war." Mandouze then realized that, while the congress had featured anti-American, anti-German, and anti-atomic accents, not a single word had yet been said against colonialism.[110] For example, American Progressive Party leader Henry Wallace's recorded message to the congress congratulated the Poles on Wrocław's return to "its legitimate proprietors" after "so many years of cruel German occupation." The Hungarian philosopher György Lukács, meanwhile, accused the United States of Nazi-inspired imperialism. Borejsza himself had offered a particularly warm welcome to "democratic Germans" from the Soviet zone who had made it to Wrocław. These were the only "Germans of good will, with whom we have found and continue to find a common language."[111]

Mandouze, meanwhile, delivered an impassioned plea for decolonization. This, he argued, was the only way to avoid another war and holocaust. In an Arendtian moment, Mandouze had offered colonialism as a partial explanation for Nazi racism and genocide. He began with the simple statement: "at the present hour, there is no peace. [ ... ] There is no peace, or it is near death, in those countries to which the West, reclaiming the heritage of Athens and Jerusalem, has pretended to bring peace and even more: I mean by this the so-called colonial countries."

Mandouze continued, "While we speak of peace, standing amidst the ruins of Wrocław, colonialism continues its massacres in Vietnam, triumphs in the trials in Antananarivo, fills prisons in Algeria, wears down the bodies of Black Africa. And I could continue for a long time in this macabre litany." For this reason, Mandouze exhorted his audience to rethink the very categories of war and peace. This was the only way to understand that any struggle for global peace needed to be also an anti-colonial struggle:

> Let us at last expunge from the world this hypocrisy that lies in thinking that colonial wars are less serious than so-called international wars and that they fall under different legal criteria. If this were the case, we would already have made a significant contribution to peace simply by revealing to the world that, though the ovens at Auschwitz have gone cold, there remain still to be extinguished the colonial furnaces that, though distant, reveal to no lesser degree how humanity, with a slow and continuously burning fire, tranquilly commits its crimes.[112]

Two hours before Mandouze called for decolonization, France's infamous "Red Priest" Boulier sounded the alarm against "Christian alliance with the forces of reaction." For Boulier, a priest who attended the congress "with neither mission, nor commission, nor permission of any sort," Wrocław was but one in a long series of unorthodox activist stands that ultimately led to his suspension from the priesthood in 1953.[113] Though a long-time professor at Paris's Catholic Institute, Boulier had no problem making common cause with Communists. Boulier had made his first trip to Communist Poland as a member of Mounier's delegation in 1946, and he would return again and again.[114]

Just the previous fall, *Peuples Amis* had featured his diatribe against Anglo-American attempts to rehabilitate Germany as a player in the international system. According to Boulier, "Seen from Washington, peace lies in making Europe's factories—German industrial power—once again market-ready." The priest argued that both Frenchmen and Poles needed to rely on the Soviet Union as guarantor that Germany would never again rise as a revanchist power: "for Poland and for Europe, Russia is the key to solving the German problem: one cannot conceive of the security of those nations threatened by Germany's resurrection without the security of Russia."[115]

When Boulier came to Wrocław in 1948, it was as a priest, wearing a cassock and preaching forcefully to the congress. The message that he delivered could hardly have been more in line with Polish Catholic socialism if *Dziś i Jutro*'s Wojciech Kętrzyński had written it himself. His goal was "to connect the proceedings to Christian thought, more precisely, Catholic thought, held under lock and key by a particularly vigilant authority." And so began Boulier's attack on Pope Pius XII. Yet this was merely a prelude. Boulier offered his own version of Catholic ethics, reduced to the following dictum: "The Christian is not an escapist. He should take his place beside his brothers in the workshop where humanity is forced to build its destiny."

At first glance, this sounds simply like a more colorful version of Jacques Maritain's call for Catholics to build a new Christendom on earth. Boulier, however, turned away from Thomism, opting instead for a radical Catholic socialism. Like *Dziś i Jutro*'s Kętrzyński a few months earlier, Boulier insisted that Catholics must first accept the social and political order in which they live as it is given to them, before they can even think about Christianizing it: "The Christian will thus be a good citizen of the modern temporal realm, and it is to be understood that, if this temporal realm is Communist, he will work with all his heart to build a socialist order, such as it is proposed to him."[116]

Fig. 7: Rev. Jean Boulier, speaking before the Congress of Intellectuals in Defense of Peace, Wrocław, Poland, August 26, 1948. Reproduced by permission of the Polish Press Agency (PAP).

Yet, even as Boulier insisted on first building socialism, and only then Christianizing it, he recoiled in horror from the idea of building capitalism: "The only truly godless man, for a Christian, is the lover of money. For a heart in which God reigns, how can money reign there as well!" The struggle for peace, as Boulier painted it, was but a thinly veiled argument for Catholic-socialist internationalism, with the socialism taking priority. As he put it, capitalists were successors of Nazi Germany, and so—"as long as Hitler's war continues, so continues the Resistance."[117]

While Boulier and Mandouze were giving their speeches, *Dziś i Jutro* had its man in the room, assigned to report back on the congress to the journal's readership. This was Andrzej Krasiński, the thirty-two-year-old former resistance fighter responsible for a personalist defense of collectivization. Unlike most of his fellow Poles in attendance at the congress, Krasiński was ecstatic when he heard Boulier and Mandouze speak. While in Wrocław, he made contact with both French luminaries. Mandouze left Europe for Algeria soon thereafter, but the "Red Priest" would return to Warsaw two years later as *Dziś i Jutro*'s guest.

Having heard these French thinkers assert the Catholic-socialist voice in Wrocław, Krasiński now set about the task of extrapolating from their example for his readership. In his eyes, the 1948 peace congress was a successful first step toward a much larger international movement. The dispossessed aristocrat saw Fadeev's speech as an act of courage rather than a reason for shame, arguing that "Fadeev does not fall prey to fascination with authority figures and has no qualms about launching the sharpest of attacks against people of a different opinion." True—the speech was "strongly political," "uncompromising," and "brutal," yet Krasiński valued Fadeev's supposed honesty. In fact, it would be intellectually dishonest, Krasiński insisted, to dismiss what had been said merely on the grounds of "good manners in the bourgeois sense of the word."[118] As a result of the congress, Krasiński could report back to Piasecki and the rest of the *Dziś i Jutro* leadership that he had witnessed a winning combination of anti-American, anti-atomic, anti-German, and anti-colonial tirades. In the eyes of the Catholic socialists, these were the ingredients for a new era of world peace.

Anti-colonialism had not, in fact, been on the Polish movement's agenda prior to the Wrocław congress. For Krasiński, Mandouze's speech was a genuine wake-up call to a new cause: "This same voice, albeit coming from different parts of the world, reveals and unmasks a basic contradiction that allows people and indeed entire countries to apply two different moralities, limiting the application of Christian principles to the narrow field of their own country, to people with the same skin color as theirs." The basic lesson was that the Catholic activists of *Dziś i Jutro* needed to avoid making the same mistake that, for example, France's Christian Democrats had. Their Catholic socialism needed to work for humanity, not merely Poland or Europe.

For both its Polish and its international participants, the Wrocław congress heralded a new European community, unlike anything proposed by the Christian Democrats of France and Italy. After the congress, Iwaszkiewicz resumed his duties as international spin doctor of choice for the peace campaign. In the fall of 1948, he set out once again on a European tour. Taking a page from *Esprit*'s Jean-Marie Domenach, the poet exhorted Parisians to ask themselves what kind of Europe they really wanted: "Europe is a very good idea, but it depends—what kind of Europe? The entire Wrocław Congress served as one single answer to this question. There met the representatives of this best of all Europes, the Europe of great humanist traditions and a great revolutionary past, fighting for a better tomorrow. They decided that they will fight for peace. [ . . . ] [A] Europe of work, of reconstruction and transformation, a Europe of progress, a Europe of international solidarity is undoubtedly a Europe of good will."[119] The choice of phrasing was both Marxist and Catholic. Iwaszkiewicz's emphasis on "reconstruction and transformation" recalled, among others, the 1945 lead articles of *Tygodnik Powszechny* and *Tygodnik Warszawski*. In these words, postwar Poles often also heard code for securing Polish sovereignty over the Recovered Territories.

For eight years after the Wrocław congress, Polish Catholic activists presented themselves as genuine and steadfast partisans of the anti-atomic and anti-colonial causes. Yet it was their alternative vision of Europe—anti-American and anti-German, in defiance of both the Marshall Plan and the Schuman Plan—that drove them into the international arena. Wojciech Kętrzyński, Andrzej Krasiński, Konstanty Łubieński, and others set to the task of establishing lasting cross-Iron Curtain linkages with like-minded Catholic activist groups in France. The global peace effort became the launching point for *Dziś i Jutro*'s efforts to build a "Catholic-socialist international."

Residual fear of German revanchism opened the eyes and ears of the French Catholic vanguard to what their Polish counterparts had to say. The Poles, after all, had the distinction of having already gone through "revolution." Moreover, it was Polish migrants to the newly reclaimed territories of Silesia and Pomerania who were expected to be the first targets of German revanchism in the event of another war. Activists on both sides of the Iron Curtain thought that they could square Catholic personalism with a deep-set antagonism toward Germany. In fact, most went so far as to argue that true personalists *should* be anti-German. After all, personalists should be devoted to the cause of preventing Nazism's resurrection.

It would take eight years, the gutting of the Polish hierarchy by show trials, and a series of condemnations from the Vatican to teach some of the French and Polish activists the error of their ways. And many would never learn.

# 6   Pastors and Catechumens

## Catholic Renewal at the Margins of Marxist Revolution

*The Church today has lost the affection and the attention of the common people. They, on their side, ask her by what right she claims to interfere with and direct from above the spiritual and moral life of men with whom she is no longer involved in the everyday events of life, the daily task of bread-winning. Having ceased to fulfill her role as nurse and mother, her doctrinal role becomes intolerable; this tender mother seems like a strange governess, her charity like condescending alms giving.*

—*Jacques Loew OP*[1]

SEVEN CENTURIES AFTER Thomas Aquinas began writing his *Summa Theologiae*, the Polish novice priest Karol Wojtyła was in Rome, studying the text for weeks at a time, always assuming the same kneeling position before starting his reading. This is how he showed reverence for the thirteenth-century Latin. The future Pope John Paul II did this neither out of ritual nor at the request of his academic supervisors.[2] Rather, he had arrived in Rome in 1946 as a product of a Polish-language Catholic world that, in the face of dictatorships and wars, had returned to Thomas Aquinas for guidance.

Karol Wojtyła had grown up in the town of Wadowice, just southwest of Kraków. He left Poland for Rome in September 1946, and he remained outside Poland until the summer of 1948. While he was in Western Europe, the Cold War began, the Iron Curtain came into existence, and Communist Poland devolved into Stalinist terror.

Wojtyła's unique vantage point—a Polish priest in his late twenties, studying in Rome—placed him at the margins of Central and Eastern

Europe's Sovietization. Removed from Polish soil, he nonetheless found himself facing some of the same decisions in Western Europe that his fellow Polish Catholic intellectuals were confronting back at home. In these years, Wojtyła learned to reconcile anti-Communism with a belief in the need for revolutionary renewal within the Catholic Church. Unlike the acolytes of Bolesław Piasecki, he did not believe that calls for reform had to go hand in hand with a politics of Catholic socialism. He returned to a newly Stalinist Poland in 1948, armed with a repertoire of pastoral practices representing the best that Francophone Europe's Catholic vanguard had to offer—without the Stalinist politics of *Dziś i Jutro*.

Wojtyła identified deeply with a pastoral project known as the "French Mission" (*Mission de France*). In the midst of the Second World War, French primate Cardinal Emmanuel Suhard had created a seminary designed specifically to train novice priests to bring France's increasingly secularized working classes back to the Church. The new seminary's curriculum followed the teachings of a group of Dominican and Jesuit priests distrusted by Vatican guardians of Church orthodoxy, who derisively labeled them "new theologians." Nevertheless, Yves Congar, Marie-Dominique Chenu, Henri de Lubac, and their colleagues eventually became the most important voices of reform in the Catholic Church, and their ideas would shape the Second Vatican Council of the 1960s.[3]

When the French Mission was founded in 1943, however, basing its curriculum around "new theology" was a bold—and risky—move. Seminarians read Marx and Lenin because Congar and Chenu had argued that, in order to fend Marxism off effectively, priests needed first to understand it. Pius XII's Holy See looked unkindly on this project from the start, and ultimately the hierarchy condemned a whole class of French Mission alumni—the so-called "worker-priests" (*prêtres-ouvriers*), who became manual laborers and worked alongside their catechumens in order to evangelize them. Before the Vatican ultimately weighed in, however, the French Mission succeeded in creating a model of Catholic "revolution" that, unlike Catholic socialism, did not treat Marxism-Leninism as a given.

These reforming priests became a sort of living textbook for the future John Paul II. At the request of the archbishop of Kraków, Wojtyła spent the summer of 1947 traveling around France, Belgium, and Holland, studying the new theology, the worker-priests, and a host of other self-styled "revolutionary" approaches to spreading the Catholic faith. Enthralled with what he encountered, he wrote at length in Polish advocating that the Catholic Church adopt these practices more widely. The graduate student Wojtyła's encounter with the French pastoral vanguard laid the groundwork for his own doctrine of the "human person."

Karol Wojtyła was one of the youngest members of a mid-century cohort of Polish Catholic intellectuals who, after the onset of Stalinism in 1948, split dramatically with the Catholic socialists of *Dziś i Jutro*. Like Piasecki's activists, this group read Mounier and found his ideas of "revolution" inspiring. And yet, when they saw the political tide turning toward Stalinism—in Fadeev's vicious denunciation of Sartre at the Wrocław peace congress, or in the arrest and public smearing of their colleagues at *Tygodnik Warszawski*—they chose a different path. They considered themselves revolutionaries, but they did not want to rubber-stamp the violence of a Communist regime. Rather, they looked to pastoral reformers in both France and Poland: to Yves Congar and to the worker-priests, but also to the interwar teachings of Laski's Władysław Korniłowicz, who had insisted that Catholics should approach the quest for social justice in an industrialized world not as ideologues, but as catechumens. This meant—for both sides in the catechetical dialogue—constantly wrestling with Catholicism's implications for the world around them.

Alongside the French pastoral reformers and the future John Paul II, this chapter introduces Jerzy Zawieyski, the last catechumen to study with Korniłowicz (who died in 1946). By the time of the Molotov-Ribbentrop Pact, Zawieyski was already an accomplished playwright. Baptized as a Catholic, he left the Church as a young adult, disgusted with its integral nationalism and its intolerance—both toward Poland's Jews, and toward his own homosexuality. During the war, Korniłowicz helped Zawieyski to rediscover his Catholic faith. In the immediate postwar, Zawieyski tried to return the favor by helping the Catholic Church to find a modus vivendi with the Communist regime.

In August 1948, however, the playwright left the Wrocław congress appalled at its evident Stalinist turn. Abandoning public life for a decade, he avoided any cooperation with the regime, or with Piasecki's Catholic socialists. A decade later, this man breathed new life into

the Polish Catholic intellectual world on the heels of de-Stalinization, launching the Catholic Intelligentsia Club movement that exists
in Poland to this day. In 1948, however, there was only one outlet in
Communist Poland to which both he and the young philosopher-priest
Wojtyła could turn: Jerzy Turowicz's *Tygodnik Powszechny*.

## MODERNITY AS A "RETURN TO THE SOURCES"

In its modern history, two intellectual giants tower over the Dominican order: Marie-Dominique Chenu and Yves Congar. Both were
French, and they worked at France's most prominent Dominican seminary, called Le Saulchoir, in the 1920s, 1930s, and 1940s. In the 1940s,
both became black sheep of the Church, targeted by Pius XII's Holy
See for sanction and silencing. Following that pontiff's death in 1958,
however, both not only returned to the Church's good graces, but in
fact became key drivers of its transformation.[4]

Le Saulchoir, founded in 1904 in the Belgian town of Tournai, moved
to Paris in 1937 under Chenu's leadership. That same year, the Dominican rector codified the seminary's intellectual methodology in a book
entitled *A School of Theology: Le Saulchoir*, which drew extensively
on the most famous theologian in the history of the monastic order:
Thomas Aquinas.[5] Together with his colleague Yves Congar, Chenu
emulated the methodology of the *Summa Theologiae*, believing that
Catholicism's renewal in a secularizing world required a return to its
sources.

Le Saulchoir's was a self-consciously "modern" methodology. The
philosopher Charles Taylor has defined modernity as "an exercise in
retrieval," and this definition suits perfectly the task that Congar and
Chenu set for themselves: to confront the sources of their faith with the
immediate challenges of the world around them.[6] The most important
element of this methodology was *ressourcement*: a literal "return to the
sources." By sources, they meant above all the Bible, but also the "pa-
tristic" writings of the founding fathers of Church doctrine: Anselm,
Ambrose, and Augustine, as well as "the historical Thomas Aquinas,
Catholic theology's authority par excellence."[7]

Since the sixteenth-century Counter-Reformation, Catholic thinkers
who wanted to apply rationalist standards of critique to the foundational source texts of Christianity had been heavily sanctioned, first

by the Roman Inquisition and then by its modern successor, the Holy Office. This, after all, is what Luther and Calvin had done. In the early twentieth century, Pope Pius X condemned this type of source critique as a form of "modernist" heresy.[8]

Yet the Saulchoir faculty refused to validate the Holy See's methods. Rejecting the "modernist" label, they argued that *ressourcement* was the only way to make good on Leo XIII's call to restore Thomas Aquinas to the center of mainstream Catholic theology.[9] Congar and Chenu welcomed the work of, among others, Jacques Maritain, but for these Dominicans his writings were not enough.[10] Unlike their lay friend, the Dominicans refused to consider the *Summa Theologiae* on the same plane as later theologians' commentaries on the text, insisting instead on the absolute priority of Aquinas's own writings. Le Saulchoir promoted what Chenu and Congar called "historical theology" over and against the "speculative theology" predominant among the Vatican's officially sanctioned scholastic theologians—especially their Dominican brother Réginald Garrigou-Lagrange. The Saulchoir theologians thereby pointed the way toward a reform of Catholicism by promoting a return to early Christian practices.

Congar and Chenu were both already generating controversy in the mid-1930s. Le Saulchoir moved to Paris in the year of Pius XI's *Divini Redemptoris*, in which the pope reminded his flock that Communism was the "scourge of Satan." Yet Chenu, in his guide to the seminary's methodology, complained that Dominicans could not effectively engage with modern philosophy without understanding Marx, Engels, and Lenin.[11] As the seminary's rector, he ordered the shelves of its library stocked full of Marxist writings. The result was Chenu's first official reprimand—by his order's Master-General—in 1938.

While Chenu led Le Saulchoir to the brink of heterodoxy, Congar vented his frustration with mainstream Catholic theology's inability to address the needs of the working poor. In 1935, Congar wrote,

> While *work* is one of the most important elements of human life and the modern states are seeking to give it status, where do we have a theology of work? There is an urgent need for us as clerics to turn our efforts and apply our vocation of "salt of the earth" to theology itself, as a human *science* of the things of faith or that touch on faith. As long as we have not done the theology of all the great human realities that must be won back for Christ, we will not have done the first thing that

is to be done. As long as we talk about Marxism and Bolshevism in Latin, as I've seen it done in classes and at conferences of theologians, Lenin can sleep in peace in his Moscow mausoleum.[12]

Clearly, Congar himself was no Marxist. Rather, the Dominicans of Le Saulchoir represented what theologian Robin Lovin has called "Christian realism."[13] Looking at the world around them, half a century after *Rerum Novarum*, they saw the proletariat slipping away from Catholicism while Church orthodoxy had trapped itself in byzantine, legalistic debates that accorded the Holy Office priority over the *Summa Theologiae*—and even the Bible. These observations led the "new theologians" to the conviction that Catholicism not only could, but in fact must study and borrow from the best in Marxist thought and practice. Congar, in particular, insisted that Catholic philosophers and theologians needed to recover an ontological link that Marx had highlighted: between personhood and the value of human work.

In the 1930s, Chenu and Congar, like Emmanuel Mounier, represented the radical vanguard of Roman Catholicism. Unlike Mounier, however, their focus was not a reordering of politics and society, but instead a revolution in what it meant to preach or evangelize the faith. Theirs was a movement of pastoral renewal, and they initiated a transnational movement of dissident Catholic theology that would include at least five European countries—Belgium, France, Germany, the Netherlands, and Poland—and multiple monastic orders: Jesuits as well as Dominicans.[14]

Even before the outbreak of World War II, the Holy Office had derisively labeled the transnational *ressourcement* movement a "new theology"—with "new" intended to be a slur—condemning those theologians for allegedly breaking with tradition and orthodoxy.[15] In February 1942, Chenu's guide to the methodology of Le Saulchoir was placed on the Vatican's Index of Banned Books. Chenu made matters worse for himself by describing his detractors' work as "theological imperialism which is nothing but intellectual clericalism."[16] The outcome was an effective silencing of the Dominican luminary. Stripped of his seminary rectorship and banned from teaching there, Chenu became a favorite punching bag of *L'Osservatore Romano* (*The Roman Observer*), the Vatican's daily newspaper. Up-and-coming Neapolitan theologian Pietro Parente, a trusted confidant of Pius XII, called Chenu and his Saulchoir colleagues "portents of a dangerous threat to Catholic teachings."[17]

The condemnation of Chenu was only the first in a series of attacks on "new theology." Chenu and Congar were kept on an ever-tightening leash after 1942, with both ultimately banned from teaching altogether in 1954.[18] Yet the Holy See's repressive measures turned the Dominicans into causes célèbres, mobilizing transnational Catholic sentiment against the Vatican even among venerable institutions of unwavering orthodoxy. Joseph Folliet, chair of the celebrated Lyon-based Social Weeks (*Semaines Sociales*), apparently experienced a breakdown on hearing of the suppression of new theology. To Yves Congar, he wrote, "What I wanted to tell you is that I feel deeply wounded by the measure to which you have fallen victim, wounded as though I myself had been its addressee."[19]

In its response to the Thomist pioneers of *ressourcement*, the Holy See demonstrated that it was completely unsuited to be the command center for Catholics who were catering to the spiritual and material needs of the working poor. This was a particularly devastating revelation at the turn of the 1940s and 1950s, when half of Europe was being remade in the Soviet Union's image.[20]

## A PASTORAL REVOLUTION

Cardinal Emmanuel Suhard, archbishop of Paris and primate of France at the time of the country's capitulation to Germany in 1940, was initially an enthusiastic supporter of Philippe Pétain's collaboration with the Third Reich.[21] What ultimately turned Suhard against Vichy and the Germans was the introduction in September 1942 of the Compulsory Labor Service (STO, *Service du Travail Obligatoire*), which conscripted French citizens to work in labor camps in the Third Reich.[22] The STO precluded any exemptions for priests, which Suhard took as an affront to the sanctity of the cloth.

Suhard's anger at the STO had consequences that far outlasted the war and occupation. After he assigned priests from his archdiocese to survey the STO's impact on clergy, he received a report that both terrified him and inspired him to create a new pastoral project focused on reaching France's working masses. Having already called for the creation of a large new seminary in 1941, the primate, acting on advice from three priests—Louis Augros, Henri Godin, and Yvan Daniel—initiated the enterprise that became the French Mission.[23]

Augros, Godin, and Daniel all had significant experience as social activists working in the interwar teams (*équipes*) of the Young Christian Workers (JOC, *Jeunesse Ouvrière Chrétienne*). Originally a Belgian derivative of Catholic Action, JOC enjoyed great success in France in the 1930s in organizing devout young industrial workers. JOC's goal was to preserve and deepen those workers' spiritual commitments. Lofty as these ideals were, they proved deeply compelling to the thousands who signed up. This was not, however, a way to reach the entirety of a given country's working classes.[24]

In August 1942, the French primate's confidant Louis Augros, pastor at the Saint-Sulpice Church in Paris, arranged a meeting with the cardinal for himself and his friends Henri Godin and Yvan Daniel. Augros's goal was to convince Suhard to dedicate the country's new seminary to evangelizing the proletariat. By the meeting's end, the priests had piqued their primate's interest. Worried about the impact of the STO on clergy and laity alike, Suhard asked Godin and Daniel to prepare a report on the "spiritual state" of France's workers. Suhard officially launched the new seminary two months later, but he held off on finalizing its curriculum until he received Godin and Daniel's report.

On the primate's authority, the two priests criss-crossed France, collecting testimony and statistical data for their report.[25] The country's occupied northern zone had been subject to labor deportations since the armistice of 1940, while the newly introduced STO policy had expanded the pool of potential conscripts to include residents of the southern, Vichy zone as well.[26] Among those interviewed by the priests were workers who had returned from forced labor in Germany. These men inspired Godin and Daniel to make the case to Suhard that forced labor had accelerated the secularization of the French proletariat, and that the Church in France needed to mount an immediate, bold response in order to fight that trend.

What so struck both the report's authors and their primate were stories that conscripted priests and JOC activists were preaching the Gospels in STO camps in order to alleviate the psychological burden on their fellow laborers.[27] One JOC activist who had just been released from a German work camp told Godin and Daniel that "Christ willed that this great misery of the war and the STO serve to spread his doctrine. He gave us a unique opportunity to touch the masses, the real masses, in permanent and profound interaction."[28]

On receiving Godin and Daniel's report in April 1943, Suhard was reportedly so moved that he spent a sleepless night reading the whole document. What so absorbed him was the priests' meticulous reconstruction of "the retreat of Christianity in France," where "in 1943, *the faith is not being preached in an entire milieu, millions of people in France are not hearing the Gospel.*"[29] Suhard's response was to publish the report later that year under the title *France, A Mission Country? (La France, pays de mission?).* The new seminary that he had just opened was christened the French Mission, and Louis Augros became its first rector.[30]

The methodology for this seminary came directly from Godin and Daniel, who argued that the modern, war-torn world needed "the renewal of the gesture of Christ, who took form and came into the world to save it." The program of the French Mission centered on the "reconversion" of those sectors of the country—above all, the industrial proletariat—that had lost contact with the Gospels and with the Church. Priests participating in the French Mission therefore needed special training—a "real missionary vocation."[31] Only this kind of pastoral approach stood a chance of helping workers feel like "human persons," and thereby winning them back to the faith, which would actually restore their personhood.

War or no war, the proletarian "person" had been dispossessed, atomized, and alienated from Christendom by the Industrial Revolution and its long-term consequences. As Godin and Daniel put it, "Yes or no, if Christ came to aid us in 1943 in the re-establishment of religion in our world, in its present state of ferment, would he not count above all, as before, on the meek, on the proletarians?"[32]

The French Mission's methodology benefited intellectually from, among others, the new theologians and the personalism of Emmanuel Mounier. Looking to help priests forge bonds of "human solidarity" by awakening a sense of "Christian community," Godin and Daniel insisted that the first step was to recognize "the priority of personhood."[33] Priests needed to understand that their project was not just about spiritual salvation, but was aimed at a recovery of the image of God in each worker they encountered.

The Dominican Chenu, whom the French primate counted as a friend, sat on the board of censors that granted *France, A Mission Country?* its stamp of Church approval. This came in May 1943, just one year after Chenu's own indictment by the Holy See's Index of Banned Books.[34] As the new French Mission seminary developed a curriculum based on the report of Godin and Daniel, Chenu played the role of advisor to the seminary's rector Louis Augros, becoming one of the French Mission's strongest public advocates.[35] After all, the new seminary brought to life the lessons that Chenu and Congar had been teaching for over a decade.[36]

It should come as no surprise then that, even though the French Mission was created by the French primate himself, the Vatican looked on it unkindly from the start.[37] Of particular concern were the Marxist literature available in the seminary's library, the "communal" style of vocational training, and the influence of the "new theologians." The French Mission operated on the assumption that evangelization was best achieved through small teams of missionaries able to fan out across several parishes and set down roots in their new communities. Ideologically, institutionally, and pastorally, the seminary was breaking new ground.

### KAROL WOJTYŁA: ROMAN PHD STUDENT

Three years after Godin and Daniel handed their report to the French primate, the young Karol Wojtyła arrived in Rome to pursue a PhD at the Collegium Angelicum, an institution devoted to the study of Thomism. It was the archbishop of Kraków, Adam Stefan Sapieha, who had decided that Wojtyła should leave Poland for his studies. The prelate had ordained the twenty-six-year-old only a few months earlier. Sapieha's initiative likely saved Wojtyła—a member of the Union resistance movement, and the alumnus of a clandestine wartime seminary—from arrest, interrogation, and possibly torture at the hands of postwar Poland's secret police.[38]

During World War II, Wojtyła survived by laboring in a limestone quarry and in the Solvay chemical factory outside Kraków. In his few free hours, he met with Christian Democratic resistance fighters and performed in an illegal theater troupe. In February 1940, he joined an underground Catholic study group organized by the tailor Jan Tyranowski, whom Salesian fathers had tasked with creating a space outside mass where young men living in Kraków could meet to pray together, hidden from the menace of the Gestapo. Running a group that he called the "Living Rosary," Tyranowski introduced Wojtyła and scores of other young men to the seventeenth-century Spanish Carmelite mystic John of the Cross. Following his early-modern hero, Tyranowski insisted that any man could be a "saint."[39]

Ultimately, Tyranowski helped Wojtyła to discover his priestly vocation. Two years' worth of weekly readings from John of the Cross led the young actor and day laborer to consider becoming a monk. Archbishop Sapieha met with and liked the young man, accepting him into the archdiocese's clandestine seminary—but also dissuading him from the path of monastic isolation.

In some ways, then, it was the Kraków tailor, who died of tuberculosis in 1946, rather than Wojtyła's Roman PhD advisor, who defined the contours of the future pope's intellectual and pastoral trajectory. And yet that advisor was Dominican theologian Réginald Garrigou-Lagrange, Pius XII's most trusted authority on Thomism.[40] Like Wojtyła, the French Dominican had, in his youth, been fascinated by John of the Cross, and he wrote extensively on how the Spanish friar's writings could aid in interpreting the *Summa*.[41]

With age, however, Garrigou-Lagrange became an intransigentist. He discouraged critical and creative readings of Aquinas, which he saw as verging on modernist heresy. Once a close friend to Maritain, Chenu, and Congar, Garrigou-Lagrange had, by the 1940s, become one of their harshest critics. In fact, he personally played a central role in publicizing the derogatory label *nouvelle théologie* for the writings of his Dominican brothers, and he ultimately drafted an encyclical for Pius XII—the 1950 *Humani Generis*—that included a wholesale condemnation of *ressourcement*.

Unlike his Polish graduate student, who had been a member of the anti-German underground, Garrigou-Lagrange had, in fact, enthusiastically endorsed Vichy's collaboration with the Third Reich.[42] This did not diminish his expertise in Thomism, but it limited his authority in the eyes of younger generations who, like Wojtyła, had either themselves witnessed Nazi atrocities or had heard extensive accounts of them. Jacques Maritain, whom Wojtyła had read in Sapieha's wartime seminary, parted ways with Garrigou-Lagrange over his insistence that theological orthodoxy and political autocracy should go hand in hand.

Maritain arrived in Rome in 1945 as France's postwar Ambassador to the Holy See, less than a year before Wojtyła began his studies at the Collegium Angelicum. When the Dominican accused his one-time lay friend of having betrayed Thomism by endorsing democracy during the war, Maritain cut to the heart of Garrigou-Lagrange's authoritarian politics: "Whatever our political differences may be, you had no right whatsoever in this regard to cast the slightest suspicion on my doctrine. When you took the side of Marshal Pétain, to the point of declaring that to support de Gaulle was a mortal sin, I felt that your political prejudices blinded you in a matter that was very serious for our country, but it did not even cross my mind to suspect your theology or to accuse you of deviation in matters of doctrine. I might add that I was very sorry about the way you compromised Thomism through your political positions that were justifiably odious to those who were struggling for the liberation of our country."[43]

Even by Roman standards, then, the future John Paul II's academic advisor was an archconservative: an ardent opponent of Marxism and liberalism alike, and one of Pius XII's most trusted theological watchdogs. Yet, in the course of two years as Garrigou-Lagrange's student, the young Wojtyła embraced a range of radical new tendencies within the Church. In his writings, he sought, for example, to square the rationalism of Thomas Aquinas with a mystical existentialism derived from John of the Cross. In his pastoral life, he grew enamored of the same "new theology" and French Mission methods that his advisor so deplored. In his first stint as a transnational intellectual, Karol Wojtyła learned to espouse both orthodoxy and radicalism. These qualities, which later defined him as a pope, grew out of the combination of lessons learned from his French intransigentist advisor and the French reformist movements that he encountered outside the halls of the Angelicum.

Wojtyła's 300-page dissertation on Aquinas and John of the Cross, written in Latin and defended in June 1948, provides the key to understanding how the young priest defined his responsibilities as "shepherd" of a "Christian flock."[44] For Wojtyła, the thesis was as much a spiritual creed as a critical reading of theology. George Huntston Williams puts it best: "It is evident from the clarity of the dissertation that the youthful brooder in the parks, woods, and mountain forests, now the priest of destiny, had himself some experience comparable to that of the Spanish mystic or he could scarcely have made that exalted realm of the spirit in faith so clear in limpid Latin with Spanish footnotes."[45]

In his dissertation, Karol Wojtyła laid out a personalist rationale for the aggressive evangelization of all mankind. Though made in God's image, human beings lack what the young cleric called an "essential likeness" to God. As a consequence, he contended, the human intellect engages in a perpetual quest for that missing essence of the divine, which is how Wojtyła defines "love." According to the young priest, only through faith can the human intellect find God, achieving a "union of likeness called by love." Only through "witness of personal experience," he wrote, can we "discover the living and dynamic reality of the virtue of faith, its activity in the human intellect, its corollaries and the effects on the movement of the soul toward union with God."[46]

These claims represent the foundations of Wojtyła's pastoral philosophy. At its core was personalism, rooted in the study of the *Summa Theologiae*. Like Maritain, Wojtyła believed that Aquinas's notion of the "human person" most properly embodied the Catholic Church's fundamental mission: to minister to all of humanity. At the same time, however, Wojtyła took liberties with Thomism, exploring "essential likeness" as a product of mystical awakening. In particular, Wojtyła emphasized that human beings find fulfillment in God as acting members of the Church. In other words, for a "human being" to become a "human person" in the fully Christian sense, he must achieve an existential likeness with God through love.

Over the next thirty years, Wojtyła's theology evolved. As Supreme Pontiff of the Roman Catholic Church, Wojtyła would contend that God had made all human beings to be "persons" in His image. This was the source of human dignity. Personhood is prior to faith, declared John Paul II in 1979, which is why humanity is able to enjoy God's gift of freedom by sharing its wealth—what the pope called "unreserved giving of the whole of one's human person."[47] That is the ultimate act of faith—surrender, following the example of Jesus Christ.

As a graduate student, however, the future pope took a very different stance. In his dissertation, he clearly suggested that personhood is not an a priori condition of being human. Instead, he presented personhood as a consequence of what we might today call a conversion experience: a uniquely personal—even mystical—encounter with God that allows human beings to experience the very essence of faith and love. For the young Wojtyła, then, only the process of becoming a consciously believing Christian could make a "human person." Because there could be no salvation outside the Church, there could also be no personhood for non-Catholics.

Rather than stop at this theologically orthodox conclusion, however, Wojtyła believed that the limits of personhood should motivate priests to be as creative as possible in their pastoral work. After all, the stakes could not possibly be higher: salvation for as many human beings as possible. Wojtyła wanted every human being to become a "human person," and that meant finding more effective ways of reaching those most alienated from the modern Church: the industrial proletariat. Paradoxically, the parochialism of the young Wojtyła's reading of Thomist philosophy drove him to take the most open-ended stance that he could conceive as a pastor: the Church should provide all human beings with every possible opportunity to love God through the witness of personal experience. Thus the theological conservative became a pastoral radical.

## KAROL WOJTYŁA: WORKER-PRIEST IN TRAINING

Terrifying as Garrigou-Lagrange was, he evinced respect for his Polish pupil, and Wojtyła's encounters with him instilled in the young priest a profound appreciation for Thomism as a source of authority within Catholicism. Yet the mentor had relatively little time for his Polish disciple. Left to his own devices, Wojtyła read widely, attended lectures, and made friends with his fellow residents of Rome's Belgian College. His extracurricular activities as a graduate student held the key to Wojtyła's emerging pastoral radicalism. When the Kraków archbishop asked him to spend the summer of 1947 exploring Catholic pastoral life in France, Belgium, and the Netherlands, the young priest had the opportunity to turn theory into practice.

Archbishop Sapieha—recently elevated to the rank of cardinal—secured for Wojtyła and Stanisław Starowieyski, his fellow Polish student at the Angelicum, a stipend to fund three months away from Rome. The bulk of what we know about their travels in the summer of 1947 comes from two of Wojtyła's own texts written two years later, following his return to Poland.[48] The Kraków cardinal tasked the two

Fig. 8: A 1948 photo of Rev. Karol Wojtyła, last row, right, during his two-year stay at the Belgian College in Rome. Wojtyła later became Pope John Paul II. (AP Photo) © 2018 The Associated Press.

young clerics with a very broad mission: "to study pastoral methods."[49] Theirs was a fact-finding trip, but it was also a pretext for Wojtyła and Starowieyski not to come home to Poland for the summer. Had they done so, they might not have been permitted to return to Rome in the fall to resume their studies.

For the twenty-first-century reader, it is hard to grasp how transformative this trip was for the twenty-seven-year-old from Wadowice. He had never before been to these countries—indeed, he had not traveled widely at all—yet here he was now representing one of Central and Eastern Europe's most venerable clerics to some of the greatest pioneers of Catholic reform. Three months' worth of first-hand encounters gave Wojtyła the opportunity to consider the practical, pastoral implications of the medieval and early-modern Latin and Spanish that he had been reading all year in Rome, locked away from the world.

Belgium and the Netherlands were no mere afterthoughts to Wojtyła and Starowieyski's itinerary. The French Mission's first graduating classes had fanned out across not only the key French industrial centers of Paris, Marseille, and Lille, but also into Walloon and Flemish port and mining communities. At its core, the Mission had Belgian roots, building on the respected interwar Young Christian Workers movement. JOC, as it was known, had debuted in Belgium before taking French Catholicism by storm. Its founder, Joseph Cardijn, was no modernist. Yet early in his priestly career, Cardijn had declared that his goal was "to end the scandal which brings death to millions of young workers, separating them from Christ and the Church."[50] In designing JOC, he adapted a mid-nineteenth-century paternalist model of Catholic workers' circles to the purposes of a mass organization that operated across national borders. The final outcome was to be a tightly supervised network of young industrial workers' circles.

Wojtyła's dormitory for both of his years in Rome was the Belgian College, just a few hundred meters from the former papal residence at the Quirinal Palace. The connection to Belgium proved fortuitous for the Polish student. In his own dormitory, Wojtyła had the chance to attend a gathering with JOC founder Cardijn in the fall of 1946; the great pastoral organizer returned to the college several times while Wojtyła resided there.

With each successive encounter JOC impressed him more. For Wojtyła, Cardijn's insistence on the "duties of a modern pastor" represented innovation: pioneering new forms of ministry that targeted specific classes of the faithful. Even as an outsider, Wojtyła immediately perceived the roots of the French Mission in JOC. Having read Godin and Daniel's book, Wojtyła could not shake one particular scene: "those who have completely lost touch with Christianity [. . .] are multiplying at a fearful rate. Take this example for instance. A group of lads come upon a statue of Christ on the cross, and study it with interest. They see the letters INRI over the top, and one of them says: 'Inri, was that the chap's name?'"[51]

Karol Wojtyła was not privy to the Church hierarchy's debates on the doctrinal standing of the French Mission, in particular its self-styled "worker-priests." Insisting that to minister effectively to the proletariat, one had to join its ranks, the *prêtres-ouvriers* themselves became wage-earning stevedores, coal miners, and assembly-line workers. In Wojtyła's eyes, this was not a radical revision of the French Mission, but rather its quintessential fulfillment: "The clergyman is a man who together with Christ and through Christ offers up every molecule of human effort and human work to the Heavenly Father. He joins this milieu in order to endow the whole of its lifeblood with the ultimate value represented by Christ's Sacrifice."[52]

The itinerary followed by Wojtyła and Starowieyski in their travels reversed the path taken by French-language pastoral reform in the 1930s and 1940s. JOC had helped to inspire the French Mission, which in turn produced worker-priests. For practical reasons, however, the Poles began in the south of France with the worker-priests, moved north to meet alumni of the French Mission, and ended with JOC. Afterwards, Wojtyła stayed behind in Belgium as a temporary replacement for the pastor of a community of Polish workers. This was, in effect, an apprenticeship in the life of a worker-priest. Entering into dialogue and witnessing the ministry of these various groups made a pastoral revolutionary of Karol Wojtyła, teaching him that "Catholic intellectual activism alone does not suffice to transform society." And yet "it is indirectly apostolic, inasmuch as it nourishes the roots of social activism."[53] This is how Wojtyła understood his purpose as a spiritual guide: translating the heady intellectualism of Doctors of the Church like Thomas Aquinas and John of the Cross into the everyday experience of those most alienated from the faith.

Hours after arriving in Marseille on July 3, 1947, Wojtyła and Starowieyski sat down with Jacques Loew, an outspoken Dominican priest who was also a prolific writer. In 1941, after he finished seminary, Loew's superiors had sent him to Marseille to minister to workers. Loew had gone to work as a stevedore, and in that capacity he became one of the first worker-priests in France's largest port city—a city filled with manual laborers, many of them immigrants, long abandoned by the French state.[54]

In Marseille, Loew realized that dockworkers and their families had become so alienated from the Church that simply visiting with them or preaching to them would achieve nothing. Loew concluded that "it was no good wasting time on paper theories: the thing to do was to buy overalls on the old-clothes market, get a job like everyone else, and then, at the end of the day's work, go off and live with the very dregs of the population—the dockers on the ports."[55] Loew told Wojtyła that he had taken up manual labor only because he felt that no other form of ministry made sense: priests first needed to re-establish the sacred trust between pastors and proletarian catechumens. Wojtyła clearly agreed.

A year before the Polish priests paid him a visit in Marseille, Jacques Loew had published an account of his worker-priest ministry in which he laid out a blueprint for pastoral revolution based on his own experiences. Just like Władysław Korniłowicz in Piłsudski's Poland, Loew learned under the Vichy regime that the Catholic Church needed a dramatically new approach to saving souls: face-to-face dialogue built on a foundation of trust and solidarity. While Korniłowicz shared the *Summa* with his catechumens, Jacques Loew shared manual labor on the docks of Marseille. From his experience he concluded that the Church could not succeed in protecting personhood in an industrialized world without "a transformation of the priesthood, which, in the service of the laity, will transform the working class." For young priests finishing seminary in postwar France, the Dominican wrote, "To be in the very heart of a mission, you don't have to set out for the Cameroons." It was enough to cross over to the "bad" side of one's own city.[56] As Karol Wojtyła later recalled, the Dominican "had reached the conclusion that a white cassock no longer stood for anything on its own."[57] Any missionary's first task was, therefore, not to force feed the Gospel to disaffected people living in infested and overcrowded tenements, but to leave his ivory tower and "to live amongst them and win their acceptance as men." In so doing, priests might have a chance to experience the deepest solidarity they had ever known.[58]

To the young philosopher-priest from Wadowice, Loew's description of worker solidarity was a revelation. Wojtyła already knew the word well from the encyclicals of Pius XI; Loew's definition, however, was born not of doctrine, but of actual missionary work among proletarians. The idea that the working poor had their own forms of solidarity—and that Catholics, in order to succeed in their work of catechism, needed to learn solidarity from the workers—made a deep impression on the future pope. As he later explained in the pages of *Tygodnik Powszechny*, "shared work breaks through antagonistic attitudes, forms bonds based on a shared skill set, a certain community of life interests; it thereby opens a path to apostolic activity."[59]

From the docks of Marseille, Wojtyła and his companion headed to the shrine at Lourdes to pray to the Virgin Mary. From this pilgrims' haven in the foothills of the Pyrenees, the Poles headed on to Paris. Rather than see the sights, they went straight to the city's industrial slums. In Colombes and Gennevilliers, in Asnières and Nanterre, the priest Georges Michonneau introduced them to the Paris Mission (*Mission de Paris*). This was Paris's answer to the French Mission, and Michonneau—formerly a parish priest in the southern suburb of Clichy—took pride in the initiative's local roots.[60] Michonneau was not a worker-priest. Instead, he followed the classical method defined by Godin and Daniel: living among the poor, establishing trust with them, but without going so far as to work for pay in factories or on ships. Michonneau explained his approach, "I consider every individual living in the neighborhood to be a parishioner. Everyone—with no exceptions on the basis of nationality, social marginality, or even opposition to organized religion. I feel responsible for their souls. I try to live as they do—at work, at leisure, and in family life."[61]

On August 5, 1947, Wojtyła and Starowieyski left Paris for Brussels. There they paid a visit to JOC founder Cardijn, who remembered them from the Belgian College in Rome.[62] In his 1946 lectures in Rome, Cardijn had seemed to call for exactly what the worker-priests were doing. A year later, however, Wojtyła heard the opposite from the future cardinal. Impassioned by his interview with Jacques Loew, the Polish student could only shake his head at Cardijn's diatribe against the worker-priest movement. The Belgian's line was simple: "The worker does not want the priest to become a worker, but instead only to be a real priest to him. A worker-priest can never be a real worker because he can choose at any moment to stop being a worker."[63]

Foundational as JOC had been for the young Wojtyła's pastoral philosophy, by the late summer of 1947 he had concluded that it was too conservative. Wojtyła put it delicately: "whether or not the path [of the worker-priests] is the correct one, must we not acknowledge the fact that this is certainly one of the most elemental manifestations of the Holy Spirit, which ceaselessly reveals in the life of the Church ever newer, previously unknown, paths and roads?"[64]

In fact, Wojtyła felt so passionately about the worker-priest example that, after a detour through Ghent, Bruges, Amsterdam, Rotterdam, and The Hague, he returned to Wallonia. While Starowieyski traveled on, Wojtyła remained by himself in the mining city of Charleroi for the entire month of September. Belgium had seen a massive influx of Poles in the nineteenth century, following two separate anti-Russian insurrections—in 1830–31 and 1863–64—and many of the Poles had become miners in the area around Charleroi.[65] Historically, the Belgian episcopate had appointed as this community's pastors Polish-born priests who had completed university studies in French.[66] For several weeks, Wojtyła became part of this tradition, temporarily replacing the pastor of the Polish Catholic émigré mission at Charleroi.

This assignment charged the young priest with the souls of several hundred Polish coal miners. Wojtyła later recalled how deeply this experience affected him, evoking memories of his own labor in a limestone quarry outside Kraków during the German occupation of Poland. More than the stevedores of Marseille or the factory workers of Paris, it was the Polish coal miners of Charleroi who spurred the young Wojtyła to identify with the worker-priests. Among the miners, he saw himself as both worker and priest. On his return to Rome at the end of the summer, Wojtyła explored this identity further, volunteering to assist in the Roman industrial parish of Garbatella.

Despite appearances, then, Wojtyła the PhD candidate and Wojtyła the young pastor were not two different personalities, but one integrated whole. What Wojtyła had taken away from John of the Cross was the need for a Catholic to place front and center both "the movement of the soul toward union with God" and "witness of personal experience." The Polish student's reading of Thomas Aquinas and John of the Cross led him to the conviction that, as a pastor, he needed to minister to atheists and Christians alike, to the most "at-risk" populations as much as to the pious—if not more so.

The French Mission resonated with Wojtyła emotionally and spiritually. Especially compelling for him were its most radical pastors: the worker-priests.[67] The Dominican dockworker Jacques Loew had—in Wojtyła's words—chosen to demonstrate his fitness as a "pastor to his colleagues and comrades" by "becoming one of them."[68] A report to the French Mission by a team of worker-priests based in Alfortville illustrated the virtues of this approach: "One of our team members, a former blue-collar worker, told us that he had been unable to enter into conversations with the workers in his neighborhood, other than by talking to them for a long time about his former work, and by showing that he knew all about the things preoccupying their minds. Only on this basis did trust get established, and only then were they able to pose [*sic!*] him the most profound questions on religion and on Christian belief."[69]

And yet, the worker-priests' days were numbered. In 1953, the order came down from the Vatican to suppress all worker-priest activity. Yves Congar spoke for several generations' worth of pastoral reformers when he denounced Pius XII's Holy See as "a police regime of betrayal."[70]

Wojtyła did not anticipate the suppression of the worker-priests, and in fact his writing from the late 1940s celebrates the pastoral radicalism that they embodied. His PhD thesis gave him the opportunity to work out the foundations of his own personalism and, in doing so, to discover the role of "witness" in helping human beings to achieve personhood. Through his encounters with JOC, the French Mission, and the worker-priest movement, Wojtyła came to understand two complementarities that defined his lifelong approach to pastorship: between human work and pastoral mission; and between priests and laity in their shared task of spreading the Catholic faith, and with it, personhood. After all, even Jesus had been a carpenter.

## JERZY ZAWIEYSKI: PLAYWRIGHT, ACTIVIST, CATECHUMEN

After World War II, priests were no longer alone in spreading the word of the Gospels. Across the European continent, Catholic laymen had stepped in to resist fascism and its collaborators while the ecclesiastical hierarchy mostly either kept to the sidelines, or itself collaborated. As Europe emerged from the war, France and Poland had vibrant Catholic intellectual worlds that acted autonomously of both their bishops and the Holy See. As Maryjane Osa writes, the prewar "feudal Church" had become a Church of activists—both laity and clergy.[71]

In this era of lay empowerment, Catholic writers played a special role as transnational authorities, even as the Iron Curtain divided the European continent. We have already seen the growing power of the men and women of *Dziś i Jutro*, *Esprit*, and *Tygodnik Powszechny* as they defined the terms of postwar debates about the future of their countries, their continent, and their faith. Within the larger class of Catholic intellectuals, however, there was a special role reserved for novelists, poets, and playwrights. In the closing months of the war, François Mauriac, who later won the Nobel Prize for Literature, vehemently protested against the wholesale purging (*épuration*) from French public life of activists, intellectuals, and officials with any connection to Vichy.[72] In so doing, Mauriac set the terms of a debate that played out not in niche Catholic publications, but in France's most widely read journals and newspapers. An assemblage of gray-haired eminences of Catholic prose—Georges Bernanos, Paul Claudel, Daniel-Rops—became not only Catholic, but indeed *French*, public intellectuals.[73]

In the 1940s, Catholic intellectuals of all persuasions believed that personhood had to be claimed through a conscious choice of faith. Anyone—Jewish, Protestant, Orthodox, or atheist—could find fulfillment as a "human person" if ably guided through catechism. This, as we have seen, is the one of the beliefs that drew Karol Wojtyła to the French model of mission to the proletariat in the late 1940s. Two decades before the launching of the French Mission, however, the Swiss-trained Polish priest Władysław Korniłowicz had already created a haven for catechumens in Poland, cutting across confessional, class, and ideological lines. Korniłowicz's last catechumen was the author and playwright Jerzy Zawieyski.

In his late fifties, Zawieyski wrote an autobiographical essay entitled "A Catechumen's Path" (*Droga katechumena*). Zawieyski made clear that he had followed a course charted by Korniłowicz and another Polish pastor, Jan Zieja. His example demonstrates just how important catechesis became in Communist Poland. This was a path to personhood that had nothing to do with the Communist agenda, but spoke to the spiritual needs of Catholics striving for social justice. In Zawieyski, we find the other face of pastoral revolution that we have already explored with Karol Wojtyła: the lay catechumen, transformed by face-to-face dialogue with a pastor, making good on the promise of revolution by dialoguing with others.

Born Henryk Nowicki in the industrial city of Łódź, Zawieyski moved to Kraków in the 1920s, and then spent three years in Paris. Although he grew up in a Catholic family, already as a teenager Zawieyski had trouble simply buying into the faith that was passed down to him. His late father had been a secularized Jewish merchant, and though his mother later converted to Catholicism in order to marry his stepfather, Zawieyski never forgot his roots. In the 1920s, he turned away from Catholicism altogether, disgusted by the Church's complicity in injustices that he saw around him. He felt that, rather than promoting social justice, Polish Catholicism was both stoking the flames of anti-Semitism and conspiring to limit the social mobility of agrarian and industrial workers.[74] Zawieyski wrote, "I must confess with sadness that the Church in the person of its institutional representatives, the clergy, constituted for us the greatest roadblock to Catholicism and faith."[75]

As a teenager and then a university student in Łódź, Zawieyski chose a path that struck him as "purer": the path of socialism.[76] He was not a Marxist, but Zawieyski's personal desire to help "bind up the bleeding wounds of the social question in the spirit of social justice" led him to join May 1st demonstrations and other protests demanding solidarity with the workers. While still a student, Zawieyski became secretary of Łódź's Workers' University Association (*Towarzystwo Uniwersytetu Robotniczego*).[77]

The three years (1929–32) that Zawieyski spent in France after his graduation exposed him to a different kind of Catholicism—one that would satisfy his desire for both spiritual guidance and social justice. In between writing his own plays and novellas, Zawieyski read Mauriac and Maritain. The émigré Polish philosopher-priest Augustyn Jakubisiak, who ran Paris's largest Polish-language parish, guided Zawieyski in his encounters with these authors. Thanks to this pastor, the young Catholic writer entered the Parisian Catholic salon culture of the 1930s, meeting Emmanuel Mounier, Gabriel Marcel, and others, and personally debating philosophy with them.[78] On Zawieyski's return to Poland, Jakubisiak also directed the playwright to his friend Korniłowicz. During World War II, Zawieyski became a regular at Laski, where he gained several spiritual mentors.

Among these was the forty-year-old Stefan Wyszyński, who developed a friendship with Zawieyski founded in part on their common passion for French thought, and for Maritain in particular. Although the priest was in hiding throughout the occupation, he led regular clandestine seminars for the resistance fighters of the wartime generation.[79]

In February 1942, guided by Korniłowicz, Zawieyski "reconverted" to Catholicism. Thereafter, until his death in 1969, he considered himself a practicing Catholic. Yet the story of Zawieyski's catechesis is both telling and unrepresentative. Zawieyski was gay. Although he maintained a relatively stable partnership for close to thirty years, the impossibility of reconciling his orientation with canon law ate away at him for the twenty-seven adult years that he lived as a practicing Catholic.[80] This was a core element of who he was: being gay did not challenge his socialism, yet he spent the final decades of his life struggling to reconcile his sexuality with his Catholic piety.

Zawieyski was remarkably well-connected on both sides of the Catholic-Marxist divide. From his student days, he retained extensive contacts with Poland's socialist movements—Marxist and non-Marxist alike. He and Władysław Gomułka had known each other for years by the time Gomułka rose to lead postwar Poland's Communist party. Because Zawieyski was a successful playwright, he became part of Poland's cultural elite; even Communists saw him in these terms, both during and after the war. The postwar Catholic activists of *Dziś i Jutro* knew about Marxist revolution only from books. Zawieyski, meanwhile, had actually lived on both sides of the barricades, struggling his entire adult life with how to reconcile the two.

Zawieyski kept an eye on both France and Poland, and he worked hard to get Polish Catholics to learn from France's successes and failures. In 1947, Zawieyski published a long essay in *Tygodnik Powszechny* entitled "The Matter of Catholic Literature." Drawing on Maritain, Zawieyski demanded that Catholics break out of their "ghetto" and engage the secular world, while at the same time arguing that a distinctively Catholic literature still had value. Catholics, the playwright argued, must take up their pens to spread their ethics in a world that teetered on the edge of nuclear holocaust: "In the secular world, Catholicism values questions pertaining to history, to social movements, to the economy, and to politics. That which is objectively good, which grows out of an intention to ennoble man and society, carries in itself Christian traits. [ ... ] In the face of the atomic bomb, there opens before all of humanity the perspective of a final horizon."[81]

Like the Catholic socialists of *Dziś i Jutro*, Zawieyski believed that every Catholic should support nuclear disarmament. When his old friend, the Marxist poet Jarosław Iwaszkiewicz, included him on the list of invited guests for the Wrocław peace congress of August 1948, Zawieyski went eagerly. But, sitting in the congress hall, Zawieyski could not believe his ears when the Soviet puppet Fadeev viciously de-

Fig. 9: Jerzy Zawieyski, seated right, with Antoni Słonimski and Julian Tuwim, in session at the Congress of Intellectuals in Defense of Peace, Wrocław, Poland, August 25, 1948. Reproduced by permission of the Polish Press Agency (PAP).

nounced Jean-Paul Sartre. Nor could he ignore the fact that the hall seemed to be teeming with plainclothes secret police officers. Sitting with esteemed writers Antoni Słonimski, Julian Tuwim, and Maria Dąbrowska, Zawieyski could not escape the feeling that secret police were simply waiting for any of them to make a political misstep.[82]

The Wrocław congress was Zawieyski's last public appearance for eight years. Less than a month after its conclusion, his old friend Władysław Gomułka was purged from the Polish Communist leadership. Meanwhile, *Dziś i Jutro*'s star was on the rise. Between 1945 and 1948, Zawieyski had published regularly in the pages of *Tygodnik Powszechny*—and, on occasion, in *Dziś i Jutro* and *Tygodnik Warszawski*, too. But, as he left Wrocław in August 1948, Zawieyski saw the writing on the wall. He wanted nothing to do with *Dziś i Jutro*'s promise to Christianize the Marxist revolution from within, or with Poland's Stalinist government.

Making Laski a second home, Zawieyski did not publish a word between 1949 and 1955. In fact, the playwright felt a moral obligation to stay silent, since publishing would have been tantamount to legitimizing *Dziś i Jutro*'s virtual monopoly over Catholic life in Stalinist Poland.[83] In 1956, Zawieyski would return to public prominence arm in arm with the rehabilitated General Secretary Gomułka and the recently freed Primate Wyszyński, their redemption marking the end of the Stalinist era in the People's Republic of Poland. In the intervening years, however, it was only the crew of *Tygodnik Powszechny* that offered some semblance of solace for the Catholic writer in Communist Poland.

## THE LEGACY OF KRAKÓW'S "ARISTOCRATIC CITADEL"

With *Dziś i Jutro* on the rise, the moderates of *Tygodnik Powszechny* focused all of their energy on one goal: keeping their voice heard. In 1946, Stomma had encouraged Catholics in a newly Communist Poland to be guided in their choices by "national interest." But his was not a political statement. Instead, the writers of *Tygodnik Powszechny* and *Znak* asked Poles to focus on cultural, intellectual, and religious life— no matter what happened in the political arena. Unlike their jailed or exiled *Tygodnik Warszawski* counterparts, the Catholics of *Tygodnik Powszechny* fell in line with the new Communist establishment to the extent that they grudgingly accepted Poland's alliance with the USSR. Unlike their *Dziś i Jutro* counterparts, however, Turowicz, Stomma, and their colleagues steadfastly refused to cross the line separating the Catholic obligation to bear witness to secular life from the new radical ideology of Catholic socialism. This was the price of their reluctant support for Communist Poland.

Until mid-1948, *Tygodnik Powszechny* had, broadly speaking, stayed loyal to the legacy of the interwar Renaissance movement: to Antoni Szymański's social Catholicism, Władysław Korniłowicz's catechetical method, and the Thomism that underlay both. After the secret police targeted Jan Piwowarczyk at the end of 1947, state censors became so aggressive toward the weekly that it seemed that substantive articles could no longer appear in print. Jerzy Turowicz soon found that the only meaningful texts his journal could put into circulation were those focused on either the life of the mind (philosophy, literature) or leisure activities (hiking, painting). And still, one editor joked that censors tied the editors' hands so tightly that even articles about mountain-climbing were a risky proposition.[84]

And yet, aside from the persecution of Piwowarczyk, the writers of *Tygodnik Powszechny* and *Znak* remained relatively unscathed by the political intrigue, arrests, and violence that touched the masses of Polish Catholics. As they watched conditions deteriorate for their co-religionists, the Kraków writers remained resolute in what they described as their neo-positivism.[85] They believed, in other words, that they could serve both Poland and the Church best by trying to square national interest with personalist ethics, thereby showing their beleaguered fellow Polish Catholics that, even under Stalinism, it was possible to have a public voice while staying true to their faith. Still, each successive issue of the journal provoked a fight with the censors.

In the early Stalinist years—1948, 1949, 1950—*Tygodnik Powszechny* offered regular commentary on how the editors' civic personalism could enrich Communist Poland. Intent on defending Catholics' right to shape Polish culture, Jerzy Turowicz wrote in January 1949 that "a man of culture, an intellectual, is bound to objectivity and to jealous defense of his independence."[86] In hopes of maintaining this independence, Turowicz was willing to help the Communist government by urging his journal's considerable readership—upwards of 50,000—to support any state policy that was in line with national interest.

As fate would have it, it was Rev. Jan Piwowarczyk who made the most persuasive Catholic case on behalf of Polish claims to the Recovered Territories. Partly out of principle, partly in anticipation of the censors' next move, Turowicz solicited texts from Piwowarczyk ever more selectively, focusing on matters where the priest was willing to criticize the Vatican. For example, Piwowarczyk opposed the Vatican's continued recognition of German jurisdiction over the dioceses of the Recovered Territories, arguing that canon law should follow the redrawing of international borders.[87]

It was on the question of Church-state relations, however, that *Tygodnik Powszechny* came closest to echoing *Dziś i Jutro*. Unlike Piasecki's movement, the writers from Kraków were far from the halls of power. And still, Jerzy Turowicz and Stanisław Stomma elected to put the full weight of their journals behind a moderate line of Church-state cooperation.

Fully aware that the "nations of the world" were deeply frustrated by the "attempt to work out the conditions for a modus vivendi [ . . . ] between Catholicism and Communism," Stomma and Turowicz nonetheless argued in a series of joint editorials that Catholics should give Communist Poland a chance. Despite their disillusionment with Mounier's 1946 visit, it is difficult not to see echoes of his thinking in their own. Like Mounier, Stomma and Turowicz emphasized Poland's uniqueness as a committedly Catholic country planted squarely within the Soviet camp. This fateful position meant that "the Polish experiment in its significance eclipses the affairs of one nation, and that its results will be judged by the entire Catholic Church." While their colleagues at *Dziś i Jutro* wanted Catholic socialism right away, Stomma and Turowicz felt that it would take "several decades at a minimum" to build the kind of trust needed for serious Catholic-Marxist cooperation.[88]

Writing this text in 1952, Stomma and Turowicz could still—arguably—ask with a straight face, "when will we be able to consider the Polish experiment a success in universalistic terms?" By the end of summer 1953, however—at the latest—it was clear that the "experiment" had been a farce. Three bishops—including the Primate of Poland—were under arrest, and the honeymoon period between Catholic intellectuals and Polish Stalinism was over.

By mid-1953, in fact, both Stomma and Turowicz were out of work. The breaking point for *Tygodnik Powszechny* and *Znak* was the massive eulogy campaign for the late Joseph Stalin that mobilized the entire Communist world following the dictator's death in March 1953. Turowicz had, in the past, agreed to publish pieces endorsing Communist policy. These included support for the Stalinist constitution of 1952, as well as a toadying sixtieth-birthday note for Polish president Bolesław Bierut in April 1952. But Turowicz drew the line at Stalin. As a result, the last Stalinist-era issue edited by Turowicz was dated March 8, 1953, and it contained articles focusing on Thomist philosophy and the ethics of the "human person."[89] Its featured author was none other than Karol Wojtyła, who since his return from Rome had been contributing regularly to the weekly.[90]

For the editors of *Tygodnik Powszechny* and *Znak*, singing the praises of Stalin was at odds with Polish *raison d'état*, and therefore a bridge too far. As a result, Poland's Office of Confessional Affairs shuttered *Znak* and transferred control over *Tygodnik Powszechny* to PAX. Thus the one non-Stalinist option for Polish Catholic intellectuals at the turn of the 1940s and 1950s—French-inspired, but guided by its own sense of national interest—was silenced for three years, until the onset of de-Stalinization.[91]

# 7  Stalinist Catholics of Europe, Unite!

## The Stockholm Appeal and the Polish Project of a Catholic-Socialist International, 1949–1953

*Let me do my job as a man and a priest and preach to all men the Lord's precept "Thou shalt not kill." Where is the Communist game in this? [ . . . ] your house and the house of the Communist, both equally, your wife and his, your children and his children, all of us together, are menaced by the atom bomb. This danger can only be eliminated by millions of signatures. Why refuse yours on this petition? Because the Communists have put theirs? Must you be evil because they have been good?*

—*Jean Boulier*[1]

THE 1948 WROCŁAW CONGRESS was but the first step on the path of Catholic-socialist internationalism chosen by the Poles of *Dziś i Jutro*. Along the way, these Catholics signed on for a whole host of Communist-led peace initiatives, handed down from Moscow by the Cominform to Communist parties across Europe. It was the Cominform that gave Wojciech Kętrzyński the idea of building his own "international." In so doing, he copied elements of both Communist internationalism, which Kętrzyński intended to complement, and Christian Democratic internationalism, which he sought to best at its own game. Catholic peace activism across the Iron Curtain may have begun as Cominform propaganda, but, to its French and Polish practitioners, it became a way of life. Budding Catholic socialists on both sides of the Iron Curtain developed personal, institutional, and intellectual friendships with their counterparts, rooted in a deep belief in their common cause.

And yet, despite genuine personalist commitments, these Catholics betrayed their own "revolution." What they said they wanted was peace and human dignity. What they actually did was to endorse the creeping expansion of Soviet power across Central and Eastern Europe. Worse still—they reified ethnonationalism, integralism, and practices of exclusion. In the process, however, they built a rich transnational network across the Iron Curtain—assuring the curtain's permeability, even as Stalinism tightened its grip on the Soviet Bloc.

For Western European progressives, Catholic socialism was a way of protesting the Cold War into which—as they saw it—their new postwar governments had dragged them, in partnership with the United States. The heads of many of these governments were Western Europe's postwar Christian Democrats, who served the "established disorder" whose elements Mounier had so fervently denounced: individualism, capitalism, and liberalism. And yet, like the men and women of *Dziś i Jutro*, the Christian Democrats who helped to unify postwar Western Europe claimed that the virtue of their approach lay in their ability to put Catholic ethics front and center in the public life of their countries. In joining forces with *Dziś i Jutro*, then, Catholic socialists from across the Iron Curtain were attempting to mount a Catholic alternative to the Christian Democrats ascendant across Western Europe. Above all, Catholic socialists opposed the project of (Western) European integration that the Christian Democrats of France, Italy, and West Germany had embraced as their own. The French technocrat Jean Monnet had designed the blueprints, but the Christian Democrats saw it as their path to "a Catholic Europe."[2]

Taking a page from their Western European opponents, *Dziś i Jutro* activists saw in transnationalism the wave of the future. This was the Soviet Bloc's transnational alternative to (Western) European integration, predicated on opposing the Cold War geopolitics of both the Vatican and the Christian Democrats.

The Catholic-socialist international based in Warsaw seemed to have a chance of success until it encountered two major roadblocks. The first was a decisive anti-Catholic turn by Poland's Stalinist establishment. The regime's attacks on bishops and laity alike gave the lie to *Dziś i Jutro*'s promise of Christianizing the revolution. Instead, multiple bishops—including Poland's primate—were taken into custody as enemies of progress.

The second obstacle came in the form of a new generation of true believers. When Kętrzyński's generation turned to Catholic-socialist internationalism, activists ten years their junior rose to the fore of *Dziś i Jutro*. This was a postwar generation, marked by the war, but—for the most part—too young to have spent those six years as clandestine students and guerrilla fighters. They were the next vanguard of Catholic "revolution." In the words of their leader Tadeusz Mazowiecki, "an authentic concern for the victory of the revolution" always took precedence over the kind of institution-building that drove Kętrzyński and Piasecki. Having joined *Dziś i Jutro* in their early twenties, these activists were nudged by Piasecki to channel their devotion to personalism toward a hybrid political program: anti-Germanism, anti-Americanism, ethnonationalism, and Stalinism. From the middle of 1950 onward, the immediate payoff became clear: avoiding a reenactment of the Korean War in the heart of Europe.

This generation's unquestioned leader was Tadeusz Mazowiecki, who, four decades later, would become a leading anti-Communist dissident and prime minister of Poland. To the young Mazowiecki, *Dziś i Jutro* represented Catholicism's chance to share in the real social advancements achieved by the Communists: breaking down Poland's historically rigid class barriers, industrializing a once-backward countryside, and working toward peace. Forty-five years later, Mazowiecki looked back on those Stalinist years with the benefit of hindsight: "What attracted me most was the movement's sensitivity to social issues. That sensitivity undoubtedly caused me to focus more on revolutionary social transformations in the new political order than on the weight of the emerging totalitarian system."[3] This was the logic of Catholic socialism, which initially blinded its most ardent exponents to the political consequences of their social ideals.

## THE PARTISANS OF PEACE

The August 1948 congress in Wrocław launched the international Communist campaign for world peace. That gathering had been the brainchild of Jerzy Borejsza, yet his fall from grace in the following months ensured that credit would instead go to his French partners.[4] That October, Joseph Stalin gave an interview to *Pravda* affirming Moscow's full support for the new "forces in favor of peace."[5]

The Wrocław peace congress supplied ready-made leaders for the Communist-inspired peace movement.[6] In its final minutes, the assembly voted to create the International Liaison Committee of Intellectuals for Peace (ILCIP). Jarosław Iwaszkiewicz became a prominent figure within the new movement, but its chairmanship fell to the eminent French radiochemist Frédéric Joliot-Curie, already active as leader of the Franco-Polish Friendship Association. The new ILCIP executive committee under Joliot-Curie included also the rabble-rouser Fadeev, who had caused such trouble in Wrocław. The appointment of the Soviet author to such a position of authority after he had so deeply offended French progressives showed that Moscow would in fact be pulling the movement's strings. With good reason, then, the British Foreign Office in December 1950 called the peace campaign "a Cominform racket."[7]

The Catholic activists of *Dziś i Jutro*, however, were not privy to the movement's high politics. In February 1949, the ILCIP—together with the Women's International Democratic Federation—issued a joint call for a World Peace Congress. An all-French committee led by Joliot-Curie became responsible for getting the assembly ready within the next two months.

The writers of *Dziś i Jutro* were overjoyed to see Jean Boulier on the committee. The self-styled Red Priest, though not a member of the French Communist Party, had their utmost confidence. Thanks to their contact with Boulier, Poland's Catholic socialists regularly bypassed official channels, making their voice heard among the French organizers of the World Peace Congress. *Dziś i Jutro* correspondent Andrzej Krasiński's networking in Wrocław had begun to pay dividends for his movement.

Meanwhile, his colleague Wojciech Kętrzyński, as *Dziś i Jutro*'s designated foreign relations specialist, attended the Paris congress, one of 2000 delegates from seventy-two countries. At the same time, a parallel congress took place in Prague, assembling those who had been refused French visas.[8] Together, Paris and Prague gave the peace movement a name—the Partisans of Peace—and a mission statement, directed against the brand-new North Atlantic Treaty Organization (NATO). Joliot-Curie put it succinctly: "We are not here to ask for peace, but to impose it. This congress is the reply of the peoples to the signers of the Atlantic pact. To the new war they are preparing, we will reply with a revolt of the peoples." The greatest threat to peace came from "one of the most spectacular misappropriations of science," the atomic bomb, intended by the United States and its Western European allies "as a weapon of mass destruction."[9]

It was the Paris congress's closing resolution, which called for a complete ban on atomic weapons, that paved the way to the Communist-led peace movement's greatest success: the Stockholm Appeal.[10] On March 15, 1950, the Partisans of Peace adopted Soviet writer Ilya Ehrenburg's text as their official line: "We demand the absolute prohibition of the atomic weapon, the weapon of terror and of mass extermination of populations. We demand the establishment of a rigorous international control to assure the application of this measure of prohibition. We consider that the government which first would use the atomic weapon against any country whatsoever would commit a crime against humanity and should be treated as a war criminal."[11]

This text provoked an international uproar. For signatories to the North Atlantic Treaty, the appeal was unacceptable because it turned the Nuremberg Trial language of "crimes against humanity" against their atomic arsenal. Even defensive warfare was to be out of the question. Since Hiroshima and Nagasaki, the United States had remained the primary target of anti-atomic protest, even though US president Harry S. Truman revealed to the world in late 1949 that the Soviet Union, too, had successfully detonated an atomic weapon.[12]

Frédéric Joliot-Curie was the perfect choice to lead the Stockholm Appeal propaganda campaign. As a Nobel Laureate in Chemistry for his work in the field of atomic energy, Joliot-Curie carried serious weight in global discussions concerning atomic weaponry—even where policy was at stake rather than science. For his announcement that he would refuse to work on a weapon that might be turned against the USSR, he had been dismissed in April 1950 from his position as the head of France's Atomic Energy Commissariat (*Commissariat à l'Énergie Atomique*), which he himself had created in 1945. Before the start of the Cold War, Joliot-Curie had been de Gaulle's right-hand man for atomic energy, putting France at the global forefront of the peaceful application of nuclear technology.[13] Joliot-Curie, despite his Communist politics, had the substantive credentials to put an acceptable face on what was essentially a Soviet plea for the UN to promise sanctions against future American action.[14]

The Stockholm Appeal shrewdly targeted religious constituencies as well as political ones. As Joliot-Curie wrote in June 1950, "We have come to a problem which involves all humanity, the American citizen as well as the English, the French, or the Russian citizen, whatever his political or religious opinions may be."[15] One month after the appeal's publication, Jean Boulier circulated a pamphlet entitled "Why I Signed the Stockholm Appeal," in which he set out to convince Catholics that their faith obliged them to lend their support. The priest reasoned that the world was careening toward armed conflict that could end in cataclysm: "from the very first moment of a conflict, atomic death threatens thousands of innocent victims, in the United States, in Europe, in the world. This abominable situation must be done away with."[16]

The best way for Christians to help humanity, Boulier argued, was to sign the Stockholm Appeal: "an appeal by peoples to governments— by people who command to governments who claim to serve them. The governing authorities must hear this appeal like a thunderclap through the snug and tight double doors of the chancelleries. Millions of voices must lend themselves to this appeal. That is why I have given my name."[17] To Christians arguing that the appeal was a Communist "publicity trap," Boulier responded that "sophistry and equivocation" were luxuries that present-day Christians could not afford.[18] And to Christians impugning Boulier personally as a "Moscow spy in a priest's frock," the cleric countered, "This danger can only be eliminated by millions of signatures. Why refuse yours on this petition? Because the Communists have put theirs? Must you be evil because they have been good?"[19]

Anticipating arguments that would enter the Catholic mainstream fifteen years later at Vatican II, Boulier made a case for Catholic dialogue with atheists. Going against over a century of papal teaching, Boulier insisted, "As a Christian I owe it to myself to welcome truth and justice whatever their source, making exceptions of nobody." Invoking Paul, Boulier declared, "I rejoice with the Communists for the good they do, and that is why I am attacked and insulted."[20]

## THE VATICAN AND THE PROGRESSIVES

Jean Boulier did not speak for the Church hierarchy. In fact, he openly flouted its teachings. And yet the arguments that he advanced spoke to thousands of Europeans who could not believe that, a mere five years after Hitler's death, the continent was once again on the brink of war. Most of these Catholics were not Soviet sympathizers. More importantly, neither were they American sympathizers.

For those who in good faith believed in peace and neutrality, the Stockholm Appeal proved an effective propaganda tool. It succeeded in pulling a broad spectrum of Christian support away from the American camp.[21] Unsurprisingly, its success frightened the Vatican: in the pope's eyes, this was the beginning of a Communist tide with the potential to sweep Catholics along as well. For this reason, Pope Pius XII later publicly condemned "pacifist efforts or propaganda originating from those who deny all belief in God."[22] Lawrence Wittner is thus wrong to suggest that "the Catholic church, for the most part, dodged the issue of the Bomb."[23]

Yet Catholics could heed Pius XII's warning and still join peace movements. Catholic socialists, after all, did not "deny all belief in God." Cold War Europe's self-styled progressive Catholics vigorously exploited this loophole. For the Catholic vanguard, this was a time of both promise and peril, especially in France. The Holy See was slowly turning the French bishops against pastoral and political radicalism. Even the episcopate's own initiatives, like the French Mission, would not escape unscathed.

Before the crackdown began, however, pockets of activism sprang up across France. Just one year after the future John Paul II encountered France's worker-priests, André Mandouze cofounded the Union of Progressive Christians (UCP, *Union des Chrétiens Progressistes*). He followed this act by publishing his widely read treatise on "progressive Christianity." Yet the UCP floundered with its patron based in Algiers, dedicating himself to anti-colonialism and the cause of Algerian independence. In 1950, inspired by the Stockholm Appeal, UCP's most die-hard progressives jumped ship to join the staff of a new biweekly journal called *La Quinzaine* (*Fortnight*).[24]

The Stockholm Appeal also breathed new life into a floundering network of Catholic discussion circles spread across France's major urban centers. These had begun during the German occupation as clandestine reading groups, led by Marie-Dominique Chenu, Henri Godin, and other well-known priests of the French vanguard. After the war, these circles joined together in a loose confederation called the Youth of the Church (*Jeunesse de l'Église*).

These reading groups became incubation sites of what Gerd-Rainer Horn has called "Western European liberation theology." They tended toward a belief that the proletariat—condemned to material poverty as an entire class—had a better chance at spiritual salvation than anyone else. To Vatican eyes, these beliefs brought the Youth of the Church dangerously close to heresy. Two decades later, the Peruvian priest Gustavo Gutiérrez would inspire a very similar approach in Latin America, famously condemned by the Vatican as "liberation theology."[25]

The Stockholm Appeal did not create French progressive Catholicism. That said, the heyday of the French vanguard coincided with a time when Catholics across Europe were quaking at the thought of impending nuclear war. Their fears only deepened when war broke out on the Korean Peninsula three months after the appeal's publication.[26] More and more Catholics wondered if maybe the Soviet camp did have a role to play in securing world peace. It is thus no surprise that, even before the start of the Korean War, Pius XII was throwing up his hands in frustration at the apparent success of progressives. Wladimir d'Ormesson, Maritain's successor as French ambassador to the Holy See, witnessed in May 1950 what he considered a deeply disturbing conversation between the Holy Father and Cardinal Pierre-Marie Gerlier of Lyon. With Gerlier complaining to the pontiff about the rising tide of "reckless and dangerous" progressive currents among French Catholics, "Pius XII responded, smiling, 'How many condemnations would you have me issue?'"[27] The condemnations would continue to flow forth until this pope's death in 1958.

Pius XII's exasperation with progressive Catholicism is understandable. Even after *Quadragesimo Anno*, *Divini Redemptoris*, the Mindszenty Affair, and the 1949 Holy Office decree, there were still Catholics who believed that making good on the Church's promises of social justice necessitated "revolution" inside and outside of Catholicism. Emmanuel Mounier's waffling response to the July 1949 decree was a case in point. Though he professed respect for the Holy See's position, he himself did not change course. *Esprit*, in fact, led the way into the heart of Soviet Bloc Stalinism.

## PEACE BEFORE JUSTICE

Less than a year after Mounier's visit to Poland, *Dziś i Jutro*'s Konstanty Łubieński traveled to Paris. At Mounier's invitation, he visited *Esprit*'s offices several times, where he struck up a friendship with Mounier's editorial assistant, Jean-Marie Domenach.[28] As an employee of the Polish Finance Ministry, Łubieński could travel abroad on a dip-lomatic passport, and he began to do so frequently, in the service of multiple agendas. On the one hand, he reported on his travels directly to secret police *éminence grise* Julia Brystygier, who used Łubieński to gather information about Polish émigré communities throughout West-ern Europe.[29] Publicly, however, Łubieński represented *Dziś i Jutro* in Paris, and in so doing he paved the way for a line of colleagues who began traveling to France later that same year.

The most important among them was Wojciech Kętrzyński. Rather than limit himself to contact with *Esprit*, he took advantage of his per-fect spoken French to introduce himself—sometimes with Mounier's help, sometimes on his own—all over Paris, and in Lyon and Brussels, too: to the Dominican "new theologians," to Mandouze's UCP, and to Joseph Folliet's Lyon-based Social Weeks—among many others.

Initially, these were courtesy visits: free copies of journal issues and books were exchanged, many cups of coffee consumed, vague promises made. But the Wrocław congress changed all of that. From among the French vanguard, only Mandouze and Boulier had come to Poland in the summer of 1948. But Kętrzyński became one of Poland's delegates to sessions of the Permanent Committee of the Partisans of Peace. This gave him an entirely new cachet in Western Europe, lending additional credibility as he began to coax his French interlocutors to sign on for long-term partnerships across the Iron Curtain.

No longer just an obscure representative of a journal based in a far-away land, Kętrzyński was now a leading Catholic peace activist func-tioning in a transnational, predominantly Communist network. When the peace movement leadership decided in advance of its April 1949 Paris congress to call for the formation of national peace committees in all participating countries, Kętrzyński became a key player in Poland's Committee of Defenders of Peace (PKOP, *Polski Komitet Obrońców Pokoju*).[30]

The Polish committee included both Party loyalists like the poet Iwaszkiewicz and Catholic socialists like Kętrzyński. Although repre-senting the Catholic faith in the Polish committee's discussions proved almost impossible due to the conflict between the *Dziś i Jutro* delega-tion and the secret police-backed "patriot priests," not a trace of these tensions made it into the pages of *Dziś i Jutro*.[31] Aside from the PKOP delegates, then, the truth about the committee's inner gridlock got out to no one. As a result, Kętrzyński was able to brag in Paris and Stockholm about the great achievements of the PKOP without any voice to the contrary, emphasizing the access that Catholic socialists had to the Polish halls of power.[32]

## THE CATHOLICS AND THE COMINFORM

The kind of argumentation that Kętrzyński presented on behalf of Catholic-socialist cooperation in the PKOP gained even more traction after the third conference of the Cominform, which took place on November 16–19, 1949. Palmiro Togliatti, long-time leader of the Italian Communist Party, gave a speech there that doubtless haunted Pius XII and deepened his sensitivity the following year to the Stockholm Appeal. The title of Togliatti's speech, "Working-Class Unity and the Tasks of the Communist and Workers' Parties," suggested nothing particularly noteworthy. The speech's content, however, portended a new Communist *main tendue*, threatening the unity of the Catholic ranks as Maurice Thorez had thirteen years before, in the face of the Spanish Civil War.

Arguing that only the Soviet Union was pursuing a "consistent policy of peace," Togliatti condemned the Marshall Plan and its contributions to Western European political integration: "When they talk of 'uniting' Europe the agents of American imperialism are really trying to disrupt cooperation between the peoples of Europe, to set up a barrier between them in order to isolate the Soviet Union and the people's democracies."[33] Only one year earlier, Italian prime minister Alcide De Gasperi's Christian Democrats had scored a stunning electoral victory over Togliatti's Communists in the April 1948 general elections. Togliatti had his party's loss to the Christian Democrats in mind when he noted the growing importance of "Catholic trade unions" and "Catholic parties" across Western Europe, lamenting that Western Europe's "Catholic parties are the principal bourgeois parties and direct the state." To remedy this state of affairs, Togliatti asked lay Catholics to step up and claim their role in faith and politics alike:

> In all the Catholic organizations, however, there is a profound contradiction between the policy of the leading circles of the Church, who are allies of imperialism and reaction and enemies of social progress, and the working masses, even the most backward, who want peace and

defense of their vital interests. This explains why it is that, despite the repressive measures taken by the church authorities, nevertheless left-wing, progressive trends constantly appear in the Catholic movement, which instinctively seek cooperation and unity with the non-Catholic workers' movement.[34]

Togliatti's message was clear: Catholics should ignore their reactionary, imperialist pontiff, Pius XII, and instead embrace "left-wing, progressive trends." The pope had, in fact, campaigned heavily on Christian Democracy's behalf. For the 1948 Italian parliamentary elections, the pontiff turned Catholic Action into a grassroots electoral organization stumping for Italian Christian Democracy.[35] Pius XII's attempts to insure Europe's "Christian future" rose to the level of systematic interference in secular politics, where he hoped to dictate policy both to national-level Christian Democratic politicians and to the Christian Democratic international. In principle, Italy was unique among European states as the Vatican's host territory, but Pius XII made it clear to Christian Democratic leaders at the time that his aspirations were European, not Italian. Western Europe's top Christian Democratic politicians—particularly Italian prime minister Alcide De Gasperi—had the challenging task of trying to limit the pope's role in secular politics.[36] Togliatti invited Catholics to ignore the pope's entanglement with Christian Democracy, and instead to partner with Communists in the most exalted among temporal causes: "[b]ringing a large section of the Catholic workers and working people into the united front for the defense of peace, freedom, and the living standards of the working people."[37]

In the wake of the Holy Office's July 1, 1949 threat to excommunicate any Catholic who worked with Communists, Togliatti was scrambling for a new approach to the Catholic rank and file. For Catholics looking for real answers in a world on the brink of nuclear war, the Italian Communist could seem more realistic than the pope. The Stockholm Appeal campaign, launched only four months after the meeting where Togliatti spoke, extended the reach of the Italian's "outstretched hand."

## A POLISH-LED CATHOLIC-SOCIALIST INTERNATIONAL

Togliatti's speech inspired Wojciech Kętrzyński to pitch a new project to the *Dziś i Jutro* leadership the following year.[38] What he presented was a blueprint for a Catholic-socialist international dedicated to the pursuit of world peace through transnational cooperation in Europe. Beginning with a half-page excerpt from Togliatti's speech, Kętrzyński framed his initiative as a response to the Italian leader's call for partnership, adapted to Poland's unique status as the most firmly Catholic country in the Soviet Bloc: "In fulfillment of the goals set out by Togliatti, it is clear that Poles, Marxists and Catholics alike, have a role to play as bringers of a sea change in the Catholic political attitudes of the masses of Western Europe: Poland is, after all, the first larger country with a predominantly Catholic population to become consistently engaged in laying the foundations of socialism."

Praising the *Dziś i Jutro* movement without identifying it by name, the document observed that, since "there have emerged in these years in Poland essentially Catholic organizations clearly founded on an acceptance of the new order"—read: *Dziś i Jutro*—"These considerations make Poles uniquely responsible to the Catholics of the Western world."

The Poles' new charge was "the creation of an international movement of Catholic socialists." Kętrzyński believed that the founding nodes of this transnational network should be countries that had established contingents of self-styled progressive Catholics: Poland, France, and Italy. The *Dziś i Jutro* leadership soon realized, however, that in Italy it lacked the kind of access to these Catholics that it enjoyed in Francophone countries.[39] For this reason, Belgium quickly replaced Italy as the group's second target country.

Kętrzyński's blueprint also specified the organizations that Polish activists should approach first. These included "the progressives [the Union of Progressive Christians], the Paris Mission, Youth of the Church, *L'Esprit*, *Témoignage Chrétien*, the French Popular Movement [*Mouvement Populaire des Français*], *L'Économie et Humanisme*."[40] Even though none of these organizations were political parties, the document assigned the larger proposed international's activities above all to the "political realm, with the reservation that ideological elements will also constitute a consolidating factor."

For the initial stages of the international's construction, the blueprint recommended secrecy, avoidance of "too ostentatious contact with Catholic groups openly condemned by the Vatican," and initial incorporation only of organizations with "significant reach."[41] Nonetheless, the blueprint clearly stated the proposed international's ultimate goals: "1) A campaign against reactionary elements within the Catholic camp; 2) Direct action against capitalism; 3) Cooperation with the socialist camp." In the end, the Catholic-socialist international was "to reach all progressive Christian elements."

This was, quite simply, a revolutionary proposal. Taking one page from the Cominform and another from its sworn opponent, Western European Christian Democracy, the *Dziś i Jutro* leadership aimed at nothing less than an institutional foundation for its alternative, anti-Marshall Plan vision of European partnerships across the Iron Curtain. It was thus a logical consequence of the Wrocław congress, Togliatti's speech, and what the *Dziś i Jutro* activists styled in their public writings as attempts to Christianize socialism from within.

*Dziś i Jutro* recognized the debt that it owed to French Catholic thought, and that is why Kętrzyński's blueprint advised securing long-term partnerships in France first. Yet the proposed Catholic-socialist international was about much more than Franco-Polish Catholic relations. Its real goal was an active network of peace-advocating Catholic organizations on both sides of the Iron Curtain, of people who would see in Catholic social teaching a principled rationale for the geopolitics of the Soviet Bloc.

In the end, the plan failed. Yet what is surprising is that it failed neither immediately nor completely. *Dziś i Jutro*'s leader Piasecki supported the project in part because he hoped that *Dziś i Jutro* could thereby win sufficient cachet to become a full-fledged political party—perhaps even to share power with the Communists.[42] Piasecki also agreed with Kętrzyński that *Dziś i Jutro* had a special mission on behalf of the entire Catholic Church. When he celebrated the movement's tenth anniversary six years later, he bragged, "The international significance of our movement lies in the fact that it sustains hope, generates creative ferment, and strengthens all Catholic thought and activism in the pursuit of social renewal. Our ideological allies abroad are the object of all sorts of moral and material attacks. Nonetheless, it is our friends who will carry ever greater weight in determining the social trajectory of Catholics in a globalizing order. [ . . . ] Without getting ahead of ourselves, we can declare in good conscience that the activities of our movement have played a serious role in giving concrete form to the pursuit of social justice."[43]

The fantastic quality of Piasecki's larger aspirations in no way prevented *Dziś i Jutro* from going about building the international just as the blueprint had proposed: via close, lasting partnerships built on personal trust and political common ground with the Catholic vanguard of France. With the peace campaign as a backdrop, the immediate goal was to multiply the number of Catholic-socialist nodes as rapidly as possible. Solid foundations in France and fortuitous contacts in Belgium turned both of those countries into promising centers of transnational Catholic-socialist cooperation.

As they set about building their international, the *Dziś i Jutro* activists took a three-pronged approach. First, they took advantage of existing contacts. The Poles' rock was *Esprit*, whose creator Mounier had, after all, provided the foundations for *Dziś i Jutro*'s Catholic socialism. The movement's international emissaries Kętrzyński and Łubieński used *Esprit* as a springboard to make new contacts in the course of their travels to Western Europe.

Second, *Dziś i Jutro* activists exploited the Partisans of Peace movement to win new acolytes. The outbreak of the Korean War just months before the planned Second World Peace Congress raised the stakes for the peace campaign. Due to a combination of sabotage and happenstance, this congress—originally to be held in Sheffield—was relocated to Warsaw at the last minute. *Dziś i Jutro* took full advantage of the opportunity to recruit various Catholic activists who had come to Warsaw in 1950.[44]

Third and finally, the *Dziś i Jutro* activists encouraged international interest in the "Polish Revolution," getting their friends to publish feature stories on Polish economic output and religious life. The point was to get the word out to Catholics in the wider world that Communist Poland represented a viable alternative model: anti-capitalist, yet still respectful of faith and personhood—or at least, so Kętrzyński and his colleagues claimed.

Together, these three approaches promised to turn Kętrzyński's dream into a reality. It did not matter that Poland had, in the interim, sunk deeper into Stalinism. A handful of Polish Catholics had decided in 1950 to take on the world, and they were gaining traction.

## *ESPRIT* AND THE SPECTER OF GERMAN REARMAMENT

Though he welcomed Kętrzyński and his *Dziś i Jutro* colleagues warmly each time one visited Paris, Mounier received no small share of criticism from his Polish acolytes. In February 1950, Kętrzyński had written to Mounier to express *Dziś i Jutro*'s regret that *Esprit* had printed a series of essays singing the praises of Tito's Yugoslavia—the pariah of Central and Eastern European Communism since its ejection from the Cominform in the summer of 1948. The essays had gotten international attention because their authors included leading lights of postwar France's literary pantheon—most notably, Resistance heroes Jean Cassou and Vercors (Jean Bruller), author of *The Silence of the Sea*.[45]

When the Polish Communist press took *Esprit* to task, *Dziś i Jutro* publicly responded with a polite defense of its French ally. Privately, however, Kętrzyński rebuked Mounier for an editorial line that seemed to be moving away from the USSR:

> It seems to me that you ought to take care that your ideological position be intelligible also to the Communist circles in our part of the world, a good portion of whom appreciate the logic of your ideas as representing honest, advanced Christians even as, on the other hand, they deign from time to time to reproach you for your anti-Communism, which they see as stemming from either opportunism or a "bourgeois mentality." For my part, I would like simply to draw your attention to the fact that you now have readers all over the world and that you have a great role to play as representatives of the point of view that should be shared by all Christians who do not want to see the triumph of a contemptuous Catholic crusade against Communism.[46]

Kętrzyński was clearly not mincing words, but, in Mounier's eyes, it came from a place of principle, not pride. Remarkably, the Pole's gambit paid off. Rather than take exception, Mounier replied in early March in a conciliatory tone, "I thank you for understanding that, if we have had to enter recently into dispute with some of the Communist positions, that in no way signifies a change in orientation on our part."[47] The world's most famous personalist revolutionary remained committed to Poland's Catholic socialists.

Traveling to Stockholm that month to vote on the appeal, Kętrzyński took Mounier's letter with him, re-read it, and evidently felt badly enough about the way that he had confronted Mounier to write him a quick, cryptic, but earnestly apologetic note from Stockholm. Promising more details about a new joint initiative—the Catholic-socialist international—Kętrzyński sent the letter off and returned to his committee meetings. Yet he would never get the chance to pitch the international to Mounier. Eight days after the announcement of the Stockholm Appeal, Mounier died of a heart attack.

Kętrzyński was utterly crushed by Mounier's death, and he was not alone. The collective emotion that *Dziś i Jutro*'s editors experienced on hearing of the forty-five-year-old philosopher's passing was expressed in the form of a commemorative special issue of *Dziś i Jutro*.[48] Mounier's death bound the Poles ever more to his successors at *Esprit*, who reciprocated the bond in no uncertain terms.

Even a quick glance at the personal correspondence between the staffs of *Dziś i Jutro* and *Esprit* reveals that these people liked and respected each other not only as brothers in arms, but indeed as friends. Behind this emerging cross-Iron Curtain partnership lay a very real human element. In the end, there was genuine interpersonal affection binding together pro-Communist personalists on both sides of the Iron Curtain.

When Kętrzyński learned of Mounier's death, he immediately sat down to draft two letters: one to Jean-Marie Domenach, the late Mounier's editorial assistant, whom Kętrzyński had first met in 1947 in Paris; and one on behalf of the entire *Dziś i Jutro* movement to the entire *Esprit* staff. In the second letter, he wrote,

> It is incumbent upon all of us Christians who are campaigning for the right of Christendom to participate in the making of history to prevent an abyss of misunderstanding from opening up between the working masses, who seek the path to liberty on the socialist road, and Christian thought, which points them to the path that leads to God. This, in our understanding of the phenomenal body of work of Emmanuel Mounier, was the message that, in defiance of the everyday difficulties and contradictions of our era, he attempted to bring to fruition for *Esprit* and for the personalist movement. We hope that our brothers, the staff of *Esprit*, will continue to carry out this mission. We will participate in this effort in all solidarity as brothers in work and in arms.[49]

Kętrzyński also pledged the balance of *Dziś i Jutro*'s credit with *Esprit* —4200 unclaimed francs for article reprints and permissions—to aid Mounier's widow and children, who were left without income by the philosopher's sudden passing.[50]

The author of *Esprit*'s reply was Jean-Marie Domenach. The former editorial assistant received a promotion to managing editor of *Esprit*, in tandem with Swiss philosopher Albert Béguin's appointment as the journal's executive editor. The one-time Christian Witness activist made it clear that he, too, was a personalist whose heart lay east of the Iron Curtain. *Dziś i Jutro*, Domenach wrote, could count on him for close, long-term cooperation: "I hope that you will want to maintain with me the amicable contact that you have shared with Emmanuel Mounier."[51]

In fact, Domenach and Kętrzyński had bonded almost immediately when Kętrzyński had first encountered the French thinker in the *Esprit* offices. These two men shared a bond much deeper than Catholic socialism: a past in the anti-Nazi wartime resistance. Although Kętrzyński was six years older than Domenach, both men belonged to the wartime generation. Though they came from different countries, they both lost dear friends at the hands of the Germans. Domenach lost his best friend, Gilbert Dru, in July 1944. Kętrzyński lost his friend Włodzimierz Pietrzak, the young fighter who came to represent not only their particular partisan movement—the Confederation of the Nation—but all of the young Catholic martyrs of Poland's wartime generation. Pietrzak had perished in the Warsaw Uprising, but his fate—for the Catholics of that generation—was emblematic also of those who had fallen in forests or camps. The two young personalists—Dru and Pietrzak—died only weeks apart at the hands of the same enemy, albeit on opposite sides of Europe.

Unlike Mounier, who despite his strong attachments had avoided open political agitation, Domenach quickly became one of the most politically outspoken Catholic authors of his generation. Neither eccentric nor marginal, he became an authority figure, following in the footsteps of the man who already in 1944 had invited him to join the staff of *Esprit*.[52] Like Mounier, Domenach had insisted since the war's end that personalists stay the course of "anti-capitalist revolution."[53] But he was also outspoken on matters of state. Though he was the junior editor to Béguin, his anti-Germanism quickly set the tone for *Esprit*'s new political agenda, delivering the journal into the welcoming embraces of both French Communists and the *Dziś i Jutro* movement. Domenach bitterly opposed both European integration and the remilitarization of Western Europe, which he saw as giving Germany the tools to launch a new war. In the late summer of 1950, Domenach wrote to Kętrzyński, "We are entering a difficult period, and the rearmament will aggravate France's situation even further. We are going to regroup in order to fight against fanaticism and the spirit of war, but in spite of the confidence that we maintain, there are days when the future seems bleak."[54]

Three months later, when he received an anti-colonialist diatribe in the mail from Kętrzyński, Domenach could only nod his head in agreement. According to the Pole, Western European Catholics had fallen victim to the lies of Christian Democrats promising peace. Among other things, Kętrzyński wanted independence for Algeria and Indochina and an end to "imperialist" warfare. According to the Pole, "out of fear, evidently, of suffering and chaos that await them on the path to a better tomorrow," even the most pious representatives of "Catholic opinion in the West" had warmly embraced "an established, yet odious, order." Instead, Kętrzyński thundered, Western Europeans needed to muster up courage as Catholics, with the moral obligation to fight oppression in all forms.

Wojciech Kętrzyński hoped that France would—sooner, rather than later—follow Poland's lead down the path of Marxist revolution, and he looked to Jean-Marie Domenach to help him share the Poles' lessons learned with as wide a French audience as possible.[55] In response, Domenach lobbied his boss, Albert Béguin, to organize a public event in France featuring Kętrzyński and other *Dziś i Jutro* representatives. The idea was to put the Poles in the same room with all of *Esprit*'s collaborators and French supporters. This public event came to fruition in the early fall of 1951.[56]

After Mounier's death, this burgeoning Catholic-socialist partnership drew *Esprit* into the global peace campaign. As fans of the Stockholm Appeal converged on Warsaw in November 1950, Domenach prepared to launch a French Committee for the Peaceful Resolution of the German Problem (*Comité Français pour la Solution Pacifique du Problème Allemand*).[57] Two years later, the *Esprit* editor gaveled the committee's first international meeting to order—in Odense, Denmark. Domenach wanted to bring Kętrzyński on board as a member of the committee's executive council. However, the first meeting location for that council was West Germany, to which Kętrzyński was denied a visa.[58] In the end, the Odense conference, held only three months after its planners first met, went nowhere. The organizers failed to coordinate with the Danish government, which ended up refusing visas to almost all of the invited participants from Austria, Czechoslovakia, East Germany, and Poland.

The fact that the East German delegation was limited to two bit players was particularly bad news. After all, the conference had been intended to persuade Germans from both republics to oppose remilitarization, and an Eastern presence was crucial to this plan. In October 1950, West Germany's remilitarization had become a concrete political prospect, following the announcement by French prime minister René Pleven of plans for a "European defense community." Opponents of the Pleven Plan feared that successful economic integration would make military integration inevitable as well, guaranteeing the dreaded outcome of West Germany's rearmament. Yet, unlike its economic counterpart, the Pleven Plan failed. In the end, France's own National Assembly torpedoed the project in 1954.[59]

As the working document produced by the Odense conference declared, the goal of protesting the Pleven Plan was not to strip Germany of its sovereignty, but to "impede the renaissance of militarism in Germany" by means of a collective "neutralization" of the region. The declaration expressed hope that definitively disarming Germany would lead to voluntary disarmament by Germany's neighbors. The fantasy driving Domenach's committee was "general simultaneous, progressive, and controlled disarmament" of the entire world.[60] These goals were entirely unrealistic, ignoring as they did the rules of *Realpolitik* that governed the emerging Cold War. In 1955, NATO in fact welcomed West Germany as a new member.

In the first half of the 1950s, however, Domenach's committee was immensely attractive to France's Catholic socialists—at least as a basis for further cooperation across the Iron Curtain. Poles, meanwhile, honed in on the call to keep Germany demilitarized—doomed though it soon proved to be. After seeing a copy of the 1952 Odense declaration, Polish Communist leaders offered *Dziś i Jutro* the chance to help put together a Polish equivalent of Domenach's committee, and Piasecki jumped at the opportunity. By the summer of 1953, Poland had its own "Committee for the Peaceful Resolution of the German Problem." It was for the purpose of advising this committee that Domenach made his first trip to Poland, in January 1954.[61]

In so doing, Domenach went further than Mounier had ever gone, extending a hand to Polish Stalinism mere months after the arrest of Primate Wyszyński and the show-trial conviction of another prelate. This initiative forever doomed any wider appeal that the joint action of *Dziś i Jutro* and *Esprit* might have had. Receptive as European masses might have been to the rallying cries to fend off German rearmament and American atomic power, Catholic socialists in the early 1950s considered the Church hierarchy expendable in their quest to serve a "revolution" conceived in distinctly exclusionary terms. Instead of a just society, they embraced a nationalist, Catholic turn to Stalinism.

## THE SECOND WORLD PEACE CONGRESS

By the fall of 1950, the Stockholm Appeal had become a household name in Poland, not just among Catholic socialists, but across the whole of society. For months, the PZPR had distributed leaflets, canvassed apartment buildings and houses, and practiced intimidation in the workplace and in universities to get everyone to sign. The June 1950 issue of the pro-Communist magazine *Peuples Amis* sported a naïve, Orientalist photograph of an elderly Polish woman in peasant garb signing the Appeal (figure 10).[62] According to the PKOP's own statistics, 136,000 three-person canvassing teams; four million printed copies of the appeal; and 88,000 local peace committees by late June 1950 had amassed the signatures of 18 million adult Poles, with only 190,000 failing to sign.[63] Even allowing for significant inflation in these statistics, first-hand accounts made clear that the campaign was extensive and effective.[64]

With the start of the Korean War in late June 1950—less than a year after Mao Tse-tung announced the creation of the People's Republic of China—the appeal campaign took on a sense of particular urgency. The predominant fear was that East Asia might provide the spark that would ignite an American-Soviet atomic showdown. Bolesław Piasecki wrote in the pages of *Dziś i Jutro* that the Korean conflict only underscored the fact that, "for Polish Catholics, their place is wherever the living interests of the Polish nation lie. [ . . . ] The engagement of Catholics in the world movement of defenders of peace is consistent with the national interest and thereby provides the proper perspective for their coexistence with Marxists."[65] Worldwide, by the end of 1950, upwards of 500 million signatures had supposedly been gathered for the appeal.

Faced with the apparent success of the Stockholm Appeal, Western

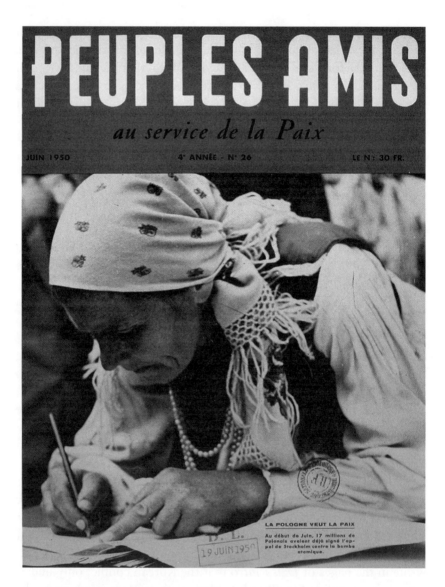

Fig. 10: Front cover of the monthly journal *Peuples Amis* (*Friendly Nations*), June 1950 issue. The caption reads, "POLAND WANTS PEACE: By the start of June, seventeen million Poles had already signed the Stockholm Appeal against the atomic bomb." Source: National Library of France (BnF).

European governments began to view the Communist-led peace movement as a tangible threat. The Second World Peace Congress, scheduled for mid-November 1950, was relocated from London to Sheffield. At the last minute, however, the British Foreign Office torpedoed the gathering by refusing visas to almost 50 percent of prospective participants.[66]

Five days before the scheduled start of the congress, Frédéric Joliot-Curie and his fellow executive committee members, who had been turned back at the port of Dover, secured the PKOP's enthusiastic support for moving the conference to Warsaw.[67] Hearing the news, *Dziś i Jutro* editors hurried to rewrite the cover of their November 19 issue, lauding their government for "not being afraid of world peace"—this, in contrast with the British, who had chosen to "seal the lips" of the peace movement in the interest of pleasing "American editors."[68] Not surprisingly, hosted as it was by a people's democracy, the congress turned into a carefully choreographed "Communist conference," complete with cheering crowds "who threw flowers and money" at arriving delegates. Polish president Bolesław Bierut delivered an address lauding the congress as "this most illustrious assembly in the history of man."[69]

The congress lasted six days, ending on November 22, 1950. For *Dziś i Jutro*, it meant an unprecedented opportunity to play host to possible new recruits to the Catholic-socialist international.[70] Scheduling around the congress's plenary sessions, Kętrzyński organized a special conference of Catholic peace activists at the Warsaw headquarters of *Dziś i Jutro*. As it happened, the congress's timing coincided with the journal's fifth anniversary, which *Dziś i Jutro* celebrated with pomp and circumstance. Piasecki hosted a banquet for guests from abroad, and Kętrzyński did the substantive programming.

The whole point of the event was to gather intelligence about the delegates, in order to develop a recruitment plan. Some were approached right away about the Catholic-socialist international, while others would first be cultivated on a trial basis, to see if they qualified to become partners at some future date. With only one day to plan everything, Kętrzyński achieved a remarkable feat of triage. Although he played host to a total of eighty Catholic participants from around the world, Kętrzyński virtually ignored the delegations from Canada, Korea, Madagascar, and Vietnam. Instead, he focused his attention almost exclusively on Catholic activists hailing from Belgium, France, and Italy. In his notes from the meeting, Kętrzyński explained that the delegates from these countries "demonstrated a deeper interest in the ideological situation of Catholics in Poland, particularly Catholics concentrated in or around our movement."[71]

The "Red Priest" Jean Boulier was there, and Kętrzyński greeted him warmly. But he spent much more time networking with the Union of Progressive Christians. In the Pole's view, UCP leader Max Stern approved of "Catholicism's peaceful rooting within socialism." Kętrzyński summed up the progressives' stance succinctly: "Let us participate in the political undertakings of Communists, and the ideological complications will fall away." In other words, the UCP delegation to the Second World Peace Congress manifested a faith akin to *Dziś i Jutro*'s in their own ability to Christianize "revolution" from within. Prospects for partnership with the UCP seemed promising.

However, on their return to Paris, Stern and the other UCP delegates learned from the organization's general secretary Marcel Moiroud that their union was falling apart. As Yvon Tranvouez points out, the Stockholm Appeal campaign hurt the progressives as much as it helped them: on the one hand, it energized them; on the other, it accentuated the deep divisions that soon broke the union apart.[72] Some UCP progressives wanted to focus on pastoral, rather than political, revolution; these men and women strongly disapproved of a growing faction within the union led by the Catholic journalist Ella Sauvageot.[73] After she published an appeal entitled "Christians against the Atomic Bomb" in the French Communist journal *L'Humanité*, Sauvageot and her supporters were denounced by every Catholic journal in France. As Moiroud put it, because of the UCP's overt engagement in the Communist-led peace movement, "we were often on the defensive for having supposedly boxed ourselves into an exclusively political approach, relegating religious concerns to the status of something less than an afterthought."[74]

The turmoil that wracked the UCP in 1950 explains why it took Moiroud several months to respond when Kętrzyński suggested that they co-organize a Franco-Polish Catholic debate about Catholicism and Marxism. Moiroud's tremulous answer underscores just how effective the anti-UCP campaign had been. Although glad to sponsor "an international gathering of Christians on the problem of peace," Moiroud categorically refused to sign off on the proposed debate on Catholicism and Marxism. After all, this was the topic that was actively tearing the UCP apart at that very moment. Moiroud demurred, "The Christianity-Marxism question is politically incorrect in France. To pose it would be to perform an act of fragmentation and to retard the development of the peace movement."[75]

What bothered Moiroud was not *Dziś i Jutro*'s Catholic socialism. It was, rather, his fear that working with the Poles might threaten his position as UCP leader. As clear as his desire was to benefit from *Dziś i Jutro*'s popularity among the French vanguard, even clearer was the weakness of the UCP. Within six months, it folded under pressure from the French episcopate.

Nonetheless, the air that had gone out of the UCP was immediately sucked in by the new journal *La Quinzaine*. Its first issue hit Parisian newsstands in November 1950, within days of the Second World Peace Congress. This was no mass-circulation journal, but all of French Catholicism reckoned with its political commentary. From politicians to pastors, every Catholic public figure of the first half of the 1950s sought it out: "For this biweekly born in—and largely of—Cold War contingency, the struggle for peace was a foundational element of a broader struggle to resolve the grave problems of French society and of the postwar world: the exploitation of the working class and the oppression of colonial peoples. One could even say that one of the principal preoccupations of this journal was to render intelligible the logical link between these concerns."[76] Likewise, anticipating the activities of Domenach's committee, *La Quinzaine* wanted "a Europe with a disarmed Germany."[77]

This is precisely the program that *Dziś i Jutro* adopted after the Wrocław peace congress of 1948. Arguably, *La Quinzaine* was even more akin to *Dziś i Jutro* than *Esprit*. While the French monthly had long focused principally on cultural and intellectual life, *La Quinzaine* was a political journal through and through. When *Esprit* did speak out on international politics, *La Quinzaine* was still more radical.

The two journals occasionally found themselves in conflict, particularly on philosophical grounds: *La Quinzaine*, for example, rejected Jacques Maritain's argument that religion should not dictate the totality of secular life. The self-styled progressives of *La Quinzaine* believed not only that everything socialist should be made Christian, but indeed that everything Christian should be made socialist. To philosopher Jean Lacroix of *Esprit*, this smacked of Charles Maurras's integral nationalism: the only difference was that, unlike French Action, *La Quinzaine*'s "revolution" focused not on the nation, but on the proletariat to the exclusion of all else. Lacroix said as much in the pages of *Esprit* in 1953—for which Domenach, as the journal's managing editor, actually apologized in a letter sent to the staff of *La Quinzaine*.[78]

When the UCP activists who had impressed Kętrzyński in Warsaw jumped ship, it was to *La Quinzaine* that they went. There they joined Ella Sauvageot's anti-nuclear PCF sympathizers as well as a wide variety of refugee progressives from across the French Catholic world. As the Vatican, operating principally through the French episcopate, derailed more and more "revolutionary" movements, ideas, and individuals over the first half of the 1950s—clamping down on "new theology" in 1950, condemning the UCP in 1951, shutting down the worker-priests and the Youth of the Church in 1953, defrocking Boulier that same year, and banning Chenu and Congar from teaching in 1954—it was *La Quinzaine* that became their refuge.

To be clear, most of these people were not "Stalinist Christians."[79] And yet, most were willing to go to great lengths with their pens and their typewriters to make the Soviet camp look good, ideally at the expense of the Cold War West—not only Germans and Americans, but anyone who got in the way of their "revolutionary" agenda. Their unwitting partners in this enterprise included other Catholic journals inspired by Mounier's personalism, among them, American social activist Dorothy Day's ground-breaking *Catholic Worker*.[80] Their commonality of philosophical and political goals made *La Quinzaine* immensely attractive to *Dziś i Jutro*, and the feeling was mutual.

One of *La Quinzaine*'s staff writers, Geneviève Clairbois, visited Poland in the spring of 1951 and prepared a series of articles for the journal relating her impressions from the trip. Her articles sound like the speeches given by Communist poet Jarosław Iwaszkiewicz on his promotional tour in advance of the Wrocław congress. Specifically, Clairbois cited world peace as a necessary condition for maintaining and deepening the social achievements of Communist Poland: "One objective: reconstruction. One means: planning. One condition: peace." On the question of whether Poles were free and happy under Stalinism, Clairbois demurred, explaining, "It is impossible to respond to these questions if one does not put oneself in the position of a new society in the process of forging itself."[81]

All told, Clairbois proved herself to be the latest in a long line of

French "useful idiots" lauding freedom where there was, in fact, oppression.[82] Most scandalous was her insistence that Stalinist Poland guaranteed universal "attachment and respect for the person of the priest."[83] In the year of her article's publication alone, Communist Poland's secret police arrested a bishop and hundreds of regular clergy.

Though not nearly as prominent as *Esprit*, *La Quinzaine* proved itself to be a stalwart ally of *Dziś i Jutro*'s Catholic-socialist project. As Polish Stalinism turned more aggressively against the Catholic Church, *La Quinzaine* offered *Dziś i Jutro* writers precious column space to publish articles in France defending the "Polish Revolution" against mainstream Western European news reports about the worsening situation of the Catholic Church in Poland.[84] In times of crisis, *La Quinzaine* proved indispensable. For the day-to-day, however, Kętrzyński pursued a moderate approach in his allegiances, always privileging *Esprit* over *La Quinzaine*, and avoiding the appearance of paying disproportionate attention to *La Quinzaine* during his visits to Paris. *La Quinzaine* constituted a perfect match for the Catholic-socialist vision of "revolution," but on its own would not suffice to get anything done.

## THE PEACE OF CHRIST

Catholic peace organizations were slower to grow and flourish in postwar Europe than their Communist-led counterparts. A French-language International Movement of Catholic Students (*Mouvement International des Étudiants Catholiques*) had been founded in 1921, based out of Fribourg, Switzerland. However, this movement—unlike the Young Christian Workers', Students', and Farmers' movements of Belgium and France—shut down completely for the duration of the Second World War. After the Vatican authorized the movement's reactivation in 1947 under the name of Pax Romana, it confronted the task of recovering its prewar stature and reach. Only in the mid-1950s would the movement blossom, turning its mission to the Third World, with a place of prominence reserved for activists from the Soviet Bloc.[85]

At the time of the Korean War's outbreak, however, there was another, much more active, transnational Catholic peace movement on the rise: Pax Christi. Initiated in 1945 and run locally out of Tours for five years by a laywoman and a bishop, both of whom had spent part of the war in labor camps, Pax Christi had one overarching goal:

Franco-German reconciliation.[86] In 1950, the French episcopate assumed control of the movement. The new leadership of Pax Christi included, as president, Cardinal Maurice Feltin, primate of France; as vice-president, the prominent lay activist Maurice Vaussard; and as secretary, the Jesuit priest Robert Bosc.

Feltin's role was largely symbolic, so it was to Vaussard and Bosc that the real responsibility fell of setting the tone for transnational Catholic peace activism in Europe. These were the men who could have put the Catholic-socialist international out of business. Instead, they embraced it and helped to sell the idea that only *Dziś i Jutro* had gotten "revolution" right.

Maurice Vaussard came to Pax Christi with a long and distinguished track record in Catholic activism. A prolific author of anti-nationalist and antiwar treatises since 1908, he had worked with Giuseppe Toniolo, the father of Italian social Catholicism; flirted briefly with French Action; and despaired at the human and material devastation of the Great War. Seeing Europe destroy itself inspired him to expose "the perils of nationalism for humanity and the means of combating it."[87] In 1915, Vaussard published *For Those Who Will Survive* (*Pour ceux qui survivront*), in which he demanded that the belligerent powers conclude the war by ensuring "a durable victory that would at the same time also be a Christian victory."[88]

Though lacking formal training as a historian, Vaussard drew on his extensive knowledge of the French and Italian languages, cultures, and political traditions to compile histories of French and Italian Catholic life. Over the next three decades, he produced foundational works of modern Franco-Italian historiography on a range of topics: Catholic intellectual life, nationalism, Christian Democracy, and Jansenism. Vaussard repeatedly underscored that nationalism was "one of the most serious, if not the most serious" problem facing the modern world, and Catholics in it.[89] After publishing a series of essays denouncing the integral nationalists of French Action, Vaussard won financial backing to create a journal devoted to "international Catholic solidarity."[90] Vaussard was, in other words, the consummate transnational Catholic peace activist. His long track record made him an attractive friend for *Dziś i Jutro*.

Unlike the Communist-led peace movement, Pax Christi was interested in bringing Christians—Catholics and Protestants—in both West and East Germany into dialogue with the French Catholic world. In this pursuit, its leadership sought all available channels to access and persuade those Christian communities to meet at a single table. As Vaussard put it in 1952, "Nothing would be worse for 'peaceful co-existence' than closed doors, for then one can believe or imagine that *anything and everything* is taking place behind them."[91] In the spirit of opening doors, Vaussard looked eastward for new allies. Having been put in touch with Kętrzyński in 1950 by several French progressives who attended the Warsaw peace congress, Vaussard decided to make *Dziś i Jutro* an offer:

> As direct contact would in any case be extremely desirable between Catholics of Europe East and West, especially between Polish and French Catholics, an analogous invitation could be addressed to you by an organization of a more official nature, presided at the international level by His Eminence the Archbishop of Paris and at the national level by a different French bishop, on the occasion of the Congress and pilgrimage that is being organized next September to Assisi. I speak of Pax Christi, whose manifesto, enclosed here, will explain briefly its goals and methods of action.[92]

In the end, *Dziś i Jutro* sent three high-ranking activists—Kętrzyński, Konstanty Łubieński, and another dispossessed aristocrat, Dominik Horodyński—to public meetings organized by Pax Christi in Paris in November 1952. Łubieński later confessed to being pleasantly "surprised by the degree of progressive social tendencies" within Pax Christi.[93] The organization only needed better information about the geopolitical concerns of the Soviet Bloc, in order to embrace more fully Poland's "convictions regarding the merits of our borders on the Oder and Neisse Rivers."[94]

In three years of correspondence, Kętrzyński and Vaussard somehow managed to avoid discussing Germany. Clearly, the two men saw mutual benefit in cross-Iron Curtain cooperation, and they did not want to squander that potential with disagreements over the German question. And yet, the Poles of *Dziś i Jutro* consistently proved to be unabashedly, vocally anti-German. Meanwhile, Pax Christi, though strongly critical of proposals for Germany's remilitarization, refused for example to echo Domenach's demands for German "neutralization." At the end of the day, Pax Christi's declared goal was reconciliation among nations, and that included West Germany.

Fig. 11: A July 1953 memo from the Polish Committee of Defenders of Peace to the Polish secret police's passport office, requesting approval for *Dziś i Jutro*'s Wojciech Kętrzyński and Andrzej Krasiński to travel to France at the invitation of Pax Christi. The document comes from the collections of Poland's Institute of National Remembrance (*Instytut Pamięci Narodowej*): AIPN BU 1532/1312.

While avoiding the German taboo, Vaussard and Kętrzyński covered a whole host of other issues: Franco-Polish cultural relations; higher education; the Catholic hierarchy; and the worker-priest initiative. Even though it was Vaussard's boss Cardinal Feltin who banned the worker-priests in 1953, Vaussard himself remained an ardent admirer of all postwar Catholic radicals. Born in 1888, Vaussard was of the same generation as the late Lublin professor Antoni Szymański; he, too, identified with social Catholicism. And yet Vaussard sympathized also with the concerns of men twenty or even thirty years younger than himself, like Kętrzyński and Domenach, and he respected their ideological convictions. What Vaussard found appealing in Catholic socialism was its declared struggle against divisions based on class and nation. On this point, however, he consistently had to look the other way, faced with the anti-German thrust of the Catholic-socialist peace campaign.

Pax Christi thus seemed a well-connected, creative, and enthusiastic partner for *Dziś i Jutro*, not least because it turned a blind eye to perhaps the most important element of the Polish movement's ideology: its attempt to juggle revolutionary personalism with exclusionary nationalism. In sidelining the German question, Vaussard gambled that it was better to win the Poles over slowly to the ethics driving his movement than to risk alienating the Polish activists all at once. In the end, however, Vaussard never actually tried to convince the Poles to pursue reconciliation with Germany.

Though Maurice Vaussard chose a distinctly accommodationist line toward *Dziś i Jutro*, his Pax Christi subordinate, Jesuit Father Robert Bosc, followed a more winding road. The priest was the author of a widely read commentary on the April 1950 accord between the Polish government and the Polish episcopate. Publishing his analysis in *Études* (*Studies*), a widely read Jesuit journal of current events, Bosc tried to maintain scholarly objectivity in his treatment of Communist Poland.

And yet, Bosc clearly understood the toxic nature of Church-State relations in postwar Poland. Three months before concluding the accord, the PZPR had seized the ecclesiastical charity Caritas on the pretext of investigating corruption. The French Jesuit acknowledged that the seizure was based on a "campaign of calumnies," yet he believed that the Party's subsequent willingness to conclude an agreement with the bishops trumped past misdeeds. The Jesuit marveled, "For the first time, the hierarchy of the Catholic Church has signed an accord with the government of a resolutely Marxist people's democracy." Bosc acknowledged that there were dangers, yet he fell back on the assertion that "the majority of Catholics" in Poland considered the accord "useful and constructive." In the end, Bosc concluded that "the rest of the Catholic world" may have frowned upon how the accord came about, but it "owed its utmost respect" to the bishops.[95]

When he wrote this article, Bosc was appealing to a specific audience: the moderates within the Society of Jesus in France. As of 1950, French Jesuits had a remarkably diverse range of political and social commitments. The Jesuits ran the *Conférence Olivaint*, an organization dating back to the late nineteenth century, which offered extracurricular academic-year seminars and a star-studded summer camp off the coast of Corsica to budding Catholic student activists, especially from the elite National School of Political Science (*Sciences Po*).[96] Meanwhile, *Études*, where Bosc published his analysis of the Church-State Accord, was a socially conservative journal that nonetheless spoke with a "politically realistic" voice.[97] Finally, there was Popular Action (*Action Populaire*), a Jesuit social-science research group created in 1905. Its monthly journal, the *Revue de l'Action Populaire*, offered guidance to priests around the world, with a particular emphasis on pastoral radicalism both inside and outside France.[98] After World War II, the laity set the terms of Catholic activism in France, and yet there were few postwar ventures in which the Society of Jesus did not have a stake.

On his appointment to Pax Christi, Bosc found himself having to serve two masters at once. His real home in the world of French Jesuit activism was Popular Action, headed by Pierre Bigo. Known mostly for his international development work in the 1960s, Bigo had debuted over a decade earlier as a top Jesuit intellectual.[99] In 1953, he published *Marxism and Humanism* (*Marxisme et Humanisme*), which looked at Marxism "in order to see what positive things one can take away from it for the edification of the modern world."[100] Bigo saw parallels between Christianity and Marxism, emphasizing the shared ontology of "creation" in both worldviews: "the creational act, constituted by work, is closely tied to the act of man's alienation in work. Sin is to be found at humanity's very origins."[101]

Bigo's openness to learning from Marxists helps to explain why he sent Father Bosc to Poland in May 1953 on a fact-finding trip (*voyage d'étude*). Shepherded for the duration of his visit by Wojciech Kętrzyński, Bosc became a test case for *Dziś i Jutro*. Kętrzyński was trying to figure out if priests could play a serious role in the Catholic-socialist international. In fact, the Jesuit would prove indispensable to Kętrzyński's public relations efforts just a few months later, after Polish authorities arrested Primate Stefan Wyszyński in September 1953.

## PAX'S YOUNG RADICALS

While Kętrzyński was building his Catholic-socialist international, Communist Poland was changing around *Dziś i Jutro*. As Catholics, the editors of *Dziś i Jutro* felt that they needed to develop Catholic justifications for Stalinist oppression. In other words, they took on the impossible task of making the arrest and imprisonment of fellow Catholics seem not only forgivable, but in fact theologically justified. In

April 1952, seeking firmer institutional grounding in a time of shifting political sands, the *Dziś i Jutro* movement reinvented itself as the PAX Association.

The change was more than cosmetic: it heralded the rise within the movement of a new generation of "revolutionary" radicals. This was the first generation too young to have served in the underground for the entirety of the war—though some had seen serious combat. Its members were born between 1926 and 1929. Some came from aristocratic stock, but most were children of small-town professionals. Janusz Zabłocki, Tadeusz Myślik, Rudolf Buchała, Ignacy Rutkiewicz—these young men were middle-class children from small towns a stone's throw from Warsaw, Lwów, Katowice, and Wilno. Together with the doctor's son Tadeusz Mazowiecki, these young men in their twenties would shatter the idealistic façade of Catholic socialism. They would do this not by challenging their movement's ideology, but by believing in it wholeheartedly and pursuing it aggressively. The story of their radicalization and subsequent deradicalization—in Mazowiecki's own words, a "totalitarian" flirtation—reminds us of the totalistic aspirations that guided Mounier from the start—and the integralism that ultimately crashed his "revolution" on the rocks of Stalinism.[102]

Unlike the wartime generation, the postwar radicals had been too young to be Piasecki's clandestine brothers in arms. In fact, many had qualms about signing on with a group led by a prominent ex-fascist. Janusz Zabłocki, for example, tested out a middle road. In February 1949, the twenty-three-year-old law student received a commission from Piasecki to publish a regular insert in *Dziś i Jutro* named *Etap* (*Phase*). Using the penname "Karol Zajczniewski," Zabłocki organized and delivered to press articles written by himself and a half-dozen other student authors; the insert appeared monthly for almost a year.[103]

The roots of *Etap* lay in informal, interdisciplinary seminars in the humanities—called the Logophage Club (*Klub Logofagów*)—run by a handful of Kraków undergraduates in the years 1946–49.[104] After the Logophage Club disbanded to evade secret police attention, some of its veterans moved to Warsaw, where they joined a "personalist reading group" run by a Warsaw University sociology student named Czesław Czapów. The seminar's heroes were Maritain, Mounier, and German sociologist Karl Mannheim; Czapów's goal was to combine the best in all three in order to create the ultimate "humanist and socialist personalism."[105]

Although it never expanded beyond twenty people, the social network that formed around these debates caught the personal attention of Julia Brystygier of the Public Safety Ministry, who planted a mole in the group. As it turned out, the Stalinist secret police took Catholic personalism very seriously when it operated outside the boundaries of officially sanctioned media like *Dziś i Jutro*. Those personalists who joined Piasecki's weekly on a permanent basis were not subject to any repressive measures. The others, however, ultimately endured arrest, interrogation, and—in some cases—torture.[106]

Without even realizing it, Zabłocki avoided arrest by joining *Dziś i Jutro* in 1950. Though only twenty-four years old, he was well-versed in personalism, which he had first encountered during the war. In 1943, at the tender age of seventeen, he became a platoon leader for the Scouts-turned-guerrilla fighters of the Gray Ranks.[107] Zabłocki and those under his command encountered personalism not through Mounier, but through Maritain. The clandestine Gray Ranks journal *Brzask* (*Dawn*) ran a series of essays recapitulating Maritain's 1936 *Integral Humanism*. To the Scouts hiding in Mazovian forests, Maritain symbolized faith, anti-fascism, and a way of organizing a Catholic society without rejecting modernity wholesale. According to Zabłocki, the concept of a "human person," wedded to Maritain's philosophy of integral humanism, "constituted the foundations of our later project"—*Etap*.[108]

When Bolesław Piasecki helped to negotiate the 1950 Church-State Accord, many of the young personalists tied to *Etap* changed their opinion of *Dziś i Jutro*. It was Piasecki's visible contribution to the accord that convinced Zabłocki to join the ex-fascist's movement.[109] With *Etap* gone and Czapów's reading group arrested, the arrival of Zabłocki and other young radicals assured *Dziś i Jutro* a virtual monopoly over personalist thought in Stalinist Poland.

When Janusz Zabłocki entered Piasecki's movement, he encountered many elders and a small handful of activists closer to his own age. The first young radical to join *Dziś i Jutro* had been Tadeusz Mazowiecki, in 1948. As a freshman law student at Warsaw University, the young refugee from SP had faced discrimination and recrimination when he made his Catholicism known to fellow students. With SP gone, *Dziś i Jutro* was appealing simply because it gave him, a Catholic who made no secret of his faith, a chance to become involved in Polish public life.

Mazowiecki became a personal favorite of Piasecki's almost overnight. Hand-picked to run *Dziś i Jutro*'s summer camps for university students—where Mazowiecki first met Zabłocki and many others of their generation—the young Catholic activist, on Piasecki's advice, quit his studies at Warsaw University to edit the student page of *Dziś i Jutro*'s daily newspaper, *Słowo Powszechne* (*The Universal Word*). He held this position only briefly before Piasecki elevated him even further.[110]

Mazowiecki's complete lack of wartime attachments put him in a unique position relative to Piasecki's old guard. The young editor's German was better than his French, and he came to *Dziś i Jutro* never having heard of either Mounier or Maritain. That said, he proved an apt pupil, and within a year he had become one of *Dziś i Jutro*'s regular commentators on how to "Christianize socialism." This was a dangerous business: Mazowiecki's visibility meant that a misstep could land him in an interrogation room. And yet the twenty-two-year-old novice essayist proved to be a natural; by the time that Zabłocki and his friends signed up, Mazowiecki was one of the movement's most influential thinkers. If anyone from among the young radicals had a position in *Dziś i Jutro* from which to speak his mind, it was Mazowiecki.

Within a month of having picked up Mounier's works for the first time, Tadeusz Mazowiecki was arguing in the pages of *Dziś i Jutro* that Catholic socialism needed to showcase the ideas of the French Catholic vanguard front and center. This had once been Wojciech Kętrzyński's line, but he moved away from writing about personalist philosophy in 1948–49 to pursue transnational networking and the peace campaign. Kętrzyński passed the baton to Mazowiecki, who believed that Poland's Catholic youth should engage body and soul in the Communist-led peace movement: the meetings in Wrocław, Stockholm, and Paris had been "plebiscites" on the "indolence of the UN." Nuclear war threatened social progress, and Mazowiecki demanded better: justice through "revolution."[111]

To explain his vision, Mazowiecki reached back past Mandouze and Mounier to draw Maritain's Thomism into his writings. As a friend of his from those years later put it, "He was a deeply pious, practicing, unopportunistic Catholic, whose social views were initially socialist, and then evolved."[112] Inspired by the example of France's Youth of the Church movement, Mazowiecki wrote in April 1950, "Catholics today have a great role to play in the construction of the new world. This is not 'smuggling Christianity' into Marxism, but rather the construction of a new, contemporary Catholic culture that will be capable of giving Christian content to the new social order."[113]

Two months later, Mazowiecki took the task of elaborating a personalist theology for *Dziś i Jutro* even further. His core conviction was that human history had advanced to the point where Marxism and Catholicism needed one another: to socialize the means of production, move to a planned economy, and advance the twin causes of internationalism and a class society. And so, he argued, "it is not the defense of even the best elements of individualism but rather **the complete development and integration of personalism into the content of the socialist revolution that ought to endow Catholic thought with the proper form.** For it is the struggle for personalism in a socialist order that falls to us as our task."[114]

Where Mazowiecki left off, his new friend Janusz Zabłocki picked up, offering the most systematic rationale to date for *Dziś i Jutro's* embrace of French Catholicism. In October 1950, Zabłocki issued a warning to his colleagues, reminding them of the story of Marc Sangnier. A legendary social organizer, Sangnier had pioneered lay activism in turn-of-the-century France, following the letter and spirit of *Rerum Novarum*—only to be silenced in 1910 when Pope Pius X condemned his organization, Furrow (*Sillon*).[115] As Zabłocki put it on the fortieth anniversary of *Sillon's* shuttering, "This anniversary ought to remind us of the fate of this group, which, despite all of its errors and the insufficiency of its political program, can be considered one of the precursors of the socially progressive wing of Catholicism today."[116] The message was clear: *Dziś i Jutro* needed to stay bold and hungry, but at the same time it needed to keep in mind the mistakes of its precursors.

In the fall of 1951, a new topic of foundational importance entered into public debate in Communist Poland: the writing of a new constitution. Ultimately ratified on July 22, 1952, this document replaced the interwar Piłsudskite compact. Among other things, it renamed Poland the "Polish People's Republic" (*Polska Rzeczpospolita Ludowa*). The November 25, 1951 issue of *Dziś i Jutro* sought to showcase the achievements of the "Polish Revolution," examining the six years of Communist rule through the lens of Catholic philosophy. The articles published in this issue measured PZPR policy against the writings of Mounier, Maritain, Mandouze, and others.

France, too, was in the midst of heated constitutional debate. Following the June 1951 parliamentary elections, French Christian Dem-

Fig. 12: Janusz Zabłocki (left) and Tadeusz Mazowiecki (right), leaders of the *Fronde,* mid-1950s. Reproduced by permission of the Widmański family.

ocrats, Gaullists, and Socialists made various proposals to amend the Fourth Republic's constitution. These included the expansion of presidential powers, as well as extension of a symbolic voice in governance to certain subjects of the French overseas empire—rechristened the "French Union" following the Second World War. Ultimately, however, the Fourth Republic's dysfunctional constitution remained unchanged, paving the way for the republic's collapse in 1958, in the face of the protracted Algerian War.[117]

Unlike the French projects for constitutional amendment, however, Polish Communists proposed to jettison Poland's entire constitution in order to refashion the country into a "People's Republic." PAX's young radicals followed the PZPR's lead, devising Catholic justifications for a new constitution. The twenty-three-year-old economics student Tadeusz Myślik made the case that personalism justified a planned economy. His point was simple: Poland should emulate the USSR. With an accent on the "communitarian" aspect of Mounier's personalism,

Myślik argued that any change in the social and economic orders fundamentally affects the capacity of the human person to flourish as a transcendent entity in possession of his own dignity. Only a planned economy, the young personalist contended, could safeguard that dignity, for "in a free-market economy there emerge, independently of will and consciousness, means of production engendering individual efforts, with the unintended consequence of removing all space for cooperation in the creation of the human personality. In contrast, in the planned economy, the means of production are consciously refashioned."

Myślik argued that economic planning was also more in line with Catholic ethics. Supposedly, it would breed a sense of responsibility for the fruits of one's labor, as well as a willingness to sacrifice individual gains for the benefit of society as a whole. Although he admitted that a Marxist-Leninist planned economy alone was not enough to help Catholics achieve "spiritual salvation," Myślik still concluded, "the basic principle of planning an economy—consciously and mindfully examining well-being—develops rather than marginalizes the human personality."[118]

Rudolf Buchała was even more direct than Myślik in claiming that French Catholic personalism justified Polish Communist policy; after all, postwar Western European countries had adopted economic planning, too. Buchała, meanwhile, argued against the principle of private property itself. This was the bread and butter of Mounier's anti-capitalism, and Buchała reinterpreted for his readers the history of French Catholic thought as a path to anti-capitalist Catholic "revolution." According to Buchała, the French had begun to lay the foundations for a Catholic critique of private property already in the *fin-de-siècle*, when the priest Antonin-Dalmace Sertillanges wrote that socialism and Christianity shared common foundations.[119] Buchała's argument was that any serious theological analysis of the concept of private property would reveal that every Christian faces a choice: whether to accumulate material possessions, or to divest himself of them for the common good. According to Buchała, then, true Christians should surrender their absolute right to private property in service to the community. This was the greatest test that a Christian could face in the modern world. Proudly, Buchała concluded, "We must therefore choose, and we choose the socialist order."[120]

Meanwhile, in the special issue's lead article, Janusz Zabłocki came as close as anyone before him to making Catholic "revolution" synonymous with Marxism. Masking his essay as an open letter to an erstwhile colleague, Zabłocki invoked the entire personalist canon en route to declaring:

> The revolutionary transformation of society is impossible without the awakening of personhood in each of the individuals constituting the masses. Before each of these individuals, there stands the task of casting off the crushing weight of yesterday's words and answering the call of history. For this reason, class struggle, which precedes revolution, ought to be a struggle for the human person. The classes that derived their greatness from the conquest of the rest of society are doing everything to prevent the awakening of that spirit.[121]

In 1948, announcing *Dziś i Jutro*'s program of Catholic socialism, neither Kętrzyński nor Łubieński had been so explicit in their endorsement of "class struggle." Zabłocki's words reveal the contradictions latent in conceiving of "revolution" as the embodiment of the ethical life. Pope Pius XI had arguably opened a door for the planned economy in the 1931 encyclical *Quadragesimo Anno*, but the young radicals went beyond this option: theirs was a program of collectivization, not merely of political economy, but of personhood as such.

The 1951 articles of *Dziś i Jutro*'s young radicals sound like Marxists experimenting with Catholicism, rather than the other way around. And the special issue's featured editorial showed no signs whatsoever of attachment to Catholic metaphysics: "We are also going to defend the core interests of the Polish nation against the bellicose, sabotaging provocations of all foreign secret agencies, as well as those Poles whose retrograde attitudes have set them on the path of service to foreign interests. In the great struggle taking place all over the world against the attempt to force a third war upon humanity, we have made clear that our place is in the Camp of Peace, for it is on our side that the infrastructure is emerging of a more progressive world; here one finds an objective will for peace."[122]

The height of the *Dziś i Jutro* movement's power coincided with postwar Poland's Stalinist turn away from reconstruction and transformation toward repression. *Dziś i Jutro* had tailored its Catholic socialism from the beginning to the political platform of the Polish Communists—from collectivization to world peace, to defense of the Recovered Territories against German revanchism. Catholic socialism followed suit—for the Poles, as for their French admirers. In their early explorations of personalism, the young radicals found themselves caught between Marxism and Catholicism.

In the nineteenth century, Karl Marx desacralized the "person." A century later, French Catholic philosophers worked hard to make personhood transcendent in God's image once again. The young radicals under Bolesław Piasecki's charge sought to square these two positions —all while remaining captive to an understanding of personhood that excluded not only the unbaptized, but also (West) Germans, Americans, and whole other swathes of humanity. In so doing, Mazowiecki's generation stretched Catholic personalism to a breaking point.

# 8   The Limits of Catholic "Revolution"

## The Vatican and Stalinism's Turn against the Church, 1953–1956

*For Katyń, for the millions of innocent victims, either already murdered or still suffering in prisons and camps, for raising a sacrilegious hand against Christ's creation through battle against the Church and against the Holy See, for the death and imprisonment of Its devotees, our innocent Clergy, for poisoning the souls of our young ones already at birth, for sucking up for profit the blood and sweat of millions through murderous enslavement, for the suffering of innocents and the tears of mothers, etc etc, you share joint responsibility.*

— "Polak-Katolik," *anonymous reader, to the*
Wrocław Catholic Weekly[1]

BETWEEN 1951 AND 1953, the Church in Poland suffered through the arrests of three bishops (including its chief prelate, Stefan Wyszyński) and two show trials—of Bishop Kaczmarek of Kielce, and of several priests who had helped the late Cardinal Sapieha to administer the Archdiocese of Kraków.[2] Not only did PAX fail to speak out against these repressions, but it even pressured Wyszyński to do whatever the Communists asked of him. In the late fall of 1953, with Primate Wyszyński under arrest and Bishop Kaczmarek sentenced, PAX ran its own propaganda campaign against the ecclesiastical hierarchy.

The French Catholic vanguard understood that PAX was part of a Polish Stalinist order. But, as Jean-Marie Domenach wrote several years later, they felt caught between Soviet Bloc Stalinism and the "Stalin of the Church"—Pius XII. One after another of Domenach's friends and colleagues in France faced silencing or condemnation at the turn of the 1940s and 1950s. Years later, *Esprit*'s editor was convinced that only the pontiff's death had saved his journal from the same fate. Faced with the choice between the "Stalin of the Church" and the political system created by the real Stalin, the French listened to their Polish friends, who repeated what Mounier had written back in 1946: that Communist Poland was blazing the trail of Catholic, personalist "revolution."

In fact, PAX's Western European friends—Domenach, Mandouze, and even the much older Vaussard—sympathized with Poland's Catholic socialists. Instead of feeling for the Polish bishops whose arrests PAX lauded, the French activists feared for PAX's safety, combining expressions of solidarity with advice on how to avoid the Holy See's watchful gaze. It was the prospect of PAX's ecclesiastical suppression, rather than its complicity in the subjugation of the Polish hierarchy, that stirred the French vanguard to action. It was not the Communists, but the bishops, whom French and Polish radicals alike accused of totalism. Saying that it was all for personhood and social justice, they chose the legacy of the real Stalin.

## THE FAILURE OF THE CHURCH-STATE ACCORD

For Piasecki's youngest disciples, the 1950 agreement became almost an obsession, its very existence a validation of their chosen path. Yet the relationship between Piasecki and Poland's bishops soured soon after the signing of the accord. In January 1951, the Public Safety Ministry arrested and imprisoned Bishop Kaczmarek of Kielce; one year later, Katowice bishop Stanisław Adamski met the same fate.[3] The one bishop who commanded the Communists' respect was Kraków's Cardinal Sapieha, but he died in July 1951. The Archdiocese of Kraków lost its protector, and the Polish secret police began to gut its administration.

Counting on backing from Rome, a few Polish bishops broke ranks with Primate Wyszyński after the April 1950 agreement, running counter-propaganda campaigns in their own dioceses. In a sense, then, the Communist establishment was right to describe as "counter-revolutionary" the prelates whom it arrested.[4] At the same time, these arrests were in clear violation of the Church-State Accord of 1950. Poland's Communist leadership was looking to cut Poland off from the Vatican, and it was off to a good start.

Then, in February 1953, Poland's Communists went in for the kill. The Polish prime minister decreed that the state had the power to control every aspect of Church life in Poland. This was to include, among other things, veto power over Church appointments, resignations, and transfers among the clergy. Modeled on Communist Hungary's successful strategy of co-opting the Church after Cardinal Mindszenty went to jail, the Polish decree meant to deprive the Polish hierarchy of control over their own clergy.[5] Understandably, the episcopate responded by turning its back on the government, announcing a policy of civil disobedience.

Poland was different from Hungary, Czechoslovakia, and Yugoslavia. Unlike his counterparts across the region, Primate Wyszyński had bent over backwards to accommodate the Communists in his quest to safeguard the Church's place in Polish society. When he was appointed in 1948, the Polish primate genuinely believed that he could avoid all-out war with the Communist leadership. After one Communist leader (Bierut) cut down another (Gomułka) within months of Wyszyński's appointment, the new primate took the hint. Starting in 1950, his goal was to make the Church-State Accord work. The PZPR leadership knew this—and yet, by the end of September 1953, Wyszyński found himself under arrest.[6]

## BISHOPS AND SPIES

In the spring of 1951, Czesław Kaczmarek was adjusting to solitary confinement. Poland's secret police had secluded the fifty-six-year-old bishop in a holding facility on suspicion of espionage. The bishop had maintained regular contact with American ambassador Arthur Bliss Lane. When forty Jews were massacred in his diocesan seat of Kielce in July 1946, Kaczmarek blamed Communist provocateurs. After Poland turned Stalinist the next year, he spoke out regularly against the regime in homilies and pastoral letters. This was not a man who would go quietly in the night. His arrest represented only "the first act of a longer drama."[7]

Geopolitical context is of foundational significance here. On March 5, 1953, Joseph Stalin died. His death left a vacuum at the apex of power not only in the USSR, but throughout the Communist world. This, in turn, sent the Soviet Bloc leadership into a tailspin. As a power struggle played out among Nikita Khrushchev, Gyorgy Malenkov, and

Lavrentiy Beria, a workers' revolt erupted in East Berlin on June 17, 1953. Although suppressed within a week, the Berlin Crisis of 1953 left Soviet Bloc leaders feeling anxious—about the USSR and about their own political futures.[8]

For Polish Catholics, 1953 was a harrowing year. Stalin had died, but Stalinism was in fact at its height in the Soviet Bloc. The Stalinist assault on Poland's Catholic Church only grew in intensity after the Soviet leader's death. Polish president Bolesław Bierut was torn about how to respond to the Polish bishops' declaration of disobedience with regard to state interference in Church appointments. East Berlin had scared Bierut, who was not at all sure of what to expect in the face of a protracted power struggle within the Soviet leadership. In the end, Bierut chose a hard course of repression against the Catholic hierarchy.[9]

Unlike its counterparts elsewhere behind the Iron Curtain, the PZPR did not immediately move to arrest the primate. But Bierut decided to make the bishop of Kielce a scapegoat for the episcopate's continued loyalty to the Vatican. Kaczmarek, like so many show-trial defendants, "confessed" to his crimes. Accused alongside him were three priests and one nun who had worked in his diocesan office; their trial lasted nine days. The prosecutor began by alleging that they had "harmed the country, betrayed their Fatherland and their compatriots; having been ready to send their flock to their deaths in exchange for the spoils of war, they made preparations for our homes to burn to the ground, set aflame by the napalm made by a foreign power, our enemy."[10] The bishop himself, who was exhausted from months of exacting interrogation and torture, drugged before the trial, and fed the story that he was to tell, declared, "Working on behalf of the foreign aims and interests that fed me my politics, I sought to drag the Polish Church into a hurtful and devastating conflict with the People's government." On September 24, 1953, he and his four co-defendants were convicted of conspiring to commit espionage and treason; they received prison sentences ranging from five to twelve years in length.[11]

While all of this was happening, Wyszyński continued to meet regularly with Piasecki, who was extremely well-informed as to what the PZPR brass were thinking. Piasecki's plan was to coax the primate into disavowing and condemning Kaczmarek for his alleged crimes. This Wyszyński consistently and categorically refused to do.[12]

Kaczmarek's story became entangled in Catholic and Communist jockeying for power in the Recovered Territories. Pius XII never agreed to redraw the boundaries of Catholic dioceses in accordance with the transfer of territory from Germany to Poland in 1945. Yet the pope had granted the Polish primate the prerogative of appointing temporary "vicars-general" to administer those lands. Wyszyński alone should have made these decisions, but the PZPR ignored his prerogative, even after concluding the Church-State Accord. This was one of the points of contention that led the episcopate to address a pointed memorandum to the Polish Council of Ministers on May 8, 1953. Known henceforth by its closing words, "*Non Possumus!*" (We cannot!), the statement dismissed any state claims upon the power to make appointments to Church offices. The explanation was simple: "We cannot place what belongs to God on the altar of Caesar."[13] This was the immediate back-drop for the show trial of the Kielce bishop.

The one Catholic to whom the PZPR consistently turned for advice on Church appointments in the Recovered Territories was Bolesław Piasecki. Perversely, then, PAX's leader often had more of a say than the primate in the choice of a given vicar-general. This was the case, for example, with Kazimierz Lagosz. Released from a secret police holding facility in 1952, the priest found his name immediately put forward for vicar-general of Wrocław, the most prominent archdiocese in the western lands. In exchange for the appointment, Lagosz promised the secret police that he would follow their instructions in the exercise of his new leadership role.[14]

Closely tied to PAX and indebted to Piasecki for support in the selection process, Lagosz set aside resources to help Piasecki start a weekly journal in Wrocław, which PAX then paid the archdiocese to distribute.[15] This was the *Wrocławski Tygodnik Katolicki* (*WTK*, *Wrocław Catholic Weekly*), which young radical Tadeusz Mazowiecki was imported from Warsaw to edit.

*WTK* debuted on August 30, 1953. Its mission was to serve as "the Catholic journal of the Western Territories, much needed for the mobilization of that area, capable of taking into account its unique concerns."[16] The weekly had something for everyone: devotional images for the elderly, comics and brain-teasers for children, and well-written articles for everyone else. Broadly speaking, it featured two types of articles: historical propaganda making the case that Silesia and Pomer-

Fig. 13: The editorial staff of the *Wrocławski Tygodnik Katolicki* (*Wrocław Catholic Weekly*), 1954. Standing center is Tadeusz Mazowiecki, the journal's editor. Photograph from the collections of Jacek Łukasiewicz, reproduced by his permission.

ania had always been Polish, and political commentary separating the "bad" from the "good" in the Polish Church.[17] In the end, the journal helped to push Catholicism in Poland toward schism—as evidenced by the venom of letters that Mazowiecki received from several readers. (This chapter's epigraph comes from a letter sent on Mazowiecki's twenty-seventh birthday.)

In particular, *WTK* came down hard on the bishop of Kielce. In his first month as editor of the new journal, Tadeusz Mazowiecki got a press pass to cover Kaczmarek's trial. Afterward, he produced an editorial that was simultaneously an attack on West Germany, the United States, and the Vatican. While admitting the "pain for Catholics of seeing pastors in the role of defendants," Mazowiecki had not a single sympathetic word for the defendants. His greatest regret from the Kaczmarek trial was that, for the faithful Catholics watching, it proved to be so "painful, creating a deep conflict within our consciences."[18]

Mazowiecki's condescension became a register for the sadness and indignation that he professed at Kaczmarek's alleged treasonous activity. The young editor insisted that the bishop had disgraced the "millions of faithful in our country who each day offer up a self-sacrificing, creative contribution to the new social and economic order." At the same time, Kaczmarek had undermined "the national interest and social progress—in the interwar era, during the occupation, and in People's Poland." Most devastatingly, Mazowiecki accused Kaczmarek of "collaboration with institutions of the American intelligence network that would use representatives of the clergy as tools to fulfill their anti-Polish plans."

Prior to assuming the duties of *WTK* editor, Mazowiecki had already been one of Poland's most impassioned Catholic socialists. Well before moving to Wrocław, he had argued not only that PAX should "pressure the episcopate to change its politics," but that the hierarchy needed to be reminded of "its proper mission": matters of "faith and morality" alone. Only the laity could fight for the "human person," while the pastor needed to confine himself to the altar: "The office of a bishop and his pastoral dignity constitute for Catholics the object of great respect. There is, after all, no Catholicism without the indefatigable, dogmatically defined Church structure, whose foundation is constituted by the bishop's office."[19] But Kaczmarek had crossed a line, Mazowiecki argued: "This is why we not only express our sorrow but indeed renounce the erroneous views of Bishop Kaczmarek, which have driven him to sabotage People's Poland."

Mazowiecki proceeded from the assumption that the trial was real and that the bishop was guilty. Kaczmarek, after all, had "confessed" to being an agent of foreign powers driven by the "imperialistic, bellicose policy of the United States government," as well as "the political views of certain members of the Roman Curia." It is to these unnamed Curia figures that the twenty-six-year-old *WTK* editor attributed designs against Poland's "national interest and social progress, as well as a destructive attitude toward the religious mission and future of the Church in Poland." Finally, Mazowiecki did exactly what André Mandouze had warned "progressives" not to do: he criticized the pope. The young editor insisted, "with all due respect to our total religious unity with the Head of the Church—the Holy Father—it is necessary to draw a definitive distinction between the ecclesiastical authority in Poland (the episcopate), including its religious mission received from the Holy See, and the politics of high-ranking members of the Church."

If there was ever a clear indication of the PAX movement's break with the ecclesiastical hierarchy, Tadeusz Mazowiecki's editorial was it. What made matters worse is that Mazowiecki was no detached observer: he had, in fact, known Kaczmarek personally since childhood. The prelate had actually been a friend of his father's.[20] And still Mazowiecki concluded that Kaczmarek—like the Holy See—was blinded by the "capitalist baggage" of his upbringing. On this point, Mazowiecki spoke for all of PAX: these were feelings long held by the Catholic socialists, but never before expressed in print. In his eyes, Pope Pius XII had become an American stooge: both Kaczmarek and the pontiff were agents of American imperialism, seeking "by means of a new war, and thus the deaths of millions of people, to force an order defined by profiteering and social harm upon countries that have chosen a new historical path."

The PZPR had been right to make an example of Kaczmarek, Mazowiecki argued, because Catholics needed to be taught that pro-American sympathies would start "a new war, a war carried out in Poland with the help of a neo-Hitlerite Wehrmacht."[21] If the Vatican continued to refuse to recognize Polish sovereignty over the Recovered Territories, it was the Polish bishops' pastoral duty to show the Holy See the error of its ways. Mazowiecki proudly concluded, "With each day of effort and self-sacrificing work by millions of Poles residing in these territories, the lands are strengthened in their ultimate assimilation into the Motherland."

This was the same year when six Western European countries—including West Germany—joined forces in the European Coal and Steel Community. And so, Mazowiecki underscored, there had never been a more important time since the end of World War II to defend Poland's claim to the formerly German lands. It was this reason that led the new *WTK* editor to conclude that the Kielce bishop himself was to blame for his misfortunes. The Polish public needed reminders of this alleged fact, moreover, because, "with all due respect to the office and dignity of a bishop, a clear assessment is required of his erroneous social and political attitude."

The editorial thus represents some of the most damaging political propaganda produced by Catholics under Stalinism. It flatly denied personhood to the accused. And yet this was no momentary whim, but a pathological consequence of PAX's fusion of integralism and personalism. PAX's young radicals were so deeply ensnared in the contradictions of their "revolution" that, in the *WTK* editor's eyes, it was Kaczmarek who was repeating Charles Maurras's error of "political immanence," not Mazowiecki himself.

Legendary dissident Adam Michnik once wrote of PAX's young radicals, "In the name of honest personalist ideals, they served totalitarianism. Thinking they were serving the Church, they actually worked against it."[22] On the surface, it is hard to see "honest personalist ideals" in Mazowiecki's condemnation of the bishop of Kielce. Yet Michnik is right that Mazowiecki's article expressed "totalitarian" aspirations, which were perfectly compatible with how PAX's young radicals understood personhood in 1953: as an exclusionary project of "revolution."

One-hundred-thirty years earlier, G. W. F. Hegel had proposed in the *Philosophy of Right* that "persons" could find fulfillment through *Sittlichkeit*, an "ethical life" that allowed the "expression of free individuality *within* the community."[23] Marx rejected this Hegelian balancing act. And yet, a century after Karl Marx, French Catholic philosopher Emmanuel Mounier tried to accommodate both individuality and community. For Mounier's followers—French and Polish alike—their hero's balancing act implied a commitment to totalistic political praxis in the pursuit of universal social justice. The paradoxical consequence for PAX's young radicals was that the project of personalist "revolution" so consumed them that, in the darkest years of Polish Stalinism, they consistently prioritized the "Polish Revolution"—read: the Communist political agenda—over the dignity of individual persons.

Ironically, then, despite their anti-German animus, Poland's young Catholic socialists were following in the footsteps of the nineteenth-century German Protestants for whom personhood had been almost synonymous with the autocratic exercise of sovereignty. The German Restorationists of the early nineteenth century dreamed of seeing Germany unified under the auspices of a pre-Enlightenment, pre-Napoleonic vision of absolute monarchy. Personalist hopes that had gone unfulfilled in the hands of Friedrich Wilhelm III and Friedrich Wilhelm IV were, paradoxically, resurrected a century later in the service of another national agenda—now anti-German. For the Polish "revolutionaries" of the 1950s, their absolute sovereign was Bolesław Bierut—Poland's own "little Stalin."[24]

Giving into personalism's "totalizing" temptation put the young radicals in a self-defeating position, leading them away from the quest for social justice that had brought them to *Dziś i Jutro*, and instead setting them on a path reminiscent of the prewar fascism of PAX's founders. Instead of condemning Jews as his elders had before the war, Mazowiecki condemned Germans, espousing a nationalistic desire to protect the Recovered Territories at all costs. Mazowiecki's article was a case study in the "captive mind" problem described by Czesław Miłosz. The public activism of PAX's young radicals seemed to be poisoning the devout Catholic within each of them.[25]

## THE BREAKING POINT

Even though he published the piece condemning Kaczmarek, Tadeusz Mazowiecki soon recoiled in horror at what he had written. In trying to defend the Recovered Territories at all costs, he had crossed an ethical line.[26] The result was what Czesław Miłosz called "Ketman": a cognitive dissonance, a split within himself, which in turn led Mazowiecki first to try to change the movement to which he belonged, and then—having failed—to seek a more righteous alternative.

Ironically, Piasecki had sent his former protégé to Wrocław not as a promotion, but rather to relocate him far from the halls of power. The thirty-eight-year-old Piasecki had begun to see his twenty-six-year-old colleague as a threat to his leadership; Piasecki may well have been personally responsible for Mazowiecki's uncompromising attack on the bishop.[27] Decades later, however, Mazowiecki would take full responsibility for the article, explaining that he had been naïve enough to take Kaczmarek's public testimony at face value: "At the time, I was speechless in the face of the bishop's own testimony during the trial. I had no idea that what he was saying was the result of drugs that he had been fed. I learned this only from him, following his release. When we met after his release, I expressed my deepest regret for having written this article."[28]

Mazowiecki's main target audience was the hundreds of thousands of Catholics engaged in "polonizing" Silesia and Pomerania. And he did a good job of reaching them. Until 1953 the Polish episcopate had seen eye to eye with Piasecki on the matter of the western lands, but PAX crossed a line by condemning a sitting bishop. Bolesław Piasecki saw Wyszyński twice in the course of the week-long trial, and on the second occasion the primate angrily rebuked the activist. Wyszyński wrote to the Council of State on July 20, demanding Kaczmarek's release. After registering an official protest with the government when the bishop was sentenced, the primate resolved to stop negotiating compromises that the state would never bother to respect.[29]

On September 24, 1953, the primate told Piasecki that he would rather go to prison than compromise again with the Communist government.[30] Expecting to be arrested the next day, he delivered an uncharacteristically inflammatory homily during an evening mass in Warsaw: "The Church will eternally demand truth and freedom. Perhaps this is why the Church has so many enemies, for Christianity will always call for resistance, for struggle against every calumny and every modus vivendi. The Church will always call out: 'sell what you have, do not carry your ballast with you.'"[31] Four hours later, the primate of Poland was in transit to a holding cell, under guard by officers of the secret police.[32]

Still, Stalinist Poland was neither Stalinist Czechoslovakia nor Stalinist Hungary. Wyszyński suffered neither torture nor a show trial. President Bierut chose to confine the cardinal—with a priest and a nun to attend to him—to a remote, vacant monastery rather than a prison cell. Already on the second day of his internment, Wyszyński noted in his diary, "Certainly, martyrdom is deeply ennobling, but God leads the Church not only down the extraordinary path of martyrdom, but also down the ordinary path of apostolic work. Indeed, I was of the opinion that what we need today is a different kind of martyrdom: martyrdom through work, not blood."[33]

And so Wyszyński continued to work, preparing himself for a return to pastoral duties, reviewing the agenda that he had pursued since becoming primate. And he prayed. While in isolation, he could receive no visitors, but he maintained a regular correspondence with his father, and he also received press materials (ironically, mostly periodicals published by PAX). One day, the primate had a mystical awakening: he became a devotee of the cult of the Virgin Mary.

One week into Wyszyński's internment, *Dziś i Jutro* published the government's official decree banning the primate from exercising his duties. Wyszyński's arrest had not been made public, so PAX's writers treated it as a "suspension." The episcopate selected a replacement for its suspended leader: Łódź bishop Michał Klepacz, who would lead the Church in Poland until Wyszyński's eventual release in October 1956.[34] The *Dziś i Jutro* editors added their own commentary to the official PZPR and Church voices. It now became clear that Mazowiecki's denunciation of Kaczmarek was no isolated incident. The PZPR had made its move against the hierarchy, and PAX was backing it to the hilt. To this end, it condemned Kaczmarek and Wyszyński together as traitors to Poland's national interest:

> At a time of victory by the most reactionary, pro-Hitlerite forces of Adenauer in West Germany, when a campaign of immense proportions has been unleashed there against the most vital interests of Poland—we cannot allow ourselves further equivocation in the face of such a harmful orientation. [ . . . ] The fact of the removal from office of an ecclesiastical leader of the rank of Primate of Poland cannot fail to touch the emotions and the Catholic conscience. All the more so given that we are bound to the person of the Cardinal-Primate not only by respect for the dignity of his ecclesiastical office, but also by respect for his pastoral stance, full of passion in the service of Christ. This decision has, nonetheless, become fact, for the objective consequences of recent ecclesiastical policy undermine the basic principles of national unity, thereby threatening the prospects of the development of the very Church whose Hierarchy ought to carry out first and foremost its religious and apostolic duties.[35]

This was the beginning of the end for the Catholic socialism of *Dziś i Jutro*. What previously had been edgy and radical now became treason to the Catholic Church. Following the Polish primate's arrest, Mazowiecki and his fellow radicals slowly moved toward a break with their movement's elders. And yet, even though PAX moved in lock-step with the PZPR's assault on the Polish ecclesiastical hierarchy, the movement's own position seemed to be in jeopardy following the primate's arrest.[36]

Piasecki, in particular, worried about what Bierut would do next to Catholics in Poland. The PAX leader decided to invest as much energy as possible in Kętrzyński's Catholic-socialist international. After all, if PAX could maintain its international cachet despite having publicly backed the removal of its own primate from office, the PZPR would have to appreciate the movement's staying power. In October 1953, Piasecki put it succinctly, "The movement of socially progressive Catholics only matters to the extent that it matters in the international arena; otherwise, it counts for little. Possibilities exist for international cooperation among Catholics, and they serve the interest of Marxists as well."[37]

## PAX'S INTERNATIONAL PARTNERS RESPOND

When the PZPR announced Wyszyński's suspension, the Catholic press across Western Europe and the United States led with the story. Journals known for their anti-Communist politics—France's *La Croix*, the United Kingdom's *Tablet*—roundly condemned the Polish People's Republic for this blatant encroachment on canon law.

Others, however, tried to see things from the Communists' side. The leading Catholic voices of sympathy for Poland's Catholic socialists belonged to French members of the Society of Jesus. Four months before Wyszyński's arrest, the Jesuit Robert Bosc had led a Pax Christi delegation to Poland. This was not an auspicious moment for Poland's Catholic hierarchy. Two months earlier, the government had claimed the right to control all personnel decisions within the Church. A few weeks later, a Kraków jury convicted the late Cardinal Sapieha's closest advisors of espionage and treason. Bosc arrived in Warsaw right in the thick of one of the stormiest periods in the history of Polish Catholicism.

Pax Christi's Maurice Vaussard had originally asked Bosc to shepherd a group of about ten French university students around Poland. In the end, however, Bosc traveled only with two companions from

Pax Christi headquarters.[38] He tried, and failed, to gain an audience with Wyszyński.[39] The Pax Christi delegation spent a total of seven days in Poland. This included one day in Lublin, one in Wrocław, and five in Warsaw. Bosc knew that he had not seen everything, but he believed that the week-long trip was "sufficient to understand the difficult experiment in which our Polish Catholic brothers find themselves engaged and to gain a sense of responsibility and obligation toward them." For Bosc, it was PAX, not the episcopate, that expressed the authentic struggle of most Polish Catholics for social justice. For this reason, whatever the evils of Stalinism, "the current regime has done real service to the homeland in terms of the social and economic order (reconstruction, industrialization, the struggle against public immorality, defense of the western borders)."[40] By leading the way for Catholics looking to join in the Communist project of postwar state-building, PAX, in Bosc's eyes, was expressing the revolutionary will of the Polish nation.

On his return to France, Robert Bosc published an extensive account of his journey in the Jesuits' *Revue de l'Action Populaire*. Bosc heaped praise on the Polish bishops as "men who know themselves to be successors of the Apostles, guided by the Holy Spirit to lead the Church along a difficult journey."[41] He acknowledged that the state's attempt to take over the appointment of clergy put the bishops in a tight spot. Yet he said not a word about any show trials. Either he did not understand what was going on, or—more likely—he did not want readers back home to get the full picture.[42]

Nor did Bosc raise the matter of PAX's anti-Germanism. Instead, the advocate of Franco-German reconciliation staunchly refused to side with West Germany against Poland: "The declared intention of the heads of state of West Germany to recover the territories on the Oder and the Neisse presses upon Europe a menace that it would be vain to try to deny. Whatever one's opinion on the matter, it is urgent for the sake of peace that a treaty intervene as soon as possible, deciding once and for all the fate of these regions that Poland considers to be unquestionably its own." Clearly, Bosc came down on PAX's side.[43]

Bosc marketed PAX to the French public as having the right priorities for life in a modern, industrialized world: social justice, personhood, international solidarity, and "our common obligation toward world peace."[44] As an example of their accomplishments on behalf of the Catholic faith, Bosc explained that, without them, no copies of the

New Testament would have been printed in postwar Poland. (This was true: the PAX publishing house had a monopoly on the printing of religious material.)

As the greatest achievement of his visit, the Jesuit bragged of having warned PAX about the dangers of Communism—not by lecturing them, but "in the spirit of brotherhood." Bosc and his colleagues sat up late into the night talking "in all sincerity" over cognac and canapés.[45] Because PAX was open to dialogue and to the concerns of others, the Jesuit asked French Catholics to reward the Poles with more invitations and collaborative projects: "exchanges among Catholics, to bear fruit, must never go in only one direction. [ . . . ] Are we ready to receive something from our brothers in Poland?"[46]

Some of PAX's leaders were also secret police informants, and their reports shed light on the overwhelmingly positive impressions that Bosc had of a Communist country at the height of postwar Stalinism. Bosc's visit preceded Stefan Wyszyński's arrest, and the French priest was apparently furious that the primate did not find the time to meet with him. The prelate—or so PAX suspected—resented Bosc's interest in the Catholic socialists. By not agreeing to see the French Jesuit, however, Wyszyński unwittingly played to his prejudice. Instead, PAX's hand-picked vicar-general of Wrocław, Kazimierz Lagosz, stepped in to play host on the part of the Church hierarchy. As a result, Bosc left Poland puzzled by "the difference between the primate, who refused any contact with him, and the warm welcome offered by Rev. Lagosz. Nonetheless, he delighted in the official reception that the ecclesiastical hierarchy offered him in Wrocław."[47]

Clearly, PAX was doing something right. A French priest representing both a Jesuit think tank and a Franco-German peace movement was singing their praises in the French press, encouraging Catholics the world over to support Poland's Catholic socialists. Even the ex-fascist Piasecki made a good impression on Bosc.[48] For Wojciech Kętrzyński, the architect of Dziś i Jutro's Catholic-socialist international, this was quite a coup. Bosc had gone to Poland to reflect on how to deal with persistent tensions between Poland and West Germany. He returned to France convinced that the Poles were right and the West Germans wrong, and he repeated this again and again to French audiences. As one of his PAX interlocutors put it, Bosc "left under the general impression that the Church in Poland is much freer than he had anticipated.

He clearly saw also the growing power of the progressive orientation among clergy and laity alike."[49]

And he was not alone. Jacques Mignon, responsible for youth affairs in Pax Christi, asked, genuinely puzzled, "What reason would we have to condemn them?"[50] In sum, through its contacts with Pax Christi, the *Dziś i Jutro*/PAX movement succeeded not only in acquiring a powerful partner for the Catholic-socialist international, but indeed in effecting a change in political attitudes within perhaps the key center of Catholic peace activism in postwar Europe.

Four months later, Primate Wyszyński was under arrest, but even this news did not shake Pax Christi's faith in PAX. Although the *Revue de l'Action Populaire* protested the primate's suspension, Bosc wrote personally to Wojciech Kętrzyński to assure him that nothing had changed between their movements.[51] Calling himself one of Communist Poland's "best friends and defenders," the Jesuit apologized for the negative reactions of many Western European Catholics. Bosc wrote, "we understand well that the primate has not always been as accommodating and understanding as he needed to be, this is possible; but he was a man who wanted the best for the new Poland, who made himself one of the staunchest defenders (at least, in the eyes of French Catholics) of Poland's new western borders. Thus, we are all waiting, and we hope that it will be possible to find an honorable means of restoring the primate to his functions."[52]

Bosc—and with him, Vaussard and the rest of Pax Christi—remained a good friend to the PAX leadership at a time when more orthodox Catholics were falling in lockstep behind the anti-Communism of Pope Pius XII. In a time of crisis for PAX, the Catholic-socialist international proved indispensable. PAX's partners stayed loyal despite the Poles' betrayal of their primate.

This loyalty showed even in the pages of *Le Monde*, France's highest-circulating daily newspaper. In addition to his Pax Christi activism, Maurice Vaussard worked as an editor at *Le Monde* starting in 1945. His boss, the paper's executive editor Hubert Beuve-Méry, was in fact a Mounier acolyte who, like his hero, had taught at Vichy's "leadership school" at Uriage.[53] Beuve-Méry therefore needed no convincing to endorse Mounier's Polish disciples, only information and guidance from his employee, Vaussard. Following Wyszyński's arrest, *Le Monde* ran a two-part feature on the Catholic Church in Poland, written by the philosopher Odette Laffoucrière, in back-to-back issues. The feature's title said it all: "The Church of Poland [caught] between Rome and the state." Laffoucrière began her first article,

> For several years, and especially since the imprisonment of [Czechoslovak primate] Monsignor Beran, a game has been in progress in Poland whose outcome will weigh on the Church: the point is to know if Rome and the people's democracies can reach a modus vivendi. It is paradoxical that this encounter has taken place in this country of profound faith that is, nonetheless, traditionalist and relatively poorly educated. On September 25, a new episode in this drama played out. Around 10 pm, as he was returning from preaching at the interim cathedral, Cardinal Wyszyński, archbishop of Warsaw and primate of Poland, was apprehended by the police.[54]

What made Laffoucrière's piece so important was the interpretation that she offered for the 1949 Holy Office decree. Her point was that, under canon law, the threat of excommunication could not possibly apply to Catholics living in Communist countries. For this reason, the men and women of PAX were "neither heterodox nor dissidents." Responding to those who called PAX "disloyal" to the Church, she replied that this was a "misunderstanding of the origins of their approach in the very history of the Church." In other words, PAX was leading the way for both Church and state toward a "certain reconciliation" with a new, revolutionary world.[55] Even if a few bishops had to go to jail first—Laffoucrière argued—PAX was doing for the Church under Communism what Marc Sangnier and the first French Christian Democrats had done at the dawn of French republicanism.[56]

Even though the Vatican objected most strongly to the Polish stance on the Recovered Territories, this was the question around which Western European Catholic activists rallied most enthusiastically. Seeing in the primate's arrest a test of Catholics' commitment to Polish sovereignty, *La Quinzaine* and *Esprit* actually intensified their ties with PAX in the wake of Wyszyński's arrest.[57] *La Quinzaine* editor Jean Verlhac explained that France's progressives refused to get sucked into anti-Polish propaganda because that would automatically benefit West Germany and the cause of European integration. As he put it, "the Cardinal's suspension is one thing, and the European army is something else entirely. There is, of course, an attempt by the extreme Right to use the suspension of the Cardinal to justify a crusade." Verlhac accepted without question Wojciech Kętrzyński's version of the primate's arrest, which placed blame squarely on the prelate himself: "All efforts had been made to incline the primate toward reasonable solutions. This was deemed impossible. What could the Polish government do in these conditions but invoke the decree authorizing it to intervene in ecclesiastical affairs? Above the primate there is only the Vatican, which had no desire of playing the role of mediator in this conflict. [ . . . ] What is hidden in the West is the fact that the bishops have not followed the primate in this conflict, that his successor has managed to establish relations with the government."[58]

By this time, the Pleven Plan was a household name in Western Europe, and the French were bitterly divided on the perils and promise of a European defense community. With a preliminary treaty having already been signed in May 1952, the Catholic socialists of *La Quinzaine*, *Esprit*, and *Dziś i Jutro* feared that Europe was doomed to face German revanchism. For this reason, a mere three months after the arrest and imprisonment of Primate Wyszyński, Verlhac declared, "friendship toward Poland is growing in France, and the question of the Oder-Neisse border is making great progress in public opinion."[59] In the fall of 1953, anti-Germanism saved the Catholic-socialist international.

## JEAN-MARIE DOMENACH VS. EUROPEAN INTEGRATION

In the fall of 1953, Kętrzyński asked Piasecki to approve a limited-edition, French-language version of *Dziś i Jutro* in time for Christmas. The result was *Aujourd'hui et demain*, an eight-page highlight reel of the journal's most important articles from the past year. It was so successful as propaganda among PAX's French friends that PAX repeated the exercise in 1954 and again in 1955, mailing copies of the edition to its acolytes across Europe. Kętrzyński prepared a list of recipients based on his target areas for the Catholic-socialist international. The 1953 lead article carried the title "We place our trust in France," calling on French readers to protest the proposed European defense community. In fact, almost every text included in *Dziś i Jutro*'s first French edition concerned peace and the neutralization of (West) Germany.[60]

PAX's main partner on these issues was *Esprit*'s managing editor, Jean-Marie Domenach. Two years after founding a French committee for the "peaceful resolution of the German problem," the writer had become a renowned peace activist. In mid-1953, the PZPR and PAX joined forces to create a counterpart to Domenach's French committee. Six months later, the Polish committee brought Domenach to Poland to lead a workshop on anti-German peace activism. In late January 1954, Domenach spent just over a week in Poland, visiting Kraków and Lublin in addition to Warsaw. This was his first visit to Poland, and it gave him a better understanding of the Poles' "traditions and hopes for the future."[61] In these, he found a perfect synergy with his own.

During his time in Poland, the thirty-two-year-old Domenach made the acquaintance of thirty-eight-year-old *Dziś i Jutro* writer Andrzej Krasiński. Although Krasiński had largely withdrawn to the sidelines of PAX to nurse himself back to health after a struggle with tuberculosis, he volunteered to be Domenach's guide to Poland. Krasiński, like Domenach, was a product of the Catholic resistance of World War II. The two men bonded instantly, laying the groundwork for a lifelong friendship. Four months later, it was Krasiński who wrote to Domenach to inform him that PAX had awarded him its highest honor—the Włodzimierz Pietrzak Prize.[62] Krasiński showed great tact in his announcement of the prize to Domenach. The award letter ended by asking the *Esprit* editor if he would permit the Poles to advertise his acceptance of the prize: "The decision of the Jury was unanimous, but in taking it the Jury deemed it necessary to consult first your opinion regarding publicity for the Prize. In particular, the jury wanted to spare you possible attacks on the part of conservative Catholic circles in France and avoid inflaming the growing campaign against the so-called 'Catholic progressive international.'"[63]

This caution proved unnecessary. Although Domenach did not announce the Pietrzak Prize in the pages of *Esprit*, he invested considerable time, thought, and passion into planning his second voyage to Poland. The French activist was very much taken by the similarities between Pietrzak and his own fallen personalist friend, Gilbert Dru. These parallels between the two fallen heroes only deepened his solidarity with the Polish Catholic socialists.

Domenach returned to Poland in mid-July 1954, a man on a mission. To his mind, France and Poland faced the same grave danger to peace and personhood: Germany. Although the European Coal and Steel Community had existed for a year by this point, Franco-German reconciliation was anything but a fait accompli. Two mainstream French political parties—the Socialists as well as the Communists—feared for Alsace, Lorraine, and whatever other territory might come into play in the event of German revanchism. Common coal and steel market or no, French memory of Pétain's capitulation in 1940, and even of France's humiliation at Prussian hands in 1870, remained fresh.

As he accepted the Pietrzak Prize in Warsaw, Domenach declared, "If countless Christian activists—both Catholics and Protestants—have decided to struggle, together with peace fighters, against the remilitarization of Germany, they have done so above all for moral reasons: the example of Munich has taught us all that a nation that betrays its friends prepares its own demise."[64] What Domenach said in public matched what he said in private correspondence: "our Polish friends' cause is in solidarity with our own."[65]

This solidarity bred hope for success in mounting a transnational, Catholic alternative to (Western) European integration. Kętrzyński's international was a good starting point, but Domenach was setting his sights even higher. His starting point was Germany's permanent neutralization, but the end goal was a global Catholic peace campaign. Since the Vatican had already chosen "American imperialism," Catholic socialists needed to take the lead.

The *Esprit* editor saw eye to eye with his Polish friends, and they loved him for it. Wojciech Kętrzyński delivered an impassioned congratulatory speech when conferring the prize:

> To Mr. Jean-Marie Domenach—for his selfless activism in defense of peace, for his struggle against the ratification of the Bonn and Paris treaties that have divided Europe into two opposing blocs, and for his work on behalf of the peaceful reconciliation of all European nations. The jury takes this opportunity to underscore the significance of the participation of French Catholic circles in our shared fight for a peaceful resolution to the German question, participation valued particularly by the Polish nation, which is bound to the French nation by unbreakable bonds of friendship and common national interests. The jury wishes also to single out in its decision both the personal contribution of Jean-Marie Domenach and the contribution of the *Esprit* journal that he edits to general European efforts for the defense of civilization, encompassing, regardless of differences of worldview, all people of good faith.[66]

For both the Frenchman and the Poles, geopolitics and Christian faith were indelibly intertwined as motivations for organized activism by the Catholic laity. As personalists in the tradition of Emmanuel Mounier, they believed that the imperative of waging "revolution" warranted dissent from the Vatican. This is why they saw themselves as Catholic activists even though the Catholic hierarchy was opposed to their activism. In his acceptance speech, Domenach declared,

> You Poles are our friends, as you have suffered more than we at the hands of German barbarity. I declare this in the name of all of my colleagues: when we became involved in the fight against German remilitarization and against a "false" Europe, we were thinking above all of you. [ . . . ] When we are asked to mobilize Christian Europe "against Bolshevism," we reply "no," for we remain loyal to the cause for which we are fighting and loyal to the friends with whom we fight. We do not forget that this supposed "Christian Europe" has betrayed itself, creating conflict and awakening hatred between nations and races. This Europe has already died, buried under the ruins of the Ghetto, under the millions of corpses at Auschwitz. This Europe was not Christian.

This was Domenach's rationale for protesting (Western) European integration. What he proposed instead was a "Europe reaching back to the traditions of struggle against all exploitation, and particularly the most recent struggles for liberation from fascist occupation—a Europe of the past but also of the future, which, in a mutually assured peace, will seek the path to the reconciliation of nations, cultures, and peoples."[67]

This was more than just Domenach talking; this was a bond with the whole *Esprit* circle. Domenach's boss Albert Béguin came to Poland for a week in April 1955, accompanied by renowned philosopher Jean Lacroix, sociologist Henri Bartoli, and historian Henri Bédarida. They held lectures and seminars in Kraków, Lublin, Warsaw, and Wrocław, with PAX shepherding them around as foreign dignitaries.[68] All were so impressed with their time in Poland that they pledged to return seven months later for *Dziś i Jutro*'s tenth-anniversary celebration.[69] They seemed entirely unconcerned that the Poles were using their visit for its propaganda value: "The visit of the French Catholic intellectuals came at a time when the entire Polish nation was signing the Vienna [Peace] Appeal. The fact of mass signings by Polish society made an enormous impression on our guests, who appreciate in full the significance of the struggle for peace. Prof. Lacroix voiced this appreciation in his farewell address, in which he underscored Poland's great role in the work of maintaining peace."[70]

One year after Wyszyński's arrest, none of PAX's international partners seemed to give him a second thought. Willing as they were to turn a blind eye to their Polish colleagues' complicity in Stalinist attacks on the Church, PAX's French friends urged PAX to push their lived experience of Catholic "revolution" onto the transnational stage.

## THE HOLY OFFICE AT MID-CENTURY

For Catholics in Europe, the 1950s were a decade of disenchantment. Fearing nuclear annihilation, watching their continent surrender one colony after another, Catholics felt that Rome was playing less and less of a role in their lives.[71] This is why some Catholics took it upon themselves to bring about a sea change in their faith. Only a small number of French Catholics wrote for journals like *Esprit* and *La Quinzaine*, but those who did were just the tip of a much larger iceberg of Catholic discontent.

France, in particular, was hard-hit by frustration with Rome. Many Catholics continued to read *La Croix* and stick by the pope. But in a country experiencing "Coca-Colonization" since the end of World War II, anti-Americanism was on the rise, and Pius XII's Cold War alliance with the USA was ill-received—all the more so as it seemed to go hand in hand with a Vatican policy of silencing one French Catholic voice after another in the postwar decade.[72]

The Vatican's quest for theological orthodoxy in France had already begun during World War II, with the 1942 condemnation of Marie-Dominique Chenu's *School of Theology*. In 1950, however, the full weight of the Holy Office came down on France's Dominican and Jesuit vanguard with the encyclical *Humani Generis*. Since the 1930s "new theologians" had been calling for the Vatican to take Marx and Lenin seriously; like the French Mission, they taught novice priests to study and understand Communism, rather than simply condemn its practitioners. Pius XII's 1950 encyclical, however, cast these reformers as the enemies of the Catholic Church's eternal truth.[73] For the bulk of the 1950s, it seemed that Yves Congar, Marie-Dominique Chenu, and the other great French voices of Catholic reform might be silenced forever.

The man behind *Humani Generis* was the future John Paul II's PhD advisor, Réginald Garrigou-Lagrange. Under prodding from the Angelicum professor, Pius XII decided to sweep the Church clean of "new theology." For this pope, Congar and Chenu were on par with the modernist heretics of the early twentieth century. His encyclical closely followed the letter of his predecessor Pius X's condemnation of that trend in *Pascendi Dominici Gregis*. Like its 1907 forerunner, *Humani Generis* condemned not one specific proposition, but a whole spectrum of ill-defined "new opinions [ . . .] not always advanced in the same degree, with equal clarity nor in the same terms, nor always with unanimous agreement of their authors." The encyclical was first and foremost a cracking of the whip. Though unnamed by the pope, his chief targets were clear: anyone who returned to "historical sources" was to be suspected of "overthrowing the foundation of all truth and absolute law."[74] Chenu, Congar, and their Jesuit counterparts had a bull's eye on their backs.

In fact, *Humani Generis* was only the beginning. Theologians and political activists united by opposition to the Holy See formed an alliance that played right into the hands of Vatican propaganda. The encyclical drove the Dominican new theologians, for example, to write under assumed names for *La Quinzaine* in order to stay intellectually active in the wake of their dismissal from Le Saulchoir.[75] The Second Vatican Council was still more than a decade in the future, unthinkable under Pius XII. It seemed only a matter of time before the vigilant eye of the Holy See would purge French Catholicism altogether of its self-styled vanguard elements.

Pius XII's reluctant henchmen were the French bishops—whose Gallican traditions Pius XII resented and whose initial support of the reformers the Vatican blamed for opening the door to heterodoxy.[76] Cardinals Maurice Feltin of Paris, Pierre-Marie Gerlier of Lyon, and Achille Liénart of Lille spent the early 1950s shutting down the French radicals and reformers. Feltin directed the suppression of the UCP in 1951 and the Youth of the Church in 1953. Liénart, meanwhile, took a more measured approach to the French Mission, suspending its rector and relocating the seminary away from proletarian communities.[77] When this failed to silence the worker-priests, the French episcopate ordered the recalcitrant pastors to cease their factory work and their mining and to report to their bishops for reassignment. Of the hundred or so worker-priests in the field in March 1954, only about half submitted to these new marching orders.[78]

Neither theologians nor politicians, the worker-priests carried enormous appeal as a human interest story for global mass audiences: hands-on grassroots idealists shut down by an unenlightened autocrat. As Karol Wojtyła had pointed out to Polish readers, the worker-priests were the one missionary initiative in Catholic Europe sending its clergy to integrate with the proletariat, and thereby to win their trust. Pastorally, this was the equivalent of Kętrzyński's promise that *Dziś i Jutro* would Christianize socialism from within, but with a key difference. The worker-priests were on the frontlines every day, not just writing articles. Their suppression caught the attention of mainstream media worldwide.[79]

In Poland, too, the Communist press found propaganda value in the suppression of the worker-priests. Writing to *La Quinzaine*, Wojciech Kętrzyński expressed fear that the Catholic Church was reverting to the days of Pius X,

> We are watching from here with great attentiveness, as well as great disquiet, the events that have recently taken place in France. The affair of the worker-priests seems to us particularly tragic. I truly believe that, next to the condemnation of Marc Sangnier, this is the most tragic moment in twentieth-century Christendom. It must be said that the entire experiment of the worker-priests has been annihilated at one fell swoop, in the most unfortunate of ways. In reading the declarations of the French hierarchy, I have the impression that it is defending a cause that is not its own, that the call to order that has come from Rome has been carried out in France *à contre-cœur*. [ . . . ] In sum it must be clearly stated that the decision taken by the Vatican and carried out by the French Hierarchy has turned into an irreparable disaster, as much on a spiritual as on a social level.[80]

The Vatican had lumped together pastoral radicals and philo-Communists, and this could have worked to the advantage of the Catholic socialists. Seeing the writing on the wall for reformist clergy, Kętrzyński nonetheless instructed *La Quinzaine*, "In these conditions, it is only the laity who have the possibility of representing Catholics in the working man's world and of taking part in his fight. Your role is thus all the greater, and more dangerous at the same time." With these words, he was describing not only *La Quinzaine*, but also himself and PAX. As he and his fellow Catholic socialists understood it, the task of the Church in a world propelled by the progress of Marxist revolution was to offer spiritual guidance at the vanguard, not the rear-guard, of the world's events.

For Poland as for France, the whole point of a Catholic-socialist partnership was to create a social environment in which all human beings—whatever their class background or heritage—could flourish as "human persons." In the Catholic socialists' hands, the Church was to be both agent and object of change—partnering with "revolution," and thereby reforming itself. Catholics who threw in their lot with Stalinism ultimately proved that they could never make good on this promise, but the Holy See seemed to be giving them more, rather than less, ammunition to sustain their campaign.

At the time, the most pressing issues on the table were the legacy of war (and the prospect of yet another), Marxist revolution in Central and Eastern Europe, and the twilight of colonialism in the Third World. With Pius XII's Holy See throwing overboard the only European clergy working to remake Catholic society from the ground up, more lay activists felt that it was their time to step in.

## THE "NEW THEOLOGY" OF BOLESŁAW PIASECKI

PAX's founder was no political hack. When Mounier came to Poland in 1946, most Poles still thought of Piasecki as a fascist. This is why the young leader quickly learned to draw on the strengths of his top recruits. Piasecki met Mounier, but he delegated the personalist philosophical writing to his well-read, French-speaking colleagues—most notably Wojciech Kętrzyński, who had in fact completed several years of high school in Brussels.[81] Meanwhile, Piasecki jockeyed to position his movement on the postwar Polish political scene.

At the same time, Piasecki shaped the ideology and printed content of *Dziś i Jutro* from the moment of the weekly's inception. True, Kętrzyński and Konstanty Łubieński declared in 1948 that *Dziś i Jutro* had a mission to Christianize socialism from within. But it was Piasecki's commentaries that defined the contours of the emerging partnership between Catholicism and Marxism in Poland. Prone though he was to borrowing abstruse Marxist terminology, Piasecki's intellectual contribution helped to establish *Dziś i Jutro* and PAX as a presence in Poland and in the world.

Piasecki's writings were not born in an intellectual vacuum. He read and listened carefully to the great French minds who interacted with *Dziś i Jutro* in the course of their visits to Poland. These included Mounier, Mandouze, Boulier, and Domenach—just to name a few. Piasecki was also an avid reader of Congar and Chenu, whom *Dziś i Jutro* reprinted in Polish translation. New theology became a major source of inspiration for Piasecki's own ideas. In particular, he shared their emphasis on the need for a Catholic theology of work that would, in Chenu's words, encourage a "spirituality of labor" to humanize the modern world's technological civilization.

By the time of the suppression of the worker-priests, Piasecki had been scribbling away for a decade at his own political theology. It all started in 1945, as he sat in an NKVD prison cell, writing a memo for Polish Communist chief Władysław Gomułka. Ten years later, the worker-priest condemnation seemed to Piasecki to open a door for him to make his mark on Catholic theology worldwide. In December 1954, he published his collected writings, opening with a forty-two-page theological manifesto that combined personalism with a theology of labor. Although few outside PAX read the book, and many who did mocked it, Piasecki saw it as his magnum opus.[82] After its publication in Warsaw, the PAX leader dispatched a friend of his living in Rome to make inquiries into having the book translated and published in Italian. Piasecki's goal was for the book to circulate at the highest levels of the Vatican, perhaps even reach the Holy Father himself.[83] The PAX leader earnestly believed that he had the power to win over not only Polish Communists to his theology, but in fact also Pope Pius XII.

He was, of course, out of his mind. And yet the book had an impact, and it remains a serious intellectual artifact of personalism and labor theology at mid-century. What Piasecki set out to do in *Essential Questions* was to provide the Church with a new foundation for understanding the value of human work. In so doing, Piasecki was answering a call issued by Congar as early as the mid-1930s. His preface neither names nor quotes any theologians or philosophers, but the influence of personalism and new theology is apparent throughout the text. Though meant to be as much a political gambit as a theological tract, *Essential Questions* would leave its mark on European Catholic intellectual life.

Piasecki began by declaring that his was a manifesto of all "socially progressive circles in global Catholicism." The world could celebrate the tenth anniversary of "People's Poland," a country both Communist and Catholic. What Piasecki wanted was to define a "common structure of the base of believing citizens and non-believing citizens and their shared freedom in the superstructure." In plain English— he wanted to explain why Catholic socialism was the only choice for Catholics looking to protect human dignity and social justice. Fighting for these quintessentially Catholic goals required "qualitative and quantitative expansion of the camp of peace."[84] For Piasecki, this was the link between personalism and world peace. Like Kętrzyński before him, PAX's leader believed that old papal encyclicals written for a "capitalist" order needed a new interpretive framework, put entirely in the service of "revolution." And so, Piasecki declared, "the thrust of Catholic thought on how to foster a conscience has been an utter failure." What needed to change immediately was the misguided assumption that "the world will always be as unjust as the capitalist or feudal world."[85] This mistake, according to Piasecki, came from a long-standing failure by Catholic theologians to distinguish between the two roles of the Christian God: Creator and Redeemer. Christianity had historically privileged "the task of Redemption to the evident exclusion of the work of Creation. This one-dimensionality has resulted in a range of far-reaching social consequences."

As he built an intellectual scaffolding for his claims, Piasecki followed closely not only the Dominican new theologians, but also Jacques Maritain. Echoing Marie-Dominique Chenu's condemned *School of Theology*, Piasecki decried, among other shortcomings, "the abstruseness and flatness of [mainstream] theological casuistry."[86] Like Maritain in *Integral Humanism*, PAX's founder insisted that, without letting the Church control the secular world, Christians must do all that they can to shape that world according to Christian ethics. He then continued,

> Christianity is optimistic. The root of its optimism in the register of Redemption is mercy; the root of its optimism in the register of Creation is work. God the Redeemer brought mercy to the earth, opening for man the path to achieving the ultimate outcome. God the Creator brought work to the earth, placing man between experienced reality and desired, latent reality. A plan for the future perfectibility of the earth was contained within the act of Creation, demanding of people the translation of its latent possibilities into lived reality. The means for transforming the world is human work, which thus has the dignity of continuing the activities of God the Creator.[87]

Scholars have given much more attention to Piasecki's next big claim: that "leading forces of the party of the working class" were "loving

God ontologically," while Christians could only love God "intention-ally."[88] At face value, Norbert Żmijewski is right: "In his doctrine athe-ism does not seem to be possible at all." After all, "intentional" atheists are really just "ontological" theists.[89] In this way, virtually any Com-munist could gain salvation with no strings attached, while Christians, despite intense work, might very well get nothing. What, then, was the point of Christianizing socialism if "ontologically" God-loving social-ists were already better poised to achieve salvation than "intentionally" God-loving—yet invariably sinful—Christians?

These contentions soon became the object of a major international controversy surrounding Piasecki and *Dziś i Jutro*. That controversy has, unfortunately, meant that the first part of Piasecki's argument—about a Catholic theology of work—has been almost totally ignored. Like Chenu, Congar, and the young Karol Wojtyła, Piasecki believed that Christian evangelization among the proletariat was the linchpin of all possible advancement in the secular world. For this reason, he wanted to be both Catholic and socialist—like Emmanuel Mounier before him. If not for the misguided excursus on ontological and intentional love—rightly interpreted by historians as toadying to Communists—Piasecki could have produced a theology of labor that respected the intellectual conventions of the French vanguard.

Seen in another light, *Essential Questions* was a compendium of the ideological and theological ground that *Dziś i Jutro* and PAX had covered over the span of a decade. This is why Piasecki insisted on the "sanctity" of the Recovered Territories. This is why he theologized the Communist peace campaign: "For the camp of peace, the matter of thought and work of the masses of the faithful is a question not of tactical significance, but of strategy in the struggle against the bellicose plans of imperialism. Catholicism has a decisive position here, for its attitude has a determin-ing influence on all of Christianity, and Christianity in turn profoundly shapes humanity as a whole."[90] This was Piasecki's definitive gambit to justify his version of "revolution." The outcome, however, was heresy.

### THE FRONDE

Even before Piasecki tried to get the pope to take his advice, *Essen-tial Questions* stirred considerable controversy within PAX itself. It was the impassioned young writers in their twenties who started the trouble. By the end of 1955, both *Dziś i Jutro* and *Essential Questions* would land on the Index of Banned Books, and PAX's intrepid young radicals would be ejected from PAX. Catholic "revolution" was through.

Four years earlier, twenty-four-year-old Tadeusz Mazowiecki had been hard at work on a philosophical treatise intended to reconcile personalism with Marxism. The year was 1951, and Mazowiecki was the most established and most powerful of the young radicals. He was both deputy editor-in-chief of the daily newspaper *Słowo Powszechne* and a member of Piasecki's closely guarded Political Committee. He began writing the book at Piasecki's request; the leader commissioned it for the PAX publishing house.

The purpose of Mazowiecki's book was to map out ground within both Catholicism and Marxism for the shared pursuit of dignity of the "human person." This project built on years' worth of claims in the pages of *Dziś i Jutro*—by Kętrzyński as well as Mazowiecki—that the "human person" and "socialist revolution" needed one another. Mazowiecki's goal was nothing less than a reversal of Marx's secularization of personhood—in other words, an attempt to reinscribe God into a Marxist conception of sovereignty and social justice. The young Mazowiecki would certainly have agreed with historian Warren Breckman that "moving the theme of personality from the periphery to the center of our awareness illuminates the political and social concerns of Hegelians from Feuerbach to Marx."[91]

The young personalist conceived of this work as a Catholic affirmation of French Communist Roger Garaudy's 1949 *The Church, Communism, and the Christians* (*L'Église, le communisme et les chrétiens*).[92] Garaudy had argued that, even though the Vatican's politics were counter-revolutionary, new currents in Catholic thought—especially personalism—could be squared with "revolution." Mazowiecki hoped to give teeth to Garaudy's ideas, showing Marxists that a Catholic from behind the Iron Curtain was ready to answer the call.

The timing of Mazowiecki's work proved fateful. Within the next year, the PZPR would begin arresting bishops, and Piasecki—sensing a sea change in the Communists' approach to the Church—applied to the government to incorporate the *Dziś i Jutro* movement under the legal name "PAX Association." In the course of debates over the association's founding charter, it became clear that Mazowiecki and friends were parting ways ideologically with Piasecki. By the summer of 1952,

Mazowiecki's book—never completed, never published—and a series of memos by his fellow radical Janusz Zabłocki threatened to break the movement apart.

Bolesław Piasecki was, by this time, well on his way to the political theology of *Essential Questions*. Meanwhile, Mazowiecki, Zabłocki, and their closest colleagues were moving slowly, but steadily, toward a pluralist worldview. They broke ranks with Piasecki by insisting that Catholics needed to separate theology from politics. In some sense, this claim represented a retreat from this cohort's earlier writings—including Mazowiecki's 1950 declaration that it is "the socialist revolution that ought to endow Catholic thought with its proper form."[93] Instead, in *Marxism and Personalism on the Human Person*, Mazowiecki insisted, "The idea that 'the human being is a person' means that a human being living in nature, in history, embedded in the social relationships around him, transcends in his essence nature, history, and those very same social relationships. These words must not be twisted."[94]

Mazowiecki's manuscript made an impassioned case for the compatibility and complementarity of Marxism and Catholic personalism. Already in his unfinished manuscript's first pages, he clearly identified himself as a socialist: "We declare this unequivocally. We are socialists, too. Socialism, for us, is a concrete historical idea of contemporary life, inhabited by personalism—an idea that transcends historical contingency."[95]

Unlike the Mazowiecki of 1950, however, the Mazowiecki of 1951 and 1952 took seriously the evident contradictions between Catholic metaphysics and Marxist materialism. Specifically, the recovery of personhood within Marxism did not imply the surrender of the "human person" to dialectical materialism, but rather the opening of both to a "pluralism of social goals, of part of the social group and of the person; a pluralism of goals in which the personalist approach ought always to provide salutary foundations for creative action." Mazowiecki did not shy away from criticizing key Marxist tenets, admitting that at the heart of the encounter between Catholicism and socialism there lies "a conflict between materialistic monism and pluralism in the study of existence."[96]

One word in particular stands out within the twenty-four-year-old's vocabulary: "pluralism." Piasecki himself would eventually come to advocate the idea of a "plurality of worldviews" (*wieloświatopoglądowość*). This is how he explained why a Communist country needed a Catholic political party, which is what he wanted PAX to become.[97]

Yet "pluralism" and "plurality" were very different things. Mazo-wiecki's use of the word "pluralism" carried dangerous implications for Piasecki's movement. Instead of merely calling for Catholic participation in "revolution"—one of the messages of Piasecki's introduction to *Essential Questions*—Mazowiecki called for a whole new attitude. What he wanted was dialogue, not monism, and openness to cooperative social action in many different forms. It is in Mazowiecki's unpublished manuscript that we find the roots of the approach to freedom and human dignity that he carried with him decades later as co-founder of Solidarity and as prime minister of Poland—flying in the face of his 1950s vision of "revolution."[98]

In 1952, however, these ideas were dangerous for PAX. The movement had gained an international following by advocating Catholic socialism. Pluralism, on the other hand, was something else entirely. Even Mazowiecki was torn as to how far he should take this new approach—as we have already seen in his Stalinist diatribe against the bishop of Kielce. Rather than attack Mazowiecki for his work on a manuscript that Piasecki himself had commissioned, PAX's leader conceived a delicate game of political intrigue beginning in the spring of 1952. On the one hand, he spread gossip about Mazowiecki's loyalty to the movement; on the other, Piasecki set his young protégé up for failure by promoting him to a position that tested the limits of his politics and ideology. This is how Tadeusz Mazowiecki became the founding editor of the most important Catholic periodical in the Recovered Territories.

Janusz Zabłocki, too, started in 1952 to get the impression that PAX's elders wanted nothing to do with the ideas that he pitched at meetings. Over several months, the twenty-six-year-old editor circulated a half-dozen working papers to the PAX leadership—under the rubric of "Catholicism and Politics"—reflecting on the nature and purpose of Catholic participation in public life. In a paper entitled "Depoliticizing the Church—Politicizing Catholic Citizens," Zabłocki began by reconstructing Jacques Maritain's Thomist personalism as a way of jumpstarting debate within PAX.[99] Drawing on Maritain's 1936 *Integral Humanism*, Zabłocki insisted that confessional faith and politics should never mix. Quoting one of the most famous passages in the Synoptic Gospels, the young activist reiterated that some things are God's, while others are exclusively Caesar's. He wrote, "No self-aware Catholic can demand" the introduction of religion into politics, "for in so doing, he would be demanding the degradation of the Church as a guardian of Revealed Truth from its transcendence of politics to political immanence."[100] Charles Maurras, the integralist leader of French Action, had wanted to turn the Catholic Church into an instrument of secular politics; this idea is what resulted in his condemnation by the Vatican in 1926. And this is what ultimately doomed Catholic "revolution" in Poland.[101]

What Zabłocki denounced as political immanence, the radicals began to call by a familiar name: integralism. Zabłocki's senior colleagues in PAX understood the parallel that he was drawing with Maurras. Meanwhile, Zabłocki saw himself as a latter-day Maritain; after all, the Thomist had spent several years in French Action before turning around and condemning Maurras in 1927. The treatise that Maritain published that year, *Primacy of the Spiritual*, exposed what he saw as the evils that Maurras had introduced into Catholicism.[102] No fan of an intransigentist Vatican, Zabłocki was nonetheless even more antagonistic toward the kind of integral nationalism that Maurras had pioneered. By the spring of 1952, the young editor had begun to suspect Bolesław Piasecki of following in the French ultranationalist's footsteps—and thereby reverting to his prewar fascist roots. After all, when Piasecki co-founded his first political movement in 1934, it was as a disciple of Roman Dmowski, Poland's most famous integralist.[103]

Zabłocki's gutsy memoranda earned the respect of his peers and the fury of his elders. When Piasecki came after him, the young radicals rallied around him. Overnight, these radicals became reformers, seeking to move PAX away from the micro-empire that Piasecki was building and toward the goals for which they had signed up in the first place: human dignity and social justice.

By the late spring of 1952, it was clear that Piasecki no longer had any intention of publishing Mazowiecki's book. Every time the two scheduled a meeting, Piasecki either rescheduled at the last minute, or failed to show altogether. By the time the PAX Association was formally chartered, Mazowiecki and Zabłocki were meeting regularly on their own, drawn together by a close friendship and a shared feeling of marginalization within the movement. Despite his own nationalism, Mazowiecki shared Zabłocki's concerns about Piasecki, and Zabłocki embraced Mazowiecki's call for pluralism and dialogue. These shared tenets turned them into an independent political force.[104]

Then, in May 1952, Piasecki shocked the radicals by appointing the twenty-five-year-old Mazowiecki to chair the committee tasked with preparing the movement's new charter. Even odder was that Piasecki invited Mazowiecki's closest collaborators—Zabłocki, as well as Rudolf Buchała, Ignacy Rutkiewicz, and Wojciech Wieczorek—to sit on the committee. Janusz Zabłocki explains, "We saw no reason not to use our numerical advantage in this group. We decided to open up the debate on the dangers of 'political immanence' within Catholicism—which thus far had been confined to the Political Committee—to the forum of the entire Central Committee." This "Central Committee" was simply a plenary assembly of all of the movement's members. On May 16, Mazowiecki wrote to everyone, requesting "all sorts of corrections, motions, or opinions regarding changes to the charter."[105] Within two weeks, the document was ready.

Not surprisingly, Piasecki was unhappy with the text. Having escalated tensions around the young radicals' reformist ideas, he maneuvered PAX's Central Committee into voting down their proposal. Then he wrote his own counterproposal, which replaced the committee's affirmation of "Christian responsibility in politics" with the slogan "Church, Nation, Socialism." For PAX activists who remembered the interwar era, this was eerily similar to the integralist slogans of National Democracy.[106] It seemed like Piasecki had simply copied Roman Dmowski's slogan "Church, Nation, State," replacing the word "State" with "Socialism." Mazowiecki and colleagues protested with fighting words about the need to tackle "the integralist disease."

Yet, rather than sideline the young radicals when they complained, Piasecki ultimately set forth a compromise proposal. He succeeded in preserving a façade of consensus within the movement, while his younger colleagues, too, felt like they had succeeded at least in forcing important questions about the movement's future. In the end, everyone signed the new charter, which declared, "The committee recognizes the achievements of the doctrines of Marx, Engels, Lenin, and Stalin insofar as they do not contradict the doctrine of the Catholic faith, defined *ex cathedra* by the teaching authority of the Church, and thereby serve eternal religious truth. [ . . . ] The committee assumes joint responsibility for the revolution. This means that the committee wishes to do its part in conquering all difficulties arising on the road to socialism's victory."[107]

Although none of the substantive ideological disagreements within the PAX leadership had been resolved, the reformers' redemption and institutional reintegration seemed complete. In the summer of 1952,

Zabłocki received the Włodzimierz Pietrzak Prize "for his activism up to this point in the domain of Catholic thought, with particular attention to his writings on neo-Thomism and personalism."[108] It seemed that the very working papers that had caused him a year's worth of grief had now earned him an award.

Accepting the award, Zabłocki gave a speech entitled "One Must Become Simultaneously an Authentic Catholic and an Authentic Revolutionary." Here the young personalist set out a vision of how Catholics could reshape public life in accordance with Catholic ethics, without falling prey to the kind of political immanence of which he had accused Piasecki. Setting forth a remarkable synthesis of Maritain, Mounier, and the whole canon of nineteenth-century writings on revolution, Zabłocki insisted that, "in order for a culture grounded in a Catholic worldview to fulfill its present transcendent goals," Catholics needed to accept

> **the conscious assertion of service both to the Church and to the natural social aspirations of the human person within a socialist revolution.** In order to serve these causes effectively, one must first achieve a difficult synthesis within oneself, before attempting it in the wider world: one must simultaneously become an authentic Catholic and an authentic revolutionary. The authenticity of the revolutionary stance is predicated on fidelity to the social struggle of the masses, begun in the name of the natural rights of man; on a sober view of its prospects and necessities; on vigilance and implacability with respect to all temptations to compromise, all subtly masked "third ways." The authenticity of Catholicism is, above all, full living of the life of the Church—a Church not downgraded to "Catholic civilization" or to the "Catholic camp."[109]

Promoted from the Kraków regional office of *Słowo Powszechne* to its Warsaw editorial headquarters, Zabłocki arrived in the nation's capital just as Mazowiecki was leaving Warsaw to open the *Wrocławski Tygodnik Katolicki*. Mazowiecki and Zabłocki were both immensely excited by these opportunities, but Zabłocki in particular could not shake the impression that Piasecki had ulterior motives.[110]

Meanwhile, Mazowiecki would shine in Wrocław, earning the Pietrzak Prize in 1954 for running an organization that had substantially "strengthened Polishness in the Western Territories."[111] This was the same year that Jean-Marie Domenach received a special edition of the Pietrzak Prize for his work to neutralize West Germany.

The prize committee took into account Mazowiecki's wide-ranging public activism in Wrocław. Less than a year after his arrival, Mazowiecki was running a journal and a press, preparing a "Catholic Social Days" conference for all of Silesia, and even serving as a councilman for Wrocław. Yet Mazowiecki was increasingly uncomfortable with the growing volume of negative feedback from readers—and even more so, Piasecki's attempts to steer field operations from his Warsaw headquarters. PAX's leader could see this, as could the Communist secret police, which began spying on the twenty-seven-year-old editor in the fall of 1954. By that time, the secret police saw Mazowiecki as one of his generation's most prominent "potential enemies" of Communist Poland.[112] By March 1955, Mazowiecki was allegedly complaining about the "mafia-like activity of Piasecki's inner circle" at the top of the PAX hierarchy, for whom "the pursuit of money prevents the expansion of the Catholic social and political movement."[113]

The publication of Piasecki's *Essential Questions* at the tail end of 1954 had reopened old wounds. Mazowiecki strongly objected to the book, as did Janusz Zabłocki. After circulating a short critical review of the work among friends in early 1955, Zabłocki became a symbol of intellectual opposition within PAX. Though his memo did not dismiss Piasecki's theses, his argument for a "Christian ideal of political action" was irreconcilable with Piasecki's bizarre theory of ontological and intentional love of God. Zabłocki proposed that PAX change its approach in two key ways: first—"disavow struggle for Marxist recognition of a 'separate Catholic political movement'"; and second—"struggle for the fulfillment within one socialist movement of equal standing for different worldviews on the condition that they all accept one common socialist philosophy of society: socialist ideological pluralism."[114]

Zabłocki, drawing on his personalist heroes Maritain and Mounier, had dismantled a key piece of his leader's theology. Implicit in Piasecki's argument regarding the compatibility of Communists' "ontological love of God" with the "intentionalist" Christian worldview was the idea that the two sides should work together in their joint appreciation of God. As Mikołaj Kunicki has noted, Piasecki was adamantly lobbying the PZPR to grant PAX the rights of a full coalition partner. His political theology neatly followed this line. Yet both came under threat when Zabłocki revived the arguments that he and Mazowiecki had been making three years earlier.

Piasecki wanted to continue peddling his theology, which he believed could be marketed far and wide. Underlying this belief was his vision of turning PAX into a Trojan horse, to undermine Polish Stalinism. As Norbert Żmijewski has put it, Piasecki's "doctrine was thus not the basis for subordination of the Church to the Marxist regime but rather for claiming sole political power."[115] The young radicals' interference in this delicate balancing act threatened Piasecki's theological claim to political power. The movement leader reacted accordingly.

As it happened, Piasecki picked the worst possible time to enforce orthodoxy and ideological discipline within his movement. Feeling their positions threatened, Mazowiecki and Zabłocki got together as they had three years earlier, compared notes, and found that they had a lot to protest. Closing ranks with their closest colleagues in the movement, they led a campaign against Piasecki and his oldest, closest friends. The radicals charged these ex-fascists with "an un-socialist style of work and leadership" and a "bourgeois and consumerist lifestyle." The point was that PAX was not living up to the promises of Catholic socialism at all, and was instead merely filling the coffers of its top leadership.[116]

These young activists shared two motivations: one ideological—making good on the personalism and the Catholic socialism on which they had been weaned within PAX; and the other institutional—seeking less centralization and more democracy within the movement. They did not want a "rapprochement with mainstream Catholicism."[117] Instead, they wanted PAX to take its own Catholic socialism seriously—by renouncing Stalinism and shifting toward pluralism and dialogue.

For their pains, Mazowiecki, Zabłocki, and their six closest friends—termed the "Fronde" (*Fronda*) by one of their elders, with Piasecki as their Cardinal Mazarin—were put through the ringer.[118] Failing to build a majority opposition to Piasecki, Mazowiecki and Zabłocki agreed to submit to self-criticism, only to be demoted, with significant cuts in pay. They then renewed their complaints, and this time they refused self-criticism. By the end of the year, they were out. The "revolution" had eaten its young.

### HERESY

In January 1955, Bolesław Piasecki received a letter from his friend, the Catholic novelist Jan Dobraczyński, who was traveling in France.

This letter put Piasecki in a foul mood. Dobraczyński called into question the value of the Catholic-socialist international, suggesting that PAX's French allies would run at the slightest hint of trouble. He wrote, "An 'intellectual terror' predominates here in Paris, depriving people of the possibility of expressing themselves and acting honestly. The affair of the worker-priests and its outcome tells us that Catholic circles are prepared to deal ruthlessly with rebels from within. Both Domenach and Vaussard will only back us to a point. When this support for us begins to threaten them—they will pull out immediately!"[119]

Dobraczyński's prediction would soon be put to the test. Though Domenach and Vaussard both proved him wrong, Dobraczyński was certainly right about the atmosphere in Western Europe. Reeling from the silencing of Congar and Chenu, with the worker-priest affair still fresh in their memories, the rest of the French Catholic vanguard feared that it was just a matter of time before they, too, fell prey to ecclesiastical sanction.

On February 4, 1955, the French ambassador to the Vatican telegrammed the Foreign Ministry that "*L'Osservatore Romano* published a decree this evening of the Supreme Congregation of the Holy Office dated the 3rd of this month condemning and banning the journal *La Quinzaine*."[120] Jean Verlhac, Max Stern, and the rest of this most radical bastion of French Catholic socialism learned of their imminent demise from the Vatican's daily newspaper. At once defiant and obedient, the *Quinzaine* staff submitted to the decree, while insisting in their final editorial, "After the worker-priests, the Dominican theologians, and many others, Rome has condemned *La Quinzaine* and banned it from being read. [ . . . ] The Roman declaration obliges our conscience to cease publication of the journal. The disappearance of *La Quinzaine* does not, however, in any way signify a renunciation on our part of the struggles shared with all of our comrades to save the world from the reign of war and profit."[121]

Wojciech Kętrzyński learned about *La Quinzaine*'s fate from the pages of *Le Monde*. He immediately wrote to Verlhac to express his outrage and his solidarity with his *Quinzaine* colleagues. Kętrzyński lamented, "And so the drama continues—after the worker-priests, after the Dominicans—it is now you. [ . . . ] Please accept, dear friends, our most profound sense of solidarity and our complete confidence in you."[122]

Little did he know that Piasecki's theological treatise would soon bring the same fate to *Dziś i Jutro*. On June 29, 1955, *Osservatore Romano* published an editorial entitled "The Necessity of Two Condemnations" alongside a decree dated one day earlier. The decree "condemns and prohibits 1) the book written by Bolesław Piasecki, *Zagadnienia istotne*, Warszawa, PAX, 1954; 2) the weekly journal named *Dziś i Jutro*, Warsaw."[123]

The editorial accompanying the Vatican condemnation explained at length why not only Piasecki's treatise, but also his flagship journal had earned the Holy Office's ire. Describing the ex-fascist and his "progressive Catholics" along with their journal as "the most zealous propagandists of several false affirmations," *Osservatore Romano* upbraided PAX for spreading lies among Catholics behind the Iron Curtain. The Vatican journal decried, moreover, Piasecki's "fanaticism" and "quasi-messianic" belief in "Communism as the sole savior of humanity."

The Holy Office took a harsh view of Piasecki's core message: "Christianity is in error, up to and including the present day." This was heresy, plain and simple. For the cardinals of the Holy Office, his transgression was even worse for having been committed behind the Iron Curtain: "While Cardinal Wyszyński and other Polish bishops are in prison or impeded in the exercise of their episcopal office, we are witnessing an indescribable attempt to pass off the Communist regimes as respecting the liberty of the Catholic Church."

And yet, if Piasecki and *Dziś i Jutro* were so bad, why had so many Western European colleagues been condemned first? And why condemn both the book and the journal, if the journal had operated for a decade without attracting the least bit of attention from the Vatican?[124]

The answer is that Piasecki dug his own grave by working so hard to win international recognition for his book. At Piasecki's request, his sister-in-law Janina Kolendo sent a copy of the book to the Dominican priest Józef Maria Bocheński, an émigré philosophy professor —later rector—at the University of Fribourg. Piasecki had hoped for an endorsement from Bocheński, who was the brother of one of *Dziś i Jutro*'s co-founders. The book so appalled Bocheński, however, that he personally translated the preface into French and prepared a memorandum systematically refuting its theses. He then delivered these documents to Archbishop Józef Gawlina, chaplain of the Polish exile community in Rome, for submission to the Holy Office.[125]

*Le Monde*'s Odette Laffoucrière had been right to declare in 1953 that the Holy Office decree against Communism had left considerable leeway for Catholics in the Soviet Bloc. In light of the political constraints they faced as citizens of Communist countries, these Catholics could, under canon law, make the case that they were neither "consciously" nor "freely" choosing collaboration with Marxism. This, in part, explains why the Vatican's censors had been far more focused on Western than on Eastern Europe. With his claims about "ontological love of God," however, Piasecki went beyond what the Holy See was willing to countenance, even behind the Iron Curtain. With Bocheński doing the Holy Office the favor of furnishing both the book and a list of its theological errors, the movement's fate was sealed.

This was the end of the line for the Catholic-socialist international. The project—never publicly announced, yet pursued over half a decade —now endangered PAX's remaining Western European partners. Having condemned *Dziś i Jutro* and "its most fanatical leader," the Holy Office hoped to have "cut off definitively the ideological confusion brought about by 'progressives' in the Catholic camp, from both sides of the Iron Curtain."[126]

The Vatican condemnation did not destroy PAX, but it put Piasecki in an impossible position. As Kętrzyński wrote to Robert Bosc the following month, "Do not worry, Reverend Father. We are sons of the Church, and so we shall remain."[127] And indeed, Piasecki's personal piety took precedence over political tactics. Yet when he went to ask the Communist leadership for permission to submit to the Holy Office decree by shuttering *Dziś i Jutro*, they said no.[128] Fortunately for PAX, canon law gave him several months to make things right. This gave Piasecki time to negotiate a solution acceptable to both the PZPR and Poland's interim head bishop, Michał Klepacz.

## "NOTHING RECALLED THE FACT THAT WE WERE SUPPOSEDLY AMONG CHRISTIANS"

Klepacz gave him ecclesiastical cover, but Piasecki still had to sort out his theological commitments. Mazowiecki, Zabłocki, and their fellow Fronde activists wanted PAX to be more authentically socialist, while the Vatican obviously wished it to be less so. Nonetheless, both sets of critics rooted their complaints against PAX in Catholic social teaching.

The more Piasecki pushed his one-time disciples to the movement's margins, the more radical they became in their Catholic socialism. By the time of their exclusion from PAX, Mazowiecki and Zabłocki were claiming that the movement's ideological hypocrisy dated back to its very beginnings. A key example was PAX's failure to respond to a 1953 diatribe against personalism in the Communist journal *Nowe Drogi* (*New Roads*). Its author was an up-and-coming, twenty-six-year-old Marxist philosopher named Leszek Kołakowski. At the apogee of Polish Stalinism, this future revisionist icon wrote, "So-called Christian personalism constitutes a collection of mendacious slogans, which, under the appearance of care for human dignity and the rights of man, serve to offer a theoretical justification for all of the dirtiest political practices of imperialism and its servant, the Vatican, as well as providing a foundation for the most reactionary political doctrines."[129]

A decade later, following his own turn to revisionism, Leszek Kołakowski would embrace many of the personalists whom he condemned in the early 1950s. Although it would take the election of Karol Wojtyła to the papacy for Kołakowski to see personalism as more than an ideological smokescreen for the Church's material interests, he and his students began to work together with the Fronde after its exit from PAX in 1955. Three years later, Mazowiecki, Zabłocki, and their colleagues founded a monthly journal named *Więź* (*Bond*), to which Kołakowski's students contributed as well, seeking an "authentic" Catholic-Marxist dialogue unencumbered by Stalinism.[130] In 1963, Kołakowski even agreed to take on Janusz Zabłocki as his PhD student. Marxist revisionism and Catholic socialism would thus meet and engage in serious dialogue following Poland's de-Stalinization, brought together by the "human person."

When Kołakowski published his initial attack on personalism in 1953, however, PAX chose not to respond publicly. The twenty-six-year-old Mazowiecki actually drafted a critique of Kołakowski's article, in which he drew a distinction between PAX's advocacy of personalist revolution and the kind of old-fashioned scholasticism that Kołakowski was condemning.[131] PAX hosted a lively debate on this paper, attended mostly by the organization's youngest members. The future Frondists resoundingly endorsed Mazowiecki's reply to Kołakowski, but Piasecki refused to publish it, and no one outside the organization had access to the text.[132] Following on Piasecki's decision one year earlier to drop Mazowiecki's book about Marxism and personalism, this newest snub was a major blow to the young radicals' confidence in PAX's chief.

By mid-August 1955, the Fronde were in Piasecki's crosshairs. On the night of August 11, its members were summoned to the Warsaw office to speak with a committee of PAX elders, only to find themselves isolated on arrival and interrogated separately from one another. Disgusted by the experience, three days later the Fronde went over Piasecki's head and submitted a joint letter of protest to the Communist party's Central Committee that spelled out their various criticisms of PAX. By early September, Piasecki had suspended the Fronde's memberships in the PAX Association. That fall, Mazowiecki and his fellow Wrocław-based Frondists made a gambit to retain control of WTK and to withdraw it from PAX. Lacking Communist support, however, the Fronde succeeded only in obtaining pink slips.[133]

Throughout this stormy time for the Polish movement, PAX's French Catholic-socialist partners remained doggedly loyal. Just in the previous five years, they had seen so many Holy See condemnations that the decree against Dziś i Jutro seemed to be but one more unjust act of oppression.

And yet a small group of Francophone writers from Belgium started a wave of public criticism against PAX. Only three months after the Holy Office decree, Kętrzyński was sending out invitations to Dziś i Jutro's tenth-anniversary gala. Among the responses that he received was a thoughtful note from Jean Delfosse, the personalist managing editor of La Revue Nouvelle (The New Review). The Walloon publisher—a long-time friend of Emmanuel Mounier—politely refused the invitation, explaining, "I am at once too well and insufficiently well-versed in the current Polish situation to permit myself to engage La Revue Nouvelle in the taking of positions that are terribly complex."[134]

Meanwhile, Delfosse's compatriot Guy de Bosschère—who belonged to the Belgian-based International Movement for Action for Peace (Mouvement International d'Action pour la Paix)—accepted Kętrzyński's invitation. Having been in Warsaw in July and August 1955 for the massive International Youth Festival, he returned to Poland for three days in late October of the same year.[135] Enjoyable as the anniversary gathering was, de Bosschère could not reconcile its tenor with the professed Catholicism of its organizers. Even though he came to Poland with strong Marxist sympathies, de Bosschère was a Catholic peace activist, and he looked for piety in other activists. As a guest at the PAX gala, he could not get over the absence of any crosses, or of prayers to open and close the meeting sessions; he was equally struck by the absence of any representatives of the proletariat.

After his return to Brussels, de Bosschère wrote, "apart from a small number of priests' cassocks in the audience, nothing recalled sufficiently the fact that we were supposedly among Christians." In fact, even de Bosschère's request to "commune with our brothers from the East in the liturgical simplicity of a community mass" was rejected because, not having anticipated such a need, Kętrzyński could not obtain last-minute permission from state authorities to take the delegates to a mass anywhere near the meeting space.[136]

The Belgian activist's feeling that Christianity itself was absent from the PAX proceedings illustrates just one of the many contradictions that defined that movement. Though Piasecki ultimately submitted to the Holy Office decree, he got the PZPR to sign off on *Dziś i Jutro*'s closure only by promising to open a substitute weekly. This he did already in May 1956, under the title of *Kierunki* (*Directions*).[137] *Essential Questions*, meanwhile, was out of print by the time of the decree's publication, so all that Piasecki had to do was to cancel plans for future editions. On the surface, the movement seemed to comply with the Vatican's wishes, yet its tactical approach did not change.

This tension created problems for PAX, both domestically and internationally. Never having renounced the theses advanced in *Essential Questions*, Piasecki, who had already alienated the Fronde, remained a heretic in their eyes. They took the Vatican's condemnation seriously, but they read it as a personal indictment of Piasecki, not of Catholic socialism as such. While leaving Stalinism in the dust, these radicals would continue to believe in Catholic participation in a Marxist order until successive acts of repression by the regime taught them the folly of their ways. Janusz Zabłocki ultimately remained within the system, trying—and failing—to start a concessioned Christian Democratic party. Tadeusz Mazowiecki, in the end, went on to cofound Solidarity in 1980.[138] The roots of that anti-Communist dissidence lay in these young radicals' disenchantment with PAX.

In the international realm, meanwhile, *La Quinzaine* was no more, but *Esprit* and Pax Christi held firm in their continued support of PAX. Commenting on the death of Pius XII in his diary three years after *Dziś i Jutro*'s condemnation, Jean-Marie Domenach breathed a sigh of relief: "I learned this evening that this illustrious pope died just in time for *Esprit*. A text condemning us had already been prepared."[139] Seeing *Esprit* and *Dziś i Jutro* in the same light, Domenach thought not about the substance of what the Vatican was condemning, but about the politics. Maurice Vaussard at Pax Christi followed suit.

Domenach only abandoned PAX after the one-time Fronde created *Więź* in 1958. Vaussard never gave up on PAX.

## CONCLUSIONS

Despite the persistence of ideological affinities and personal friendships, Communist Poland's turn from reconstruction to Stalinist oppression doomed the Catholic-socialist international. PAX's run as laboratory of Catholic "revolution" had ended, leaving only integralism and heresy.

PAX nominally survived even beyond the fall of Poland's Communist regime in 1989. But never again after 1956 did it command the kind of ideological loyalty that it had enjoyed in the Stalinist era, both from its young adherents and from its French partners. The final word on PAX as a model for Catholic socialism came from a rather unexpected source: the British Catholic novelist Graham Greene. A superstar to many Catholic intellectuals, Greene came to Poland in late 1955 to promote the Polish translation of his novel *The Heart of the Matter*. While there, he decided to investigate the state of Catholic life.[140] Writing in the *Sunday Times* after he returned to London, Greene put it simply: "The old independent Catholic press is dead."[141]

And yet, though Greene pulled no punches in his criticism of PAX, Greene took seriously the issues into which Piasecki, Kętrzyński, and their colleagues had tapped: fear of nuclear annihilation and frustration with the Vatican. These were genuine, widespread concerns among Catholics in Communist Poland. The issues that had made *Dziś i Jutro* and PAX attractive abroad reflected real worries, and these did not disappear after Piasecki's condemnation. Rather, the coming of de-Stalinization to Poland in 1956 opened the door for other Catholic movements that would take up the twin causes of personhood and social justice.[142]

Graham Greene diagnosed quickly and tersely the reasons why Poles had wanted to believe in both France and the USSR:

> Peace, Democracy, Patriotism—these words when spelt with a capital letter have been taken over in a special sense in Eastern Europe. [ . . . ] It is too easy for us to condemn them. We have no Auschwitz to remember. The girl we entertain to dinner has no prison number tattooed upon her arm. [ . . . ] German rearmament to these people—Catholics as well as Communists—is a betrayal. No crimes have been committed

by Communists equal to what Poland has suffered from Germany. [ . . . ] At the moment Vatican policy seems directed as much against the Catholic people of Poland as against the Communist Government. No one in Poland today—except perhaps some old lady dreaming of the past in her denuded apartment—wants the return of an émigré Government, and yet the Vatican recognizes an émigré ambassador. It is as if the Pope still received as the ambassador of Russia some White Russian Grand Duke from the days of Nicholas II. Nor are any Poles prepared to consider the return of the Western Territories to a Germany responsible for such immeasurable suffering, yet when the Bishopric of Breslau [Wrocław] fell vacant a German cleric was appointed who now lives in the comfort and security of Western Germany. Every Catholic in Poland feels a pin-prick to his pride when letters to administrators in the Western Territories are addressed by the Roman Curia to "Germania," and prays for the day when the realities of the situation shall be recognized by the Vatican.[143]

Writing about some of the Marxists with whom Piasecki's people worked closest, Marci Shore concludes, "For those who offered body and soul, poetry and prose to support the new regime, it was a time of unprecedented power over life and death."[144] Like their atheist colleagues who wielded "unprecedented power," Poland's Catholic socialists shared in these years' dramatic hopes for revolutionary transformation of the world. Continuing to advertise their activism as personalist and "social-Catholic," the men and women of PAX sought partners at home and abroad. After the arrest of their primate, PAX became a crass caricature of the contradictions that had plagued Catholic visions of "revolution" since the dawn of social Catholicism. Anti-Germanism knit together Catholic life in Communist Poland's first decade, taking anti-Semitism's place in the wake of the Holocaust and the pogroms of the postwar years. In the 1960s, PAX would return to this anti-Semitism, contributing to the regime's vicious anti-Semitic propaganda during and after the Six-Day War in the Middle East, followed in 1968 by the so-called "anti-Zionist purges" within the Polish Communist establishment. By then, however, all of the Catholic socialists had abandoned PAX, leaving only the ex-fascists to circle back to their starting ideology from the 1930s.[145]

The consensus opinion of Piasecki among historians is very low, but, when it comes to the rest of the movement, by and large there is no consensus. We may never know for sure if Wojciech Kętrzyński believed in everything that he wrote and said. But—inspired by the solidarity of anti-Nazi resistance in World War II—he had done his homework, and he presented his ideas in a serious, compelling way. Mazowiecki and his fellow young radicals then followed in Kętrzyński's footsteps. The French enthusiasm for those writings shows that *Dziś i Jutro* had a serious impact on Catholic agendas on both sides of the Iron Curtain.

In the mid-nineteenth century, the Protestant thinkers of the German Restoration had insisted that only a sovereign autocrat could protect the dignity of every Christian "person"—inspiring their opponents, the young Hegelians, to secularize the idea of personhood itself.[146] A century later, a generation of young Polish radicals—inspired by the Catholic magisterium's turn to social justice, and by their own country's turn to Marxism—stood the old Protestant argument on its head. Bolesław Piasecki had attempted to harness personalism in the service of Stalinist autocracy. In response, the young radicals whom Piasecki had brought into public life—Tadeusz Mazowiecki, Janusz Zabłocki, Tadeusz Myślik, Rudolf Buchała—called him a closet integralist and chose to go their own way: back to the sources, seeking to recover Marx's own personalist roots, before Lenin or Stalin had corrupted the great master's writings. In their eyes, both Aquinas and Marx needed to be at the heart of Catholic socialism.

In Stalinist Poland, this kind of thinking was a pipe dream, and it earned the young radicals a one-way ticket out of PAX. In the process, they confronted their own exclusionary commitments. Their path of redemption drew the attention of Leszek Kołakowski and other prominent young Marxists.[147] One year after Piasecki expelled the Fronde from PAX, Catholics and Marxists alike made the jump to humanism and revisionism. Poland's Catholic socialists spent the next two decades trying to carve out an official space in Communist Poland for the rights of the "human person"—only to give up and turn to political dissidence in the 1970s.

Like the German Restoration or Vichy, Polish Stalinism showed how personalism's inability to eject integralism could be co-opted in the service of a "total" reorganization of politics and society. As Vladimir Tismaneanu suggests, "In these worlds of disarray, there is propitious ground for the most eccentric discourses of resentment."[148] Catholic socialism could never gain enough power to earn respect for the "human person" as the organizing unit of a just society—except by selling personhood out to autocracy. Yet, for principled activists who took seriously—hope against hope—the promise of social justice on which the Communist system was built, Catholic socialism held real power as the ultimate vision of "revolution" for Catholics. Believers on both sides of the Iron Curtain wanted more than the Vatican was willing to offer, and many—at least, at first—were willing to give Communism the benefit of the doubt.

But this was no ethical life. Worse still, just as the anonymous "Catholic Pole" had warned Mazowiecki in 1954, the act of taking "joint responsibility for the revolution" came back to haunt many Catholic socialists, entrapping them within an integralist ethos of exclusion. The cross-generational Catholic romance with this "fantasy of salvation"— hoping for personalism to save "revolution" not only from capitalism, but also from its own exclusionary pathology—helps to explain why it took the deradicalized Catholic socialists another twenty-five years to help form the Solidarity trade union, and then another decade after that to help bring down the Iron Curtain.

# Epilogue

*O, blessed Innocence! You and I, we were both active in our respective*
*Communist parties in the '40s and '50s which means that, whatever*
*our noble intentions and our charming ignorance (or refusal to get rid*
*of ignorance) were, we supported, within our modest means, a regime*
*based on mass slave labor and police terror of the worst kind in human*
*history. Do you not think that there are many people who could refuse*
*to sit at the same table with us on this ground? No, you are innocent,*
*while I do not feel, as you put it, the "sense of the politics of those*
*years" when so many Western intellectuals were converted to Stalinism.*
                                                    —*Leszek Kołakowski*[1]


IN 1973, THE PHILOSOPHER Leszek Kołakowski received an open
letter from renowned British historian E. P. Thompson. Kołakowski
—the twentieth century's greatest authority on Marxism—had in his
youth been a Stalinist. In the mid-1950s, he led a revisionist turn in Marxist philosophy that became the intellectual force behind de-Stalinization
in Poland.[2] Ultimately, however, the regime and the revisionists parted
ways. Stripped of his Warsaw University professorship in 1968 for
his public defense of student protesters who were savagely beaten by
the regime's "civic militia," Kołakowski left behind both Poland and
Communism.

To E. P. Thompson, a lifelong "Western" Marxist, Kołakowski was
a traitor.[3] Disgusted by the Soviet invasion of Hungary in November
1956, Thompson had left the Communist Party of Great Britain, but he
never abandoned the faith.[4] Subjected by Thompson to a public scold-
ing in the pages of Britain's *Socialist Register*, Kołakowski responded
in kind, sardonically dubbing his response "My Correct Views on Everything." This exchange cemented Kołakowski's reputation as an authoritative ex-Marxist. Like Arthur Koestler, Ignazio Silone, and others
before him, the Pole had "seen the light" after learning the hard way

that Marxist philosophy and Marxism in power were not the same thing. Unlike his predecessors, however, Kołakowski came from the Soviet Bloc. He had helped to build the system that ultimately betrayed him.[5]

Seven years after Leszek Kołakowski's exchange with E. P. Thompson, labor strikes paralyzed the shipyards of Communist Poland. The strikes of August 1980 were not the first time that masses of workers had humiliated the "workers' state" with collective protest. Unlike the Polish strikes of 1956, 1970, or 1976, however, the scale of the solidarity strike made the Communist leadership think twice about using violence.[6] Weeks of negotiation—with strikers and the intellectuals advising them seated at the same table with their autocratic rulers, as equals—produced the Gdańsk Accord. For the first time, a Communist state possessing its own, "official" unions recognized an independent, self-governing union—evocatively named "Solidarity" (*Solidarność*). Overnight, a peaceful revolution followed: unions sprang up across the country, in every profession. Soon, ten million Poles belonged to Solidarity.[7]

Sixteen months later, on December 13, 1981, Communist leader Wojciech Jaruzelski introduced martial law, banning *Solidarność*. Its leaders went into internment camps; its membership disbanded. And yet, the tinder that had been set remained in place. The spark came in 1989, and it brought down the Communist system of Central and Eastern Europe.[8]

The Solidarity movement was born both *thanks to* and *in spite of* the ideas and individuals explored in this book. Karol Wojtyła—Pope John Paul II—learned about workers' solidarity first as a day laborer during World War II, then ministering to coal miners in Belgium in 1947. In 1980–81, the personalist pope became Solidarity's most important spokesperson on the world stage. Tadeusz Mazowiecki, a fallen angel of Catholic "revolution," became one of Solidarity's co-founders in 1980. In 1989, he was its nominee for prime minister of Poland, and he became the Soviet Bloc's first non-Communist head of state.

Like Leszek Kołakowski, Mazowiecki had helped to lay the foundations of Communist Poland, only to dismantle them decades later. The reversal was so complete that the young radical who warned of German revanchism in 1953 became, in 1990, the prime minister who joined West German chancellor Helmut Kohl in a public embrace. To-gether, they resolved in Poland's favor the long-outstanding matter of the Recovered Territories. In one fell swoop, Mazowiecki swept away the rationale for the ethnonational anti-Germanism that had united Catholics and Marxists since World War II, even in the darkest years of Stalinism. The long-time Catholic socialist made Poland a candidate state for NATO membership and for European integration. His gov-ernment introduced one of the world's most unabashedly neoliberal programs of economic reform. The Catholic socialist had become one of the liberal democrats he had spent his youth criticizing.[9]

The story of Europe's Catholic vanguard is not, however, a simple story of a "God that failed." These were Catholics, after all: their God never failed. They also never ceased to be personalists. The quest for the dignity of the "human person" took our book's heroes from the *fin-de-siècle,* through two world wars and decades of empires and re-publics in collapse, into the throes of Moscow-imposed postwar "rev-olution" and Stalinism. By 1956, the Catholic vanguard in France and Poland alike had to confront the meaning of de-Stalinization: the de-legitimation of the Stalinist order that they had justified on putatively Catholic grounds.

The social drama of Europe's Industrial Revolution and socialist promises of a just society merged in the years 1891–1956, triggering a series of transnational conversations and political projects with am-bitious goals of "revolution." After all, ideas travel even when regimes take away passports. When the Stalinist bubble ultimately burst in the years 1955–56, Catholic Poland's non-Stalinist "revolutionaries"—Jerzy Turowicz, Jerzy Zawieyski, and the young Karol Wojtyła—joined forces with the dispossessed Catholic socialists from PAX, Tadeusz Mazowiecki and Janusz Zabłocki. Together, they looked to reform not only Communist Poland, but Catholicism, too.

Theirs is both a Polish and a transnational story. It was not only Mazowiecki and Wojtyła who became "prophets of Solidarity," but also Jacques Maritain, Władysław Korniłowicz, and even—despite having led generations of Catholic intellectuals down a path to Stalinism—Emmanuel Mounier. What makes this more than a story of pseudo-Catholics cynically fomenting "revolution" is the set of *bona fide* commitments to personalism demonstrated by the entirety of the twentieth-century Catholic vanguard—French and Polish.

### DE-STALINIZING "REVOLUTION"

On October 22, 1956, a dozen Catholic activists met in the Warsaw apartment of Władysław Seńko, recently departed from PAX. Others chimed in over the telephone, huddling together around the receiver in Jerzy Turowicz's Kraków apartment. This was the birth of the movement that ultimately took the name Catholic Intelligentsia Clubs (KIK, *Kluby Inteligencji Katolickiej*). The new movement's founder and leader was the fifty-four-year-old playwright Jerzy Zawieyski, who had foresworn public activism altogether rather than work with *Dziś i Jutro* after 1948. Yet standing right alongside him were Mazowiecki and Zabłocki, the former young radicals of PAX. Turowicz and Stomma, from whom Bolesław Piasecki had stolen *Tygodnik Powszechny*, stayed on the line with their Warsaw colleagues all night.

This was the night that the PZPR's Central Committee voted to restore Władysław Gomułka—in the mid-1940s, Poland's Communist leader; under Stalinism, its political prisoner—to the position of general secretary. This was Poland's so-called "October Revolution"—the end of the line for Polish Stalinism.[10]

Nikita Khrushchev's February 1956 revelations about Stalin's purges and terror, delivered in the so-called "Secret Speech" at the Twentieth CPSU Party Congress, reached Poland together with the news that Polish president Bierut had died in Moscow, having attended that very congress. These two revelations knocked the legs out from under Poland's Stalinist establishment. After soldiers fired that summer on hungry, protesting workers in the city of Poznań, Polish Communists turned to their former leader, Władysław Gomułka.

Having just spent the better part of five years under house arrest, the reinstated general secretary understood the plight of Catholics in Poland. In his first days as general secretary, he released Poland's primate, Cardinal Wyszyński, from a house arrest that had lasted three years. Gomułka also looked to the Catholic laity, rewarding intellectuals who showed a willingness to get involved in the life of Communist Poland without embracing Stalinist tactics, as PAX had.[11]

When Gomułka returned to power, Jerzy Zawieyski asked for and was granted a meeting with his old friend. His timing was perfect, and Gomułka approved the playwright's request to establish the Catholic Intelligentsia Clubs. In fact, the general secretary even offered the new movement its own small group of MPs in Poland's parliament. Beginning in 1957, Zawieyski represented the movement in the powerful Council of State.[12]

When Zawieyski opened the October 1956 phone call to Kraków, he thundered, "I speak to you in the name of revolutionary Warsaw!" But he did not mean only Gomułka's revolution against Stalinism and against Soviet hegemony.[13] In fact, he was thinking first and foremost of Bolesław Piasecki, who had contended that there was no other way for Catholics behind the Iron Curtain to shape the world around them, except through an embrace of Stalinism.

KIK's founding members were a motley crew indeed, including *Tygodnik Powszechny* editors, Lublin professors, and the displaced former radicals of PAX. They spanned four generations, and the full range of educated professions. Some—like *Tygodnik Warszawski*'s Jerzy Braun—had done hard time under Stalinism, while others had benefited from their colleagues' fall. But all agreed that personalism should remain their watchword. It was Stalinism that had been wrong, not the idea of wedding the Church's fate to the revolutionary pursuit of human dignity and social justice. These men and women hoped that Gomułka, as a victim of Stalinism, would give them the freedom to be "authentic Catholics and authentic revolutionaries," without becoming puppets of autocracy.[14]

Once again, the promise of "revolution" would fail them. But it did so neither completely nor immediately. In fact, freed of its Stalinist shackles, Catholic socialism helped the men and women of KIK to change the world. After 1956, KIK's leading activists—Mazowiecki and Turowicz, Zabłocki and Zawieyski—repeatedly traversed the Iron Curtain. Former *Dziś i Jutro* partners like Jean-Marie Domenach showed the younger generations a "West" that, while still threatened by nuclear war, at least offered a chance at dignity.[15] Anti-capitalists they remained, but what they saw in their travels taught them that even Gomułka's government was a pathetic excuse for Communist dictatorship, a betrayal of the workers' cause and of the ideal of social justice. As a result, they looked for new ways to bring Catholicism into the world around them. This led them to interfaith dialogue—with Jews, Catholics, and Russian Orthodox; to international dialogue—with Germans; and, ultimately, to a leading role in bringing down the Communist system. Michael Gubser has put it best: "To remain relevant in a crisis-ridden age when religions competed for loyalty with secular and materialist ideologies, the Church had to address the specific needs of modern men by grounding its doctrine in a rigorous engagement with contemporary life."[16]

At the forefront of this engagement was the laity. By the time of Pius XII's death in 1958, French and Polish lay activists alike had ample experience rolling up their sleeves and representing their faith in the world. They still sought to create a just society, divested of individualism—a world that would afford "human persons" living their secular lives the dignity due them as beings made in God's image. The personalists sought to achieve this through "revolution." When Pope John XXIII convoked the Second Vatican Council in 1962, they hoped against hope that their revolution's time had come at last.[17]

## MODERNITY AND REVOLUTION

In a literal sense, "revolution" implies a return to the sources, coming full circle. In their various visions for a Catholic reordering of the modern world, Maritain, Mounier, Yves Congar, and their Polish disciples —from Władysław Korniłowicz to John Paul II—proposed exactly this: a return to the sacred, the restoration of a personhood abandoned in the course of the world's secularization, from the Renaissance and Reformation through the Industrial Revolution. It is difficult to imagine that Thomas Aquinas would have chosen Marxists as partners in this enterprise, yet it was to his method—a return to the source, to God—that the twentieth-century vanguard declared its loyalty.

This is why, in their eyes, the restoration of the "human person" went hand in hand with a return to the textual sources of Catholicism: primarily the New Testament, but also the writings of Augustine, Anselm, Ambrose, and Aquinas. They certainly would have agreed with the philosopher Charles Taylor that "Understanding modernity aright is an exercise in retrieval."[18] For the Catholic vanguard of France and Poland, personalist revolution could only be modern, just as modernity must be remade personalist. It is for this reason that so many of their ideas seemed to presage the teachings of the Second Vatican Council of the 1960s, which ultimately affirmed that the Church's mission included ministry to the modern world.[19]

Passing in and out of Rome throughout the conciliar era, Maritain and Mazowiecki, Congar and Wojtyła, all felt a sea change. To some extent, they were personally responsible for the Council's reforms.

Congar, Maritain, and Wojtyła, in particular, were actively involved in its work. More broadly, however, the transnational partnerships built across the European continent by the mid-century vanguard helped to prepare the conciliar ethos—what has become known as the "spirit of Vatican II." As John W. O'Malley describes it, "Vatican II thus took greater account of the world around it than any previous council and assumed as one of its principal tasks dialogue or conversation with that world in order to work for a better world, not simply a better Church."[20] From the ethos of the French and Polish vanguard, the "spirit of Vatican II" took not the pathologies of exclusionary national-ism, integralism, or Stalinism, but instead humanism, modernism, and radicalism. To these, it added pluralism and universalism.

The twentieth-century Catholic revolution was a joint labor of French and Polish intellectuals. What brought the French and the Poles together was the shared experience, first of liberalism's collapse before 1939, and then of the anti-Nazi resistance of World War II. After the war, all believed in the promise of peace and personalism; by 1948, however, this promise was predicated on blind loyalty to an agenda dictated by Moscow. By this logic, the USSR was better than the United States, Stalinist terror better than European integration, and Stalin himself better than the Holy Father. "Revolution" on these terms was a lie. This, however, was the line followed by *Dziś i Jutro* and its French Catholic-socialist partners to the west of the Iron Curtain.

Yet, when push came to shove, it was clear that PAX never really put workers in conversation with Catholicism. Kętrzyński and Piasecki, Mazowiecki and Zabłocki—these were no worker-priests, evangeliz-ing in factories and mines alongside the members of the proletariat to build their trust in the Catholic faith. PAX failed completely at Cath-olic ministry to the working class. Quite the opposite—the movement created its own *nomenklatura*, a mini-empire of wealth and influence, at a moment when many Poles (including Catholic bishops) languished in Stalinist holding cells. When PAX not only failed to defend the eccle-siastical hierarchy, but indeed reinforced the establishment's attacks on it, it betrayed personalism.

## PERSONHOOD FOR THE WORLD

By the time of Piasecki's death in 1979, it was clear that his integralist approach to personalism and social justice had failed.[21] And yet some of his recruits to *Dziś i Jutro* extricated themselves from his Stalinist politics, instead turning pluralist in their transnationalism. Tadeusz Mazowiecki explored how to end the anti-Germanism that kept Polish Catholic integralism alive under Communist rule. Janusz Zabłocki, fascinated by European integration, entered into dialogue with Western Europe's Christian Democrats.[22] In so doing, both Mazowiecki and Zabłocki helped to reshape the ethos of European Catholicism in the 1950s, 1960s, and 1970s.

The Catholic Intelligentsia Clubs, cofounded by Mazowiecki, Turowicz, Zabłocki, and Zawieyski sought to recover from Stalinism the core values of personalist revolution—personal dignity, a just society—and to purge them of any "totalitarian" content. When Communist Poland signed the Helsinki Final Act of 1975, promising to protect "the inherent dignity of the human person," Mazowiecki and his colleagues rushed to show the world how Polish Communists were harming the very proletariat in whose name they claimed to rule.[23] In this endeavor, they enjoyed the support of former French members of the Catholic-socialist international. Jean-Marie Domenach had shifted his allegiance from PAX to KIK in the late 1950s; twenty years later, when the Catholic Intelligentsia Clubs needed a Western European platform for their appeals to "Christian human rights" in the spirit of Helsinki, *Esprit* eagerly came to their aid. Once Poland's Catholic intellectuals met the workers of the Gdańsk Shipyard in 1980, Solidarity was born.[24]

But there were also "revolutionaries" in the mid-century vanguard who had never been down the road of Catholic socialism. They had, however, believed that personhood was contingent, that only active Catholics could be "human persons." Jews, Protestants, and atheists were to be aggressively and respectfully evangelized, but, compared to Catholics, they were essentially different—human beings, not "human persons." On the cusp of Vatican II, the Catholic vanguard's pastoral radicals dramatically revised their vision of personhood: evangelization remained a priority, but just as important was recognizing the givenness of personhood in the world.

The embodiment of this personalist revolution in Catholic thought was the vanguard thinker who became pope in 1978: Karol Wojtyła, John Paul II. At mid-century, the Roman-trained prelate from Wadowice had drawn inspiration from the French pastoral radicals of "new theology" and the French Mission. He had also refused to partner with Marxist revolution after his return to a Stalinist Poland in 1948.

At that point, Karol Wojtyła had not yet established himself as a personalist philosopher. After his defense at the Collegium Angelicum, he turned to the phenomenology of German philosopher Max Scheler.[25] Following his 1953 habilitation thesis on the compatibility of Scheler's writings with Christian ethics, another sixteen years would pass before the publication of Wojtyła's personalist *magnum opus, The Person and the Act (Osoba i czyn)*. By this time, he was already a cardinal who had made his mark at Vatican II.[26]

The Council was the turning point in his intellectual and spiritual trajectory. It was in Rome, as a member of the drafting commission for *Gaudium et Spes (Joy and Hope)*, that Wojtyła realized that personhood was not contingent on faith, but was instead fulfilled in the actions of a believer. He and his colleagues insisted that the Catholic Church was not the sole source, but rather the "sign and safeguard of the transcendent character of the human person"—a phrase that found its way verbatim into *Gaudium et Spes*, Vatican II's celebrated teaching on "the Church in the modern world."[27] The turn to a universalist understanding of personhood made possible Vatican II's formal recognition of the personhood of non-Catholics—including a dramatic reversal of Catholicism's long-standing persecution of Jews and Judaism. In the document *Nostra Aetate (In Our Time)*, the Council announced, "the Church, mindful of the patrimony she shares with the Jews and moved not by political reasons but by the Gospel's spiritual love, decries hatred, persecutions, displays of anti-Semitism, directed against Jews at any time and by anyone."[28]

Wojtyła's 1969 *The Person and the Act* further elaborated the Council's unprecedented—and, at long last, universalist—revolution in Catholic thought. The cardinal argued that action merely "fulfills" personhood, as an individual takes "possession" of his personhood through action.[29] A secular notion of "transcendence" replaced the specifically Catholic vision of God that had defined personhood in Wojtyła's PhD thesis. In the wake of Vatican II, he accepted that personhood was present in every human being. This remained a core conviction of the man who a decade later was elected Pope John Paul II, with two foundational consequences for his work as pastor and pontiff: all human beings were deserving of dignity as persons, but all human beings also needed solidarity and dialogue with others in order to find fulfillment in their personhood.

There were two intellectual keys to this shift: human work and the laity. For Marie-Dominique Chenu, Yves Congar, and the other Dominican "new theologians" who had inspired and animated the French Mission, the theological intertwining of work and the laity was obvious and essential to any pastoral work. Congar, who in 1935 had appealed for a theology of work that might actually give priests a chance to roll back the tide of Communism, in 1953 published a seminal work entitled *Markers for a Theology of the Laity*. In it, he argued, "Lay people will always be a subordinate order in the Church; but they are on the way to the recovery of a fuller consciousness of being organically active members thereof, by right and by fact."[30]

By the time that he returned to Poland from his studies in Rome, Wojtyła was already working on the assumption that clergy and laity must both do their part in pastoral work. In an article published six months later, he explained what he called the new role of the "pioneering lay apostle":

> Everyone who shares in the supernatural gift of the Heavenly Father thereby becomes responsible. They are responsible for its incontrovertibility and its distribution. Hence the necessity, hence the responsibility, of apostolic life. The apostolic nature of the Catholic Church lies in the continuity of collective effort by all believers for the preservation and spread of faith. On this basis are the new parishes producing an ideal-type of the lay Catholic. He is to be the proper author of the Christian character of his milieu; he is responsible for the social fulfillment and propagation of the Mystery of Transubstantiation.[31]

Thirty-five years later, celebrating the Solidarity movement, Wojtyła concluded that it was bearing witness through work to God's creation that made human beings "persons" in God's image.[32] Among human beings, this was universal. Hence, all human beings were, by nature, "human persons."

As pope, John Paul II turned against the "liberation theologians" of Brazil, Mexico, and Peru—not in spite of his belief in evangelizing among the poor, but because of it.[33] In September 1981, he wrote, "In order to achieve social justice in the various parts of the world, in the various countries, and in the relationships between them, there is a need for ever new *movements of solidarity of* the workers and *with* the workers."[34] The Catholic trade-unionism of Solidarity was his approach to protecting the dignity of human persons—not anti-colonial revolution. In John Paul II's eyes, Polish personalists had finally gotten it right, while the Latin American emphasis on "orthopraxis" risked subordinating faith to politics—and, ultimately, justifying violence. From the standpoint of much of the Global South, his vision was short-sighted.[35] But, for the Soviet Bloc, it was the right message at the right time.

In 1982, with martial law in effect in Communist Poland, Canadian historian John Hellman penned an essay entitled "The Prophets of Solidarity."[36] It was the men and women of *Tygodnik Powszechny*— Hellman held—who since 1945 had heralded the coming of the labor union movement that would prove to be the undoing of the Communist system. Hellman is right that Jerzy Turowicz, the future John Paul II, and other *Tygodnik Powszechny* authors were "prophets of solidarity," and that they drew inspiration from France, but in the final analysis it was not from Emmanuel Mounier. In their eyes, by 1948, he had sold them down the river in favor of the revolutionary utopia of *Dziś i Jutro*.

Instead, it was the conscious cultivation of dialogue that helped *Tygodnik Powszechny* to lay the foundations for the emergence of the Solidarity movement. French thought was absolutely indispensable here, and the young Karol Wojtyła was perhaps its single most important mediator. As Stalinism was beginning in Poland, he opened Polish Catholic intellectuals' eyes to the Dominican "new theologian" Yves Congar, to the Dominican dockworker Jacques Loew, and to the world of the French Mission. The postwar French promise of pastoral revolution found a warm welcome amidst alumni of the interwar Renaissance movement, for whom Laski's Władysław Korniłowicz had been a pastor well ahead of his time with his belief in dialogue-driven, face-to-face catechism. What Jacques Loew had taught Wojtyła about "worker solidarity" would come full circle three decades later, when as pope he would support the creation of a movement of workers called Solidarity.

## THE ETHICAL LIFE

From a twenty-first century perspective, it is tempting to see a *telos* of failure in this story, despite the various moments of exhilaration that came in 1956, 1965, 1980, and 1989. Following the end of Communism in Poland, the Catholic intellectuals left the workers and their outdated means of production to rust on the global marketplace.[37] Integralism re-emerged, reviving strong currents of anti-Semitism and xenophobia (anti-Germanism included).[38] In France as in Poland, critiques of "modernism" still abound within the Catholic Church—targeting above all "genderism," defined by one Polish commentator as the successor to "communism and Nazism."[39] The legacy of Vatican II itself seems at risk.

Yet the lessons of Catholics' twentieth-century quest for "revolution" dwarf the vicissitudes of Church and state, pointing a way to the "ethical life" sought by Catholic thinkers since the Industrial Revolution. In 1999, Polish philosopher-priest Józef Tischner—a personalist disciple of Karol Wojtyła before the latter became pope—wrote, "He who encounters, steps outside—transcends—himself in both senses of the word: toward one on whose behalf he bears witness (becoming ever closer with that other); and toward the One, before whom he bears witness (in other words, before God—the One who demands witness). This is why it should be said: to encounter is to experience Transcendence."[40] Put another way—"an authentic encounter between two persons in this world reveals the transcendental horizons leading to Salvation." On the cosmic balance sheet of the believing Catholic, the "encounter is the deepest and richest of the experiences that a human being can enjoy in his life."[41]

Tischner's words may seem directed more toward Heaven than earth, but his metaphysical commitments translate into very real ethical guidelines for behavior in this world. The "encounter" is the highest standard to which Catholics can aspire. Meeting that standard involves establishing the kind of genuine interpersonal solidarity that, by bringing "human persons" closer to one another, also brings them all as close to God as they can ever get before the Last Judgment. This is the twentieth-century personalists' answer to G. W. F. Hegel's dilemma of how to live the "ethical life": to seek genuine encounters with other "persons" on a similar quest for social justice, human dignity, and a sense of solidarity and rootedness in the world—whatever the Judgment of Heaven to come.

# Notes

INTRODUCTION

1. Tadeusz Mazowiecki, *Rozdroża i wartości* (Warsaw: Biblioteka WIĘZI, 1970), 33.

2. Norman Davies, *Rising '44: The Battle for Warsaw* (New York: Viking, 2004).

3. Quoted in Hiroaki Kuromiya, *Stalin: Profiles in Power* (New York: Pearson, 2005), 160. According to another version, Stalin first made this statement not to Churchill, but to French foreign minister Pierre Laval—a future prime minister of the Vichy regime—in 1935.

4. Jean-Marie Domenach, *Beaucoup de gueule et peu d'or: Journal d'un réfractaire (1944–1977)* (Paris: Seuil, 2001), 190.

5. Jean-Marie Domenach and Robert de Montvalon, *The Catholic Avant-Garde: French Catholicism since World War II*, trans. Brigid Elson *et al.* (New York: Holt, Rinehart, and Winston, 1967). Instead of *avant-garde*, I use the English equivalent "vanguard."

6. Andrzej Friszke, *Między wojną a więzieniem 1945–1953* (Warsaw: Biblioteka WIĘZI, 2015).

7. Padraic Kenney, *Rebuilding Poland: Workers and Communists, 1945–1950* (Ithaca, NY: Cornell University Press, 1997), 336.

8. The usage of these terms here follows Jerry Z. Muller, *The Other God That Failed: Hans Freyer and the Deradicalization of German Conservatism* (Princeton, NJ: Princeton University Press, 1987); François Furet, *The Passing of an Illusion: The Idea of Communism in the Twentieth Century*, trans. Deborah Furet (Chicago: University of Chicago Press, 1999); Vladimir Tismaneanu, *The Devil in History: Communism, Fascism, and Some Lessons of the Twentieth Century* (Berkeley: University of California Press, 2012).

9. Tony Judt, *Past Imperfect: French Intellectuals, 1944–1956* (Berkeley: University of California Press, 1992); Marci Shore, *Caviar and Ashes: A Warsaw Genera-*

*tion's Life and Death in Marxism, 1918–1968* (New Haven, CT: Yale University Press, 2006).

10. Bernard Doering, *Jacques Maritain and the French Catholic Intellectuals* (Notre Dame, IN: University of Notre Dame Press, 1983); John Hellman, *Emmanuel Mounier and the New Catholic Left, 1930–1950* (Toronto: University of Toronto Press, 1981).

11. Anna Mateja, *Co zdążysz zrobić, to zostanie: Portret Jerzego Turowicza* (Kraków: Znak, 2012); Piotr H. Kosicki, "After 1989: The Life and Death of the Catholic Third Way," *TLS—Times Literary Supplement*, December 13, 2013: 13–15; George Weigel, *Witness to Hope: The Biography of Pope John Paul II, 1920–2005*, rev. ed. (New York: Harper Perennial, 2005).

12. On the role of French ideas in occupied Poland—Paweł Rodak, *Wizje kultury pokolenia wojennego* (Wrocław: Funna, 2000). On the occupation—Jan T. Gross, *Polish Society under German Occupation: The Generalgouvernement, 1939–1944* (Princeton, NJ: Princeton University Press, 1979); Jadwiga Biskupska, "Extermination and the Elite: Warsaw under Nazi Occupation, 1939–1944" (PhD diss., Yale University, 2013).

13. Quoted in Hellman, *Emmanuel Mounier and the New Catholic Left*, 221.

14. Michael Fleming, *Communism, Nationalism, and Ethnicity in Poland, 1944–50* (New York: Routledge, 2010); Martial Libera, "France and the German Economy 1945–48: An Imperialist Policy?," in *A History of Franco-German Relations in Europe: From "Hereditary Enemies" to Partners*, ed. Carine Germond and Henning Türk (New York: Palgrave Macmillan, 2008), 137–150.

15. Brian Porter-Szűcs, *Poland in the Modern World: Beyond Martyrdom* (Chichester, UK: Wiley-Blackwell, 2014).

16. Emily S. Rosenberg, *Transnational Currents in a Shrinking World: 1870–1945* (Cambridge, MA: Belknap Press of Harvard University Press, 2012); Philipp Ther, "Comparisons, Cultural Transfers, and the Study of Networks: Towards a Transnational History of Europe," in *Comparative and Transnational History: Central European Approaches and New Perspectives*, ed. Heinz-Gerhard Haupt and Jürgen Kocka (New York: Berghahn, 2010), 204–225.

17. On the eighteenth-century partitions—Jerzy Lukowski, *The Partitions of Poland: 1772, 1793, 1795* (New York: Longman, 1999); Norman Davies, *Heart of Europe: The Past in Poland's Present*, rev. ed. (New York: Oxford University Press, 2001), 138–244. On the Nazi-Soviet partitioning in 1939—Timothy Snyder, *Bloodlands: Europe Between Hitler and Stalin* (New York: Basic Books, 2010), 119–154.

18. Paul Brykczynski, *Primed for Violence: Murder, Antisemitism, and Democratic Politics in Interwar Poland* (Madison: University of Wisconsin Press, 2016). For a region-wide lens—Antony Polonsky, *The Little Dictators: The History of Eastern Europe since 1918* (Boston: Routledge & K. Paul), 1975.

19. Piotr H. Kosicki, "Masters in Their Own Home or Defenders of the Human Person? Wojciech Korfanty, Anti-Semitism, and Polish Christian Democracy's Illiberal Rights-Talk," *Modern Intellectual History* (2015), doi: 10.1017/S1479244431 4000857.

20. Snyder, *Bloodlands*, 119–312; Gross, *Polish Society under German Occupa-*

*tion*; Jan T. Gross, *Revolution from Abroad: The Soviet Conquest of Poland's West-ern Ukraine and Western Belorussia* (Princeton, NJ: Princeton University Press, 1988).

21. Jan T. Gross, "War as Revolution," in *The Establishment of Communist Regimes in Eastern Europe*, ed. Norman Naimark and Leonid Gibianskii (Boulder, CO: Westview Press, 1997), 17–40; Bradley F. Abrams, "The Second World War and the East European Revolution," *East European Politics & Societies* 16, no. 3 (2002): 623–664.

22. S. M. Plokhy, *Yalta: The Price of Peace* (New York: Viking, 2010), 241–251.

23. Though now more than five decades old, Zbigniew K. Brzeziński's observa-tion still holds that Stalinism was "an international system." Brzeziński, *The Soviet Bloc: Unity and Conflict*, rev. ed. (Cambridge, MA: Harvard University Press, 1967), 64.

24. Whereas Brzeziński suggested that Stalinism in the Soviet Bloc began in 1947, with the creation of the Cominform, and ended with Stalin's death in 1953, the consensus in recent scholarship is that it commenced later (in either 1948 or 1949) and lasted longer—until the start of de-Stalinization in 1955–56. Brzeziński, *The Soviet Bloc*, 62; Małgorzata Fidelis, *Women, Communism, and Industrializa-tion in Postwar Poland* (New York: Cambridge University Press, 2010), 15; Ken-ney, *Rebuilding Poland*, 337.

25. See, e.g., Patryk Babiracki, *Soviet Soft Power in Poland: Culture and the Making of Stalin's New Empire, 1943–1957* (Chapel Hill: University of North Carolina Press, 2015); Kenney, *Rebuilding Poland*; Kyrill Kunakhovich, *Culture for the People: Art and Politics in Communist Poland and East Germany* (Forth-coming); Katherine Lebow, *Unfinished Utopia: Nowa Huta, Stalinism, and Polish Society, 1949–56* (Ithaca, NY: Cornell University Press, 2013); Małgorzata Ma-zurek, *Społeczeństwo kolejki: O doświadczeniach niedoboru 1945–1989* (Warsaw: TRIO/ECS, 2010); Marcin Zaremba, *Wielka Trwoga, Polska 1944–1947: Ludowa reakcja na kryzys* (Kraków: Znak/ISP PAN, 2012).

26. Lebow, *Unfinished Utopia*, 6.

27. Akira Iriye, *Global and Transnational History: The Past, Present, and Future* (New York: Palgrave Macmillan, 2013), 78; Susanne Hoeber Rudolph and James Piscatori, eds., *Transnational Religion and Fading States* (Boulder, CO: Westview Press, 1997).

28. On the Church in Poland—Brian Porter-Szűcs, *Faith and Fatherland: Ca-tholicism, Modernity, and Poland* (New York: Oxford University Press, 2011). On Rome and Warsaw—Larry Wolff, *The Vatican and Poland in the Age of the Parti-tions: Diplomatic and Cultural Encounters at the Warsaw Nunciature* (Boulder, CO: East European Monographs, 1988); Neal Pease, *Rome's Most Faithful Daugh-ter: The Catholic Church and Independent Poland, 1914–1939* (Athens, OH: Ohio University Press, 2009).

29. James E. Bjork, *Neither German nor Pole: Catholicism and National Indif-ference in a Central European Borderland* (Ann Arbor: University of Michigan Press, 2008).

30. Porter-Szűcs, *Faith and Fatherland*, 328–359.

31. Charles Maurras, long-time leader of French Action, defined "integral na-

tionalism" as "the exclusive pursuit of national policies, the absolute maintenance of national integrity, and the steady increase of national power—for a nation declines when it loses its might." Quoted in Umut Özkirimli, *Theories of Nationalism: A Critical Introduction*, 2nd ed. (New York: Palgrave Macmillan, 2010), 34. On *Action Française*—Peter J. Bernardi, *Maurice Blondel, Social Catholicism, and Action Française: The Clash over the Church's Role in Society During the Modernist Era* (Washington, DC: Catholic University of America Press, 2009).

32. Eugen Weber, *Action Française: Royalism and Reaction in Twentieth-Century France* (Stanford, CA: Stanford University Press, 1962), 197–201, 504; Brian Porter, *When Nationalism Began to Hate: Imagining Modern Politics in Nineteenth-Century Poland* (New York: Oxford University Press, 2000), esp. 10, 157–188.

33. John Connelly, *From Enemy to Brother: The Revolution in Catholic Teaching on the Jews, 1933–1965* (Cambridge, MA: Harvard University Press, 2012); Timothy Snyder, *Sketches from a Secret War: A Polish Artist's Mission to Liberate Soviet Ukraine* (New Haven, CT: Yale University Press, 2005), 23–98.

34. Fleming, *Communism, Nationalism, and Ethnicity in Poland*, 2.

35. Longina Jakubowska, *Patrons of History: Nobility, Capital, and Political Transitions in Poland* (Burlington, VT: Ashgate, 2012), 3.

36. The Polish word *inteligencja* (often rendered in English as "intelligentsia") is not a literal translation of the French word *intellectuels*, but given the transnational nature of this book, I—following the reasoning of Polish historian Jerzy Jedlicki—consistently use the English word "intellectuals" to describe both. Jerzy Jedlicki, *The Vicious Circle 1832–1864*, trans. Tristan Korecki (Frankfurt am Main: Peter Lang, 2014).

37. François Furet, *Revolutionary France, 1770–1880*, trans. Antonia Nevill (Oxford: Blackwell, 1992).

38. Marcin Kula, *Mimo wszystko bliżej Paryża niż Moskwy: Książka o Francji, PRL i o nas, historykach* (Warsaw: Wydawnictwo Uniwersytetu Warszawskiego, 2010).

39. Tyler Stovall, *Transnational France: The Modern History of a Universal Nation* (Boulder, CO: Westview Press, 2015); Patricia M. E. Lorcin and Todd Shepard, eds., *French Mediterraneans: Transnational and Imperial Histories* (Lincoln: University of Nebraska Press, 2016).

40. Jotham Parsons, *The Church in the Republic: Gallicanism and Political Ideology in Renaissance France* (Washington, DC: Catholic University of America Press, 2004).

41. Dale K. Van Kley, *The Jansenists and the Expulsion of the Jesuits from France, 1757–1765* (New Haven, CT: Yale University Press, 1975); Austin Gough, *Paris and Rome: The Gallican Church and the Ultramontane Campaign, 1848–1853* (Oxford: Clarendon Press, 1986).

42. Carl Schorske, *Fin-de-siècle Vienna: Politics and Culture* (New York: Vintage Books, 1981); Venita Datta, *Heroes and Legends of Fin-de-siècle France: Gender, Politics, and National Identity* (New York: Cambridge University Press, 2011).

43. Philip G. Nord, "Three Views of Christian Democracy in *Fin-de-siècle* France," *Journal of Contemporary History* 19, no. 4 (1984): 713–727; Caroline

Ford, *Creating the Nation in Provincial France: Religion and Political Identity in Brittany* (Princeton, NJ: Princeton University Press, 1993); Janet Horne, *A Social Laboratory for Modern France: The Musée Social and the Rise of the Welfare State* (Durham, NC: Duke University Press, 2001); J. P. Daughton, *An Empire Divided: Religion, Republicanism, and the Making of French Colonialism, 1880–1914* (New York: Oxford University Press, 2006).

44. Émile Poulat, *Église contre bourgeoisie* (Tournai: Castermann, 1977), 173–206.

45. Darrell Jodock, ed., *Catholicism Contending with Modernity: Roman Catholic Modernism and Anti-modernism in Historical Context* (Cambridge: Cambridge University Press, 2000).

46. The two key documents were both papal encyclicals: Pius X, *Pascendi Dominici Gregis*, September 8, 1907, available at http://w2.vatican.va/content/pius-x/en/encyclicals/documents/hf_p-x_enc_19070908_pascendi-dominici-gregis.html; Pius XII, *Humani Generis*, August 12, 1950, available at http://w2.vatican.va/content/pius-xii/en/encyclicals/documents/hf_p-xii_enc_12081950_humani-generis.html.

47. Lloyd S. Kramer, *Threshold of a New World: Intellectuals and the Exile Experience in Paris, 1830–1848* (Ithaca, NY: Cornell University Press, 1988), 176–228.

48. Larry Wolff, *Inventing Eastern Europe: The Map of Civilization on the Mind of the Enlightenment* (Stanford, CA: Stanford University Press, 1994).

49. John Marenbon, *Boethius* (New York: Oxford University Press, 2003), esp. 70–79.

50. Warren Breckman, *Marx, the Young Hegelians, and the Origins of Radical Social Theory: Dethroning the Self* (New York: Cambridge University Press, 1999), e.g. 299.

51. Emmanuel Mounier, "Refaire la Renaissance," *Esprit* no. 1 (1932): 5–51.

52. Stefanos Geroulanos, *An Atheism That is Not Humanist Emerges in French Thought* (Stanford, CA: Stanford University Press, 2010), 112.

53. Joseph Amato, *Maritain and Mounier: A French Catholic Understanding of the Modern World* (Tuscaloosa: University of Alabama Press, 1975), 3.

54. This formulation dates to Hegel's 1820 *Philosophy of Right*. On personalism as ethics see, e.g., E.-Martin Meunier and Jean-Philippe Warren, *Sortir de la "Grande noirceur": L'horizon "personnaliste" de la révolution tranquille* (Sillery, QC: Septentrion, 2002), 83–164.

55. As Warren Breckman writes, "Mutual recognition of the individual and the universal ensures that each sees himself confirmed as the *end* of the other even as he is the means to the end of others." Breckman, *Marx, the Young Hegelians, and the Origins of Radical Social Theory*, 75. Italics in the original.

56. Jacques Maritain, *The Person and the Common Good*, trans. John J. Fitzgerald (New York: Charles Scribner's Sons, 1947), 13; Samuel Moyn, "Personalism, Community, and the Origins of Human Rights," in *Human Rights in the Twentieth Century*, ed. Stefan-Ludwig Hoffmann (Cambridge: Cambridge University Press, 2010), 85–106, at 87.

57. Breckman, *Marx, the Young Hegelians, and the Origins of Radical Social Theory*, 9.

58. Anson Rabinbach, *Begriffe aus dem Kalten Krieg: Totalitarismus, Antifaschismus, Genozid* (Göttingen: Wallstein, 2009).

59. Muller, *The Other God That Failed*, 10.

60. Emmanuel Mounier, *Révolution personnaliste et communautaire* (Paris: F. Aubier, 1935); Michel Winock, *Histoire politique de la revue "Esprit" 1930–1950* (Paris: Seuil, 1975), 176–181.

61. Maritain introduced this argument in Jacques Maritain, *Primauté du spirituel* (Paris: Plon, 1927).

62. Zeev Sternhell, *Neither Right nor Left: Fascist Ideology in France*, trans. David Maisel (Princeton, NJ: Princeton University Press, 1996), xv–xvii, 216, 272, 280; Geroulanos, *An Atheism That is Not Humanist Emerges in French Thought*, 124–125.

63. Amato, *Maritain and Mounier*, 14.

64. This approach keeps in view not only the ideas themselves, but also the agency of their authors and proponents, to avoid the fallacy that Quentin Skinner has described: "that the doctrine to be investigated so readily becomes hypostasized into an entity [ . . . ]. The fact that ideas presuppose agents readily disappears as the ideas get up to do battle on their own behalf." Skinner, *Visions of Politics*, vol. 1, *Regarding Method* (Cambridge: Cambridge University Press, 2002), 62.

65. Muller, *The Other God That Failed*, 12. Italics in the original.

66. Slavoj Žižek, *Did Somebody Say Totalitarianism? Five Interventions in the (Mis)use of a Notion* (London: Verso, 2001), 3. Italics in the original.

67. Giovanni Gentile, Speech to the Italian Senate, April 12, 1930, in *Giovanni Gentile: Discorsi parlamentari*, ed. Francesco Perfetti (Bologna: Mulino, 2004), 157–172, at 171.

68. Barbara Geddes, *Paradigms and Sand Castles: Theory Building and Research Design in Comparative Politics* (Ann Arbor: University of Michigan Press, 2003), 50–53.

69. This trend was exemplified, e.g., by the peer-reviewed journal originally named *Totalitarian Movements and Political Religions*—renamed *Politics, Religion, & Ideology* in 2011.

70. Abbott Gleason, *Totalitarianism: The Inner History of the Cold War* (New York: Oxford University Press, 1995), 14.

71. Breckman, *Marx, the Young Hegelians, and the Origins of Radical Social Theory*, 302.

72. James Chappel, "The Catholic Origins of Totalitarianism Theory in Interwar Europe," *Modern Intellectual History* 8, no. 3 (2011): 561–590, at 563; Udi Greenberg, *The Weimar Century: German Émigrés and the Ideological Foundations of the Cold War* (Princeton, NJ: Princeton University Press, 2014), 120–168.

73. Muller, *The Other God That Failed*, 12.

74. Adam Michnik, *The Church and the Left*, trans. and ed. David Ost (Chicago: University of Chicago Press, 1993), 174.

75. Gerd-Rainer Horn, *Western European Liberation Theology: The First Wave (1924–1959)* (Oxford: Oxford University Press, 2008), 98–101.

76. Domenach and de Montvalon, *The Catholic Avant-garde*, 3–4.

77. Domenach and de Montvalon, *The Catholic Avant-garde*, 4.

78. Paul Misner, *Social Catholicism in Europe: From the Onset of Industrialization to the First World War* (New York: Crossroads, 1991); Horn, *Western European Liberation Theology*, 58–59.

79. Quoted in Amato, *Maritain and Mounier*, 136.

80. Wolfram Kaiser, *Christian Democracy and the Origins of European Union* (Cambridge: Cambridge University Press, 2007), 22.

81. Janet Horne has argued that turn-of-the-century French social Catholics "offered an explanatory model that enabled social policy questions to be framed in a new humanist language, one that was not incompatible with the secular republic." And yet, in Mounier's eyes, republicanism eviscerated any humanist content. Horne, *A Social Laboratory for Modern France*, 113.

82. Bernard Doering writes that the expression "Christian democracy," coined by Pope Leo XIII, "had occasioned many bitter disputes. It had been shelved in Catholic circles as promptly as the principles of social reform contained in the pope's encyclical *Rerum Novarum.*" Doering, *Jacques Maritain and the French Catholic Intellectuals*, 179.

83. Jan-Werner Müller describes Christian Democracy at mid-century as "the party of anti-Communism par excellence and as a movement that retained connections to a real religion—as opposed to the fake religion of fascism." Müller, *Contesting Democracy: Political Thought in Twentieth-Century Europe* (New Haven, CT: Yale University Press, 2011), 6.

84. Wojciech Kętrzyński, "Konsekwencje encyklik społecznych," *Dziś i Jutro*, June 6, 1948.

85. Jan-Werner Müller, ed., *Memory and Power in Post-War Europe: Studies in the Presence of the Past* (New York: Cambridge University Press, 2002).

86. Philip Nord, *France's New Deal: From the Thirties to the Postwar* (Princeton, NJ: Princeton University Press, 2010), 12–13; Gross, "War as Revolution."

87. Zaremba, *Wielka Trwoga*, 24. The term "continuum of mobilization and violence" comes from Peter Holquist, *Making War, Forging Revolution: Russia's Continuum of Crisis, 1914–1921* (Cambridge, MA: Harvard University Press, 2002).

88. Samuel Moyn, *The Last Utopia: Human Rights in History* (Cambridge, MA: Belknap Press of Harvard University Press, 2010), 120–175; Samuel Moyn, *Christian Human Rights* (Philadelphia: University of Pennsylvania Press, 2015).

89. Mikołaj Stanisław Kunicki, *Between the Brown and the Red: Nationalism, Catholicism, and Communism in Twentieth-Century Poland—The Politics of Bolesław Piasecki* (Athens, OH: Ohio University Press, 2012).

CHAPTER 1. THE ROOTS OF CATHOLIC "REVOLUTION"

1. Jerzy Turowicz, "O Maritain'ie czyli o najlepszym katolicyzmie," *Prosto z Mostu*, May 24, 1936.

2. Martin Conway, *Catholic Politics in Europe, 1918–1945* (London: Routledge, 1997), 18; Philip Nord, "Catholic Culture in Interwar France," *French Politics, Culture, and Society* 21, no. 3 (2003): 1–20, at 1.

3. Herman Lebovics, *The Alliance of Iron and Wheat in the Third French Republic, 1860–1914: Origins of the New Conservatism* (Baton Rouge: Louisiana

State University Press, 1988); Caroline Ford, *Creating the Nation in Provincial France: Religion and Political Identity in Brittany* (Princeton, NJ: Princeton University Press, 1993), 97–134.

4. Leo XIII, *Rerum Novarum*, May 15, 1891, available at http://w2.vatican.va/content/leo-xiii/en/encyclicals/documents/hf_l-xiii_enc_15051891_rerum-novarum.html.

5. James Chappel, *Spiritual Welfare: Catholic Political Economy in Twentieth-Century Europe* (Cambridge, MA: Harvard University Press, 2018).

6. Bernard McGinn, *Thomas Aquinas's "Summa Theologiae": A Biography* (Princeton, NJ: Princeton University Press, 2014), 80.

7. McGinn, *Thomas Aquinas's "Summa Theologiae,"* 74.

8. McGinn, *Thomas Aquinas's "Summa Theologiae,"* 5.

9. Hunt Janin, *The University in Medieval Life, 1179–1499* (Jefferson, NC: McFarland, 2008), 98.

10. Arthur P. Monahan, *From Personal Duties towards Personal Rights: Late Medieval and Early Modern Political Thought, 1300–1600* (Montreal: McGill-Queen's University Press, 1994), 166–184.

11. McGinn, *Thomas Aquinas's "Summa Theologiae,"* 160–162.

12. Lillian Parker Wallace, *Leo XIII and the Rise of Socialism* (Durham, NC: Duke University Press, 1966), 212.

13. Leo XIII, *Aeterni Patris*, August 14, 1879, available at http://w2.vatican.va/content/leo-xiii/en/encyclicals/documents/hf_l-xiii_enc_04081879_aeterni-patris.html.

14. Thomas D. McGonigle and James F. Quigley, *A History of the Christian Tradition: From the Reformation to the Present* (Mahwah, NJ: Paulist Press, 1996), 125.

15. Leo XIII, *Rerum Novarum*, May 15, 1891, available at http://w2.vatican.va/content/leo-xiii/en/encyclicals/documents/hf_l-xiii_enc_15051891_rerum-novarum.html.

16. Brian Porter-Szűcs, *Faith and Fatherland: Catholicism, Modernity, and Poland* (New York: Oxford University Press, 2011), 130.

17. Quoted in Brian Porter, *When Nationalism Began to Hate: Imagining Modern Politics in Nineteenth-Century Poland* (New York: Oxford University Press, 2000), 194.

18. Jacques Prévotat, *Les catholiques et l'Action française: Histoire d'une condamnation* (Paris: Fayard, 2001), 176–179.

19. Porter, *When Nationalism Began to Hate*, 200.

20. Porter-Szűcs, *Faith and Fatherland*, 179–183; Grzegorz Krzywiec, *Szowinizm po polsku: Przypadek Romana Dmowskiego (1886–1905)* (Warsaw: Neriton, 2009).

21. Roman Dmowski, *Myśli nowoczesnego Polaka*, 12th ed. (Wrocław: Nortom, 2002), 127.

22. Roman Dmowski, *Kościół, Naród, Państwo*, 1927, available at http://www.romandmowski.pl/default.php?id=30&dzial=teksty.

23. Charles Maurras, *L'Action française et la religion catholique*, 1914, available at http://maurras.net/textes/100-3.html; Jacques Prévotat, "L'Action française et les catholiques: Le tournant de 1908," *Mil neuf cent* no. 1 (2001): 119–126.

24. Dmowski, *Myśli nowoczesnego Polaka*, 102.

25. Ryszard Bender, *Społeczne inicjatywy chrześcijańskie w Królestwie Polskim, 1905–1918* (Lublin: TN KUL, 1978); Daniel L. Unowsky, *The Pomp and Politics of Patriotism: Imperial Celebrations in Habsburg Austria, 1848–1916* (West Lafayette, IN: Purdue University Press, 2005), 74–75.

26. Tomasz Sikorski and Marcin Kulesza, *Niezłomni w epoce fałszywych proroków: Środowisko "Tygodnika Warszawskiego" (1945–1948)* (Warsaw: von Borowiecky, 2013), 25–26.

27. Karl Marx, "Communism, Revolution, and a Free Poland," February 1848, available at https://www.marxists.org/archive/marx/works/1848/02/22a.htm; Friedrich Engels, "What Have the Working Classes to do with Poland?," 1866, available at https://www.marxists.org/archive/marx/works/1866/03/24.htm; Timothy Snyder, *Nationalism, Marxism, and Modern Central Europe: A Biography of Kazimierz Kelles-Krauz, 1872–1905* (Cambridge, MA: Harvard Ukrainian Research Institute, 1997), 80–81.

28. Porter, *When Nationalism Began to Hate*, 220.

29. Norman M. Naimark, *The History of the "Proletariat": The Emergence of Marxism in the Kingdom of Poland, 1870–1887* (Boulder, CO: East European Quarterly, 1979), xiii.

30. Quoted in Neal Pease, *Rome's Most Faithful Daughter: The Catholic Church and Independent Poland, 1914–1939* (Athens, OH: Ohio University Press, 2009), 53.

31. Antony Polonsky, *Politics in Independent Poland, 1921–1939: The Crisis of Constitutional Government* (Oxford: Clarendon Press, 1972), 210–212.

32. Peter J. Bernardi, *Maurice Blondel, Social Catholicism, and Action Française: The Clash over the Church's Role in Society During the Modernist Era* (Washington, DC: Catholic University of America Press, 2009), 214–215.

33. Porter-Szűcs, *Faith and Fatherland*, 181; Krzysztof Kawalec, *Roman Dmowski* (Warsaw: Éditions Spotkania, 1996), 325.

34. Dmowski, *Kościół, Naród, Państwo*.

35. Porter-Szűcs, *Faith and Fatherland*, 328–359.

36. Dmowski, *Kościół, Naród, Państwo*.

37. Mikołaj Stanisław Kunicki, *Between the Brown and the Red: Nationalism, Catholicism, and Communism in Twentieth-Century Poland—The Politics of Bolesław Piasecki* (Athens, OH: Ohio University Press, 2012), 30–36; Szymon Rudnicki, *Obóz Narodowo-Radykalny: Geneza i działalność* (Warsaw: Czytelnik, 1985).

38. John Connelly, *From Enemy to Brother: The Revolution in Catholic Teaching on the Jews, 1933–1965* (Cambridge, MA: Harvard University Press, 2012), 103–107.

39. Antoni Szymański, *Poglądy demokracyi chrześcijańskiej we Francyi, 1892–1907* (Poznań: Księgarnia św. Wojciecha, 1910), 19.

40. Antoni Kość, "Antoni Szymański (1881–1942)," in *Dziekani Wydziału Prawa, Prawa Kanonicznego i Administracji Katolickiego Uniwersytetu Lubelskiego Jana Pawła II*, ed. Antoni Dębiński, Wojciech Staszewski, Monika Wójcik (Lublin: Wydawnictwo KUL, 2008), 199–205.

41. Szymański immediately followed this book with a 56-page pamphlet on social Catholicism in France: Szymański, *Katolicyzm socyalny we Francyi* (Włocławek: Redakcja "Ateneum Kapłańskiego," 1911).

42. Szymański, *Poglądy demokracyi chrześcijańskiej we Francyi*, 143; Philip G. Nord, "Three Views of Christian Democracy in *Fin-de-siècle* France," *Journal of Contemporary History* 19, no. 4 (1984): 713–727.

43. As Brian Porter-Szűcs has shown, the learned Lwów archbishop Józef Bilczewski preceded the younger Szymański as a voice of social Catholicism in Poland. However, Bilczewski, who died in 1923, would exercise little influence in interwar Poland. Porter-Szűcs, *Faith and Fatherland*, 130–131.

44. Szymański, *Poglądy demokracyi chrześcijańskiej we Francyi*, 131.

45. Idzi Radziszewski, "Uniwersytet katolicki w Polsce," *Wiadomości Towarzystwa Uniwersytetu Lubelskiego* 1, no. 1 (1923): 9–23.

46. Stanisław Litak, "Problematyka badań nad studentami," in *Katolicki Uniwersytet Lubelski: Wybrane zagadnienia z dziejów Uczelni*, ed. Grażyna Karolewicz, Marek Zahajkiewicz, and Zygmunt Zieliński (Lublin: Redakcja Wydawnictw KUL, 1992), 321–326, at 321.

47. Porter-Szűcs, *Faith and Fatherland*, 136–138. On Catholic Action—Gerd-Rainer Horn, *Western European Liberation Theology: The First Wave (1924–1959)* (Oxford: Oxford University Press, 2008), 5–53.

48. Janet Horne, *A Social Laboratory for Modern France: The Musée Social and the Rise of the Welfare State* (Durham, NC: Duke University Press, 2001), 118–120.

49. Quoted in Porter-Szűcs, *Faith and Fatherland*, 139.

50. On the French "Social Weeks," see, e.g., Philippe Lécrivain, "Les Semaines sociales de France," in *Le mouvement social catholique en France au XXe siècle*, ed. Denis Maugenest (Paris: Cerf, 1990), 151–165.

51. Michał Jagiełło, *Próba rozmowy: Szkice o katolicyzmie odrodzeniowym i "Tygodniku Powszechnym,"* vol. 1, *1945–1953* (Warsaw: Biblioteka Narodowa, 2001), 79–92.

52. Konstanty Turowski, *"Odrodzenie": Historia Stowarzyszenia Katolickiej Młodzieży Akademickiej* (Warsaw: ODiSS, 1987); Stefan Kaczorowski, *Historia, działalność i tradycje "Odrodzenia"* (London: Odnowa, 1980).

53. Interwar Poland's Lwów is today's Ukrainian city of L'viv; interwar Poland's Wilno is today's Lithuanian capital of Vilnius. I use Polish orthography for these cities because I discuss them only in the context of a time when a Polish state governed both.

54. Szymon Rudnicki, "From 'Numerus Clausus' to 'Numerus Nullus,'" *Polin* no. 2 (1987): 246–268; Dariusz Libionka, "Obcy, wrodzy, niebezpieczni: Obraz Żydów i 'kwestii żydowskiej' w prasie inteligencji katolickiej lat trzydziestych w Polsce," *Kwartalnik Historii Żydów* no. 3 (2002): 318–338.

55. This argument is most clearly articulated in Stefan Swieżawski, "Nowe sformułowania Deklaracji ideowej 'Odrodzenia,'" *Prąd* no. 2 (1930); Piotr H. Kosicki, "Masters in their own Home or Defenders of the Human Person? Wojciech Korfanty, Anti-Semitism, and Polish Christian Democracy's Illiberal Rights-Talk," *Modern Intellectual History* (2015), doi 10.1017/S1479244314000857.

56. Renata Latala, "Władysław Korniłowicz (1884–1946): Artisan d'une Église communautaire, ouverte au service des hommes," *Notes et Documents* nos. 1–4 (2007): 25–35.

57. Robert Blobaum, "The Revolution of 1905–1907 and the Crisis of Polish Catholicism," *Slavic Review* 47, no. 4 (1988): 667–686.

58. *Catechism of the Catholic Church* (New York: Doubleday, 1995), 4.

59. Stefan Frankiewicz, "Ojciec Władysław Korniłowicz," in *Ludzie Lasek*, ed. Tadeusz Mazowiecki (Warsaw: Biblioteka WIĘZI, 1987), 90–106, esp. 94.

60. Quoted in Frankiewicz, "Ojciec Władysław Korniłowicz," 90.

61. S. Teresa Landy and S. Rut Wosiek, *Ksiądz Władysław Korniłowicz* (Warsaw: Biblioteka WIĘZI, 1978), 58.

62. S. Krystyna Rottenberg, *Les traces des relations franco-polonaises dans les archives de l'Œuvre de Laski 1918–1939* (Paris: Association des Archivistes de l'Église de France, 1982 [Pro manuscripto]), 33–35.

63. M. Elżbieta Czacka, *Notatki*, ed. Katarzyna Michalak (Warsaw: Wydawnictwo Uniwersytetu Kardynała Stefana Wyszyńskiego, 2006), 61.

64. S. Rut Wosiek, "Św. Tomasz w środowiskach młodzieży akademickiej i młodej inteligencji polskiej okresu międzywojennego," in *Studia z dziejów myśli świętego Tomasza z Akwinu*, ed. Stefan Swieżawski and Jan Czerkawski (Lublin: TN KUL, 1978), 351–366, at 353.

65. Maria Błońska, Maria Kunowska-Porębna, Stefan Sawicki, eds., *"Verbum" (1934–1939): Pismo i środowisko*, 2 vols. (Lublin: Towarzystwo Naukowe KUL, 1976); Agnieszka Bielak, *Krytyka literacka w "Verbum"* (Lublin: Wydawnictwo KUL, 2013).

66. Michel Fourcade, "Feu la Modernité? Maritain et les maritainismes" (PhD diss., Université Montpellier III—Paul Valéry, 1997), 873–875; Piotr H. Kosicki, "Polskie personalizmy 1918–1948, Część I: Od tomizmu przedwojennego po 'nowe chrześcijaństwo' Maritaina," *Więź* no. 4 (2014): 82–92.

67. Quoted in Frankiewicz, "Ojciec Władysław Korniłowicz," 95.

68. John Connelly has importantly described Catholic converts of this era as "border crossers": Connelly, *From Enemy to Brother*, 63–64.

69. Thomas Bokenkotter, *Church and Revolution: Catholics in the Struggle for Democracy and Social Justice* (New York: Image Books, 1998), 341.

70. Philippe Chenaux, *Entre Maurras et Maritain: Une génération intellectuelle catholique (1920–1930)* (Paris: Cerf, 1999).

71. Jacques Maritain, *Trois réformateurs: Luther—Descartes—Rousseau: Avec six portraits* (Paris: Plon, 1925), 16.

72. Maritain, *Trois réformateurs*, 121. Italics in the original.

73. Jacques Maritain, *Primauté du spirituel* (Paris: Plon, 1927).

74. Quoted in Tadeusz Mrówczyński, *Personalizm Maritaina i współczesna myśl katolicka* (Warsaw: Książka i Wiedza, 1964), 22.

75. Jakób [Jacques] Maritain, "Jedność kultury chrześcijańskiej," *Prąd* no. 3 (1929).

76. Jakób [Jacques] Maritain, "Jedność kultury chrześcijańskiej (dokończenie)," *Prąd* no. 4 (1929).

77. John F. Pollard, *The Vatican and Italian Fascism, 1929–32: A Study in Conflict* (New York: Cambridge University Press, 1985), 133–166; Hubert Wolf, *Pope and Devil: The Vatican's Archives and the Third Reich*, trans. Kenneth Kronenberg (Cambridge, MA: Belknap Press of Harvard University Press, 2010).

78. Pease, *Rome's Most Faithful Daughter*, 30–53.

79. Pius XI, *Quadragesimo Anno*, May 15, 1931, available at http://w2.vatican.va/content/pius-xi/en/encyclicals/documents/hf_p-xi_enc_19310515_quadragesimo-anno.html.

80. Pius XI, *Quadragesimo Anno*.

81. Landy and Wosiek, *Ksiądz Władysław Korniłowicz*, 68–69.

82. Władysław Korniłowicz, Letter to Jacques Maritain, December 1, 1921, Ladislas Korniłowicz Correspondence, AJRM.

83. Landy and Wosiek, *Ksiądz Władysław Korniłowicz*, 68.

84. Paul Brykczynski, *Primed for Violence: Murder, Antisemitism, and Democratic Politics in Interwar Poland* (Madison: University of Wisconsin Press, 2016), 43–60.

85. Stefan Swieżawski, *Wielki przełom 1907–1945* (Lublin: Redakcja Wydawnictw KUL, 1989), esp. 104–107.

86. Swieżawski, *Wielki przełom*, 117–164.

87. Wosiek, "Św. Tomasz," 353.

88. Swieżawski, "Nowe sformułowania Deklaracji ideowej 'Odrodzenia.'"

89. The two corresponded about their deepest spiritual anxieties, including the authenticity of their own conversions. For example—Zofia Landy, Letter to Raïssa Maritain, December 19, 1923, Sophie Landy, Sœur Thérèse Correspondence, AJRM. On Raïssa Maritain—Brenna Moore, *Sacred Dread: Raïssa Maritain, the Allure of Suffering, and the French Catholic Revival (1905–1944)* (Notre Dame, IN: University of Notre Dame Press, 2013).

90. S. Teresa Landy, "Dlaczego św. Tomasz?," *Prąd* no. 12 (1930).

91. The text was Jacques Maritain, "L'impossible antisémitisme," in Paul Claudel *et al.*, *Les Juifs* (Paris: Plon, 1937); on Maritain's evolution—Richard Francis Crane, *Passion of Israel: Jacques Maritain, Catholic Conscience, and the Holocaust* (Scranton, PA: University of Scranton Press, 2010), 7–34.

92. For a complete Polish-language bibliography of Maritain's work (up to 1963), see Zenon Kałuża and Wacław Tkaczuk, "Jacques Maritain w Polsce," *Więź* no. 2 (1963): 38–56.

93. Fourcade, "Feu la Modernité?," 873–874; Kazimierz Szalata, "La présence de la pensée de Maritain dans la culture polonaise," in *Jacques Maritain en Europe: La réception de sa pensée: Actes du colloque sur "La réception de la pensée de Jacques Maritain dans divers pays d'Europe organisé par l'Association chrétienne de culture européenne le 18 et 19 novembre 1993 à l'Institut catholique de Toulouse*, ed. Bernard Hubert (Paris: Beauchesne, 1996), 223–236, at 227–228.

94. Piotr J. Wróbel, "The Rise and Fall of Parliamentary Democracy in Interwar Poland," in *The Origins of Modern Polish Democracy*, ed. M. B. B. Biskupski, James S. Pula, and Piotr J. Wróbel (Athens, OH: Ohio University Press, 2010), 110–164.

95. Julian Jackson, *The Popular Front in France: Defending Democracy, 1934–38* (Cambridge: Cambridge University Press, 1988), 17–22.

96. Richard J. Evans, *The Third Reich in Power* (New York: Penguin Press, 2005), 20–41.

97. Connelly, *From Enemy to Brother*, 116.

98. Paul Preston, *The Spanish Civil War: Reaction, Revolution, and Revenge* (New York: W.W. Norton, 2006), 66–101.

99. René Rémond, preface to *Humanisme intégral: Problèmes temporels et spirituels d'une nouvelle chrétienté* by Jacques Maritain (Paris: Aubier, 2000), ii-iii.

100. Quoted in Charles Molette, "Jacques Maritain et la Conférence de Seelisberg," *Nova et Vetera* no. 3 (1994): 208.

101. See the reports on the congress in "Chronique: Pologne—Congrès," *Bulletin Thomiste* no. 2 (1934); "Chronique: Pologne—Congrès," *Bulletin Thomiste* no. 3 (1934). See also "Międzynarodowy Kongres Tomistyczny w Poznaniu," *Verbum* no. 3 (1934).

102. Fourcade, "Feu la Modernité?," 875. Italics in the original.

103. The published English translation distorts Maritain's original meaning, refashioning "integral" humanism as "true" humanism. Jacques Maritain, *True Humanism*, trans. Margot Robert Adamson (New York: C. Scribner's Sons, 1938).

104. Philippe Chenaux, *"Humanisme intégral" (1936) de Jacques Maritain* (Paris: Cerf, 2006), 7.

105. Stefanos Geroulanos, *An Atheism That is Not Humanist Emerges in French Thought* (Stanford, CA: Stanford University Press, 2010), 114–116.

106. Bokenkotter, *Church and Revolution*, 344.

107. Since there is no separate word for Christendom or *chrétienté* in Polish, the translators substituted in different instances either *cywilizacja chrześcijańska* (Christian civilization) or *porządek chrześcijański* (Christian order).

108. Jakób [Jacques] Maritain, "O nową cywilizację chrześcijańską (c.d.)," *Prąd* no. 6 (1935).

109. José M. Sánchez, *The Spanish Civil War as a Religious Tragedy* (Notre Dame, IN: University of Notre Dame Press, 1987).

110. Jacques Maritain, "De la guerre sainte," *Nouvelle Revue Française*, July 1, 1937.

111. Bernard Doering, *Jacques Maritain and the French Catholic Intellectuals* (Notre Dame, IN: University of Notre Dame Press, 1983), 88.

112. John Hellman, *Emmanuel Mounier and the New Catholic Left, 1930–1950* (Toronto: University of Toronto Press, 1981), 128–131.

113. Doering, *Jacques Maritain and the French Catholic Intellectuals*, 97.

114. Pius XI, *Divini Redemptoris*, March 19, 1937, available at https://w2.vatican.va/content/pius-xi/en/encyclicals/documents/hf_p-xi_enc_19370319_divini-redemptoris.html.

115. Pius XI, *Divini Redemptoris*.

116. Francis J. Murphy, "*La Main tendue*: Prelude to Christian-Marxist Dialogue in France, 1936–1939," *Catholic Historical Review* 60, no. 2 (1974): 255–270; Giuliana Chamedes, "The Vatican, Nazi-Fascism, and the Making of Transnational Anti-Communism in the 1930s," *Journal of Contemporary History* 51, no. 2 (2016): 261–290, at 284–286.

117. Quoted in Maurice Thorez, *Communistes et catholiques: La main tendue* (Paris: Éditions du comité populaire de propagande, 1937), 11.

118. Quoted in Thorez, *Communistes et catholiques*, 12.

119. Thorez, *Communistes et catholiques*, 16, 17.

120. Jacques Tessier, *La CFTC, comment fut maintenu le syndicalisme chrétien* (Paris: Fayard, 1987); Magali Della Sudda, "La suppression de l'hebdomadaire dominicain *Sept*: Immixtion du Vatican dans les affaires françaises (1936–1937)?," *Vingtième Siècle: Revue d'histoire* no. 4 (2009): 29–44; Oscar L. Arnal, "Stillborn Alliance: Catholic Divisions in the Face of the *Main Tendue*," *Journal of Modern History* 51, no. 1 (1979): 1001–1027, at 1022.

121. Gaston Fessard, *La main tendue? Le dialogue catholique-communiste est-il possible?* (Paris: Grasset, 1937).

122. *Humanité*, May 17–28, 1936; Murphy, "*La Main Tendue*," 260.

123. Pius XI, *Divini Redemptoris*.

124. "Rozmowy o Emanuelu Mounier," *Więź* no. 2 (1958): 42–51, at 42.

125. Emmanuel Mounier, Letter to Jerzy Turowicz, July 26, 1937, *Esprit* Correspondence, AAJT BN.

126. Jerzy Turowicz, "Wielkość i upadek 'Odrodzenia,'" *Odrodzenie* nos. 11-12 (1937).

127. Turowicz, "O Maritain'ie czyli o najlepszym katolicyzmie."

128. Adam Doboszyński, "Sprawa Maritaina," *Prosto z Mostu*, June 7, 1936.

129. "Rozmowy o Emanuelu Mounier," 42.

130. Nord, "Catholic Culture in Interwar France."

131. Gerd-Rainer Horn, *Western European Liberation Theology: The First Wave (1924–1959)* (Oxford: Oxford University Press, 2008), 28; Wolfram Kaiser, *Christian Democracy and the Origins of European Union* (Cambridge: Cambridge University Press, 2007), 56.

132. I follow here the interpretations of "non-conformism" offered by Jean-Louis Loubet del Bayle and by Stefanos Geroulanos—with one significant departure from the latter: unlike Geroulanos, I consider Mounier's non-conformism not as an alternative to Catholicism, but as a crucial intervention within Catholicism as well. Geroulanos, *An Atheism That is Not Humanist Emerges in French Thought*, 118–125; Jean-Louis Loubet del Bayle, *Les Non-conformistes des années 30, une tentative de renouvellement de la pensée politique française* (Paris: Seuil, 1969), esp. 248–253.

133. Emmanuel Mounier, "Refaire la Renaissance," *Esprit* no. 1 (1932): 19.

134. Bokenkotter, *Church and Revolution*, 359.

135. Emmanuel Mounier, *Révolution personnaliste et communautaire*, 1935, in *Œuvres* (Paris: Seuil, 1961), 1: 140.

136. Emmanuel Mounier, *Manifeste au service du personnalisme* (Paris: Aubier, 1936), 42.

137. Emmanuel Mounier, "Appel à un rassemblement pour une Démocratie personnaliste," *Esprit* no. 12 (1938): 424–432; Hellman, *Emmanuel Mounier and the New Catholic Left*, 147, 190.

138. Lucien Pélissier, "Mounier et les communistes," in *Emmanuel Mounier ou le combat du juste* (Bordeaux: Guy Ducros, 1968), 65–117, at 68.

139. Quoted in André Mandouze, "Mounier et les communistes," in *Le Personnalisme d'Emmanuel Mounier: Hier et demain: Pour un cinquantenaire: Colloque organisé par l'Association des Amis d'Emmanuel Mounier* (Paris: Seuil, 1985), 97–109, at 99.

140. As Samuel Moyn has pointed out, "Maritain opposed Mounier's drifts into apparent proximity to fascism, but would never have become a political thinker without Mounier's example." Moyn, "Personalism, Community, and the Origins of Human Rights," in *Human Rights in the Twentieth Century*, ed. Stefan-Ludwig Hoffmann (Cambridge: Cambridge University Press, 2010), 85–106, at 90–91.

141. Mounier, *Manifeste au service du personnalisme*, 5.

142. Jean-Claude Delbreil, *Centrisme et Démocratie-Chrétienne en France: Le Parti Démocrate Populaire des origins au M. R. P. 1919–1944* (Paris: Publications de la Sorbonne, 1990); Kaiser, *Christian Democracy and the Origins of European Union*, 42–118.

143. Delbreil, *Centrisme et Démocratie-Chrétienne en France*, 121–123.

144. Tyler Stovall, *Transnational France: The Modern History of a Universal Nation* (Boulder, CO: Westview Press, 2015), 201.

145. Quoted in Susan B. Whitney, *Mobilizing Youth: Communists and Catholics in Interwar France* (Durham, NC: Duke University Press, 2009), 221.

146. Pélissier, "Mounier et les communistes," 105.

147. For example—Jakób [Jacques] Maritain, "O nową cywilizację chrześcijańską (pocz.)," *Prąd* no. 5 (1935).

148. I owe this notion of *Augenblick*—"the existential moment of making a decision on which everything is staked"—to Marci Shore, "The Bloody History between Poland and Ukraine Led to their Unlikely Solidarity," *The New Republic*, March 10, 2014.

149. Emmanuel Mounier, *Be Not Afraid: Studies in Personalist Sociology*, trans. Cynthia Rowland (New York: Harper, 1954), 195.

150. Warren Breckman, *Marx, the Young Hegelians, and the Origins of Radical Social Theory: Dethroning the Self* (New York: Cambridge University Press, 1999).

151. Mounier, *Feu la Chrétienté*, 1950, in *Œuvres* (Paris: Seuil, 1962), 3:614.

152. Jacques Maritain, *Paysan de la Garonne*, 1966, in *Œuvres complètes* (Paris: Éditions Saint-Paul, 1992), 12: 736.

153. Jean-Marie Domenach, *Beaucoup de gueule et peu d'or: Journal d'un réfractaire (1944–1977)* (Paris: Seuil, 2001), 190.

154. John Hellman, "The Prophets of Solidarity," *America*, November 6, 1982.

155. Ronald Modras, "The Catholic Press in Interwar Poland and the 'Jewish Question': Metaphor and the Developing Rhetoric of Exclusion," *East European Jewish Affairs* 24, no. 1 (1994): 49–69; Connelly, *From Enemy to Brother*, 11–35; Paul Hanebrink, *In Defense of Christian Hungary: Religion, Nationalism, and Antisemitism, 1890–1944* (Ithaca, NY: Cornell University Press, 2006), 170–192; Samuel Moyn, *Christian Human Rights* (Philadelphia: University of Pennsylvania Press, 2015), 11.

CHAPTER 2. PERSONALISM AT WAR

1. Quoted in Bernard Doering, *Jacques Maritain and the French Catholic Intellectuals* (Notre Dame, IN: University of Notre Dame Press, 1983), 173.

2. Andrzej Krzysztof Kunert, ed., *"Żegota": The Council for Aid to Jews 1942–1945, Selected Documents preceded by An Interview with Władysław Bartoszewski by Andrzej Friszke* (Warsaw: Rada Ochrony Pamięci Walk i Męczeństwa, 2002).

3. Władysław Bartoszewski, *Warto być przyzwoitym* (Poznań: W Drodze, 2005), 62–63.

4. Bartoszewski, *Warto być przyzwoitym*, 88–91.

5. For opposing viewpoints, see, e.g., Jan Grabowski, *Hunt for the Jews: Betrayal and Murder in German-Occupied Poland* (Bloomington: Indiana University Press, 2013); Irene Tomaszewski and Tecia Werbowski, *Code Name Żegota: Rescuing Jews in Occupied Poland, 1942–1945: The Most Dangerous Conspiracy in Wartime Europe* (Santa Barbara, CA: Praeger, 2010).

6. John Connelly, *From Enemy to Brother: The Revolution in Catholic Teaching on the Jews, 1933–1965* (Cambridge, MA: Harvard University Press, 2012), 11–35; Paul Hanebrink, *In Defense of Christian Hungary: Religion, Nationalism, and Antisemitism, 1890–1944* (Ithaca, NY: Cornell University Press, 2006), 170–192.

7. The turning point was Maritain's 1941 protest against Vichy France's "Statutes on the Jews" (*Statuts des juifs*) of 1940–41: Jacques Maritain, "On Antisemitism," *Christianity and Crisis*, October 6, 1941. Although Maritain wrote on Judaism and anti-Semitism prior to World War II, he did so from the exclusionary position of a Catholic seeking Jews' conversion in order to bring about the Second Coming—not a universalist notion of personhood. John Hellman, "The Jews in the 'New Middle Ages': Anti-Semitism in Its Times," in *Jacques Maritain and the Jews*, ed. Robert Royal (Notre Dame, IN: American Maritain Association/University of Notre Dame Press, 1994), 89–103, at 102–103.

8. Hubert Wolf, *Pope and Devil: The Vatican's Archives and the Third Reich*, trans. Kenneth Kronenberg (Cambridge, MA: Belknap Press of Harvard University Press, 2010), 126–178.

9. James Mace Ward, *Priest, Politician, Collaborator: Jozef Tiso and the Making of Fascist Slovakia* (Ithaca, NY: Cornell University Press, 2013).

10. Quoted in Sergio I. Minerbi, "Pius XII: A Reappraisal," in *Pope Pius XII and the Holocaust*, ed. Carol Rittner and John K. Roth (London: Leicester University Press, 2002), 85–104, at 95.

11. Oscar Cole-Arnal, "The *Témoignage* of the Worker-Priests: Contextual Layers of the Pioneer Epoch (1941–1955)," in *Left Catholicism 1943–1955: Catholics and Society in Western Europe at the Point of Liberation*, ed. Gerd-Rainer Horn and Emmanuel Gerard (Leuven: Leuven University Press, 2001), 118–141, at 139.

12. István Deák, Jan T. Gross, and Tony Judt, eds., *The Politics of Retribution in Europe: World War II and Its Aftermath* (Princeton, NJ: Princeton University Press, 2000).

13. See, e.g., the model of "advocacy networks" developed in Margaret E. Keck and Kathryn Sikkink, *Activists Beyond Borders: Advocacy Networks in International Politics* (Ithaca, NY: Cornell University Press, 1998).

14. Nicholas Atkin, "*Ralliés* and *Résistants*: Catholics in Vichy France, 1940–44," in *Catholicism, Politics, and Society in Twentieth-Century France*, ed. Kay Chadwick (Liverpool: Liverpool University Press, 2000), 97–118; Julian Jackson,

*France: The Dark Years, 1940–1944* (Oxford: Oxford University Press, 2003), 402–487.

15. Feliks Gross, "Some Sociological Considerations on Underground Movements," *The Polish Review* 2, nos. 2–3 (1957): 33–56; Paul Latawski, "The *Armia Krajowa* and Polish Partisan Warfare, 1939–43," in *War in a Twilight World: Partisan and Anti-Partisan Warfare in Eastern Europe, 1939–45*, ed. Ben Shepherd and Juliette Pattinson (New York: Palgrave Macmillan, 2010), 137–155.

16. Jackson, *France*, 402–487; Krystyna Kersten, *The Establishment of Communist Rule in Poland, 1943–1948*, trans. John Micgiel and Michael H. Bernhard (Berkeley: University of California Press, 1991), 3–117.

17. Paweł Rodak, *Wizje kultury pokolenia wojennego* (Wrocław: Funna, 2000).

18. Marc Bloch, *Strange Defeat: A Statement of Evidence Written in 1940*, trans. Gerard Hopkins (New York: Norton, 1968).

19. See the special issue of the *Cahiers Jacques Maritain* subtitled "Le philosophe dans la guerre (1939–1945)" (April 1988).

20. After the war, this institution relocated to Paris and became the progenitor of the School for Advanced Studies in the Social Sciences (*École des Hautes Études en Sciences Sociales*), which functions to this day as one of France's most prestigious institutions of higher learning. Claus-Dieter Krohn, *Intellectuals in Exile: Refugee Scholars and the New School for Social Research*, trans. Rita Kimber and Robert Kimber (Amherst: University of Massachusetts Press, 1993), 59–72.

21. For example—Jacques Maritain, Letter to Oskar Halecki, November 20, 1943, Jacques Maritain file 17/04, Jacques Maritain Center, University of Notre Dame.

22. René Mougel, "Les années de New York, 1940–1945," *Cahiers Jacques Maritain* nos. 16–17 (1988): 7–28.

23. Desmond FitzGerald, "Maritain and Gilson on the Challenge of Political Democracy," in *Reassessing the Liberal State: Reading Maritain's "Man and the State,"* ed. Timothy Fuller and John P. Hittinger (Washington, DC: American Maritain Association/Catholic University of America Press, 2001), 61–72, at 63.

24. Quoted in Michel Fourcade, preface to *Christianisme et démocratie suivi de Les droits de l'homme* by Jacques Maritain (Paris: Desclée de Brouwer, 2005), 7–16, at 12. On the consequences of Maritain's wartime writings more generally—Charles Blanchard, "Jacques Maritain, 1940–1944: Le refus de la défaite et ses relations avec le général de Gaulle," *Cahiers Jacques Maritain* nos. 16–17 (1988): 39–58.

25. John Hellman, *The Knight-Monks of Vichy France: Uriage, 1940–1945* (Montreal: McGill-Queen's University Press, 1993), 34–37; Philip Nord, *France's New Deal: From the Thirties to the Postwar* (Princeton, NJ: Princeton University Press, 2010), 164.

26. Zeev Sternhell, *Neither Right nor Left: Fascist Ideology in France*, trans. David Maisel (Princeton, NJ: Princeton University Press, 1996), 275.

27. Hellman, *The Knight-Monks of Vichy France*, 53. Mounier's own account is that "the order was given from Vichy to the School of Leaders at Uriage to dispense with my services [. . .] the 'National Revolution' is, for two-thirds of its leaders, a

revolution of party and class, while the reality is one of national submission." Emmanuel Mounier, *Mounier et sa génération*, in *Œuvres* (Paris: Seuil, 1963), 4: 704.

28. Michel Bergès, *Vichy contre Mounier: Les non-conformistes face aux années 40* (Paris: Economica, 1997).

29. Tyler Stovall, *Transnational France: The Modern History of a Universal Nation* (Boulder, CO: Westview Press, 2015), 324.

30. Renée Bédarida, *Les armes de l'esprit: Témoignage chrétien (1941–1944)* (Paris: Éditions Ouvrières, 1977).

31. The full texts of the *Cahiers* and *Courriers* have been reprinted in *Cahiers et Courriers clandestins du Témoignage chrétien, 1941–1944*, ed. Renée Bédarida (Paris: Témoignage Chrétien, 1980).

32. André Mandouze, "Front spirituel," *Témoignage Chrétien*, November 4, 1944.

33. Hellman, *The Knight-Monks of Vichy France*, 224.

34. Quoted in André Mandouze, *Mémoires d'outre-siècle: D'une résistance à l'autre* (Paris: Viviane Hamy, 1998), 1: 102.

35. Ignatius Loyola, *Spiritual Exercises*, trans. Louis J. Puhl (New York: Vintage Books, 2000).

36. Jean-Marie Domenach and Robert de Montvalon, *The Catholic Avant-Garde: French Catholicism since World War II*, trans. Brigid Elson et al. (New York: Holt, Rinehart, and Winston, 1967), 232.

37. Jean-Marie Domenach, *Gilbert Dru, celui qui croyait au ciel* (Paris: ELF, 1947).

38. On Miłosz's wartime activities, see Andrzej Franaszek, *Miłosz: Biografia* (Kraków: Znak, 2011), 331–383.

39. Franaszek, *Miłosz*, 281.

40. Czesław Miłosz, *Zaraz po wojnie: Korespondencja z pisarzami 1945–1950* (Kraków: Znak, 1998), 18.

41. Franaszek, *Miłosz*, 332; Władysław Bartoszewski, *1859 dni Warszawy*, rev. ed. (Kraków: Znak, 2008), 320.

42. [Czesław Miłosz], "Od tłumacza," in Jacques Maritain, *Drogami klęski* (Warsaw: Oficyna Polska w Warszawie, 1942), 5–9, at 6. The text is available also in French: Czesław Miłosz, "À travers le désastre, clandestin à Varsovie," *Cahiers Jacques Maritain* nos. 16–17 (1988): 29–33.

43. [Miłosz], "Od tłumacza," 8.

44. Czesław Miłosz, *Native Realm: A Search for Self-Definition*, trans. Catherine S. Leach (Garden City, NY: Doubleday, 1968), 69–90.

45. Stefan Zweig, *The World of Yesterday: An Autobiography*, trans. Anthea Bell (Lincoln: University of Nebraska Press, 2009).

46. Jan Karski, *Story of a Secret State: My Report to the World* (Washington, DC: Georgetown University Press, 2013), 2.

47. Rodak, *Wizje kultury pokolenia wojennego*, 14. A crucial caveat is that this observation applies only to Poles who were actually literate as of the outbreak of war.

48. Jerzy Jedlicki, *A Suburb of Europe: Nineteenth-Century Polish Approaches to Western Civilization* (New York: Central European University Press, 1999), 173–292.

49. Norman Davies, *White Eagle, Red Star: The Polish-Soviet War, 1919–20* (New York: St. Martin's Press, 1972).

50. Jan T. Gross, *Polish Society under German Occupation: The Generalgouvernement, 1939–1944* (Princeton, NJ: Princeton University Press, 1979), 29–41, 213–291. Jadwiga Biskupska has, however, argued that education and armed resistance in fact "came into direct competition with one another over a commodity made increasingly scarce by Nazi murder policies: young Polish men with ambitions for advanced education." Jadwiga Biskupska, "Extermination and the Elite: Warsaw under Nazi Occupation, 1939–1944" (PhD diss., Yale University, 2013), 190.

51. Biskupska, "Extermination and the Elite," 190.

52. *Dziś i Jutro* no. 2 (1941).

53. Rodak, *Wizje kultury pokolenia wojennego*, 22; Aneta Ignatowicz, *Tajna oświata i wychowanie w okupowanej Warszawie: Warszawskie Termopile, 1939–1945* (Warsaw: Fundacja Warszawa Walczy 1939–1945, 2009).

54. As Jadwiga Biskupska writes, "The civilians of Warsaw were 'militarized' by the siege. The civilian-military distinction grew porous within the city." Biskupska, "Extermination and the Elite," 117.

55. Rodak, *Wizje kultury pokolenia wojennego*, 38.

56. Biskupska, "Extermination and the Elite," 196–210, 235.

57. Stefan Korboński, *The Polish Underground State: A Guide to the Underground, 1939–1945* (Boulder, CO: East European Quarterly, 1978).

58. Jerzy Jabrzemski, *Harcerze z Szarych Szeregów* (Warsaw: PWN, 1997); Kazimierz Krajewski, *Uderzeniowe Bataliony Kadrowe 1942–1944* (Warsaw: PAX, 1993); Krzysztof Kaczmarski and Mariusz Krzysztofiński, eds., *Polska Partia Robotnicza, Gwardia Ludowa/Armia Ludowa na ziemiach polskich 1942–1944/1945* (Rzeszów: IPN-KŚZpNP, 2013).

59. Rodak, *Wizje kultury pokolenia wojennego*, 28.

60. Czesław Miłosz, "Turowicz i Jacques Maritain," *Tygodnik Powszechny*, January 15, 2009.

61. Zygmunt Głuszek, *Szare Szeregi: Słownik encyklopedyczny, hasła rzeczowe* (Warsaw: Oficyna Wydawnicza RYTM, 2010).

62. The group took its name from the title of Brzozowski's classic 1908 novelistic manifesto. On the Flames group more generally—Andrzej Mencwel, *Przedwiośnie czy potop: Studium postaw polskich w XX wieku* (Warsaw: Czytelnik, 1997), 193–268.

63. The number is from Zofia Kobylańska, *Konfederacja Narodu w Warszawie* (Warsaw: PAX, 1999), 13.

64. Mikołaj Stanisław Kunicki, *Between the Brown and the Red: Nationalism, Catholicism, and Communism in Twentieth-Century Poland—The Politics of Bolesław Piasecki* (Athens, OH: Ohio University Press, 2012), 62–131, 132–193; Jacek Majchrowski, *Geneza politycznych ugrupowań katolickich: Stronnictwo Pracy, grupa "Dziś i Jutro"* (Paris: Libella, 1984), 81–98, 126–148.

65. Kunicki, *Between the Brown and the Red*, 52–76.

66. "Deklaracja ideowa Konfederacji," October 1940, in Kobylańska, *Konfederacja Narodu w Warszawie*, 18.

67. Kobylańska, *Konfederacja Narodu w Warszawie*, 19.

68. Jacek Woźniakowski, *Ze wspomnień szczęściarza* (Kraków: Znak, 2008), 144.

69. "Personalizm w Szarych Szeregach," February 26, 1952, AIPN BU 01224/5/CD/1.

70. Jadwiga Biskupska traces the unlikely alliances forged in occupied Warsaw back to the "melting pot of the siege" of September 1939. Biskupska, "Extermination and the Elite," 120.

71. Wacław Auleytner, "Oświadczenie," *Więź* no. 4 (2013): 252–253; Wacław Auleytner, *Spotkania i rozstania* (Katowice: Unia, 1999), 121.

72. Stanisław Ossowski, *Class Structure in the Social Consciousness*, trans. Sheila Patterson (New York: Free Press, 1963); Jan Strzelecki, *Próby świadectwa* (Warsaw: Czytelnik, 1975). On Strzelecki—Magdalena Grochowska, *Strzelecki: Śladem nadziei* (Warsaw: Świat Książki, 2014).

73. Auleytner, *Spotkania i rozstania*, 100–101.

74. Bogdan Suchodolski, *Skąd i dokąd idziemy* (Warsaw: Muza, 1999), 41.

75. "Rozmowy o Emanuelu Mounier," *Więź* no. 2 (1958): 42–51, at 47.

76. Andrzej Walicki, *Stanisław Brzozowski and the Polish Beginnings of "Western Marxism"* (Oxford: Clarendon Press, 1989).

77. Before his death, Brzozowski lamented in his diary, "How horribly and hopelessly alone I am." Stanisław Brzozowski, *Pamiętnik: Fragmentami listów autora i objaśnieniami uzupełnił Ostap Ortwin* (Lwów: B. Połoniecki, 1913), 143. On Brzozowski's life and death—Eugeniusz Kabatc, *Ostatnie wzgórze Florencji: Opowieść o Stanisławie Brzozowskim* (Warsaw: Studio Emka, 2011).

78. Robert Blobaum, "The Revolution of 1905–1907 and the Crisis of Polish Catholicism," *Slavic Review* 47, no. 4 (1988): 669–670; Bohdan Cywiński, *Rodowody niepokornych* (Warsaw: Biblioteka WIĘZI, 1971), 444–460.

79. Bohdan Cywiński, "Narodowe i ludzkie myśli Brzozowskiego," *Więź* no. 4 (1972): 48–59, at 56–57.

80. In his 1909 *Legend of Young Poland* (*Legenda Młodej Polski*), Brzozowski contended, "labor, productivity, are for man his only organs of truth, the only way which leads him beyond himself and establishes him in something other than himself." Quoted in Walicki, *Stanisław Brzozowski and the Polish Beginnings of "Western Marxism,"* 296.

81. Leszek Kołakowski, *Main Currents of Marxism: The Founders, The Golden Age, The Breakdown* (New York: W.W. Norton, 2005), 529.

82. "Rozmowy o Emanuelu Mounier," 47.

83. Rodak, *Wizje kultury pokolenia wojennego*, 229.

84. Timothy Snyder, *Nationalism, Marxism, and Modern Central Europe: A Biography of Kazimierz Kelles-Krauz, 1872–1905* (Cambridge, MA: Harvard Ukrainian Research Institute, 1997).

85. Rodak, *Wizje kultury pokolenia wojennego*, 227.

86. Mencwel, *Przedwiośnie czy potop*, 210.

87. [Jan Strzelecki], "Drogami klęski i nadziei," *Płomienie* no. 3 (1942).

88. Auleytner, *Spotkania i rozstania*, 107. On "open Catholicism," see Juliusz Eska, *Kościół otwarty* (Kraków: Znak, 1964).

89. "Rozmowy o Emanuelu Mounier," 49–50; Y. K., "Poussées personnalistes hors de France—En Pologne: Une idée au combat," *Esprit* no. 1 (1946).

90. Wiesław Chrzanowski, interview with author, November 3, 2005.

91. Roman Graczyk, *Chrzanowski* (Warsaw: Świat Książki, 2013), 32–81.

92. Aniela Urbanowicz, Letter to Jerzy Turowicz, May 26, 1950, Aniela Urbanowicz Correspondence, AAJT BN.

93. "Personalizm w Szarych Szeregach," AIPN BU 01224/5/CD/1; "Rozmowy o Emanuelu Mounier," 51.

94. Tadeusz Sołtan, *Motywacje i fascynacje* (Warsaw: PAX, 1978), 92–93.

95. Mencwel, *Przedwiośnie czy potop*, 203.

96. Adolf Gozdawa-Reutt, preface to *Konfederacja Narodu w Warszawie* by Zofia Kobylańska, 9.

97. Gozdawa-Reutt, preface to *Konfederacja Narodu w Warszawie*, 5.

98. Kobylańska, *Konfederacja Narodu w Warszawie*, 13, 19.

99. "Personalizm w Szarych Szeregach," AIPN BU 01224/5/CD/1.

100. Kobylańska, *Konfederacja Narodu w Warszawie*, 29.

101. "Tezy programowe Nowej Polski," *Nowa Polska* no. 69 (1944).

102. Zygmunt Lichniak *et al.*, *Księga o nagrodzie imienia Włodzimierza Pietrzaka (1948–1972)* (Warsaw: PAX, 1978), 7–23. The prize still exists, awarded annually by PAX's post-Communist successor organization, the *Civitas Christiana* Catholic Association.

103. Kobylańska, *Konfederacja Narodu w Warszawie*, 28.

104. Rodak, *Wizje kultury pokolenia wojennego*, 33.

105. Michał Komar, *Władysław Bartoszewski—skąd Pan jest? Wywiad rzeka* (Warsaw: Świat Książki—Bertelsmann Media, 2006).

106. Rodak, *Wizje kultury pokolenia wojennego*, 299.

107. [Władysław Bartoszewski], "O odwagę myślenia i konsekwencję działania," *Prawda Młodych*, February 1943; Rodak, *Wizje kultury pokolenia wojennego*, 301.

108. Wolfram Kaiser, *Christian Democracy and the Origins of European Union* (Cambridge: Cambridge University Press, 2007), 58–59.

109. Waldemar Bujak, *Historia Stronnictwa Pracy: 1937–1946–1950* (Warsaw: ODiSS, 1988), 1–43.

110. Haller was, by this point, a retired career officer who had fought alongside Piłsudski during World War I. Jarosław Rabiński, *Stronnictwo Pracy we władzach naczelnych Rzeczypospolitej Polskiej na uchodźstwie w latach 1939–1945* (Lublin: Wydawnictwo KUL, 2012), 285–295.

111. Mirosław Biełaszko, "Ksiądz Zygmunt Kaczyński (1894–1953)—duchowny, polityk, redaktor," in *Niezłomni ludzie Kościoła: Sylwetki*, ed. Jan Żaryn (Kraków: IPN-KŚZpNP/Wydawnictwo WAM, 2011), 95–122; Bujak, *Historia Stronnictwa Pracy*, 44–48. Popiel left a remarkably complete archive at his death, encompassing also the war years, deposited in the Karol Popiel Political Papers, APIASA; some of his papers—including unpublished manuscripts—are in the Konrad Sieniewicz Collection, BUKUL.

112. Majchrowski, *Geneza politycznych ugrupowań katolickich*, 52–64; Bujak, *Historia Stronnictwa Pracy*, 49–109.

113. On the story of how these two men—who met only in 1942—shaped the course of Catholic resistance to the General Government, see Mirosław Piotrowski, *Służba idei czy serwilizm? Zygmunt Felczak i Feliks Widy-Wirski w najnowszych dziejach Polski* (Lublin: Red. Wydawnictw KUL, 1994), 131–192.

114. Waldemar Bujak, "Stronnictwo Pracy—partia generała Władysława Sikorskiego," *Przegląd Polonijny*, no. 2 (1981).

115. Halik Kochanski, *The Eagle Unbowed: Poland and the Poles in the Second World War* (Cambridge, MA: Harvard University Press, 2012), 257–290.

116. A copy of the original agreement for the 1942 merger of the SP and Union clandestine movements is in APIASA 9.126; Bujak, *Historia Stronnictwa Pracy*, 84–90.

117. On Braun—Rafał Łętocha, "Unia człowieka z człowiekiem, narodu z narodem, człowieka z Bogiem: Wizja ładu międzynarodowego w publicystyce Jerzego Brauna i organizacji Unia," in *Kultura chrześcijańska w zjednoczonej Europie*, ed. Tomasz Sikorski and Andrzej Dymer (Szczecin: Centrum Edukacyjne Archidiecezji Szczecińsko-Kamieńskiej, 2007).

118. James E. Bjork, *Neither German nor Pole: Catholicism and National Indifference in a Central European Borderland* (Ann Arbor: University of Michigan Press, 2008), 214–266.

119. Piotr H. Kosicki, "Masters in their own Home or Defenders of the Human Person? Wojciech Korfanty, Anti-Semitism, and Polish Christian Democracy's Illiberal Rights-Talk," *Modern Intellectual History* (2015), doi: 10.1017/S1479244314000857.

120. Wojciech Korfanty, "Czy Pan Bóg jest na prawicy czy na lewicy?," June 16, 1936, in *Naród, Państwo, Kościół: Wybór publicystyki katolicko-społecznej* (Katowice: Księgarnia św. Jacka, 1992), 282–286, at 285; Wojciech Korfanty, "Tezy programowe Stronnictwa Pracy (Dokończenie)," October 23, 1937, in *Naród, Państwo, Kościół*, 314–317, at 317.

121. Jerzy Braun, *Nowy świat kultury* (Warsaw: Stowarzyszenie Kulturowe Fronda, 2003), 236. On corporatism and Christian Democracy—Kaiser, *Christian Democracy and the Origins of European Union*, 55.

122. Stanisław Gebhardt, public remarks at "Christian Democracy and the European Union—Poland, Central Europe, Europe" conference, John Paul II Catholic University of Lublin, May 6, 2015.

123. On the Union's program—Bujak, *Historia Stronnictwa Pracy*, 110–116; Majchrowski, *Geneza politycznych ugrupowań katolickich*, 62–64.

124. Krzysztof Kozłowski and Michał Komar, *Historia z konsekwencjami* (Warsaw: Świat Książki, 2009), 82.

125. Jerzy Turowicz and Tadeusz Kraśko, *Wierność* (Poznań: Kantor Wydawniczy SAWW, 1995), 21.

126. In his first editorial, Turowicz wrote, "If there is to be war again, then afterward there must come an economic and spiritual reconstruction of Europe." Jerzy Turowicz, "Po co znowu wojna," *Głos Narodu*, July 21, 1939.

127. "Kultura pracy jako mit społeczny," *Kultura Jutra* no. 2 (1943).

128. "W poszukiwaniu uniwersalizmu," *Sztuka i Naród* no. 8 (1943). The author is identified here following Rodak, *Wizje kultury pokolenia wojennego*, 184.

129. Kozłowski and Komar, *Historia z konsekwencjami*, 79; Marek Lasota, *Donos na Wojtyłę: Karol Wojtyła w teczkach Bezpieki* (Kraków: Znak, 2006), 36–38.

130. Miłosz, "Turowicz i Jacques Maritain."

131. Sołtan, *Motywacje i fascynacje*, 92.

132. The term "border-crosser" comes from Connelly, *From Enemy to Brother*, e.g. 64.

133. Auleytner, *Spotkania i rozstania*, 113.

CHAPTER 3. CATHOLICISM IN A NEWLY COMMUNIST WORLD

1. August Hlond, "Chrześcijaństwo czy materializm," *Tygodnik Warszawski*, December 2, 1945.

2. Karol Popiel, Letter to Patricia M. Lawlor, January 22, 1968, HIA RFE/RL Corporate Records, Box 257.3. Popiel's protest was successful, though only for a time: transitioned from Free Europe's "Exile Support and Post-termination Assistance Plan" to a hastily created—and short-lived—category of "Meritorious Exiles," Popiel received his last check in 1972, leaving him without steady income for the final five years of his life; see HIA RFE/RL Corporate Records, Washington Office File, Financial Statements (Provisional Box 976).

3. A recent example of the *Stunde null* approach is Ian Buruma, *Year Zero: A History of 1945* (New York: Atlantic Books, 2013).

4. S. M. Plokhy, *Yalta: The Price of Peace* (New York: Viking, 2010).

5. Mark Kramer, "Stalin, Soviet Policy, and the Consolidation of a Communist Bloc in Eastern Europe, 1944–53," in *Stalinism Revisited: The Establishment of Communist Regimes in East-Central Europe*, ed. Vladimir Tismaneanu (New York: Central European University Press, 2009), 51–102.

6. Karol Popiel, Letter to [n.n.], October 17, 1951, BUKUL Rkps 2018; Konrad Sieniewicz, Bolesław Biega, and Karol Popiel, Letter to Józef Haller, October 26, 1952, BUKUL Rkps 2018.

7. Rafael Caldera, Letter to Janusz Śleszyński, October 2, 1958, HIA RFE/RL Corporate Records, Box 161.1; Janusz Śleszyński, Letter to Archibald Alexander, September 24, 1959, HIA RFE/RL Corporate Records, Box 161.1; "Procès-verbal de la VIIme Réunion Internationale des directeurs et responsables de la formation politique des partis démocrates-chrétiens d'Europe, organisée par le Centre Régional de Formation Civique d'Aix-en-Provence sous le patronage de M. François Garcia du MRP et de M. Jean Chélini, tenue à Aix-en-Provence, les 3, 4 et 5 décembre 1965 [sic!—1964]," March 1, 1965, HIA RFE/RL Corporate Records, Box 258.9.

8. James Mace Ward, *Priest, Politician, Collaborator: Jozef Tiso and the Making of Fascist Slovakia* (Ithaca, NY: Cornell University Press, 2013), 246–283.

9. Pedro Ramet, "Catholicism and Politics in Socialist Yugoslavia," *Religion in Communist Lands* no. 10 (1982): 257–260.

10. Peter C. Kent, *The Lonely Cold War of Pope Pius XII: The Roman Catholic Church and the Division of Europe, 1943–1950* (Montreal: McGill-Queen's University Press, 2002), 217–236.

11. Maryjane Osa, "Resistance, Persistence, and Change: The Transformation of the Catholic Church in Poland," *East European Politics and Societies* 3, no. 2 (1989): 268–299, at 296.

12. Jacek Czajowski, *Kardynał Adam Stefan Sapieha* (Wrocław: Zakład Narodowy im. Ossolińskich, 1997).

13. Osa, "Resistance, Persistence, and Change," 296.

14. Michael Fleming, *Communism, Nationalism, and Ethnicity in Poland, 1944–50* (New York: Routledge, 2010), 103.

15. Jonathan Luxmoore and Jolanta Babiuch, *The Vatican and the Red Flag: The Struggle for the Soul of Eastern Europe* (New York: Geoffrey Chapman, 1999), 62–63.

16. James Ramon Felak, *After Hitler, Before Stalin: Catholics, Communists, and Democrats in Slovakia, 1945–1948* (Pittsburgh, PA: University of Pittsburgh Press, 2009), xi.

17. Unwelcome, "fascist" parties included the National Democracy-inspired National Party (*Stronnictwo Narodowe*). For Mikołajczyk's version of the events, see Stanisław Mikołajczyk, *The Rape of Poland: Pattern of Soviet Aggression* (New York: Whittlesey House, 1948).

18. Andrzej Paczkowski, *The Spring Will Be Ours: Poland and the Poles from Occupation to Freedom*, trans. Jane Cave (University Park: Pennsylvania State University Press, 2003), 161–162.

19. Molly Pucci, "Security Empire: Building the Secret Police in Communist Eastern Europe, 1944–1952" (PhD diss., Stanford University, 2015).

20. Piotr J. Wróbel, "The Rise and Fall of Parliamentary Democracy in Interwar Poland," in *The Origins of Modern Polish Democracy*, ed. M. B. B. Biskupski, James S. Pula, and Piotr J. Wróbel (Athens, OH: Ohio University Press, 2010), 110–164.

21. Czesław Strzeszewski, *Katolicka nauka społeczna* (Warsaw: ODiSS, 1985).

22. Marci Shore, *Caviar and Ashes: A Warsaw Generation's Life and Death in Marxism, 1918–1968* (New Haven, CT: Yale University Press, 2006), 141–149.

23. Mikołaj Stanisław Kunicki, *Between the Brown and the Red: Nationalism, Catholicism, and Communism in Twentieth-Century Poland—The Politics of Bolesław Piasecki* (Athens, OH: Ohio University Press, 2012), 81.

24. Inessa Iazhborovskaia, "The Gomułka Alternative," in *The Establishment of Communist Regimes in Eastern Europe, 1944–1949*, ed. Norman Naimark and Leonid Gibianskii (Boulder, CO: Westview Press, 1997), 126–135; Władysław Gomułka, *Pamiętniki*, ed. Andrzej Werblan (Warsaw: BGW, 1994), vol. 1.

25. On Borejsza—Barbara Fijałkowska, *Borejsza i Różański: Przyczynek do dziejów stalinizmu w Polsce* (Olsztyn: Wyższa Szkoła Pedagogiczna, 1995); Eryk Krasucki, *Międzynarodowy komunista: Jerzy Borejsza biografia polityczna* (Warsaw: PWN, 2009).

26. For the original text, see Jerzy Borejsza, "Rewolucja łagodna," *Odrodzenie*, January 15, 1945; Krasucki, *Międzynarodowy komunista*, 112.

27. Marcin Zaremba, *Wielka Trwoga, Polska 1944–1947: Ludowa reakcja na kryzys* (Kraków: Znak/ISP PAN, 2012), 15; Jacques Revel, "Great Fear," in *A Critical Dictionary of the French Revolution*, trans. Arthur Goldhammer, ed. François

Furet and Mona Ozouf (Cambridge, MA: Belknap Press of Harvard University Press, 1989), 74–80.

28. Krasucki, *Międzynarodowy komunista*, 111–119; Shore, *Caviar and Ashes*, 269–270.

29. On the concordat's origins—Neal Pease, "Poland and the Holy See, 1918–1939," *Slavic Review* 50, no. 3 (1991): 521–530.On its abrogation—Jan Żaryn, *Kościół a władza w Polsce (1945–1950)* (Warsaw: DiG, 1997), 88–144.

30. Bartłomiej Noszczak, *Polityka państwa wobec Kościoła rzymskokatolick-iego w Polsce w okresie internowania prymasa Stefana Wyszyńskiego 1953–1956* (Warsaw: IPN-KŚZpNP, 2008), 29–31.

31. Barbara Fijałkowska, *Partia wobec religii i Kościoła w PRL* (Olsztyn: Uniwersytet Warmińsko-Mazurski w Olsztynie, 1999), 1: 95–107; Noszczak, *Polityka państwa wobec Kościoła*, 31–37.

32. Andrzej Micewski, *Współrządzić czy nie kłamać? Pax i Znak w Polsce 1945–1976* (Paris: Libella, 1978), 34.

33. On the civil war between the Communist establishment and guerrilla organizations in the countryside—Krystyna Kersten, *The Establishment of Communist Rule in Poland, 1943–1948*, trans. John Micgiel and Michael H. Bernhard (Berkeley: University of California Press, 1991), 384–385; John Micgiel, "'Bandits' and 'Reactionaries': The Suppression of the Opposition in Poland, 1944–6," in *The Establishment of Communist Regimes in Eastern Europe, 1944–1949*, ed. Norman Naimark and Leonid Gibianskii (Boulder, CO: Westview Press, 1997), 93–110.

34. Karol Popiel, *Od Brześcia do "Polonii"* (London: Odnowa, 1967), 8.

35. Jerzy Braun, Karol Popiel, Konrad Sieniewicz, *Człowiek ze spiżu* (London: Odnowa, 1981), 208.

36. Kaczyński's reasoning, as recorded by Popiel on June 25, 1945, was that "millions of organized Catholics, not only in parishes, but also social, professional, and political organizations, have a right to expect our help and that we simply cannot allow ourselves to fail to meet this obligation." Popiel, *Od Brześcia do "Polonii,"* 55; Antoni Dudek and Ryszard Gryz, *Komuniści i Kościół w Polsce (1945–1989)* (Kraków: Znak, 2003), 22.

37. Quoted in Janusz Kurtyka and Jacek Pawłowicz, *Generał Leopold Okulicki, 1898–1946* (Warsaw: IPN-KŚZpNP, 2010), 384.

38. Kersten, *The Establishment of Communist Rule in Poland*, 154; Norman Davies, *Rising '44* (New York: Viking, 2004), 457, 460–467; Zbigniew Mierzwiński, *Generałowie II Rzeczypospolitej* (Warsaw: Wydawnictwo Polonia, 1990), 193.

39. Janusz Zabłocki, *Chrześcijańska Demokracja w kraju i na emigracji 1947–1970* (Lublin: Ośrodek Studiów Polonijnych i Społecznych PZKS, 1999), 53 n. 73.

40. Longina Jakubowska, *Patrons of History: Nobility, Capital, and Political Transitions in Poland* (Burlington, VT: Ashgate, 2012), 142.

41. Kunicki, *Between the Brown and the Red*, 82.

42. Paweł Sękowski, *Polskie Stronnictwo Ludowe w Krakowie i powiecie krakowskim w latach 1945–1949* (Warsaw: IPN-KŚZpNP, 2011).

43. Popiel, *Od Brześcia do "Polonii,"* 76.

44. Mirosław Piotrowski, *Służba idei czy serwilizm? Zygmunt Felczak i Feliks*

*Widy-Wirski w najnowszych dziejach Polski* (Lublin: Red. Wydawnictw KUL, 1994), 193–278.

45. For example—Feliks Widy-Wirski and Mieczysław Lityński, Letter to Konstanty Turowski, July 18, 1946, BUKUL Rkps 1153. See Popiel's official protest and accompanying resignation from the assembly at Karol Popiel, Letter to National Constituent Assembly Presidium, September 17, 1946, BUKUL Rkps 1153.

46. Quoted in Zabłocki, *Chrześcijańska Demokracja w kraju i na emigracji*, 11; Jan Draus, *Stronnictwo Pracy w województwie rzeszowskim 1945–1946–1950* (Rzeszów: Instytut Europejskich Studiów Społecznych w Rzeszowie, 1998).

47. Feliks Widy-Wirski, *Polska i Rewolucja* (Poznań: Spółdzielnia Wydawnicza "Zryw," 1945), 14, 360; Bujak, *Historia Stronnictwa Pracy*, 119–121.

48. Karol Popiel, Letter to Zygmunt Felczak [1946], BUKUL Rkps 1153.

49. Kersten, *The Establishment of Communist Rule in Poland*, 281–282.

50. "The bishops are pained to declare that, in the sector that based its program on a Catholic worldview and sought the fulfillment of Christian social principles, a splintering has been effected, with the consequence that the party in its new form no longer promises to base its actions on Catholic thought and principles." Quoted in Popiel, *Od Brześcia do "Polonii,"* 283.

51. Quoted in Popiel, *Od Brześcia do "Polonii,"* 284; "Poland: M. Bierut Reassures the Church," *Tablet*, January 25, 1947.

52. Micewski, *Współrządzić czy nie kłamać?*, 29; Tadeusz Przeciszewski, "Wspomnienia z dramatycznych lat 1945–1948," in *Błękitne sztandary: Zarys dziejów Sodalicji Mariańskiej Akademików w Warszawie 1945–1949*, 2nd ed. (Warsaw: Wydawnictwo ASKON, 2008), 46–66, at 53.

53. Przeciszewski, "Wspomnienia z dramatycznych lat," 54.

54. Popiel's decision to leave the country by legal means required considerable legwork on his part and on the part of his lieutenants from the disbanded SP. It took more than a month to obtain a passport for him, even with the personal intervention of Prime Minister Józef Cyrankiewicz and the justification that his wife, residing in London, was gravely ill.

55. Idesbald Goddeeris, "Exiles' Strategies for Lobbying in International Organizations: Eastern European Participation in the Nouvelles Équipes Internationales," *European Review of History—Revue européenne d'Histoire* 11, no. 3 (2004): 383–400. See also, for example, Centre Belge des Nouvelles Équipes Internationales, Invitation to Konrad Sieniewicz, 1947, APIASA 9.26.

56. Konrad Sieniewicz, Letter to Tadeusz Bór-Komorowski, July 12, 1948, BUKUL Rkps 2011.

57. On Free Europe—George Urban, *Radio Free Europe and the Pursuit of Democracy* (New Haven, CT: Yale University Press, 1997); Scott Lucas, *Freedom's War: The US Crusade against the Soviet Union 1945–56* (Manchester: Manchester University Press, 1999). On Free Europe's "political warfare"—"Purposes and Objectives of DER," March 7, 1955, HIA RFE/RL Corporate Records, Box 198.5.

58. Karol Popiel, Letter to Eugene Metz, November 24, 1961, BUKUL Rkps 2018; West European Operations Division—Free Europe Committee, "Appendix to WEOD Survey of European East-West Contact Programs," March 1965, HIA RFE/RL Corporate Records, Box 258.9.

59. *Free Europe Committee, Inc. Budget, Fiscal Year 1962–1963, West European Operations Division,* 3, HIA RFE/RL Corporate Records Box 358.3.

60. Piotr H. Kosicki, "Masters in their own Home or Defenders of the Human Person? Wojciech Korfanty, Anti-Semitism, and Polish Christian Democracy's Illiberal Rights-Talk," *Modern Intellectual History* (2015), doi: 10.1017/S1479244 314000857, 28–32.

61. Micewski, *Współrządzić czy nie kłamać?*, 25.

62. Kunicki, *Between the Brown and the Red*, 83.

63. Władysław Gomułka, *Pamiętniki*, ed. Andrzej Werblan (Warsaw: BGW, 1994), 2: 516–517.

64. Quoted in Micewski, *Współrządzić czy nie kłamać?*, 26–27.

65. Jerzy Pietrzak, "Prymas Polski kardynał August Hlond a grupa katolików 'Dziś i Jutro,'" in *Komu służył PAX: Materiały z sympozjum 'Od PAX-u do Civitas Christiana' zorganizowanego przez Katolickie Stowarzyszenie Civitas Christiana 30–31 stycznia 2008 roku*, ed. Sabina Bober (Warsaw: Instytut Wydawniczy Pax, 2008), 93–106.

66. Jakubowska, *Patrons of History*, 136–137.

67. Kunicki, *Between the Brown and the Red*, 86, 91.

68. Piasecki's movement later played a crucial role in disseminating anti-Semitic propaganda in the 1960s, in the run up to the Polish United Workers' Party's infamous 1968 anti-Semitic purges. Kunicki, *Between the Brown and the Red*, 140–161.

69. The letter appeared later that same year in Polish translation as anti-German, anti-Vatican propaganda: Pius XII, *Papież Pius XII do biskupów niemieckich: Pełny tekst listu z dnia 1 marca 1948* (Katowice: Odra, 1948).

70. See, e.g., Gregor Thum, *Uprooted: How Breslau Became Wrocław During the Century of Expulsions*, trans. Tom Lampert and Allison Brown (Princeton, NJ: Princeton University Press, 2011), 43–52.

71. Fleming, *Communism, Nationalism, and Ethnicity in Poland*, 105.

72. Particularly unforgiving has been the judgment of Adam Michnik, who has described the relationship between *Dziś i Jutro* and PAX on the one side and the PPR and PZPR on the other as a dialogue "between two totalitarians." Adam Michnik, *The Church and the Left*, trans. and ed. David Ost (Chicago: University of Chicago Press, 1993), 176.

73. Hélène Miard-Delacroix, *Question nationale allemande et nationalisme: Perceptions françaises d'une problématique allemande au début des années cinquante* (Villeneuve d'Ascq, FR: Septentrion, 2004), 41–46.

74. "The New Polish 'Parliament': The Lack of True Catholic Representation," *Tablet*, February 8, 1947.

75. Brought into Catholic Action by Czesław Kaczmarek—then head of Płock's Catholic Action, soon to become bishop of Kielce (1938)—Bronisław Mazowiecki became vice president of the Men's Catholic Association (*Katolickie Stowarzyszenie Mężczyzn*) and prepared two brochures for Catholic Action: *Eugenics and Catholic Concerns regarding the Polish Project of a Eugenics Law* (*Eugenika i zastrzeżenia do projektu polskiej ustawy eugenicznej ze stanowiska katolickiego*) and *Abortion of a Pregnancy and the Catholic Perspective on the Matter of Legalizing this Procedure* (*Przerywanie ciąży i katolicki punkt widzenia na sprawę legal-*

*izacji tego zabiegu*). Jan Śledzianowski, *Ksiądz Czesław Kaczmarek—biskup kie-lecki 1895–1963* (Kielce: Kuria Diecezjalna, 1991), 57.

76. Tadeusz Mazowiecki, interview with author, January 25, 2006.

77. "Credo polityka: Z Tadeuszem Mazowieckim rozmawia Jerzy Turowicz," *Tygodnik Powszechny*, May 5, 1990.

78. Mazowiecki, interview with author.

79. Hanna Świda-Ziemba, *Człowiek wewnętrznie zniewolony: Mechanizmy i konsekwencje minionej formacji: Analiza psychosocjologiczna* (Warsaw: Instytut Stosowanych Nauk Społecznych, Uniwersytet Warszawski, 1997), 241.

80. Zygmunt Skórzyński, "Zeznania własne," May 1953, AIPN BU 01224/5/CD/1.

CHAPTER 4. THE TWILIGHT OF SOCIAL CATHOLICISM?

1. Emmanuel Mounier, "L'ordre règne-t-il à Varsovie?," *Esprit* no. 6 (1946): 970–1003, at 998.

2. Emmanuel Mounier, Letter to Jerzy Turowicz, July 26, 1937, Emmanuel Mounier Correspondence, AAJT BN.

3. Mounier, "L'ordre règne-t-il à Varsovie?," 998.

4. Jean-Marie Domenach, Letter to Jerzy Turowicz, October 29, 1948, *Esprit* Correspondence, AAJT BN.

5. "Rozmowy o Emanuelu Mounier," *Więź* no. 2 (1958): 42–51, at 43.

6. Jerzy Turowicz, Letter to Emmanuel Mounier, December 7, 1949, IMEC ESP2.C1–02.06.

7. Emmanuel Mounier, Letter to Jerzy Turowicz, December 16, 1949, Emmanuel Mounier Correspondence, AAJT BN.

8. Quoted in Gottfried Claussen, *Virtues of Power: Boris Trajkovski's Pursuit of Jesus in Politics and Government*, trans. Margaret Kahlberg (Norderstedt: Herstellung und Verlag, 2013), 78. The full text of the March 24, 1946 speech is available at http://www.konrad-adenauer.de/dokumente/reden/uni-koln.

9. For statistics regarding the press in postwar Poland, see "The Catholic Press in Poland: Screened but Not Hidden Vigor," *Tablet*, May 25, 1946.

10. Bolesław Piasecki, "Ruch nie nazwany," *Dziś i Jutro*, April 6–13, 1947; Mikołaj Stanisław Kunicki, *Between the Brown and the Red: Nationalism, Catholicism, and Communism in Twentieth-Century Poland—The Politics of Bolesław Piasecki* (Athens, OH: Ohio University Press, 2012), 98.

11. Tomasz Sikorski, preface to *Niezłomni w epoce fałszywych proroków: Środowisko "Tygodnika Warszawskiego" (1945–1948)* by Tomasz Sikorski and Marcin Kulesza (Warsaw: von Borowiecky, 2013), 17.

12. Maryjane Osa, "Resistance, Persistence, and Change: The Transformation of the Catholic Church in Poland," *East European Politics and Societies* 3, no. 2 (1989): 268–299.

13. John Micgiel, "'Bandits' and 'Reactionaries': The Suppression of the Opposition in Poland, 1944–6," in *The Establishment of Communist Regimes in Eastern Europe, 1944–1949*, ed. Norman Naimark and Leonid Gibianskii (Boulder, CO: Westview Press, 1997), 93–110; Lucyna Kulińska, *Narodowcy: Z dziejów Obozu Narodowego w Polsce w latach 1944–1947* (Warsaw: PWN, 1999).

14. Jolanta Mysiakowska-Muszyńska, "Grupa *Dziś i Jutro* wobec podstawowych założeń ideowych polskiego ruchu narodowego," *Politeja* no. 8 (2011): 487–504; Zygmunt Woźniczka, *Trzecia wojna światowa w oczekiwaniach emigracji i podziemia w kraju w latach 1944–1953* (Katowice: Wydawnictwo Uniwersytetu Śląskiego, 1999).

15. Stories abound of Piasecki trading on his good contacts with the Communist secret police after 1945 to save this or that nationalist from prison, or even death. See, e.g., Kunicki, *Between the Brown and the Red*, 93.

16. The estimate comes from a review of *Tygodnik Powszechny*'s activities since 1945 produced for the Central Committee of the Polish United Workers' Party in 1963. "Ocena *Tygodnika Powszechnego* za rok 1963 (od nr 1 do 50): Dokument Biura Administracyjnego KC PZPR," December 1963, AAN KC PZPR 237/XIX/171, reprinted at *Więź* no. 4 (2011): 125–135, at 125.

17. Małgorzata Strzelecka, *Między minimalizmem a maksymalizmem: Dylematy ideowe Stanisława Stommy i Janusza Zabłockiego* (Toruń: Wydawnictwo Naukowe Uniwersytetu Mikołaja Kopernika, 2015), 133–169; Christina Manetti, "Sign of the Times: The Znak Circle and Catholic Intellectual Engagement in Communist Poland, 1945–1976" (PhD diss., University of Washington, 1998), 140–158.

18. "Oświadczenie wydawnictwa," *Tygodnik Powszechny*, March 24, 1945.

19. "W poszukiwaniu uniwersalizmu," *Sztuka i Naród*, no. 8 (1943).

20. Jerzy Turowicz, preface to *Wobec nowego czasu (z publicystyki 1945–1950)* by Jan Piwowarczyk, ed. Jerzy Kołątaj (Kraków: Znak, 1985), 5–10, at 6–7; Jan Piwowarczyk, *Kryzys społeczno-gospodarczy w świetle katolickich zasad* (Kraków: Skład Główny w Księg. Krakowskiej, 1932).

21. Cecylia Kuta, *"Działacze" i "Pismaki": Aparat bezpieczeństwa wobec organizacji katolików świeckich w Krakowie w latach 1957–1989* (Kraków: Dante/IPN-KŚZpNP, 2009), 17–18.

22. Jerzy Turowicz and Tadeusz Kraśko, *Wierność* (Poznań: Kantor Wydawniczy SAWW, 1995), 21.

23. John Paul II, Letter to Jerzy Turowicz, April 5, 1995, in Turowicz and Kraśko, *Wierność*, 205–210, at 206.

24. Jan Piwowarczyk, "Ku katolickiej Polsce," *Tygodnik Powszechny*, March 24, 1945; "'Poland Cannot Be Communist': The Lenten Pastoral Letter of the Polish Archbishops and Bishops," *Tablet*, April 27, 1946.

25. Antoni Szymański, *Poglądy demokracyi chrześcijańskiej we Francyi, 1892–1907* (Poznań: Księgarnia św. Wojciecha, 1910).

26. Jacques Maritain, *The Things That Are Not Caesar's*, trans. J. F. Scanlan (New York: C. Scribner's Sons, 1931).

27. Turowicz, preface to *Wobec nowego czasu* by Jan Piwowarczyk, 8.

28. Jan Piwowarczyk, "Wierność wobec Kościoła," *Tygodnik Powszechny*, February 2, 1947.

29. Emmanuel Mounier, "Appel à un rassemblement pour une Démocratie personnaliste," *Esprit* no. 12 (1938): 424–432, at 427–428. Capitalization in the original.

30. On Wilno (today's Vilnius) in interwar Poland, see Timothy Snyder, *The Reconstruction of Nations: Poland, Ukraine, Lithuania, Belarus, 1569–1999* (New

Haven, CT: Yale University Press, 2003), 52–72. On the future *Tygodnik Powszechny* writers' migration to Kraków, see Józefa Hennel and Roman Graczyk, *"Bo jestem z Wilna": Z Józefą Hennelową rozmawia Roman Graczyk* (Kraków: Znak, 2001).

31. Quoted in Janet Horne, *A Social Laboratory for Modern France: The Musée Social and the Rise of the Welfare State* (Durham, NC: Duke University Press, 2001), 119. Léon Bourgeois began publicizing solidarism in 1895.

32. Marci Shore, *Caviar and Ashes: A Warsaw Generation's Life and Death in Marxism, 1918–1968* (New Haven, CT: Yale University Press, 2006), 10–32.

33. Tom Junes, *Student Politics in Communist Poland: Generations of Consent and Dissent* (Lanham, MD: Lexington Books, 2015), 103–122; Padraic Kenney, *A Carnival of Revolution: Central Europe 1989* (Princeton, NJ: Princeton University Press, 2002), 1–5.

34. Norbert Żmijewski, *The Catholic-Marxist Ideological Dialogue in Poland, 1945–1980* (Aldershot, UK: Dartmouth, 1991), 35.

35. Jerzy Turowicz, "Droga do Europy," *Tygodnik Powszechny*, April 8, 1945.

36. Jerzy Jedlicki, *A Suburb of Europe: Nineteenth-Century Polish Approaches to Western Civilization* (New York: Central European University Press, 1999), 173–292.

37. Piwowarczyk, "Ku katolickiej Polsce."

38. John Connelly, *Captive University: The Sovietization of East German, Czech, and Polish Higher Education, 1945–1956* (Chapel Hill: University of North Carolina Press, 2000), 101–102, 140–141; Piotr H. Kosicki, "Nauka polska a Kościół—Kościół wobec życia naukowego," in *Historia Nauki Polskiej*, vol. 10.3, ed. Joanna Schiller-Walicka and Leszek Zasztowt (Warsaw: IHN PAN, 2015), 87–166, at 103–112.

39. Andrzej Micewski, *Cardinal Wyszyński: A Biography*, trans. William R. Brand and Katarzyna Mroczkowska-Brand (San Diego, CA: Harcourt, Brace, Jovanovich, 1984); Ewa K. Czaczkowska, *Kardynał Wyszyński: Biografia*, 2nd ed. (Kraków: Znak, 2013).

40. Piotr H. Kosicki, "*Caritas* across the Iron Curtain? Polish-German Reconciliation and the Bishops' Letter of 1965," *East European Politics and Societies* 23, no. 2 (2009): 213–243; Bartłomiej Noszczak, *"Sacrum" czy "profanum"? Spór o istotę obchodów milenium polskiego (1949–1966)* (Warsaw: Towarzystwo Naukowe Warszawskie, 2002).

41. Piotr Nitecki, *Włocławskie dzieje ks. Stefana Wyszyńskiego 1917–1946* (Warsaw: Soli Deo, 2008).

42. Stefan Wyszyński, "Naturalny ustrój społeczny," *Tygodnik Warszawski*, January 27, 1946.

43. Janusz Zabłocki, *Chrześcijańska Demokracja w kraju i na emigracji 1947–1970* (Lublin: Ośrodek Studiów Polonijnych i Społecznych PZKS, 1999), 35–36.

44. Stefan Wyszyński, "'Problem' Watykanu," *Tygodnik Warszawski*, March 17, 1946.

45. "Od redakcji," *Tygodnik Warszawski*, November 11, 1945.

46. Zabłocki, *Chrześcijańska Demokracja w kraju i na emigracji*, 36.

47. Jacek Czajowski, *Kardynał Adam Stefan Sapieha* (Wrocław: Zakład Narodowy im. Ossolińskich, 1997), 192–205.

48. On *Kolumna Młodych*—Wiesław Chrzanowski, Piotr Mierecki, Bogusław Kiernicki, *Pół wieku polityki, czyli rzecz o obronie czynnej* (Warsaw: Inicjatywa Wydawnicza <<ad astra>>, 1997), 174–180.

49. Tadeusz Przeciszewski, "Wspomnienia z dramatycznych lat 1945–1948," in *Błękitne sztandary: Zarys dziejów Sodalicji Mariańskiej Akademików w Warszawie 1945–1949*, 2nd ed. (Warsaw: Wydawnictwo ASKON, 2008), 46–66, at 52–59.

50. "Ze Stronnictwa Pracy," *Tygodnik Warszawski*, November 25, 1945.

51. Karol Popiel, *Od Brześcia do "Polonii"* (London: Odnowa, 1967), 206. The Ministry of Public Safety kept an eye on the circulation of this pamphlet: see AIPN BU 1572/2419.

52. Maciej M. Łętowski, "Dwa tygodniki: *Tygodnik Warszawski* i *Tygodnik Powszechny* (1945–1953) w życiu katolicyzmu społecznego w Polsce," *Chrześcijanin w Świecie: Zeszyty ODiSS* no. 146 (1985): 41–56.

53. August Hlond, "Chrześcijaństwo czy materializm," *Tygodnik Warszawski*, December 2, 1945.

54. Sikorski and Kulesza, *Niezłomni w epoce fałszywych proroków*, 76.

55. Kazimierz Studentowicz, "Radykalizm ruchu chrześcijańsko-społecznego w Polsce," *Tygodnik Warszawski*, January 12, 1947; Kazimierz Studentowicz, "Ojcowie Kościoła a kapitalizm," *Tygodnik Warszawski*, July 18, 1948.

56. Konstanty Turowski, "Ruch ludowy w Polsce a katolicyzm," *Tygodnik Warszawski*, January 6, 1946.

57. Piotr H. Kosicki, "Masters in their own Home or Defenders of the Human Person? Wojciech Korfanty, Anti-Semitism, and Polish Christian Democracy's Illiberal Rights-Talk," *Modern Intellectual History* (2015), doi: 10.1017/S1479244 314000857, 21–27.

58. Jan Piwowarczyk, "Stronnictwo Pracy," *Tygodnik Powszechny*, January 13, 1946. Piwowarczyk wrote only one other article explicitly concerning SP: Jan Piwowarczyk, "Sprawa nowego Stronnictwa," *Tygodnik Powszechny*, June 22, 1945.

59. Adam Doboszyński, *Adam Doboszyński o ustroju Polski*, ed. Bogumił Grott (Warsaw: Wydawnictwo Sejmowe, 1996).

60. Kuta, *"Działacze" i "Pismaki,"* 17–20.

61. Sikorski and Kulesza, *Niezłomni w epoce fałszywych proroków*, 76–77.

62. The quotations are from *Rzeczpospolita*, August 27, 1947. The attacks on Braun came in, for example, "Hitlerowiec chce zabierać głos," *Głos Ludu*, July 25, 1947. See also *"Tygodnik Warszawski* czy *Tygodnik Wall Street,"* *Głos Ludu*, April 24, 1947.

63. "Nasza generalna linia," *Tygodnik Warszawski*, October 19, 1947.

64. Wiesław Chrzanowski, interview with author, November 3, 2005; "Likwidacja *Tygodnika Warszawskiego*—Rozmowa z Andrzejem Kozaneckim i Tadeuszem Przeciszewskim," *Ład*, September 18, 1988.

65. Karol Popiel, "Oświadczenie K. Popiela w sprawie *Tygodnika Warszawskiego* z 10.IX.1948 r.," September 10, 1948, BUKUL Rkps 2014.

66. Popiel, "Oświadczenie."

67. *Sojusznicy Gestapo: Proces Kwasiborskiego i innych* (Warsaw: Książka i Wiedza, 1951).

68. Andrzej Paczkowski, "Aresztowanie ks. Zygmunta Kaczyńskiego," *Więź* no. 4 (1991): 109–114.

69. Bolesław Piasecki, "Zagadnienia istotne," *Dziś i Jutro*, November 25, 1945.

70. Kunicki, *Between the Brown and the Red*, 87; Żmijewski, *The Catholic-Marxist Ideological Dialogue in Poland*, 66.

71. Longina Jakubowska, *Patrons of History: Nobility, Capital, and Political Transitions in Poland* (Burlington, VT: Ashgate, 2012), 5.

72. See, e.g., a translation of Yves Congar's commentary on "Sainthood and Sin in the Church": Congar, "Świętość i grzech w Kościele," *Dziś i Jutro*, January 1–4, 1948.

73. Kunicki, *Between the Brown and the Red*, 85; Shore, *Caviar and Ashes*, 269.

74. Władysław Gomułka, *Pamiętniki*, ed. Andrzej Werblan (Warsaw: BGW, 1994), 2: 516–517.

75. Goulven Boudic, *"Esprit," 1944–1982: Les métamorphoses d'une revue* (Paris: IMEC, 2005), 219.

76. Angèle de Radkowski, interview with author, October 22, 2005.

77. Magdalena Grochowska, *Strzelecki: Śladem nadziei* (Warsaw: Świat Książki, 2014), 145–148. On Glasberg—Lucien Lazare, *L'Abbé Glasberg* (Paris: Cerf, 1990).

78. These details and dates are drawn from the private records kept by Mounier in his diary over the course of the voyage, held at IMEC MNR2.D5–06.01. I have verified these details to the greatest degree possible with Angèle de Radkowski, the sole member of the French delegation who was still alive when I began preparing the present work.

79. The text of this lecture appeared in print in the third issue of the newly created journal *Znak*: Emmanuel Mounier, "Przekrój ideowy Francji roku 1946," *Znak* no. 3 (1946): 287–305.

80. Piotr H. Kosicki, "Promieniowanie personalizmu: Mounier, *Esprit* i początki *Więzi*," *Więź* nos. 2–3 (2008): 113–114.

81. Mounier, "L'ordre règne-t-il à Varsovie?," 973, 997.

82. Mounier, "L'ordre règne-t-il à Varsovie?," 985, 976.

83. Jan Tomasz Gross, *Upiorna dekada: Trzy eseje na temat Żydów, Polaków, Niemców i komunistów: 1939–1948* (Kraków: Universitas, 1998).

84. John Hellman, *Emmanuel Mounier and the New Catholic Left, 1930–1950* (Toronto: University of Toronto Press, 1981), 211.

85. R. E. M. Irving, *Christian Democracy in France* (London: Allen and Unwin, 1973), 141.

86. Mounier, "L'ordre règne-t-il à Varsovie?," 999.

87. See, e.g., John Hellman, "The Jews in the 'New Middle Ages': Jacques Maritain's Anti-Semitism in Its Times," in *Jacques Maritain and the Jews*, ed. Robert Royal (Notre Dame, IN: American Maritain Association/University of Notre Dame Press, 1994), 89–103; John Hellman, *The Communitarian Third Way: Alexandre Marc's Ordre Nouveau, 1930–2000* (Montreal: McGill-Queen's University Press, 2002), 6–11.

88. Jan T. Gross, *Fear: Anti-Semitism in Poland after Auschwitz: An Essay in Historical Interpretation* (New York: Random House, 2006); Kosicki, "Masters in their own Home or Defenders of the Human Person?"

89. Quoted in Jan T. Gross, *Strach: Antysemityzm w Polsce tuż po wojnie: Historia moralnej zapaści* (Kraków: Znak, 2008), 62–63.

90. Bożena Szaynok, *Pogrom Żydów w Kielcach 4 lipca 1946* (Warsaw: Bellona, 1992).

91. "Oświadczenie," *Tygodnik Powszechny*, July 28, 1946. Accessible archival documents indicate that Piwowarczyk was away from Kraków at the time recovering from an illness, and that he advised Jerzy Turowicz to consult either the cardinal or his second-in-command in the archdiocese "in the event of pressure on *Tygodnik Powszechny* to take a position regarding the events in Kielce." Jan Piwowarczyk, Letter to Jerzy Turowicz, July 10, 1946, Jan Piwowarczyk Correspondence, AAJT BN.

92. Gross, *Fear*, 135, 146–151.

93. The Hlond quotation is from "First Shots against the Church in Poland: The Exploitation of the Kielce Pogrom," *Tablet*, July 20, 1946; see also "The Attempt to Implicate the Church," *Tablet*, August 10, 1946.

94. Quoted in Richard Francis Crane, *Passion of Israel: Jacques Maritain, Catholic Conscience, and the Holocaust* (Scranton, PA: University of Scranton Press, 2010), 107.

95. Mounier, "L'ordre règne-t-il à Varsovie?," 998.

96. Jerzy Turowicz, *La Pologne au coeur*, trans. Monika Bordier *et al.* (Paris: Cana, 2002), 76–117.

97. Kunicki, *Between the Brown and the Red*, 140–161.

98. Emmanuel Mounier, "Odnowa katolicyzmu we Francji," *Wiadomości Literackie*, January 7, 1934.

99. F. B. Otto Forst de Bataglia, "Zgon tygodnika *Sept*," *Przegląd Powszechny*, no. 11 (1937).

100. Janusz Zabłocki, "Myśl Mouniera w Polsce—rola personalizmu mounierowskiego w kształtowaniu się polskiego 'katolicyzmu otwartego,'" 28, unpublished manuscript (1963), deposited in AAN KIK 224.

101. Radkowski and Angèle Fumet fell in love in the course of her visit to Kraków with Mounier's delegation, leading Radkowski to escape Poland illegally in 1947 to France, where he settled, married Fumet, and changed his name to Georges-Hubert de Radkowski. He would be a crucial contact for all Polish activists passing through Paris or attempting to channel information to French contacts there. See the letters exchanged between Turowicz and Radkowski in Jerzy Radkowski Correspondence, AAJT BN; Christine Orsini, "Monde ouvert et pensée nomade: Présentation du séminaire consacré à Georges-Hubert de Radkowski organisé le 20 mai 1998," in *Monde ouvert, pensée nomade: En l'honneur de Georges-Hubert de Radkowski*, ed. Yann Lepape (Paris: Harmattan, 1999), 7–20, at 9.

102. This invitation came during Thorez's speech to the Communist congress at Montreuil on April 10, 1949. John Hellman, "The Opening to the Left in French Catholicism: The Role of the Personalists," *Journal of the History of Ideas* 34, no. 3 (1973): 381–390, at 387.

103. Emmanuel Mounier, Diary, May 1946, IMEC MNR2.D5–06.01.

104. Mounier, "L'ordre règne-t-il à Varsovie?," 998.

105. On Maritain in *Tygodnik Powszechny*—Antoni Gołubiew, "Nasz stosunek do średniowiecza," *Tygodnik Powszechny*, March 31, 1946; Hanna Malewska, "Dwa widnokręgi," *Tygodnik Powszechny*, July 21, 1946; J. K. [Jerzy Kalinowski], "Gilson o Maritainie," *Tygodnik Powszechny*, February 9, 1947.

106. Michał Jagiełło, *Próba rozmowy: Szkice o katolicyzmie odrodzeniowym i "Tygodniku Powszechnym," 1945–1953* (Warsaw: Biblioteka Narodowa, 2001), 1: 87–88.

107. "Z dyskusji redakcyjnej," *Znak* no. 3 (1946): 276–283.

108. Stanisław Stomma, "Maksymalne i minimalne tendencje społeczne katolików," *Znak* no. 3 (1946): 257–275.

109. Tomasz Sikorski and Marcin Kulesza have even nicknamed his putative minimalism: "stommism." Sikorski and Kulesza, *Niezłomni w epoce fałszywych proroków*, 77; Strzelecka, *Między minimalizmem a maksymalizmem*.

110. Stomma, "Maksymalne i minimalne tendencje społeczne katolików," 259, 261.

111. Stomma drew a noteworthy analogy here between the Christian Democratic parties of France and Poland. SP, according to Stomma, was trying to achieve a "power-sharing" arrangement with Poland's new Communist establishment, just as the MRP had opted for power-sharing with the Socialist and Communist parties in France. Stomma, "Maksymalne i minimalne tendencje społeczne katolików," 261–262.

112. Stomma used the term "social consequences of Catholicism," borrowed from Jerzy Turowicz's essay in the inaugural issue of *Znak*. Jerzy Turowicz, "W stronę uspołecznienia," *Znak* no. 1 (1946): 63–92.

113. Stomma, "Maksymalne i minimalne tendencje społeczne katolików," 265–266.

114. Stomma, "Maksymalne i minimalne tendencje społeczne katolików," 267.

115. Stomma, "Maksymalne i minimalne tendencje społeczne katolików," 271.

116. Stomma, "Maksymalne i minimalne tendencje społeczne katolików," 271, 270, 272.

117. Stomma, "Maksymalne i minimalne tendencje społeczne katolików," 274, 275.

118. Stomma, "Maksymalne i minimalne tendencje społeczne katolików," 266, 273.

119. Strzelecka, *Między minimalizmem a maksymalizmem*, 13.

120. The articles from this debate were collected by Janusz Zabłocki and Jędrzej Bukowski in an untitled, unpublished manuscript (1963) deposited in AAN KIK 224; Zabłocki, *Chrześcijańska Demokracja w kraju i na emigracji*, 38–42.

121. Jerzy Braun, "W cieniu dekadencji (Psychoza klęski w katolicyzmie francuskim)," *Tygodnik Warszawski*, March 30, 1947.

122. Braun laid bare his lack of patience for the French even more clearly in Jerzy Braun, "Kryzys moralny Europy," *Tygodnik Warszawski*, March 23, 1947.

123. Tadeusz Kietlicz [Tadeusz Przeciszewski], "Minimalizm czy maksymalizm społeczny?," *Tygodnik Warszawski*, April 13, 1947. The use of the pen name is explained in Przeciszewski, "Wspomnienia z dramatycznych lat," 52.

124. Stanisław Stomma, "Pozytywizm od strony moralnej," *Tygodnik Powszechny*, April 14, 1957.

125. Andrzej Żur [Wiesław Chrzanowski], "Neopozytywizm na tle rzeczywistości," *Tygodnik Warszawski*, June 8, 1947.

126. This special double issue of *Esprit* featured texts by a diverse array of Francophone thinkers and activists (some Catholic, some not), including Julien Benda, Nikolai Berdiaev, Jean Boulier, Henri de Lubac, Denis de Rougement, Étienne Gilson, François Mauriac, and Pierre Teilhard de Chardin. The goal of *Esprit*'s staff was to offer their readers a sweeping survey of writings on Christianity and modernity, centered on the unresolved tension between them. "Monde moderne, monde chrétien: Enquête," *Esprit* nos. 8–9 (1946): 185–187.

127. The French-American philosopher René Girard, who became one of Radkowski's closest friends following his escape to France, succinctly summed up the war years' impact on his friend: "The ferocious hostility that he felt toward the notion of need was more than a matter of theory. Georges-Hubert [Jerzy] had passed the entire Second World War in the European country whose occupation by Germans had been the longest and the most terrible, Poland. And he lived through this period in conditions certainly rendered more harrowing by his participation in the Polish national resistance." René Girard, "Le désir dans l'œuvre de Georges-Hubert de Radkowski," in Lepape, *Monde ouvert, pensée nomade*, 21–34, at 22.

128. "Z dyskusji redakcyjnej," 280.

CHAPTER 5. WORLD PEACE ON NATIONALIST TERMS

1. Konstanty Łubieński, "List otwarty do Pana Juliusza Łady (Na marginesie notatki w *the Tablet*)," *Dziś i Jutro*, December 5, 1948.

2. Norman M. Naimark, *The Russians in Germany: A History of the Soviet Zone of Occupation, 1945–1949* (Cambridge, MA: Belknap Press of Harvard University Press, 1995), 194, 310.

3. In a classic formulation, Zbigniew K. Brzeziński in fact dates the beginnings of Stalinism to the creation of the Cominform. Brzeziński, *The Soviet Bloc: Unity and Conflict*, rev. ed. (Cambridge, MA: Harvard University Press, 1967), 67–68; Giuliano Procacci, foreword to *The Cominform: Minutes of the Three Conferences 1947/1948/1949*, ed. Giuliano Procacci *et al.* (Milan: Fondazione Giangiacomo Feltrinelli, 1994), xi-xxii.

4. Wolfram Kaiser, *Christian Democracy and the Origins of European Union* (Cambridge: Cambridge University Press, 2007), 191–252; Jean-Dominique Durand, *L'Europe de la Démocratie chrétienne* (Brussels: Éditions Complexe, 1995).

5. John Lewis Gaddis, *The Cold War: A New History* (New York: Penguin Books, 2005), 5–47.

6. Michael D. Gordin, *Red Cloud at Dawn: Truman, Stalin, and the End of the Atomic Monopoly* (New York: Farrar, Straus, and Giroux, 2009); Lawrence S. Wittner, *One World or None: A History of the World Nuclear Disarmament Movement through 1953* (Stanford, CA: Stanford University Press, 1993).

7. James Chappel, "The Catholic Origins of Totalitarianism Theory in Interwar Europe," *Modern Intellectual History* 8, no. 3 (2011): 561–590; Samuel Moyn, *Christian Human Rights* (Philadelphia: University of Pennsylvania Press, 2015), 17.

8. Peter C. Kent, *The Lonely Cold War of Pope Pius XII: The Roman Catholic Church and the Division of Europe, 1943–1950* (Montreal: McGill-Queen's University Press, 2002), 217–236, 257–262.

9. Stephen Kotkin, *Magnetic Mountain: Stalinism as a Civilization* (Berkeley: University of California Press, 1995), 2.

10. Katherine Lebow, *Unfinished Utopia: Nowa Huta, Stalinism, and Polish Society, 1949–56* (Ithaca, NY: Cornell University Press, 2013), 9; Padraic Kenney, *Rebuilding Poland: Workers and Communists, 1945–1950* (Ithaca, NY: Cornell University Press, 1997), 335–346.

11. Czesław Miłosz, *The Captive Mind*, trans. Jane Zielonko (New York: Knopf, 1953), 54.

12. Longina Jakubowska, *Patrons of History: Nobility, Capital, and Political Transitions in Poland* (Burlington, VT: Ashgate, 2012), 2, 4–5.

13. Jakubowska, *Patrons of History*, 137.

14. For the corresponding Italian case—Renato Moro, "The Catholic Church, Italian Catholics, and Peace Movements: The Cold War Years, 1947–1962," *Contemporary European History* 17, no. 3 (2008): 365–390.

15. Antoni Dudek and Ryszard Gryz, *Komuniści i Kościół w Polsce (1945–1989)* (Kraków: Znak, 2003), 10, 16–18, 33–36, 56, 66–68; Jan Żaryn, *Stolica Apostolska wobec Polski i Polaków w latach 1944–1958 w świetle materiałów Ambasady RP przy Watykanie: Wybór dokumentów* (Warsaw: Neriton/IH PAN, 1998).

16. Kent, *The Lonely Cold War of Pope Pius XII*, 217–236; Philippe Chenaux, *Une Europe Vaticane? Entre le Plan Marshall et les Traités de Rome* (Brussels: Éditions Ciaco, 1990), 31–43.

17. Decree of the Holy Office of the Roman Catholic Church, July 1, 1949, in Yvon Tranvouez, *Catholiques et communistes: La crise du progressisme chrétien, 1950–1955* (Paris: Cerf, 2000), 42.

18. George Weigel, *The Final Revolution: The Resistance Church and the Collapse of Communism* (New York: Oxford University Press, 1992).

19. This is the central theme of "Red Cardinal or Strategic Genius," the third part of Ewa K. Czaczkowska, *Kardynał Wyszyński* (Warsaw: Świat Książki, 2009), 85–172; Stefan Wyszyński, "Od Ziemi Lubuskiej po Nysę: Rozmowa red. Jerzego Turowicza z Prymasem Polski," *Tygodnik Powszechny*, December 16, 1951.

20. This propaganda campaign accompanied mass deportations and population transfers. With the re-allocation of Silesia, Pomerania, and the interwar "free city" of Danzig (Gdańsk) to Poland, German former inhabitants of these lands were sometimes given the chance to leave voluntarily, sometimes forcibly expelled. Norman M. Naimark, *Fires of Hatred: Ethnic Cleansing in Twentieth-Century Europe* (Cambridge, MA: Harvard University Press, 2001), 108–138.

21. Andrzej Paczkowski, *The Spring Will Be Ours: Poland and the Poles from Occupation to Freedom*, trans. Jane Cave (University Park: Pennsylvania State University Press, 2003), 151–154.

22. Sheldon Anderson, *A Cold War in the Soviet Bloc: Polish-East German Relations, 1945–1962* (Boulder, CO: Westview Press, 2000), 52–75.

23. Alexander Grab, *Napoleon and the Transformation of Europe* (New York: Palgrave Macmillan, 2003), 176–187.

24. Zygmunt Kaczyński, "Po powrocie," *Tygodnik Warszawski*, November 11, 1945.

25. Mieczysław Kurzyna, "Polska prawda Wrocławia," *Dziś i Jutro*, August 8, 1948.

26. Jan Piwowarczyk, "Zbiorowa odpowiedzialność narodu niemieckiego," *Tygodnik Powszechny*, June 27, 1948. The work that Piwowarczyk had in mind is Karl Jaspers, *The Question of German Guilt*, trans. E. B. Ashton (New York: Dial Press, 1947).

27. Michael Fleming, *Communism, Nationalism, and Ethnicity in Poland, 1944–50* (New York: Routledge, 2010), 3.

28. Barbara Fijałkowska, *Partia wobec religii i Kościoła w PRL* (Olsztyn: Uniwersytet Warmińsko-Mazurski w Olsztynie, 1999), 1: 41.

29. Andrzej Micewski, *Współrządzić czy nie kłamać? Pax i Znak w Polsce 1945–1976* (Paris: Libella, 1978), 28; Janusz Zabłocki, *Prymas Stefan Wyszyński: Opór i zwycięstwo, 1948–1956* (Warsaw: Grupa Wydawnicza Bertelsmann Media/ Fakty, 2002).

30. Quoted in Micewski, *Współrządzić czy nie kłamać?*, 35.

31. Quoted in Zabłocki, *Prymas Stefan Wyszyński*, 145.

32. Quoted in Zabłocki, *Prymas Stefan Wyszyński*, 148.

33. Joanna Wawrzyniak, *ZBoWiD i pamięć drugiej wojny światowej 1949–1969* (Warsaw: TRIO, 2009).

34. News of the Main Priests' Commission's creation occasioned a jealous Piasecki to exclaim, "We need our own priests!" Micewski, *Współrządzić czy nie kłamać?*, 41.

35. "Porozumienie zawarte między przedstawicielami rządu Rzeczypospolitej Polskiej i Episkopatu Polski w dniu 14 kwietnia 1950 roku," in Zabłocki, *Prymas Stefan Wyszyński*, 233–236; Kent, *The Lonely Cold War of Pope Pius XII*, 232–234.

36. Fijałkowska, *Partia wobec religii i Kościoła w PRL*, 1: 82–94.

37. Jakubowska, *Patrons of History*, 155–157; Micewski, *Współrządzić czy nie kłamać?*, 43–45.

38. Wojciech Kętrzyński, "List otwarty do p. Jerzego Brauna, redaktora *Tygodnika Warszawskiego*," *Dziś i Jutro*, September 7, 1947; "Oświadczenie w sprawie *Dziś i Jutro*," *Tygodnik Powszechny*, September 21, 1947.

39. Odette Laffoucrière, "L'Église de Pologne entre Rome et l'État. I: Un accord de raison," *Le Monde*, November 1–2, 1953.

40. Gaston Fessard, *La main tendue? Le dialogue catholique-communiste est-il possible?* (Paris: Grasset, 1937).

41. Stefanos Geroulanos, *An Atheism That is Not Humanist Emerges in French Thought* (Stanford, CA: Stanford University Press, 2010), 116.

42. R. E. M. Irving, *Christian Democracy in France* (London: Allen and Unwin, 1973), 86–91.

43. Henry Rousso, *The Vichy Syndrome: History and Memory in France since*

*1944*, trans. Arthur Goldhammer (Cambridge, MA: Harvard University Press, 1991).

44. Gaston Fessard, *France, prends garde de perdre ta liberté* (Paris: Témoignage Chrétien, 1946), 9.

45. Fessard, *France, prends garde de perdre ta liberté*, 22, 10.

46. Fessard, *France, prends garde de perdre ta liberté*, 19.

47. Emmanuel Mounier, "Récents critiques du communisme," *Esprit* no. 10 (1946): 472–483, at 473, 478, 479.

48. Micewski, *Współrządzić czy nie kłamać?*, 32.

49. John F. Cronin, Letter to Jane [Janina] Kolendo, September 17, 1947, AKSCC V/82.

50. Karol Popiel, *Od Brześcia do "Polonii"* (London: Odnowa, 1967), 277; Stefan Kisielewski, *Abecadło Kisiela / Testament Kisiela* (Warsaw: Prószyński i s-ka, 2011), 56.

51. Auberon Herbert, "Poland in the Doldrums: Impressions of a Recent Visit," *Tablet*, April 19, 1947; Auberon Herbert, "Poland in the Doldrums II: The Extent of Communist Penetration," *Tablet*, April 26, 1947.

52. See the "News, Notes and Texts" column in the *Tablet*, May 17, 1947 and the *Tablet*, July 26, 1947. The quotation is from "M. Boleslaw Piasecki," *Tablet*, July 26, 1947.

53. Wojciech Kętrzyński, "Konsekwencje encyklik społecznych," *Dziś i Jutro*, June 6, 1948.

54. Jotham Parsons, *The Church in the Republic: Gallicanism and Political Ideology in Renaissance France* (Washington, DC: Catholic University of America Press, 2004).

55. Micewski, *Współrządzić czy nie kłamać?*, 32.

56. Konstanty Łubieński, "Referat wygłoszony przez Łubieńskiego w gronie zespołu *Dziś i Jutro* z okazji 4-letniej rocznicy tego samego zespołu," November 27, 1949, AIPN BU 0648/118/1. A redacted version of the text appeared in print: Konstanty Łubieński, "Jubileuszowe refleksje," *Dziś i Jutro*, December 11, 1949.

57. See the special issue of *Esprit* devoted to the "Crisis of the People's Democracies," *Esprit* no. 11 (1949).

58. André Mandouze, "Prendre la main tendue," in *Les Chrétiens et la politique* (Paris: Éditions du Temps Présent, 1948), 39–78, at 41.

59. Roger Garaudy, *L'Église, le communisme et les chrétiens* (Paris: Éditions Sociales, 1949), 366.

60. Mandouze, "Prendre la main tendue," 44.

61. Mandouze, "Prendre la main tendue," 51.

62. Philip Nord, *France's New Deal: From the Thirties to the Postwar* (Princeton, NJ: Princeton University Press, 2010), 145, 372; Jean-Claude Delbreil, "The French Catholic Left and the Political Parties," in *Left Catholicism, 1943–1955: Catholics and Society in Western Europe at the Point of Liberation*, ed. Gerd-Rainer Horn and Emmanuel Gerard (Leuven: Leuven University Press, 2001), 45–63.

63. Mandouze, "Prendre la main tendue," 56.

64. Mandouze, "Prendre la main tendue," 52.

65. Mandouze, "Prendre la main tendue," 62. Italics in the original.

66. Mandouze, "Prendre la main tendue," 73.

67. Mandouze, "Prendre la main tendue," 46.

68. Mandouze's essay was also reprinted in Polish translation by *Dziś i Jutro* as a front-page article: André Mandouze, "Chrześcijanin społecznie postępowy," *Dziś i Jutro*, February 19, 1950.

69. Łubieński, "List otwarty do Pana Juliusza Łady."

70. Łubieński, "Referat wygłoszony przez Łubieńskiego."

71. Emmanuel Mounier, "Le Décret du Saint-Office," *Esprit* no. 8 (1949): 305–314, at 312–313.

72. Micewski, *Współrządzić czy nie kłamać?*, 29.

73. Zabłocki, *Chrześcijańska Demokracja w kraju i na emigracji*, 14.

74. Leo XIII, *Rerum Novarum*, May 15, 1891, available at http://w2.vatican.va/content/leo-xiii/en/encyclicals/documents/hf_l-xiii_enc_15051891_rerum-novarum.html.

75. Kętrzyński, "Konsekwencje encyklik społecznych."

76. Wojciech Kętrzyński, "Rzeczywistość," *Dziś i Jutro*, April 18, 1948.

77. Paczkowski, *The Spring Will Be Ours*, 207–215.

78. Andrzej Flis, "E. Abramowski's Social and Political Thought," in *Masters of Polish Sociology*, ed. Piotr Sztompka (Wrocław: Zakład Narodowy im. Ossolińskich, 1984), 27–52.

79. Andrzej Krasiński, "Przebudowa wsi," *Dziś i Jutro*, December 12, 1948.

80. Wojciech Kętrzyński, "Idzie rok 1948," *Dziś i Jutro*, February 1, 1948.

81. A. A. Zhdanov, "Comrade Zhdanov's Report: On the International Situation," September 25, 1947, in Procacci *et al.*, *The Cominform*, 216–250; Anna DiBiagio, "The Cominform as the Soviet Response to the Marshall Plan," in *The Failure of Peace in Europe, 1943–48*, ed. Antonio Varsori and Elena Calandri (New York: Palgrave, 2002), 297–305.

82. "Pokój jest niepodzielny," *Dziś i Jutro*, August 18, 1946.

83. Dominik Horodyński, "W Paryżu: Dokąd idzie Europa," *Dziś i Jutro*, December 1, 1946.

84. Michael Sutton, *France and the Construction of Europe, 1944–2007: The Geopolitical Imperative* (New York: Berghahn Books, 2007), 17–23.

85. Jeffrey Herf, *Divided Memory: The Nazi Past in the Two Germanys* (Cambridge, MA: Harvard University Press, 1997), 267–333; Norbert Frei, *Adenauer's Germany and the Nazi Past: The Politics of Amnesty and Integration*, trans. Joel Golb (New York: Columbia University Press, 2002).

86. The transcript of the Congress of Europe proceedings is available as *Congress of Europe, Verbatim Report* (The Hague: The European Movements, 1949); Josep R. Llobera, "The Concept of Europe as an *Idée-force*," *Critique of Anthropology* 23, no. 2 (2003): 155–174.

87. Artur Zatopiński, "Jeszcze o Europie," *Dziś i Jutro*, April 25, 1948.

88. Jean-Marie Domenach, "Quelle Europe?," *Esprit* no. 11 (1948): 639–656. It appeared six years later in the pages of *Dziś i Jutro*: Jean-Marie Domenach, "Jaka Europa?," *Dziś i Jutro*, February 21, 1954.

89. Wittner, *One World or None*, 175–177; Marci Shore, *Caviar and Ashes: A*

*Warsaw Generation's Life and Death in Marxism, 1918–1968* (New Haven, CT: Yale University Press, 2006), 270–273; Tony Judt, *Past Imperfect: French Intellectuals, 1944–1956* (Berkeley: University of California Press, 1992), 224; Jacek Ślusarczyk, *Polityczna działalność ruchu obrońców pokoju na tle rozwoju sytuacji międzynarodowej 1948–1989* (Białystok: Dział Wydawnictw i Poligrafii, 2000); Eryk Krasucki, *Międzynarodowy komunista: Jerzy Borejsza biografia polityczna* (Warsaw: PWN, 2009); Dominique Desanti, *Les Staliniens (1944–1956): Une expérience politique* (Paris: Fayard, 1975), 107.

90. Shore, *Caviar and Ashes*, 269–270.

91. Shore, *Caviar and Ashes*, 270.

92. Shore, *Caviar and Ashes*, 271.

93. Jarosław Iwaszkiewicz, *Sprawa pokoju: Wiersze i przemówienia* (Warsaw: Czytelnik, 1952), 7.

94. Iwaszkiewicz, *Sprawa pokoju*, 9–10.

95. "Un congrès mondial des intellectuels pour la paix," *Peuples Amis* nos. 6–7 (1948): 9–10.

96. While this may indeed have been "Borejsza's congress," much of its script had been written well in advance by French, Polish, and of course Soviet Communists: Krasucki, *Międzynarodowy komunista*, 160.

97. Boris Kuznecov, *Fryderyk Joliot-Curie, uczony i bojownik o pokój*, trans. Stefan Nowak (Warsaw: Iskry, 1953).

98. Frédéric Joliot-Curie, "Raison d'être d'une amitié," *Peuples Amis* nos. 1–2 (1947): 3–9; Stanislas Fumet, "Rien n'a pu détruire l'âme de la Pologne," *Peuples Amis* nos. 7–8 (1947): 19–22.

99. "Congrès Mondial des Intellectuels pour la Paix," Invitation Template, reprinted in *Odra* no. 2 (1978): 3; Gertje R. Utley, *Picasso: The Communist Years* (New Haven, CT: Yale University Press, 2000), 118–120.

100. *Congrès mondial des intellectuels pour la paix: Wrocław—Pologne, 25–28 août 1948. Compte-rendu présenté par le Bureau du secrétaire général* (Warsaw: [n.p.], 1949), 16.

101. Maria Dąbrowska, *Dzienniki powojenne 1945–1965*, vol. 1, *1945–1949*, ed. Tadeusz Drewnowski (Warsaw: Czytelnik, 1997), 273.

102. *Congrès mondial des intellectuels pour la paix*, 24. This is the statement that Fadeev made, according to the official congress transcript, corroborated also by the account of Kingsley Martin, the American editor of *The New Statesman* and another delegate to the congress. Marci Shore provides a slightly different version of the speech, quoted via the account of French journalist Dominique Desanti, who was actually fusing together two separate portions of the speech. The other, even more controversial, passage in Fadeev's speech went as follows: "If jackals could learn to type on typewriters, and if hyenas knew how to use pens, what they would 'compose' would doubtless resemble the books of the Millers, the Eliots, the Malraux, and, among others, Sartre." Kingsley Martin's version is quoted in Wittner, *One World or None*, 175.

103. Quoted in Shore, *Caviar and Ashes*, 272.

104. Teresa Torańska, *Oni* (Warsaw: Omnipress, 1990), 365.

105. Edward Baring, "Humanist Pretensions: Catholics, Communists, and Sar-

tre's Struggle for Existentialism in Postwar France," *Modern Intellectual History* 7, no. 3 (2010): 581–609, at 592.

106. Jean Boulier, *J'étais un prêtre rouge* (Paris: L'Athanor, 1977); Jean Boulier, *Świadectwo prawdzie*, trans. Marcin Czerwiński (Warsaw: Czytelnik, 1950).

107. André Mandouze, "Prévenons la guerre d'Afrique du Nord: Impossibilités algériennes ou le mythe des trois départements," *Esprit* no. 7 (1947): 10–30.

108. Darcie Fontaine, *Decolonizing Christianity: Religion and the End of Empire in France and Algeria* (New York: Cambridge University Press, 2016), 49, 103–104.

109. André Mandouze, *Mémoires d'outre-siècle: D'une résistance à l'autre* (Paris: Viviane Hamy, 1998), 1: 185.

110. Mandouze, *Mémoires d'outre-siècle*, 1: 186.

111. *Congrès mondial des intellectuels pour la paix*, 37, 80, 89.

112. Mandouze, *Mémoires d'outre-siècle*, 1: 187, 188.

113. *Congrès mondial des intellectuels pour la paix*, 78, 77.

114. Magdalena Grochowska, *Strzelecki: Śladem nadziei* (Warsaw: Świat Książki, 2014), 145–146.

115. Jean Boulier, "Une paix vue de Varsovie," *Peuples Amis* nos. 7–8 (1947): 8, 5.

116. *Congrès mondial des intellectuels pour la paix*, 77.

117. *Congrès mondial des intellectuels pour la paix*, 78.

118. Andrzej Krasiński, "Pokongresowe notatki," *Dziś i Jutro*, September 12, 1948.

119. Iwaszkiewicz, *Sprawa pokoju*, 29–30.

## CHAPTER 6. PASTORS AND CATECHUMENS

1. M. R. [Jacques] Loew, *Mission to the Poorest*, trans. Pamela Carswell (New York: Sheed and Ward, 1950), 100.

2. Mieczysław Maliński, *Pope John Paul II: The Life of Karol Wojtyła*, trans. P. S. Falla (New York: Seabury Press, 1979), 93.

3. John W. O'Malley, *What Happened at Vatican II* (Cambridge, MA: Belknap Press of Harvard University Press, 2008), 43, 87, 119.

4. S. Janette Gray, "Marie-Dominique Chenu and Le Saulchoir," in *Ressourcement: A Movement for Renewal in Twentieth-Century Catholic Theology*, ed. Gabriel Flynn and Paul D. Murray (New York: Oxford University Press, 2012), 205–218; Gabriel Flynn, "*Ressourcement*, Ecumenism, and Pneumatology: The Contribution of Yves Congar to *Nouvelle Théologie*," in Flynn and Murray, *Ressourcement*, 219–235.

5. Marie-Dominique Chenu, *Une école de théologie: Le Saulchoir*, ed. Giuseppe Alberigo (Paris: Cerf, 1985).

6. Charles Taylor, *Sources of the Self: The Making of the Modern Identity* (Cambridge, MA: Harvard University Press, 1989), xi.

7. Jürgen Mettepenningen, *Nouvelle théologie—New Theology: Inheritor of Modernism, Precursor of Vatican II* (New York: T&T Clark, 2010), 11.

8. Gabriel Daly, "Theological and Philosophical Modernism," in *Catholicism Contending with Modernity: Roman Catholic Modernism and Anti-Modernism in*

*Historical Context*, ed. Darrell Jodock (Cambridge: Cambridge University Press, 2000), 88–112, at 88–90.

9. Bernard McGinn, *Thomas Aquinas's "Summa Theologiae": A Biography* (Princeton, NJ: Princeton University Press, 2014), 163–209; Lillian Parker Wallace, *Leo XIII and the Rise of Socialism* (Durham, NC: Duke University Press, 1966).

10. Gerd-Rainer Horn, *Western European Liberation Theology: The First Wave (1924–1959)* (Oxford: Oxford University Press, 2008), 103–109; Mettepenningen, *Nouvelle théologie—New Theology*, 47–56.

11. Chenu, *Une école de théologie*, 122.

12. Quoted in Mettepenningen, *Nouvelle théologie—New Theology*, 44. Italics in the original.

13. Robin W. Lovin, *Christian Realism and the New Realities* (New York: Cambridge University Press, 2008).

14. Sarah Shortall, "Soldiers of God in a Secular World: The Politics of Catholic Theology, 1905–1962" (PhD diss., Harvard University, 2015).

15. Mettepenningen, *Nouvelle théologie—New Theology*, 3–7.

16. Chenu, *Une école de théologie*, 122.

17. Pietro Parente, "Nuove tendenze teologiche," *L'Osservatore Romano*, February 9–10, 1942.

18. Yves Congar, *Journal d'un théologien: 1946–1956*, ed. Étienne Fouilloux (Paris: Cerf, 2001).

19. Joseph Folliet, Letter to Yves Congar, March 27, 1954, Archives de la Province Dominicaine de France: V-832–14 (Journaux—Congar), Chronique de la Purge (février 54). On Folliet—Antoine Deléry, *Joseph Folliet (1903–1972): Parcours d'un militant catholique* (Paris: Cerf, 2005).

20. François Leprieur, *Quand Rome condamne: Dominicains et prêtres ouvriers* (Paris: Plon/Cerf, 1989).

21. Jean Vinatier, *Le cardinal Suhard (1874–1949): L'évêque du renouveau missionnaire en France* (Paris: Centurion, 1983).

22. Oscar Cole-Arnal, "The *Témoignage* of the Worker-Priests: Contextual Layers of the Pioneer Epoch (1941–1955)," in *Left Catholicism, 1943–1955: Catholics and Society in Western Europe at the Point of Liberation*, ed. Gerd-Rainer Horn and Emmanuel Gerard (Leuven: Leuven University Press, 2001), 118–141, at 120.

23. Vinatier, *Le cardinal Suhard*, 227–230.

24. Oscar L. Arnal, "Toward a Lay Apostolate of the Workers: Three Decades of Conflict for the French *Jeunesse Ouvrière Chrétienne* (1927–1956)," *Catholic Historical Review* 73, no. 2 (1987): 211–227, esp. at 218–224.

25. For a detailed chronology, see Horn, *Western European Liberation Theology*, 227–234.

26. Patrice Arnaud, *Les STO: Histoire des Français requis en Allemagne nazie, 1942–1945* (Paris: CNRS, 2010).

27. Cole-Arnal, "*Témoignage* of the Worker-Priests," 120.

28. Henri Godin and Yvan Daniel, *La France, pays de mission?* (Paris: Cerf, 1943; Paris: Union Générale d'Éditions, 1962), 34. Pagination and quotations are from the 1962 edition.

29. Godin and Daniel, *La France, pays de mission?*, 9, 50. Italics in the original.

30. Louis Augros, *De l'Église de hier à l'Église de demain: L'aventure de la Mission de France* (Paris: Cerf, 1980), 46–73.

31. Godin and Daniel, *La France, pays de mission?*, 18, 51.

32. Godin and Daniel, *La France, pays de mission?*, 64.

33. Godin and Daniel, *La France, pays de mission?*, 19.

34. Godin and Daniel, *La France, pays de mission?*, 4. Despite having earned the ire of the Holy See, Chenu retained teaching positions at Paris's Catholic Institute and at the Sorbonne thanks in part to the personal support of Cardinal Suhard.

35. Marie-Dominique Chenu, "L'Église en état de mission," in Augros, *De l'Église d'aujourd'hui à l'Église de demain*, 7–13; Horn, *Western European Liberation Theology*, 105.

36. Marie-Dominique Chenu, *Spiritualité du travail* (Liège: La pensée catholique, 1947).

37. Horn, *Western European Liberation Theology*, 280.

38. George Huntston Williams, *The Mind of John Paul II: Origins of His Thought and Action* (New York: Seabury Press, 1981), 81–92.

39. Jacek Moskwa, *Droga Karola Wojtyły*, vol. 1, *Na tron Apostołów 1920–1978* (Warsaw: Świat Książki, 2010), 40–48, 58–62.

40. See, e.g., Réginald Garrigou-Lagrange, "La mystique et la doctrine de Saint Thomas sur la foi," *La Vie Spirituelle* no. 1 (1920): 361–382; Réginald Garrigou-Lagrange, *The Essence and Topicality of Thomism*, trans. n.n. (Rome: LULU Press, 2013).

41. Rocco Buttiglione, *Karol Wojtyła: The Thought of the Man Who Became Pope John Paul II*, trans. Paolo Guietti and Francesca Murphy (Grand Rapids, MI: Eerdmans, 1997), 45.

42. Richard Peddicord, *The Sacred Monster of Thomism: An Introduction to the Life and Legacy of Réginald Garrigou-Lagrange* (South Bend, IN: St. Augustine's Press, 2005).

43. Quoted in Bernard Doering, *Jacques Maritain and the French Catholic Intellectuals* (Notre Dame, IN: University of Notre Dame Press, 1983), 223.

44. Prepared under the title *Doctrina de Fide apud S. Joannem a Cruce*, the dissertation has been published in English as Karol Wojtyła, *Faith According to St. John of the Cross*, trans. Jordan Aumann (San Francisco: Ignatius Press, 1981).

45. Williams, *The Mind of John Paul II*, 109.

46. Wojtyła, *Faith According to St. John of the Cross*, 42, 103, 23.

47. John Paul II, *Redemptor Hominis*, March 4, 1979, available at http://w2 .vatican.va/content/john-paul-ii/en/encyclicals/documents/hf_jp-ii_enc_040319 79_redemptor-hominis.html.

48. Karol Wojtyła, "Mission de France," *Tygodnik Powszechny*, March 6, 1949; Karol Wojtyła, "Katolicyzm uporu," *Tygodnik Powszechny*, May 19, 2002.

49. Maliński, *Pope John Paul II*, 93.

50. Quoted in Williams, *The Mind of John Paul II*, 112.

51. Quoted in Maliński, *Pope John Paul II*, 97. (INRI is an acronym for the

Latin phrase *Iesus Nazarenus Rex Iudaeorum* meaning "Jesus of Nazareth, King of the Jews.")

52. Wojtyła, "Mission de France."

53. Ibid.

54. Mary Dewhurst Lewis, *The Boundaries of the Republic: Migrant Rights and the Limits of Universalism in France, 1918–1940* (Stanford, CA: Stanford University Press, 2007), 84–117.

55. Loew, *Mission to the Poorest*, 22.

56. Loew, *Mission to the Poorest*, 72, 67.

57. Wojtyła, "Mission de France."

58. Loew, *Mission to the Poorest*, 70, 23.

59. Wojtyła, "Mission de France."

60. Georges Michonneau, *Paroisse, communauté missionnaire: Conclusions de cinq ans d'expérience en milieu populaire* (Paris: Cerf, 1945); Michèle Rault and Nathalie Viet-Depaule, "'Missionnaires au travail' en banlieue parisienne," in *Ouvriers en banlieue, XIXe-XXe siècle*, ed. Jacques Girault (Paris: Éditions de l'Atelier/Éditions Ouvrières, 1998), 290–314, at 301–302.

61. Quoted in Moskwa, *Droga Karola Wojtyły*, 1: 91.

62. Williams, *The Mind of John Paul II*, 109–110.

63. Quoted in Moskwa, *Droga Karola Wojtyły*, 1: 89.

64. Wojtyła, "Mission de France."

65. Idesbald Goddeeris, *La grande émigration polonaise en Belgique (1831–1870): Élites et masses en exil à l'époque romantique* (Frankfurt am Main: Peter Lang, 2013).

66. For example—the future bishop of Kielce, Czesław Kaczmarek. Jan Śledzianowski, *Ksiądz Czesław Kaczmarek—biskup kielecki 1895–1963* (Kielce: Kuria Diecezjalna, 1991), 33–44.

67. Williams, *The Mind of John Paul II*, 111.

68. Wojtyła, "Mission de France."

69. Quoted in Horn, *Western European Liberation Theology*, 244.

70. Congar, *Journal d'un théologien*, 195.

71. Maryjane Osa, "Resistance, Persistence, and Change: The Transformation of the Catholic Church in Poland," *East European Politics and Societies* 3, no. 2 (1989): 268–299, at 296; Paul Lakeland, *The Liberation of the Laity: In Search of an Accountable Church* (New York: Continuum, 2003).

72. See, e.g., François Mauriac in *Le Figaro*, October 19, 1944. On Mauriac's postwar advocacy, see Tony Judt, *Past Imperfect: French Intellectuals, 1944–1956* (Berkeley: University of California Press, 1992), 66–74.

73. Claire Toupin-Guyot, *Les intellectuels catholiques dans la société française: Le Centre catholique des intellectuels français, 1941–1976* (Rennes: Presses Universitaires de Rennes, 2002).

74. On the *numerus clausus*—Szymon Rudnicki, "From 'Numerus Clausus' to 'Numerus Nullus,'" *Polin* 2 (1987): 246–268.

75. Jerzy Zawieyski, "Droga katechumena," in *Droga katechumena* (Warsaw: Biblioteka WIĘZI, 1971), 32–63, at 35. This is a text reprinted posthumously in 1971 as the centerpiece of a volume of various essays of Zawieyski's collected by

Tadeusz Mazowiecki under the same title. The original is at Zawieyski, "Droga katechumena," *Znak* no. 1 (1958): 14–35.

76. Zawieyski, "Droga katechumena," 35.

77. Ryszard Konowski, *Towarzystwo Uniwersytetu Robotniczego: 1923–1939* (Wrocław: Zakład Narodowy im. Ossolińskich, 1980).

78. Augustin [Augustyn] Jakubisiak, *Essai sur les limites de l'espace et du temps* (Paris: PUF, 1927). On the salon culture of the "non-conformists"—Jean-Louis Loubet del Bayle, *Les Non-conformistes des années 30, une tentative de renouvellement de la pensée politique française* (Paris: Seuil, 1969).

79. Wacław Auleytner, *Spotkania i rozstania* (Katowice: Unia, 1999), 143.

80. This was one of postwar Warsaw's worst-kept secrets, copiously documented and manipulated by the secret police: AIPN BU 0785/4, AIPN BU 0785/5.

81. Jerzy Zawieyski, "Zagadnienie literatury katolickiej," *Tygodnik Powszechny*, June 8, 1947.

82. Maria Dąbrowska, *Dzienniki powojenne 1945–1965*, vol. 1, 1945–1949, ed. Tadeusz Drewnowski (Warsaw: Czytelnik, 1997), 273.

83. Andrzej Friszke, "Posłowie," *Karta* no. 10 (2010): 87–89, at 88; Jan Z. Brudnicki, *Jerzy Zawieyski* (Warsaw: Państwowy Instytut Wydawniczy, 1985).

84. Jacek Woźniakowski, *Ze wspomnień szczęściarza* (Kraków: Znak, 2008), 52. The issue's lead article was: Jacek Woźniakowski, "Tatry," *Tygodnik Powszechny*, March 30, 1952. Virtually every text printed in that issue concerned either the Tatra Mountains or hiking etiquette.

85. Stefan Kisielewski, "Czy neopozytywizm?," *Tygodnik Powszechny*, December 25, 1956; Stanisław Stomma, "Pozytywizm od strony moralnej," *Tygodnik Powszechny*, April 14, 1957.

86. Jerzy Turowicz, "Kultura i polityka," *Tygodnik Powszechny*, January 23, 1949.

87. Jan Piwowarczyk, "Zbiorowa odpowiedzialność narodu niemieckiego," *Tygodnik Powszechny*, June 27, 1948.

88. Stanisław Stomma and Jerzy Turowicz, "Eksperyment Polski," *Tygodnik Powszechny*, February 3, 1952.

89. See, for example, Jacques Maritain, "Własne i cudze prawdy," *Tygodnik Powszechny*, October 26, 1952; Jerzy Kalinowski, "Liturgia na codzień," *Tygodnik Powszechny*, April 27, 1952; Stefan Swieżawski, "Co filozofia zawdzięcza Awicennie?," *Tygodnik Powszechny*, June 22, 1952.

90. Karol Wojtyła, "Instynkt, miłość, małżeństwo," *Tygodnik Powszechny*, October 19, 1952; Karol Wojtyła, "Religijne przeżywanie czystości," *Tygodnik Powszechny*, February 22, 1953.

91. Christina Manetti, "Sign of the Times: The Znak Circle and Catholic Intellectual Engagement in Communist Poland, 1945–1976" (PhD diss., University of Washington, 1998), 123–126.

## CHAPTER 7. STALINIST CATHOLICS OF EUROPE, UNITE!

1. Jean Boulier, *Why I Signed the Stockholm Appeal to Ban the Atom Bomb* (Sydney: New South Wales Peace Council, 1950), 8–9, 10–11.

2. Wolfram Kaiser, *Christian Democracy and the Origins of European Union* (Cambridge: Cambridge University Press, 2007), 251.

3. Tadeusz Mazowiecki, "Plan referatu o wytycznych ideowych Zespołu 'Dziś i Jutro'" [1952], TMPP; "Credo polityka: Z Tadeuszem Mazowieckim rozmawia Jerzy Turowicz," *Tygodnik Powszechny*, May 5, 1990.

4. Lawrence S. Wittner, *One World or None: A History of the World Nuclear Disarmament Movement through 1953* (Stanford, CA: Stanford University Press, 1993), 177. See the September 15, 1948 issue of the tellingly named Cominform bulletin *For a Lasting Peace, for a People's Democracy*.

5. Quoted in Wittner, *One World or None*, 177.

6. Weston Ullrich, "Preventing 'Peace': The British Government and the Second World Peace Congress," *Cold War History* (iFirst 2010), doi:10.1080/14682741 003686123, 5.

7. Quoted in Philip Deery, "The Dove Flies East: Whitehall, Warsaw, and the 1950 World Peace Congress," *Australian Journal of Politics and History* 48, no. 4 (2002): 449–468, at 465.

8. See the entire series of articles published by Kętrzyński in the wake of the peace congress, based on his time in Paris: Wojciech Kętrzyński, "Światła i cienie nad Wielkim Miastem," *Dziś i Jutro*, October 9, 1949; Wojciech Kętrzyński, "Republiki przemijają," *Dziś i Jutro*, October 23, 1949; Wojciech Kętrzyński, "'Życie łatwe,'" *Dziś i Jutro*, November 13, 1949; Wojciech Kętrzyński, "Na politycznym wachlarzu," *Dziś i Jutro*, November 20, 1949. On the Paris and Prague congresses, see Wittner, *One World or None*, 177–180.

9. Quoted in Wittner, *One World or None*, 178.

10. Yvon Tranvouez, *Catholiques d'abord: Approches du mouvement catholique en France (XIXe—XXe siècle)* (Paris: Éditions Ouvrières, 1988), 132–171; Wittner, *One World or None*, 182–184.

11. Reprinted in Frédéric Joliot-Curie, "A Proposal toward the Elimination of the Atomic Danger," *Bulletin of the Atomic Scientists* no. 6 (1950): 166–167, at 166.

12. Michael D. Gordin, *Red Cloud at Dawn: Truman, Stalin, and the End of the Atomic Monopoly* (New York: Farrar, Straus, and Giroux, 2009), 247–284.

13. Gabrielle Hecht, *The Radiance of France: Nuclear Power and National Identity after World War II* (Cambridge, MA: MIT Press, 2009), 55–90. On Joliot-Curie's dismissal, see Hecht, *The Radiance of France*, 59.

14. Frédéric Joliot-Curie, *Cinq années de lutte pour la paix* (Paris: Éditions Défense de la paix, 1954).

15. Joliot-Curie, "A Proposal toward the Elimination of the Atomic Danger," 167.

16. Boulier wrote the original in French, but the Australian Communist Party translated the pamphlet into English and circulated it widely within months of its publication in France. Boulier, *Why I Signed the Stockholm Appeal to Ban the Atom Bomb*, 4.

17. Boulier, *Why I Signed the Stockholm Appeal to Ban the Atom Bomb*, 6.

18. Boulier, *Why I Signed the Stockholm Appeal to Ban the Atom Bomb*, 7.

19. Boulier, *Why I Signed the Stockholm Appeal to Ban the Atom Bomb*, 8–9, 10–11.

20. Boulier, *Why I Signed the Stockholm Appeal to Ban the Atom Bomb*, 12.

21. As Yvon Tranvouez writes, "The Stockholm Appeal became a Christian problem." Tranvouez, *Catholiques d'abord*, 141.

22. Quoted in Wittner, *One World or None*, 189.

23. Wittner, *One World or None*, 193.

24. Yvon Tranvouez, *Catholiques et communistes: La crise du progressisme chrétien, 1950–1955* (Paris: Cerf, 2000), 47, 94.

25. Thierry Keck, *Jeunesse de l'Église: 1936–1955, aux sources de la crise progressiste en France* (Paris: Karthala, 2004); Gustavo Gutiérrez, *A Theology of Liberation: History, Politics, Salvation*, trans. and ed. Caridad Inda and John Eagleson (London: SCM Press, 1974).

26. Geoffrey Roberts, "Averting Armageddon: The Communist Peace Movement, 1948–1956," in *The Oxford Handbook of the History of Communism*, ed. S. A. Smith (New York: Oxford University Press, 2014), 322–338, at 327.

27. Quoted in Tranvouez, *Catholiques et communistes*, 46.

28. The visit took place in mid-May 1947. See Konstanty Łubieński, Letter to Emmanuel Mounier, March 13, 1947, IMEC ESP2.C1–02.06; Jean-Marie Domenach, Letter to Konstanty Łubieński, March 18, 1947, IMEC ESP2.C1–02.06.

29. Julia Brystygier, "Zapis rozmowy z Konstantym Łubieńskim ws. memoriału 'Problem emigracji,'" October 7, 1948, AIPN BU 0648/118/1. There is, however, no evidence to suggest that Łubieński's MBP marching orders included *Esprit*. This was an agenda worked out separately with Piasecki, Kętrzyński, and others in keeping with *Dziś i Jutro*'s ideological and institutional interests.

30. Jerzy Borejsza, Letter to Ministry of Public Administration, February 27, 1950, AIPN BU 1532/1312.

31. Jacek Żurek, *Ruch "Księży Patriotów" w województwie katowickim w latach 1949–1956* (Warsaw-Katowice: IPN-KŚZpNP, 2009), 230–249.

32. Wojciech Kętrzyński, "Zagadnienie szwedzkie," *Dziś i Jutro*, April 23, 1950.

33. Palmiro Togliatti, "Comrade Togliatti's Report: Working-Class Unity and the Tasks of the Communist and Workers' Parties," November 17, 1949, in *The Cominform: Minutes of the Three Conferences 1947/1948/1949*, ed. Giuliano Procacci *et al.* (Milan: Fondazione Giangiacomo Feltrinelli, 1994), 783–803, at 789.

34. Togliatti, "Comrade Togliatti's Report," 797.

35. Robert A. Ventresca, *From Fascism to Democracy: Culture and Politics in the Italian Election of 1948* (Toronto: University of Toronto Press, 2004), 100–137, 177–197.

36. Robert A. Ventresca, *Soldier of Christ: The Life of Pope Pius XII* (Cambridge, MA: Belknap Press of Harvard University Press, 2013), 241–248; Andrea Riccardi, *Pio XII e Alcide De Gasperi: Una storia segreta* (Rome: Laterza, 2003).

37. Togliatti, "Comrade Togliatti's Report," 797.

38. "Notatka w sprawie możliwej roli Katolików polskich na terenie Europy Zachodniej," 1950, AKSCC V/87.

39. For Italy, these included holdovers from the prewar "Catholic Communist" movement; the small "left" wing of the postwar Christian Democratic party, known as the *dossettiani* (after their leader, Giuseppe Dossetti); and intellectuals gathered around, for example, the journal *Adesso* (*Now*). Giorgio Vecchio, "'Left Catholi-

cism' and the Experiences 'on the Frontier' of the Church and Italian Society (1939–1958)," in *Left Catholicism, 1943–1955: Catholics and Society in Western Europe at the Point of Liberation*, ed. Gerd-Rainer Horn and Emmanuel Gerard (Leuven: Leuven University Press, 2001), 174–195; Francesco Malgeri, *"Voce operaia": Dai cattolici comunisti alla Sinistra Cristiana (1943–1945)* (Rome: Studium, 1992).

40. On the activists of *Économie et Humanisme*—Giuliana Chamedes, "The Catholic Origins of Economic Development after World War II," *French Politics, Culture, & Society* 33, no. 2 (2015): 55–75; Denis Pelletier, *"Économie et Humanisme": De l'utopie communautaire au combat pour le tiers-monde, 1941–1966* (Paris: Cerf, 1996).

41. "Notatka w sprawie możliwej roli Katolików polskich na terenie Europy Zachodniej."

42. Antoni Dudek and Grzegorz Pytel, *Bolesław Piasecki: Próba biografii politycznej* (London: Aneks, 1990), 212–214; Mikołaj Stanisław Kunicki, *Between the Brown and the Red: Nationalism, Catholicism, and Communism in Twentieth-Century Poland—The Politics of Bolesław Piasecki* (Athens, OH: Ohio University Press, 2012), 129–131.

43. Quoted in Andrzej Jaszczuk, *Ewolucja ideowa Bolesława Piaseckiego 1932–1956* (Warsaw: DiG, 2005), 128–129 n54.

44. Deery, "The Dove Flies East"; Ullrich, "Preventing 'Peace.'"

45. Vercors, "Réponses," *Esprit* no. 12 (1949): 949–953.

46. The original is at Wojciech Kętrzyński, Letter to Emmanuel Mounier, February 15, 1950, IMEC ESP2.C1–02.06. A copy was retained in Kętrzyński's master file of outgoing correspondence, preserved in the papers of *Dziś i Jutro*: Wojciech Kętrzyński, Letter to Emmanuel Mounier, February 15, 1950, AKSCC V/87.

47. Emmanuel Mounier, Letter to Wojciech Kętrzyński, March 8, 1950, AKSCC V/88.

48. The obituary is at "Emanuel Mounier," *Dziś i Jutro*, April 9–16, 1950. The special issue devoted to Mounier includes Wojciech Kętrzyński, "Emanuel Mounier umarł w połowie drogi," *Dziś i Jutro*, May 7, 1950; Emmanuel Mounier, "Wiara chrześcijańska a cywilizacja (Fragmenty z większej całości)," trans. Wanda Urstein, *Dziś i Jutro*, May 7, 1950; "Prasa francuska o Emanuelu Mounier," *Dziś i Jutro*, May 7, 1950; "Mounier—o *Dziś i Jutro*," *Dziś i Jutro*, May 7, 1950.

49. *Dziś i Jutro* Staff [Wojciech Kętrzyński], Letter to *Esprit* Staff, March 28, 1950, AKSCC V/87.

50. Wojciech Kętrzyński, Letter to Jean-Marie Domenach, August 5, 1950, AKSCC V/87.

51. Jean-Marie Domenach, Letter to Wojciech Kętrzyński, April 10, 1950, AKSCC V/88.

52. Michel Winock, *Histoire politique de la revue "Esprit" 1930–1950* (Paris: Seuil, 1975), 245–246.

53. Philip Nord, *France's New Deal: From the Thirties to the Postwar* (Princeton, NJ: Princeton University Press, 2010), 198.

54. Jean-Marie Domenach, Letter to Wojciech Kętrzyński, August 30, 1950, AKSCC V/88.

55. Wojciech Kętrzyński, Letter to Jean-Marie Domenach, December 5, 1950, AKSCC V/87.

56. Albert Béguin, Letter to Konstanty Łubieński, August 17, 1951, AKSCC V/90.

57. Martin Strickmann, "Französische Intellektuelle als deutsch-französische Mittlerfiguren 1944–1950," in *Am Wendepunkt: Deutschland und Frankreich um 1945—zur Dynamik eines "transnationalen" kulturellen Feldes / Dynamiques d'un champ culturel "transnational"—L'Allemagne et la France vers 1945*, ed. Patricia Oster and Hans-Jürgen Lüsebrink (Bielefeld: transcript, 2008), 17–49, at 42.

58. Jean-Marie Domenach and Michel Bruguier, Letter to [Wojciech Kętrzyński], March 10, 1952, AKSCC V/92.

59. Michael Sutton, *France and the Construction of Europe, 1944–2007: The Geopolitical Imperative* (New York: Berghahn Books, 2007), 64–68.

60. "Document de Travail élaboré à l'occasion de la Conférence d'Odense en vue de la recherche d'une solution pacifique du problème allemand," June 15, 1952, AKSCC V/92. For a published (revised) version of the document, see "Avertissement adopté à la Conférence d'Odense sur la solution du problème allemand," *Routes de la Paix*, July 1952: 10–11.

61. Dominik Horodyński, Letter to Jean-Marie Domenach, July 20, 1953, IMEC ESP2.C1–02.06; Dominik Horodyński and Ostap Dłuski, Letter to Jean-Marie Domenach, September 26, 1953, IMEC ESP2.C1–02.06. By this time, Domenach had already argued publicly on Poland's behalf: Jean-Marie Domenach, "Au nom de la 'Civilisation Chrétienne,'" *Peuples Amis* no. 10 (1952): 7–8.

62. The image accompanied the article "Poland wants peace" (*La Pologne veut la paix*), *Peuples Amis* no. 6 (1950).

63. Wittner, *One World or None*, 237.

64. As Lawrence S. Wittner sardonically observes, "Indeed, at one point the announced number of signers from Bulgaria exceeded that country's population, and in other countries, such as Hungary, children under five years of age would have had to be included to justify the figures." Wittner, *One World or None*, 183.

65. Bolesław Piasecki, "Za pokojem—jedność narodu," *Dziś i Jutro*, October 1–8, 1950.

66. Ullrich, "Preventing 'Peace,'" 16.

67. Deery, "The Dove Flies East," 463.

68. W. K. [Wojciech Kętrzyński], "Kongres Pokoju odbędzie się w Warszawie," *Dziś i Jutro*, November 19, 1950.

69. The first quotation is from Roger Wilson, an Australian participant of the 1950 congress interviewed in Deery, "The Dove Flies East," 466. Bierut is quoted in Wittner, *One World or None*, 184.

70. For the official congress transcript, see *Second World Peace Congress, Warsaw, November 16–22, 1950* (Warsaw: [n.p.], 1951).

71. "Notatka sprawozdawcza ze spotkania katolików, biorących udział w II Kongresie Pokoju," November 1950, AKSCC V/87.

72. Tranvouez, *Catholiques et communistes*, 83–99.

73. Jacqueline Sauvageot, *Ella Sauvageot: L'audace d'une femme de presse, 1900–1962* (Paris: L'Atelier, 2006).

74. Marcel Moiroud, "La participation des chrétiens français au Mouvement de la Paix," quoted in Tranvouez, *Catholiques et communistes*, 89. On the UCP's decline and collapse, see Tranvouez, *Catholiques et communistes*, 84–89.

75. Marcel Moiroud, Letter to Wojciech Kętrzyński, May 24, 1951, AKSCC V/90.

76. Michel Winock, "Les générations intellectuelles," *Vingtième Siècle: Revue d'histoire* no. 22 (1989): 17–38, at 31.

77. Tranvouez, *Catholiques et communistes*, 139.

78. Jean Lacroix, "Intégrisme et liberté," *Esprit* no. 2 (1953): 293–306. Jean-Marie Domenach later wrote: "I am glad that the too-strong words of Lacroix in his *Esprit* article have not given rise to an inopportune controversy." Domenach, Letter to Jacques Chatagner, March 9, 1953, quoted in Tranvouez, *Catholiques et communistes*, 181. These accusations are similar to ones that Piasecki was facing at the same time from PAX's young radicals, led by Tadeusz Mazowiecki and Janusz Zabłocki.

79. I take this term from the title of Yvon Tranvouez's fifth chapter—"Des chrétiens staliniens?"—at Tranvouez, *Catholiques et communistes*, 137.

80. There was crossover between the French Catholic socialists and some of Day's top associates, like *Catholic Worker* editorial board member Michael Harrington. In November 1952, he wrote a piece for *La Quinzaine* accusing many Americans of having difficulty "distinguishing between Christ and NATO." Harrington, "Il y a des Américains qui distinguent difficilement le Christ du NATO," *La Quinzaine*, November 15, 1952. As his biographer puts it, Harrington "wasn't just America's socialist; he was also a socialist of international prominence." Maurice Isserman, *The Other American: The Life of Michael Harrington* (New York: PublicAffairs, 2000), 350.

81. Geneviève Clairbois, "Impressions de Pologne, I: La paix et le Plan de 6 ans," *La Quinzaine*, May 15, 1951; Clairbois, "Impressions de Pologne, II: Les Polonais travaillent . . . ," *La Quinzaine*, June 1, 1951; Clairbois, "Impressions de Pologne, III: Peut-on conduire?," *La Quinzaine*, June 15, 1951. See also Geneviève Clairbois, "Problèmes religieux de la Pologne nouvelle," *La Quinzaine*, June 15, 1951.

82. On French "*idiots utiles*," see Tony Judt, *Past Imperfect: French Intellectuals, 1944–1956* (Berkeley: University of California Press, 1992), 225.

83. Clairbois was not alone in this exercise in obfuscation and prevarication. Just a few months earlier, Pierre Debray—another French progressive whom Kętrzyński was considering as a potential recruit—had insisted in the pages of *Peuples Amis* that "the Polish Church is free." Pierre Debray, "L'Église polonaise est libre," *Peuples Amis* nos. 1–2 (1952): 8–9.

84. *La Quinzaine*, for example, translated and reprinted a number of texts from PAX's *Dziś i Jutro* weekly and *Słowo Powszechne* daily. See, for example, "Traduire la notion d'amour du prochain en langage du XXe siècle," *La Quinzaine*, June 15, 1954; Jerzy Krasnowolski, "Valeur du catholicisme dans le monde socialiste?," *La Quinzaine*, January 15, 1955.

85. Philippe Chenaux, *Une Europe Vaticane? Entre le Plan Marshall et les Traités de Rome* (Brussels: Éditions Ciaco, 1990), 67–74; Ramon Sugranyes de Franch, *Die internationalen katholischen Organisationen* (Aschaffenburg: Paul Pattloch Verlag, 1972).

86. François Mabille, *Les catholiques et la paix au temps de la guerre froide: Le mouvement catholique international pour la paix Pax Christi* (Paris: Harmattan, 2004).

87. Ilaria Biagioli, "Maurice Vaussard, un cristiano contro l'"eresia' nazionalista," in *Cattolicesimo e totalitarismo: Chiese e culture religiose tra le due guerre mondiali (Italia, Spagna, Francia)*, ed. Daniele Menozzi and Renato Moro (Brescia: Morcelliana, 2004), 223–246, at 223.

88. Maurice Vaussard, *Pour ceux qui survivront* (Paris: Beauchesne, 1915), 3.

89. Maurice Vaussard, *Enquête sur le nationalisme* (Paris: Spes, 1924), 374.

90. Vaussard's most influential critique of French Action was "L'aurore de l'Internationale catholique," *Les Lettres*, February 1, 1921; Enrico Serra, "Maurice Vaussard," *Rivista Storica Italiana*, 1997: 245–260.

91. Vaussard, in "Quelques textes d'écrivains catholiques de France," *Routes de la Paix* no. 7 (1952): 17. Italics in the original.

92. Vaussard, Letter to *Dziś i Jutro* Editor, March 8, 1952, AKSCC V/92.

93. Maurice Vaussard, Letter to Wojciech Kętrzyński, July 8, 1952, AKSCC V/92; Konstanty Łubieński, "Ogólne sprawozdanie z pobytu w Paryżu w okresie od 1.XI do 14.XI.52," 1, AIPN BU 0648/118/1.

94. Łubieński, "Ogólne sprawozdanie z pobytu w Paryżu w okresie od 1.XI do 14.XI.52," 8.

95. Robert Bosc, "L'Accord du 14 avril 1950 entre le gouvernement et l'Épiscopat polonais," *Études*, September 1950: 258–262, at 258, 262.

96. A June 1950 recruitment pamphlet for *Conférence Olivaint* offered the following snapshot: "Nearly a hundred years old, the *Conférence Olivaint*, with spiritual and professional goals in mind, has assembled students in Paris in the fields of law, humanities, and political science. New circumstances have obliged it to narrow its objectives. Ever faithful to its traditional orientation, it will advertise itself from now on as 'A PRIVATE CENTER FOR POLITICAL EDUCATION, UNAFFILIATED WITH ANY POLITICAL PARTY.' Its demanding recruitment process calls for signs of VOCATION: a taste and aptitude for disinterested, competent POLITICAL ACTION." "Ce qu'est la Conférence Olivaint," January 1950, APJF I Pa 735/1. Capitalization in the original. See also David Colon, "Les jeunes de la Conférence Olivaint et l'Europe, de 1919 à 1992," *Histoire@Politique: Politique, culture, société* no. 10 (2010).

97. Łubieński, "Ogólne sprawozdanie z pobytu w Paryżu w okresie od 1.XI do 14.XI.52," 1.

98. As of June 1953, the *Revue de l'Action Populaire* had over 3,850 paid subscribers, likely producing double that number of copies for wider circulation. See the pamphlet *Jésuites: De l'Assistance de France* no. 4 (1955), archived in APJF I Pa 735/1.

99. Étienne Fouilloux, "L'Action populaire au temps de la reconstruction, 1946–1958," *Chrétiens et Sociétés: XVIe-XXIe Siècles* no. 11 (2004).

100. Jean Marchal, preface to *Marxisme et Humanisme: Introduction à l'œuvre économique de Karl Marx* by Pierre Bigo (Paris: PUF, 1953), vii-xxxii, at xxxi.

101. Bigo, *Marxisme et Humanisme*, 141.

102. "Credo polityka"; Adam Michnik, *The Church and the Left*, trans. and ed. David Ost (Chicago: University of Chicago Press, 1993), 174.

103. According to Zabłocki, it was *Dziś i Jutro* that came to him with this proposition—not the other way around—in the fall of 1948, several months before the insert's first issue appeared. Zabłocki, e-mail correspondence with author, December 3, 2013.

104. Andrzej Wielowieyski, *Losowi na przekór* (Warsaw: Agora, 2015), 78–85.

105. Karol Zajczniewski [Janusz Zabłocki], "Etap humanizmu chrześcijańskiego," *Dziś i Jutro*, February 20, 1949; Andrzej Friszke, *Między wojną a więzieniem 1945–1953* (Warsaw: Biblioteka WIĘZI, 2015), 312–379.

106. Julia Brystygier, Note to Józef Różański, November 8, 1951, AIPN BU 01224/5/CD/1. According to the MBP team's report to Julia Brystygier and her immediate subordinates, Czapów was responsible for compiling two different manuscripts, one devoted to "personalism and humanist socialism, intended for academic groups," the other an "ideological and political program for personalism entitled *Foundations and Principles of a Politics of Humanist Socialism*." "Streszczenie materiałów dot. agenturalnego opracowania pod krypt. 'WILKI,'" April 19, 1951, AIPN BU 01224/5/CD/1.

107. Janusz Zabłocki, *Kawałki pociętego sztandaru: Nieznane karty z dziejów "Szarych Szeregów" 1945–1947* (Warsaw: Fundacja "Szarych Szeregów"/ODiSS, 1992), 10, 28.

108. Zabłocki, e-mail correspondence with author.

109. Janusz Zabłocki, *Prymas Stefan Wyszyński: Opór i zwycięstwo, 1948–1956* (Warsaw: Grupa Wydawnicza Bertelsmann Media/Fakty, 2002), 104.

110. Andrzej Brzeziecki, *Tadeusz Mazowiecki: Biografia naszego premiera* (Kraków: Znak Horyzont, 2015), 46–48.

111. Tadeusz Mazowiecki's first analysis of "progressive" French Catholic thought was in "Prawo do twórczej pracy," *Dziś i Jutro*, August 14, 1949; Tadeusz Mazowiecki, "Notatki do referatu o tezach ideowo-politycznych Zespołu i aktualnej sytuacji obozu katolickiego" [1950], TMPP.

112. Jacek Łukasiewicz, "Koniec Robra," *Odra* no. 12 (2013): 18–20, at 19.

113. Tadeusz Mazowiecki, "Konieczne wyjaśnienia," *Dziś i Jutro*, April 23, 1950; Maurice Montuclard, *Lettre aux impatients* (Petit-Clamart, FR: Jeunesse de l'Église, 1947).

114. Tadeusz Mazowiecki, "Kierunek myśli społecznej," *Dziś i Jutro*, July 2, 1950. Boldface type in the original.

115. Denis Lefèvre, *Marc Sangnier: L'aventure du catholicisme social* (Paris: Marne, 2008).

116. Janusz Zabłocki, "Sprawa 'Sillon,'" *Dziś i Jutro*, October 1–8, 1950.

117. Isser Woloch, "Left, Right, and Center: The MRP and the Post-War Moment," *French History* 21, no. 1 (2007): 85–106, at 105–106; Roy Pierce, "France Reopens the Constitutional Debate," *American Political Science Review* 46, no. 2 (1952): 422–437.

118. Tadeusz Myślik, "Gospodarka planowa a osobowość ludzka," *Dziś i Jutro*, November 25, 1951.

119. A.-D. Sertillanges, *Socialisme et christianisme* (Paris: V. Lecoffre, 1905).

120. Rudolf Buchała, "Prawo własności prywatnej," *Dziś i Jutro*, November 25, 1951. Buchała demonstrated an impressive command of the source texts that he was interpreting, for example citing Jacques Maritain chapter and verse: Jacques

Maritain, *Les droits de l'homme et la loi naturelle* (New York: Éditions de la Maison française, 1942), 72.

121. Janusz Zabłocki, "Personalizm a rewolucja," *Dziś i Jutro*, November 25, 1951.

122. "Przed siódmym rokiem pracy," *Dziś i Jutro*, November 25, 1951.

CHAPTER 8. THE LIMITS OF CATHOLIC "REVOLUTION"

1. *Polak-Katolik*, Letter to *WTK* editor (Tadeusz Mazowiecki), April 18, 1954, TMPP.

2. For the broader context of Stalinist show trials in Eastern Europe, see George H. Hodos, *Show Trials: Stalinist Purges in Eastern Europe, 1948–1954* (New York: Praeger, 1987).

3. See, e.g., Tadeusz Mazowiecki, "Uwagi wokół tezy szóstej 'Wytycznych'" [1952], 10, TMPP; Jan Śledzianowski, *Ksiądz Czesław Kaczmarek—biskup kielecki 1895–1963* (Kielce: Kuria Diecezjalna, 1991), 225–305; Adam Dziurok, *Kruchtoizacja: Polityka władz partyjno-państwowych wobec Kościoła katolickiego w latach 1945–1956 w województwie śląskim/katowickim* (Katowice: IPN-KŚZpNP, 2012).

4. Jan Żaryn, *Dzieje Kościoła katolickiego w Polsce (1944–1989)* (Warsaw: Neriton/IH PAN, 2003), 116–117, 132–133, 146–147; Filip Musiał, "Kulisy 'Procesu Kurii Krakowskiej,'" *Dziennik Polski*, January 17, 2003.

5. On the Hungarian case, see Nicolas Bauquet, "Les élites religieuses de la Hongrie communiste, de la contre-élite à la proto-nomenklatura," in *Le communisme et les élites en Europe centrale*, ed. Nicolas Bauquet and François Bocholier (Paris: PUF, 2006), 187–202.

6. Teresa Torańska, *Oni* (Warsaw: Omnipress, 1990), 401–403.

7. Andrzej Micewski, *Współrządzić czy nie kłamać? Pax i Znak w Polsce 1945–1976* (Paris: Libella, 1978), 58; on the Kielce Pogrom, see Chapter 4.

8. Hope M. Harrison, *Driving the Soviets Up the Wall: Soviet-East German Relations, 1953–1961* (Princeton, NJ: Princeton University Press, 2003), 12–48.

9. Torańska, *Oni*, 403–404; Peter Raina, *Kardynał Wyszyński*, vol. 2, *Losy więzienne* (Warsaw: von borowiecky, 1999), 89.

10. Henryk Chmielewski, "Mowa oskarżyciela publicznego," September 1953, 2, AIPN BU 0330/233/1.

11. *Proces księdza biskupa Kaczmarka i innych członków ośrodka antypaństwowego i antyludowego: Stenogram procesu odbytego przed Wojskowym Sądem Rejonowym w Warszawie w dniach 14 IX-21 IX 1953 r.* (Warsaw: Książka i Wiedza, 1953). The sentences were suspended in 1956, and the prisoners released—though the Kielce bishop was not formally cleared of the charges until after the fall of the Iron Curtain.

12. Raina, *Kardynał Wyszyński*, 2:86–95.

13. Quoted in Mikołaj Stanisław Kunicki, *Between the Brown and the Red: Nationalism, Catholicism, and Communism in Twentieth-Century Poland—The Politics of Bolesław Piasecki* (Athens, OH: Ohio University Press, 2012), 99.

14. Stanisław A. Bogaczewicz, "Ustanowienie ks. Kazimierza Lagosza wikariuszem kapitulnym i działania aparatu bezpieczeństwa wobec kurii wrocławskiej w

latach 1951–1956," in *Aparat bezpieczeństwa wobec kurii biskupich w Polsce*, ed. Adam Dziurok (Warsaw: IPN-KŚZpNP, 2009), 410–442.

15. Katolickie Wydawnictwo Wrocławskie, Letter to Wrocław Curia, August 4, 1953, TMPP; Kazimierz Lagosz, "List ordynariusza Archidiecezji Wrocławskiej," *Wrocławski Tygodnik Katolicki*, August 30, 1953.

16. Janusz Zabłocki, "Mazowiecki mój przeciwnik (10): Dni-burze, o których wiesz tylko ty," *Ład*, January 6, 1991.

17. Key examples include Tadeusz Mazowiecki, "W sprawie Niemiec," *Wrocławski Tygodnik Katolicki*, September 20, 1953; Aleksander Rogalski, "Kościół na Śląsku w XI i XII w.," *Wrocławski Tygodnik Katolicki*, October 4, 1953; Ignacy Rutkiewicz, "Między Bonn a Wrocławiem," *Wrocławski Tygodnik Katolicki*, October 11, 1953.

18. Tadeusz Mazowiecki, "Wnioski," *Wrocławski Tygodnik Katolicki*, September 27, 1953.

19. Tadeusz Mazowiecki, "Notatki do referatu o tezach ideowo-politycznych Zespołu i aktualnej sytuacji obozu katolickiego" [1950], TMPP; Mazowiecki, "Uwagi wokół tezy szóstej '"Wytycznych," 5; Mazowiecki, "Notatki do referatu"; Mazowiecki, "Wnioski."

20. Śledzianowski, *Ksiądz Czesław Kaczmarek*, 57.

21. Mazowiecki, "Uwagi wokół tezy szóstej 'Wytycznych,'" 7; Mazowiecki, "Wnioski."

22. Mazowiecki, "Wnioski"; Mazowiecki, "Uwagi wokół tezy szóstej 'Wytycznych,'" 6; Adam Michnik, *The Church and the Left*, trans. and ed. David Ost (Chicago: University of Chicago Press, 1993), 174.

23. Warren Breckman, *Marx, the Young Hegelians, and the Origins of Radical Social Theory: Dethroning the Self* (New York: Cambridge University Press, 1999), 75. Italics in the original.

24. John Connelly, *Captive University: The Sovietization of East German, Czech, and Polish Higher Education, 1945–1956* (Chapel Hill: University of North Carolina Press, 2000), 1.

25. Czesław Miłosz, *The Captive Mind*, trans. Jane Zielonko (New York: Knopf, 1953), 54.

26. As Mazowiecki put it in 1990, "I shared in this group's errors—by means of my pen, too." "Credo polityka: Z Tadeuszem Mazowieckim rozmawia Jerzy Turowicz," *Tygodnik Powszechny*, May 5, 1990.

27. Micewski, *Współrządzić czy nie kłamać?*, 75.

28. "Credo polityka."

29. "*Non possumus*: Memoriał Episkopatu Polski do Rady Ministrów na ręce prezesa Bolesława Bieruta," in Raina, *Kardynał Wyszyński*, 2: 57–76. For Wyszyński's July 1953 request that Kaczmarek be released, see Raina, *Kardynał Wyszyński*, 2: 85. For the September 24 note of protest following Kaczmarek's conviction, see Raina, *Kardynał Wyszyński*, 2: 93–95.

30. Zabłocki, *Prymas Stefan Wyszyński*, 150.

31. Raina, *Kardynał Wyszyński*, 98.

32. Bartłomiej Noszczak, *Polityka państwa wobec Kościoła rzymskokatolickiego w Polsce w okresie internowania prymasa Stefana Wyszyńskiego 1953–1956* (Warsaw: IPN-KŚZpNP, 2008), 59–67.

33. Stefan Wyszyński, *Zapiski więzienne* (Paris: Éditions du Dialogue, 1982), 19.

34. Communiqué of the Council of Ministers of the Polish People's Republic,

reprinted in *Dziś i Jutro*, October 4, 1953; Declaration of the Polish Episcopate, September 28, 1953, reprinted in *Dziś i Jutro*, October 4, 1953.

35. "Doniosły zwrot," *Dziś i Jutro*, October 4, 1953.

36. Antoni Dudek and Grzegorz Pytel, *Bolesław Piasecki: Próba biografii politycznej* (London: Aneks, 1990), 211–212.

37. Quoted in Andrzej Jaszczuk, *Ewolucja ideowa Bolesława Piaseckiego 1932–1956* (Warsaw: DiG, 2005), 127 n. 50.

38. Maurice Vaussard, Letter to Wojciech Kętrzyński, January 26, 1953, AKSCC V/94.

39. Robert Bosc, Letter to Stefan Wyszyński, April 28, 1953, AKSCC V/94.

40. Robert Bosc, "Catholiques de Pologne," *Revue de l'Action populaire* nos. 7–8 (1953): 606–613, at 606, 608.

41. Bosc, "Catholiques de Pologne," 607.

42. Bosc provides a footnote with a lengthy citation from the Polish legal code, referencing simply "Law No. 10" from February 10, 1953, whose second and third articles, in particular, were in clear violation of both the letter and spirit of the 1950 Accord: "Article 2: The creation, transformation, and suppression of ecclesiastical ministries as well as the modification of the limits of their competence require the prior agreement of competent organs of the State. Article 3§1. The filling of a vacant ecclesiastical ministry requires the prior agreement of competent organs of the State. §2. The prescriptions of §1 are valid also for vacation of a post and transfer to another post." Quoted in Bosc, "Catholiques de Pologne," 607 n. 2.

43. Bosc, "Catholiques de Pologne," 612.

44. Bosc, "Catholiques de Pologne," 609.

45. Bosc, "Catholiques de Pologne," 611.

46. Bosc, "Catholiques de Pologne," 612.

47. "Uwagi o pobycie delegacji zagranicznych w Lublinie i we Wrocławiu" [1953], AIPN BU 00169/91/1.

48. Robert Bosc, Letter to Konstanty Łubieński, June 3, 1953, AKSCC V/94.

49. "Uwagi o pobycie delegacji zagranicznych w Lublinie i we Wrocławiu."

50. Jacques Mignon, "Des catholiques français et polonais se rencontrent," *L'Actualité religieuse dans le monde*, August 1, 1953. Italics in the original.

51. Wojciech Kętrzyński, Letter to Action Populaire, December 4, 1953, quoted in Étienne Fouilloux, "L'Action populaire au temps de la reconstruction, 1946–1958," *Chrétiens et Sociétés: XVIe-XXIe Siècles* no. 11 (2004), n. 59. The original document is at APJF F 1735.

52. Robert Bosc, Letter to Wojciech Kętrzyński, November 19, 1953, AKSCC V/94.

53. Philip Nord, *France's New Deal: From the Thirties to the Postwar* (Princeton, NJ: Princeton University Press, 2010), 317.

54. Odette Laffoucrière, "L'Église de Pologne entre Rome et l'État. I: Un accord de raison," *Le Monde*, November 1–2, 1953.

55. Odette Laffoucrière, "L'Église de Pologne entre Rome et l'État. II: Dieu est-il Polonais?," *Le Monde*, November 3, 1953.

56. Philip G. Nord, "Three Views of Christian Democracy in *Fin-de-siècle* France," *Journal of Contemporary History* 19, no. 4 (1984): 713–727.

57. "C'est l'Église qui est frappée en la personne du cardinal Wyszyński," *La Quinzaine*, October 15, 1953.

58. Wojciech Kętrzyński, Letter to Jean Verlhac, February 23, 1954, AKSCC V/95.

59. Jean Verlhac, Letter to Wojciech Kętrzyński, December 16, 1953, AKSCC V/94.

60. Dominik Horodyński, "Nous faisons confiance à la France," *Aujourd'hui et demain* (*Dziś i Jutro*), December 25, 1953. This text appeared also as "Nous faisons confiance à la France," *Peuples Amis* no. 2 (1954): 3–5.

61. Jean-Marie Domenach, Letter to Dominik Horodyński and Ostap Dłuski, February 11, 1954, IMEC ESP2.C2–03.02.

62. Zygmunt Lichniak *et al.*, *Księga o nagrodzie imienia Włodzimierza Pietrzaka (1948–1972)* (Warsaw: PAX, 1978), 91.

63. Andrzej Krasiński, Letter to Jean-Marie Domenach, May 29, 1954, AKSCC V/95.

64. Jean-Marie Domenach, Speech on the occasion of the conferral of the Włodzimierz Pietrzak Prize, *Dziś i Jutro*, August 1, 1954.

65. Jean-Marie Domenach, Letter to Stanisław Michalski, July 2, 1954, IMEC ESP2.C2–03.02.

66. Lichniak *et al.*, *Księga o nagrodzie imienia Włodzimierza Pietrzaka*, 91. *Dziś i Jutro*'s coverage of the award also included other texts: Wojciech Kętrzyński, "Jean Marie Domenach," *Dziś i Jutro*, July 18, 1954; "Jean Marie Domenach laureatem nagrody im. Wł. Pietrzaka," *Dziś i Jutro*, August 1, 1954.

67. Domenach, Speech on the occasion of the conferral of the Włodzimierz Pietrzak Prize.

68. These seminars eventuated in, among other things, a series of translated publications in *Dziś i Jutro*, including Jean Lacroix, "Sens nowoczesnego ateizmu," *Dziś i Jutro*, May 8, 1955; Henri Bartoli, "O cywilizację pracy," *Dziś i Jutro*, August 28, 1955.

69. Henri Bartoli, Letter to Wanda Urstein, September 22, 1955, AKSCC V/98.

70. [Untitled front-cover note], *Dziś i Jutro*, May 8, 1955. The Vienna Appeal came just shy of the fifth anniversary of the Stockholm Appeal; it was issued by the World Council of Peace (successor organization to the Partisans of Peace), on January 17–19, 1955.

71. Mark Ruff, *The Wayward Flock: Catholic Youth in Postwar West Germany, 1945–1965* (Chapel Hill: University of North Carolina Press, 2005), 1–3; Gerd-Rainer Horn, *Western European Liberation Theology: The First Wave (1924–1959)* (Oxford: Oxford University Press, 2008), 1.

72. Vanessa R. Schwartz, *It's So French! Hollywood, Paris, and the Making of Cosmopolitan Film Culture* (Chicago: University of Chicago Press, 2007); Philippe Roger, *The American Enemy: The History of French Anti-Americanism*, trans. Sharon Bowman (Chicago: University of Chicago Press, 2005).

73. Jürgen Mettepenningen, *Nouvelle théologie—New Theology: Inheritor of Modernism, Precursor of Vatican II* (New York: T&T Clark, 2010), 35.

74. Pius XII, *Humani Generis*, August 12, 1950, available at http://w2.vatican .va/content/pius-xii/en/encyclicals/documents/hf_p-xii_enc_12081950_humani-generis.html.

75. See, e.g., Apostolus [Marie-Dominique Chenu], "Devant la mort," *La Quinzaine*, March 15, 1953.

76. As Oscar Cole-Arnal has put it, "In Lyon, some worker-priests remember

Cardinal Gerlier bursting into tears at the Roman judgment." Oscar Cole-Arnal, "The *Témoignage* of the Worker-Priests: Contextual Layers of the Pioneer Epoch (1941–1955)," in *Left Catholicism, 1943–1955: Catholics and Society in Western Europe at the Point of Liberation*, ed. Gerd-Rainer Horn and Emmanuel Gerard (Leuven: Leuven University Press, 2001), 118–141, at 141.

77. Daniel Perrot, *Les fondations de la Mission de France* (Paris: Cerf, 1987), 133–190.

78. Cole-Arnal, "The *Témoignage* of the Worker-Priests," 138.

79. This is documented extremely well throughout Cole-Arnal, "The *Témoignage* of the Worker-Priests."

80. Wojciech Kętrzyński, Letter to Jean Verlhac, February 23, 1954, AKSCC V/95.

81. Wojciech Kętrzyński, "Życiorys" [n.d.], AIPN BU 1532/1312.

82. Micewski, *Współrządzić czy nie kłamać?*, 66; Norbert Żmijewski, *The Catholic-Marxist Ideological Dialogue in Poland, 1945–1980* (Aldershot, UK: Dartmouth, 1991), 61.

83. Bolesław Piasecki, Letter to Alfred Gawroński, April 8, 1955, AKSCC V/97.

84. Bolesław Piasecki, *Zagadnienia istotne: artykuły z lat 1945–1954* (Warsaw: PAX, 1954), 5, 6.

85. Piasecki, *Zagadnienia istotne*, 6.

86. Piasecki, *Zagadnienia istotne*, 7. The reference for Chenu's phrasing is Marie-Dominique Chenu, *Une école de théologie: Le Saulchoir*, ed. Giuseppe Alberigo (Paris: Cerf, 1985), 122.

87. Piasecki, *Zagadnienia istotne*, 7.

88. Piasecki, *Zagadnienia istotne*, 9, 10.

89. Żmijewski, *The Catholic-Marxist Ideological Dialogue in Poland*, 62; Jaszczuk, *Ewolucja ideowa Bolesława Piaseckiego*, 128–132.

90. Piasecki, *Zagadnienia istotne*, 33.

91. Breckman, *Marx, the Young Hegelians, and the Origins of Radical Social Theory*, 9.

92. Roger Garaudy, *L'Église, le communisme et les chrétiens* (Paris: Éditions Sociales, 1949).

93. Tadeusz Mazowiecki, "Kierunek myśli społecznej," *Dziś i Jutro*, July 2, 1950.

94. Tadeusz Mazowiecki, *Marksizm a personalizm wobec zagadnienia osoby ludzkiej*, unpublished manuscript, May 1951, AKSCC VI/189, 10.

95. Mazowiecki, *Marksizm a personalizm wobec zagadnienia osoby ludzkiej*, 7.

96. Mazowiecki, *Marksizm a personalizm wobec zagadnienia osoby ludzkiej*, 15, 11.

97. Kunicki, *Between the Brown and the Red*, 102.

98. Piotr H. Kosicki, "After 1989: The Life and Death of the Catholic Third Way," *TLS—Times Literary Supplement*, December 13, 2013: 15; Tadeusz Mazowiecki, *Rozdroża i wartości* (Warsaw: Biblioteka WIĘZI, 1970), 195.

99. Janusz Zabłocki, "Odpolitycznienie Kościoła—Upolitycznienie obywateli-katolików," Unpublished manuscript [1952], AKSCC VI/202.

100. Zabłocki, "Odpolitycznienie Kościoła—Upolitycznienie obywateli-katolików," 2. See, e.g., Luke 20:25; Mark 12:17.

101. Peter J. Bernardi, *Maurice Blondel, Social Catholicism, and Action Française: The Clash over the Church's Role in Society During the Modernist Era* (Washington, DC: Catholic University of America Press, 2009), 208–211.

102. Tadeusz Mrówczyński, *Personalizm Maritaina i współczesna myśl katolicka* (Warsaw: Książka i Wiedza, 1964), 22.

103. Kunicki, *Between the Brown and the Red*, 23.

104. Janusz Zabłocki later recalled, "We became convinced that we were not only bound together by shared beliefs, but also that we could trust each other completely in critical situations. This realization was extremely important for both of us." Janusz Zabłocki, "Mazowiecki mój przeciwnik (10): Dni-burze, o których wiesz tylko ty," *Ład*, January 6, 1991.

105. Zabłocki, "Mazowiecki mój przeciwnik (10)"; Tadeusz Mazowiecki, Letter to the PAX Central Committee Membership, May 16, 1952, AKSCC VI/190.

106. Quoted in Dudek and Pytel, *Bolesław Piasecki*, 199.

107. Tadeusz Mazowiecki, "Uwagi w sprawie 2-go projektu nowych 'Wytycznych,'" October 27, 1952, 8, TMPP; quoted in Dudek and Pytel, *Bolesław Piasecki*, 199–200.

108. Quoted in Zabłocki, "Mazowiecki mój przeciwnik (10)."

109. "Trzeba stać się równocześnie autentycznym katolikiem i autentycznym rewolucjonistą: Przemówienie Janusza Zabłockiego," *Słowo Powszechne*, July 5–6, 1952. Boldface type in the original.

110. Zabłocki, e-mail correspondence with author; Micewski, *Współrządzić czy nie kłamać?*, 38.

111. Lichniak *et al.*, *Księga o nagrodzie imienia Włodzimierza Pietrzaka*, 91. Tadeusz Mazowiecki gave away the cash gift that accompanied the prize, ceding it to scholarships for "progressive Catholic" students at the Catholic University of Lublin.

112. Ryszard Chodubski, "Raport o zezwolenie na wszczęcie opracowania kandydata na werbunek w charakterze informatora," October 12, 1954, AIPN BU 0122/1641/CD/1.

113. Quoted in Marian Lizak, "Notatka informacyjna w sprawie Tadeusza Mazowieckiego byłego redaktora W. T. K. i Sekretarza Komisji Działaczy przy K. F. N.," August 9, 1955, AIPN BU 0122/1641/CD/1.

114. Janusz Zabłocki, "Nowa chrześcijańska koncepcja działania politycznego," 1955, AKSCC VI/269.

115. Żmijewski, *The Catholic-Marxist Ideological Dialogue in Poland*, 62.

116. "Raport Krasnowolskiego z poprawkami Janusza Zabłockiego," 1955, AKSCC VI/270.

117. Maryjane Osa, *Solidarity and Contention: Networks of Polish Opposition* (Minneapolis: University of Minnesota Press, 2003), 46.

118. Micewski, *Współrządzić czy nie kłamać?*, 68, 73–77; Daria Mazur, *Realizm socpaxowski* (Bydgoszcz: Wydawnictwo Uniwersytetu Kazimierza Wielkiego, 2013), 272.

119. Jan Dobraczyński, Note for Bolesław Piasecki, January 15, 1955, AKSCC V/97.

120. Quoted in Yvon Tranvouez, *Catholiques et communistes: La crise du progressisme chrétien, 1950–1955* (Paris: Cerf, 2000), 236.

121. "À nos lecteurs," *La Quinzaine*, March 1, 1955.

122. Wojciech Kętrzyński, Letter to Jean Verlhac, February 7, 1955, AKSCC V/97.

123. Decree of the Holy Office, June 28, 1955, printed in *L'Osservatore Romano*, June 29, 1955.

124. Kunicki, *Between the Brown and the Red*, 105–110; Peter Raina, *Piasecki na indeksie watykańskim: Geneza sprawy* (Warsaw: von Borowiecky, 2002).

125. Kunicki, *Between the Brown and the Red*, 106.

126. "La necessità di due condanne," *L'Osservatore Romano*, June 29, 1955.

127. Wojciech Kętrzyński, Letter to Robert Bosc, July 25, 1955, AKSCC V/97.

128. Micewski, *Współrządzić czy nie kłamać?*, 62, 70.

129. Leszek Kołakowski, "Neotomizm w walce z postępem nauk i z prawami człowieka," *Nowe Drogi* no. 1 (1953): 68–81, at 72.

130. See, for example, "Motywy, dążenia i braki postawy otwartej—dyskusja wokół książki Juliusza Eski *Kościół otwarty*," *Więź* no. 1 (1965): 19–46.

131. Tadeusz Mazowiecki, "Referat o zagadnieniu osobowości" [May 1953], AKSCC VI/116.

132. "Sprawozdanie z zebrania dyskusyjnego z dnia 17. maja 1953 r.," May 17, 1953, AKSCC VI/116.

133. See, e.g., Tadeusz Myślik, Letter to Bolesław Piasecki, August 13, 1955, AKSCC I/71; "Postanowienie Kierownictwa," August 13, 1955, AKSCC I/71; Stefan Bakinowski, Rudolf Buchała, Zygmunt Drozdek, Tadeusz Mazowiecki, Tadeusz Myślik, Ignacy Rutkiewicz, Wojciech Wieczorek, Janusz Zabłocki, "Wielkie sprzeniewierzenie," *Po Prostu*, November 11, 1956; Tadeusz Mazowiecki, "Notatka" ("Wrocław Woj.R.Nar." notebook), September 14, 1955, TMPP.

134. Jean Delfosse, Letter to Wojciech Kętrzyński, September 26, 1955, AKSCC V/98.

135. Pia Koivunen, "Overcoming Cold War Boundaries at the World Youth Festivals," in *Reassessing Cold War Europe*, ed. Sari Autio-Sarasmo and Katalin Miklóssy (London: Routledge, 2011), 175–192.

136. Guy de Bosschère, "Réalité catholique et structures marxistes," *Routes de Paix* no. 11 (1955): 20–23, at 21.

137. Micewski, *Współrządzić czy nie kłamać?*, 71.

138. On Zabłocki's Center for Social Documentation and Studies (ODiSS, *Ośrodek Dokumentacji i Studiów Społecznych*), see Stanisław Popławski, *Katolicko--społeczny ruch ODiSS: Powstanie, rozwój, program* (Poznań: Wydawnictwo Politechniki Poznańskiej, 1981). On Mazowiecki and Solidarity, see, e.g., Timothy Garton Ash, *The Polish Revolution: Solidarity*, 3rd ed. (New Haven, CT: Yale University Press, 2002), 22, 55–63.

139. Jean-Marie Domenach, *Beaucoup de gueule et peu d'or: Journal d'un réfractaire (1944–1977)* (Paris: Seuil, 2001), 190.

140. The Polish translation of *The Heart of the Matter* appeared in 1950—its translator, Jacek Woźniakowski of *Tygodnik Powszechny* and *Znak*, not yet at odds with the *Dziś i Jutro* movement—as Graham Greene, *Sedno sprawy*, trans. Jacek Woźniakowski (Warsaw: PAX, 1950). For evidence of Greene's importance to the *Dziś i Jutro*/PAX movement, see, e.g., Jan Dobraczyński, "Koniec sprawy czy jej początek?," *Tygodnik Powszechny*, February 10, 1952.

141. Graham Greene, "A Visit to Poland, I: The Half-defeated," *Sunday Times*, January 8, 1956; Graham Greene, "A Visit to Poland, II: Between 'PAX' and Patriotism," *Sunday Times*, January 15, 1956. All quotations are from the latter.

142. Andrzej Friszke, *Oaza na Kopernika: Klub Inteligencji Katolickiej, 1956–1989* (Warsaw: Biblioteka WIĘZI, 1997); Piotr H. Kosicki, "L'avènement des intellectuels catholiques: Le mensuel *Więź* et les conséquences polonaises du personnalisme mounierien," *Vingtième Siècle: Revue d'histoire* no. 102 (2009): 31–46.

143. Greene, "A Visit to Poland, II."

144. Marci Shore, *Caviar and Ashes: A Warsaw Generation's Life and Death in Marxism, 1918–1968* (New Haven, CT: Yale University Press, 2006), 257.

145. Kunicki, *Between the Brown and the Red*, 140–161.

146. Breckman, *Marx, the Young Hegelians, and the Origins of Radical Social Theory*, 66–71.

147. Stanisław Popławski, *Personalizm w Polsce: Problem rewolucji osobowo-wspólnotowej w mounieryzmie "Więzi"* (Warsaw: PWN, 1975).

148. Vladimir Tismaneanu, *Fantasies of Salvation: Democracy, Nationalism, and Myth in Post-Communist Europe* (Princeton, NJ: Princeton University Press, 1998), 62.

EPILOGUE

1. Leszek Kołakowski, "My Correct Views on Everything," *The Socialist Register* 11 (1974): 1–20, at 2. Thompson's original is at E. P. Thompson, "An Open Letter to Leszek Kołakowski," *The Socialist Register* 10 (1973): 1–100.

2. Leszek Kołakowski, *Toward a Marxist Humanism: Essays on the Left Today*, trans. Jane Zielonko Peel (New York: Grove Press, 1968).

3. On "Western Marxism," see Andrzej Walicki, *Stanisław Brzozowski and the Polish Beginnings of "Western Marxism"* (Oxford: Clarendon Press, 1989).

4. Bryan D. Palmer, *E. P. Thompson: Objections and Oppositions* (London: Verso, 1994), 73.

5. Richard Crossman et al., *The God That Failed* (New York: Harper, 1949); Tony Judt, "Leszek Kołakowski (1927–2009)," *New York Review of Books*, September 24, 2009.

6. Jerzy Eisler, *Polskie miesiące czyli Kryzys(y) w PRL* (Warsaw: IPN-KŚZpNP, 2008).

7. Timothy Garton Ash, *The Polish Revolution: Solidarity*, 3rd ed. (New Haven, CT: Yale University Press, 2002).

8. Andrzej Paczkowski, *Revolution and Counterrevolution in Poland, 1980–1989*, trans. Christina Manetti (Rochester, NY: University of Rochester Press, 2015), 283–299.

9. Gregory F. Domber, "Pivots in Poland's Response to German Unification," in *German Reunification: A Multinational History*, ed. Frédéric Bozo, Andreas Rödder, and Mary Elise Sarotte (New York: Routledge, 2015), 179–201; Tadeusz Kowalik, *From Solidarity to Sellout: The Restoration of Capitalism in Poland*, trans. Eliza Lewandowska (New York: New York University Press, 2011), 11–13; Piotr H. Kosicki, "After 1989: The Life and Death of the Catholic Third Way," *TLS— Times Literary Supplement*, December 13, 2013: 13–15.

10. Paweł Machcewicz, *Rebellious Satellite: Poland, 1956*, trans. Maya Latynski (Stanford, CA: Stanford University Press/Woodrow Wilson Center Press, 2009).

11. Mikołaj Stanisław Kunicki, *Between the Brown and the Red: Nationalism, Catholicism, and Communism in Twentieth-Century Poland—The Politics of Bolesław Piasecki* (Athens, OH: Ohio University Press, 2012), 117.

12. Andrzej Friszke, *Koło posłów "Znak" w Sejmie PRL 1957–1976* (Warsaw: Wydawnictwo Sejmowe, 2002).

13. Janusz Zabłocki, *Dzienniki*, vol. 1, *1956–1965* (Warsaw: IPN-KŚZpNP, 2008), 28; Andrzej Friszke, *Oaza na Kopernika: Klub Inteligencji Katolickiej, 1956–1989* (Warsaw: Biblioteka WIĘZI, 1997), 36–37.

14. This phrasing comes from the PAX-era creed of Janusz Zabłocki: "Trzeba stać się równocześnie autentycznym katolikiem i autentycznym rewolucjonistą: Przemówienie Janusza Zabłockiego," *Słowo Powszechne*, July 5–6, 1952.

15. Piotr H. Kosicki, "*Caritas* across the Iron Curtain? Polish-German Reconciliation and the Bishops' Letter of 1965," *East European Politics and Societies* 23, no. 2 (2009): 213–243, at 227–231; Zabłocki, *Dzienniki*, 1: 212.

16. Michael Gubser, *The Far Reaches: Phenomenology, Ethics, and Social Renewal in Central Europe* (Stanford, CA: Stanford University Press, 2014), 196.

17. Piotr H. Kosicki, "Vatican II and Poland," in *Vatican II Behind the Iron Curtain*, ed. Piotr H. Kosicki (Washington, DC: Catholic University of America Press, 2016), 170–184.

18. Charles Taylor, *Sources of the Self: The Making of the Modern Identity* (Cambridge, MA: Harvard University Press, 1989), xi.

19. *Gaudium et Spes*, December 7, 1965, available at http://www.vatican.va/archive/hist_councils/ii_vatican_council/documents/vat-ii_const_19651207_gaudium-et-spes_en.html.

20. John W. O'Malley, *What Happened at Vatican II* (Cambridge, MA: Belknap Press of Harvard University Press, 2008), 204; John W. O'Malley, "Vatican II: Did Anything Happen?," in *Vatican II: Did Anything Happen?*, ed. David G. Schultenover (New York: Continuum, 2007), 62.

21. Kunicki, *Between the Brown and the Red*, 177–179.

22. Kosicki, "Vatican II and Poland," 178–179.

23. Dariusz Gawin, *Wielki zwrot: Ewolucja lewicy i odrodzenie idei społeczeństwa obywatelskiego 1956–1976* (Kraków: Znak, 2013), 337–362; Hansjakob Stehle, *Eastern Politics of the Vatican 1917–1979*, trans. Sandra Smith (Athens, OH: Ohio University Press, 1981), 314–374; Samuel Moyn, *The Last Utopia: Human Rights in History* (Cambridge, MA: Belknap Press of Harvard University Press, 2010), 121–175.

24. Tadeusz Mazowiecki, "Protester et éduquer," *Esprit* nos. 7–8 (1978): 78–83; Piotr H. Kosicki, "L'avènement des intellectuels catholiques: Le mensuel *Więź* et les conséquences polonaises du personnalisme mounierien," *Vingtième Siècle: Revue d'histoire* no. 102 (2009): 31–46; David Ost, *Solidarity and the Politics of Antipolitics: Opposition and Reform in Poland since 1968* (Philadelphia: Temple University Press, 1990).

25. Karol Wojtyła, *Ocena możliwości zbudowania etyki chrześcijańskiej przy założeniach systemu Maksa Schelera* (Lublin: TN KUL, 1959); Gubser, *The Far Reaches*, 80–100, 188–210.

26. See, e.g., Yves Congar, *My Journal of the Council*, trans. Mary John Ronayne

and Mary Cecily Boulding (Collegeville, MN: Liturgical Press, 2012), 714; Kosicki, "Vatican II and Poland," 184–189.

27. *Gaudium et Spes*.

28. *Nostra Aetate*, October 28, 1965, available at http://www.vatican.va/ar chive/hist_councils/ii_vatican_council/documents/vat-ii_decl_19651028_nostra -aetate_en.html; John Connelly, *From Enemy to Brother: The Revolution in Catholic Teaching on the Jews, 1933–1965* (Cambridge, MA: Harvard University Press, 2012), 239–272.

29. Karol Wojtyła, *Osoba i czyn* (Kraków: Polskie Towarzystwo Teologiczne, 1969), 116, 110. *The Person and the Act* later appeared in English translation under the title *The Acting Person*, but I choose not to use that title here, since it misleadingly dissolves "persons" and "acts" into an "acting person." Karol Wojtyła, *The Acting Person*, trans. Andrzej Potocki, ed. Anna-Teresa Tymieniecka (Boston: D. Reidel, 1979).

30. Yves Congar, *Lay People in the Church: A Study for a Theology of the Laity*, trans. Donald Attwater (Westminster, MD: Newman Press, 1957), xxiii.

31. Karol Wojtyła, "Mission de France," *Tygodnik Powszechny*, March 6, 1949.

32. Gubser, *The Far Reaches*, 220.

33. See, e.g., Gustavo Gutiérrez, *A Theology of Liberation: History, Politics, Salvation*, trans. and ed. Caridad Inda and John Eagleson (London: SCM Press, 1974).

34. John Paul II, *Laborem Exercens*, September 14, 1981, available at http://w2 .vatican.va/content/john-paul-ii/en/encyclicals/documents/hf_jp-ii_enc_14091 981_laborem-exercens.html. Italics in the original.

35. Christian Smith, *The Emergence of Liberation Theology: Radical Religion and Social Movement Theory* (Chicago: University of Chicago Press, 1991), 224–235.

36. John Hellman, "The Prophets of Solidarity," *America*, November 6, 1982.

37. David Ost, *The Defeat of Solidarity: Anger and Politics in Post-Communist Europe* (Ithaca, NY: Cornell University Press, 2005); Kowalik, *From Solidarity to Sellout*.

38. One of the earliest, most indicative cases was the controversy over the Carmelite nuns and Catholic crosses at the Auschwitz-Birkenau extermination camp sites. Geneviève Zubrzycki, *The Crosses of Auschwitz: Nationalism and Religion in Post-Communist Poland* (Chicago: University of Chicago Press, 2006), esp. 171–201. On integralism in politics and media—Rafał Pankowski, *The Populist Radical Right in Poland: The Patriots* (New York: Routledge, 2010), 111–196.

39. See, e.g., Tomasz Teluk, "Gender jak komunizm i nazizm," *Uważam Rze*, May 27-June 2, 2013. On France and Poland, see respectively, e.g., Camille Robcis, "Catholics, the 'Theory of Gender,' and the Turn to the Human in France: A New Dreyfus Affair?," *Journal of Modern History* 87, no. 4 (2015): 892–923; Piotr H. Kosicki, "Why are the Vatican and Poland So Far Apart?," *Eurozine*, March 28, 2014.

40. Józef Tischner, *Filozofia dramatu: Wprowadzenie* (Kraków: Znak, 1998), 19. I am grateful to Marci Shore for encouraging me to think about Tischner's writings—in particular, his notion of the "encounter."

41. Józef Tischner, "Fenomenologia spotkania," *Analecta Cracoviensia* no. 10 (1978): 73–98.

# Index